Netscape
JavaScript 1.2

SECOND EDITION

BOOK

ALL PLATFORMS

Netscape
JavaScript 1.2

SECOND EDITION

BOOK

ALL PLATFORMS

NETSCAPE
N
PRESS

An Imprint of
Ventana Communications
Group

The Nonprogrammer's
Guide to Creating
Interactive Web Pages

PETER KENT
JOHN KENT

Official Netscape JavaScript 1.2 Book, Second Edition
Copyright © 1997 by Peter Kent and John Kent

Library of Congress Catalog Card Number: 97-060503

First Edition 9 8 7 6 5 4 3 2

Printed in the United States of America

Published and distributed to the trade by Ventana Communications Group
P.O. Box 13964, Research Triangle Park, NC 27709-3964
919.544.9404
FAX 919.544.9472
http://www.vmedia.com

Ventana Communications Group is a division of International Thomson Publishing.

Netscape Publishing Relations
Suzanne C. Anthony
Netscape Communications Corporation
501 E. Middlefield Rd.
Mountain View, CA 94043
http://home.netscape.com

President
Michael E. Moran

**Vice President of
Content Development**
Karen A. Bluestein

**Director of Acquisitions
and Development**
Robert Kern

Managing Editor
Lois J. Principe

Production Manager
John Cotterman

Art Director
Marcia Webb

**Technology Operations
Manager**
Kerry L. B. Foster

Brand Manager
Jamie Jaeger Fiocco

Creative Services Manager
Diane Lennox

Acquisitions Editor
JJ Hohn

Project Editor
Paul Cory

Development Editor
Richard F. Jessup

Copy Editor
Paulette Kilheffer

Technical Reviewer
Richard F. Jessup

Desktop Publisher
Lance Kozlowski

Proofreader
Tom Collins

Indexer
Sherry Massey

Interior Designer
Patrick Berry

Cover Illustrator
Laura Stalzer

About the Authors

Peter Kent of Lakewood, Colorado, is a freelance writer and consultant with 16 years experience in technical writing and software-interface design. Among his 25 book credits is *PGP Companion for Windows* (Ventana).

John Kent of London, England, owns CISS Ltd., a software development company. He programs in most of the popular languages, including SQL, Visual Basic, and C++ on mainframes, PCs, and UNIX systems.

Acknowledgments

Thanks, John, couldn't have done it without you! Thanks also to my wife and kids, who can now go on vacation.

—Peter Kent

I'd like to thank my wife, Jayne, for everything. I'd also like to thank my brother and coauthor, Peter. It was tough, but we got there in the end.

—John Kent

Dedication

Dedicated to our mother, Muriel Kent (1921-1995), the family's first author.

Contents

Introduction

Welcome to the *Official Netscape JavaScript 1.2 Book, Second Edition*, the introduction to JavaScript. This book has been written for nonprogrammers, for the hundreds of thousands of Web developers who know how to create Web pages, who've heard so much about JavaScript, and who want to see what it's all about.

You might never have programmed anything before, but that needn't stop you from getting involved in JavaScript. While JavaScript can get quite complicated—and the most sophisticated of JavaScript applets require a programmer's skills—there are many things you can do without wearing pocket protectors, drinking Jolt, and eating nothing but donuts. You don't have to turn into a programmer to use JavaScript.

We've structured this book in such a way that programming concepts are introduced slowly, in a way designed to teach nonprogrammers what they need to know to get started with JavaScript. We've also provided many scripts that you can take and drop straight into your own Web pages—modify them slightly and you'll have little JavaScripts that you can use right away. You can type these scripts from the page, or you can go to the book's Online Companion (at http://www.netscapepress.com/support/javascript1.2/) and copy the scripts off our example Web pages (each example in the book has an Online Companion reference number to help you find the correct page). You can even download the sample pages off the Online Companion and onto your hard disk (we've provided these pages in .ZIP and .TAR so you can grab them all at once).

What Do You Need?

In order to use this book, you need several things. First, you must have a JavaScript-compatible browser—that is, a World Wide Web browser with the capability of executing JavaScripts. At the time of publication, that meant Netscape Navigator 2.0 or higher. The most recent version is Netscape Navigator 4, the version of Netscape Navigator that comes with Netscape Communicator (always get the most recent available, as it will include bug fixes and enhancements). You can download that from http://www.netscape.com/ and http://www.netscape.home.com/. Microsoft Internet Explorer 3 is also a JavaScript-compatible browser, and Internet Explorer 4 will be available soon. However, note that this book is based on Netscape Navigator. In the same way that different browsers display HTML pages in slightly different ways, different JavaScript browsers act in different ways. It's inevitable that different development teams will introduce different bugs and features. At the time of writing Internet Explorer did not contain many of the JavaScript features we'll look at in this book.

You also need at least *some* knowledge of HTML; this is not a book about HTML. We have assumed that you understand how to create Web pages—when we talk about HTML forms, for instance, or paragraph formats, we don't describe them in detail. When we show you how to use JavaScript to carry out an action when the user clicks on a button, we're not going to explain everything there is to know about forms. We have enough ground to cover without worrying about these basics. We'll explain only the HTML information required to do the job. If you need more information, you'll have to refer to a book on HTML (such as *Official HTML Publishing for Netscape, Second Edition* by Stuart Harris and Gayle Kidder, Ventana) or to online HTML documentation.

You'll almost certainly need a connection to the Internet, too, though it's not absolutely essential. Once you have the browser and this book, you can do everything on your hard disk if you wish. But if you have an Internet connection, you'll be able to go to the Online Companion, as well as view JavaScript examples throughout the Web.

What about a JavaScript Developers Kit? In many programming languages, in order to create programs you need a special kit that includes a variety of tools to help you work with the system. But there is no such thing for JavaScript. JavaScript is ASCII text—it is not compiled into an executable program file. You can create JavaScripts in any text editor or word processor (assuming, of course, that you save them in ASCII text). Actually, you'll want to create your JavaScripts in the same application you use to create source documents for your Web pages—Windows Notepad, HotDog, Netscape Composer, or

Navigator Gold, or whatever. JavaScripts are simply additional instructions written into the HTML documents. (Note, however, that some authoring tools simply don't let you enter tags that the program doesn't recognize; you won't be able to use such tools to create Web pages that contain JavaScripts.)

What's Inside?

Chapter 1, "What Is JavaScript?" is an introduction to JavaScript. We explain what it is and how it's different from Java, and we show you some of the things that people have done with JavaScript.

Chapter 2, "A Few Quick JavaScript Tricks," gets you working with JavaScript right away. You'll learn a few simple things you can do with JavaScript, such as adding a document-modified date to your Web pages or displaying messages in the status bar. We won't spend a lot of time explaining exactly *how* these things work, though they are so simple you'll probably figure it out. The purpose of this chapter is to show how doing some basic things in JavaScript can be quite easy—before we move on to the more complicated stuff.

Chapter 3, "First Steps—Scripts, Functions & Comments," begins your real JavaScript education. In this chapter, you'll learn how to enter scripts into your Web pages, what functions are and how to use them, and how to enter comments.

Chapter 4, "Variables & Literals—Storing Data," continues your education. In this chapter you'll learn about how JavaScript stores data—in *variables*. You'll also learn about how you can enter data into these variables using *literals*.

Chapter 5, "Expressions & Operators—Manipulating Values," teaches you how to manipulate values using a variety of techniques.

Chapter 6, "Loops & Conditionals—Making Decisions & Controlling Scripts," explains the real power of programming—how you can use loops and conditional expressions to get your scripts to actually make decisions.

Chapter 7, "More on Functions," revisits functions, explaining how to work with them in more detail. For instance, you'll learn how information can be passed to a function when you call it.

Chapter 8, "Troubleshooting & Avoiding Trouble," talks about what you can do to fix the problems in your scripts . . . yes, you will have problems. It also discusses ways to avoid trouble in the first place and how you can write your scripts so they are easy to read and understand.

Chapter 9, "Building Arrays," explains how to create *arrays*, which are variables that can hold multiple values. You'll see how you can match arrays, so that you can pull information from one array dependent on the value held in another array—how you can search for a last name, for instance, and pull a matching address from another array.

Chapter 10, "Objects, Properties & Methods," is an easy lesson in object-oriented programming. JavaScript contains *objects—things*. Each thing has its own properties, and its associated functions (called *methods*) are used to "do things."

Chapter 11, "More About Built-in Objects," explains JavaScript's objects in more detail and covers several important objects.

Chapter 12, "JavaScript Events—When Are Actions Carried Out?" looks at how *event handlers* are used to control your scripts; you can make your scripts "do things" when you click on a button, point at a link, press the Tab key, and so on.

Chapter 13, "Advanced Topics," goes into darkest JavaScript—the sorts of topics that are quite advanced and which many JavaScript programmers might never want to touch. You'll get an overview of what else JavaScript can do.

Chapter 14, "JavaScript 1.2's Advanced Features," looks at a few things that were added to JavaScript 1.2, the version of JavaScript in Netscape 4. We've discussed subjects such as layers and style sheets.

Chapter 15, "Controlling Windows & Documents With JavaScript," shows you how you can use scripts to open secondary windows, how to write text or load HTML files into those windows, how to add confirmation boxes to links, how to let a user choose from a range of destinations, and much more.

Chapter 16, "Using JavaScript With Frames," describes how you can use JavaScript to control frames within a window—for instance, how an action in one frame can write to another.

Chapter 17, "Forms & JavaScript," describes how to write scripts that work with forms—for instance, grabbing information from a form and passing it to a function—and how to validate data within a form to make sure that the user is entering good data.

Chapter 18, "Communicating With the User," introduces you to the different methods of communicating with a user through messages.

Chapter 19, "The Area Code & Telephone Directory Applications," puts it all together. We've created a couple of working applications that you can use. The first allows you to search for area codes within the North American Numbering Plan (which covers the United States, Canada, and much of the Caribbean). You can enter an area code, city, state/province/island nation, and the program will search for the associated information. The second is a phone directory you can modify and use for your own company department. We'll show you *exactly* how these programs are put together, leading you through the scripts line by line.

Chapter 20, "Ready-to-Use Scripts," shows you the easy way to add scripts to your Web pages—borrow them! There are script libraries you can visit, from which you can take scripts and incorporate them into your documents.

We have included several appendices. In order to use JavaScript, you need to know a lot of technical details—or, rather, you have to know where to find the details when you need them.

Appendix A, "About the Online Companion," discusses what is available in the Online Companion and how to reach it.

Appendix B, "The JavaScript Objects & Arrays," is an overview of JavaScript objects. This appendix lists all the objects and describes which properties each object has and which methods and event handlers can be used with each object. In some cases it also states the "parent" object—that is, the object of which the object being described is a property.

Appendix C, "JavaScript Properties," is an overview of all of JavaScript's properties. It describes the purpose of each property and states which objects each one can be used with.

Appendix D, "JavaScript Event Handlers," describes the JavaScript event handlers and explains in what conditions they can be used.

Appendix E, "Reserved Words," is a quick list of the reserved words—words that you must not use when declaring variables, defining functions, or creating objects.

Appendix F, "Symbol Reference," contains a list of all the symbols that you'll run across in JavaScript, with a quick summary of what each one does.

Appendix G, "JavaScript Colors," is a list of all the colors you can use in Java-Script and their corresponding hexadecimal codes (though you rarely, if ever, need to use the codes—you can just use the names).

Appendix H, "Finding More Information," is your source for advanced information about JavaScript. Work your way through this book, then continue on with your education in the JavaScript newsgroups, Web pages, mailing lists, and so on.

Appendix I, "The Scripts We Used," is a list of all the scripts in the book, listed by purpose. You can look up a technique—*navigation buttons, status-bar messages,* and so on—and you'll find the page on which the script can be found, along with the Online Companion's reference number so that you can copy the script off our Web documents.

About the Online Companion

This book has an associated *Online Companion,* a special collection of Web pages at the Netscape Press Web site. These Web pages contain information to help you work with this book and to continue learning about JavaScript after you've finished this book. You'll find all the examples in this book in the Online Companion—you can read about them in the book, then try the actual scripts in the Online Companion. You can also download all the Web pages and save them on your computer's hard disk, so you can work with the scripts even when you are offline.

In addition to sample scripts, you'll also find links to other useful JavaScript sites, where you'll find many more samples, news releases, tutorials, and the latest information about JavaScript. We've included a bookmark file, so you can quickly copy all the links from Appendix H, "Finding More Information," to your bookmark system. There's also a color chart that shows you all the colors you can use—just click on a color, and the page's background changes to show you that color. Also provided is an Object Hierarchy page, which will help you understand and learn the JavaScript object hierarchy.

You can get to the Online Companion by pointing your Web browser to http://www.netscapepress.com/support/javascript1.2/.

It's Alive!

Unlike most programming languages, JavaScript is changing very fast. Most languages are fixed when they are "released," and you don't have to worry about changes until the next release. But JavaScript is almost a living thing. Once you've written a script, the way that script operates is not written in stone. Different browsers might interpret the script slightly differently, and even different versions of the same browser will work differently. We've used the Netscape Navigator 3 and 4 browsers in writing this book.

> **TIP**
>
> *When you create JavaScripts, don't get on the cutting edge. You want to be a step—or two or three steps—behind. If you write JavaScripts that use the most recent JavaScript features, most of the people viewing your Web sites won't be able to use those features and might even run into problems with them. See the discussion of this problem at the end of Chapter 1.*

We recommend that you use the very latest version of Netscape Navigator to ensure you get the "best" version of JavaScript. Subsequent versions of Netscape Navigator will undoubtedly work with JavaScript in a different manner.

You might find things that we've covered in our book that operate slightly differently. If so, please let us know. You can contact us at jscript@arundel.com (Peter Kent) and 100553.1346@compuserve.com (John Kent). We'll keep the Online Companion updated with any changes we find.

So let's get started. We're going to start slowly, explaining what JavaScript is, showing a few sophisticated uses of JavaScript, and then demonstrating how you can quickly use JavaScript to add a few simple things to your Web pages. Turn to Chapter 1 and we'll begin.

Peter Kent
John Kent

What Is JavaScript?

If you've been working on the Web for more than a week or two, you almost certainly have run across the terms *JavaScript* and *Java*. What are they, and what can you do with them? If you've bought this book, you probably already know that they enable you to create little programs that are run from your Web browser. Before we get started working with JavaScript, however, let's spend a few moments taking a look at what it is, how it compares to Java, and what you can do with it.

First There Was Oak

It all began with *Oak*. The story begins in 1990—before the World Wide Web had even begun—when a special team was set up at Sun Microsystems. The team was intended to create a new product using the sort of inspiration and initiative that had originally inspired companies such as Apple and NeXT Computer, Inc.—the qualities that many felt were lacking at Sun. The team decided—they had a remarkable amount of autonomy and operated to some degree in secrecy, cut off from the rest of the company—that they would create a new operating system that could run on anything, even things that people couldn't yet imagine requiring software: refrigerators, televisions, radios, toasters, door locks, anything. This team saw the next computing revolution as an extension of consumer electronics. Software would find its way into every electronic product, and their new operating system would be there first. Furthermore, the operating system had to be reliable—as reliable as the electronic devices that would use it. The high level of bugs accepted as the norm in most PC software would be unacceptable in consumer electronics.

If all these devices used the same software—and if the software was smart enough to make all these devices easy to use—life could be a lot simpler. Instead of being confronted by a multitude of different ways to use different devices, they'd all be familiar. The language the team began work on was known as *Oak*. They also created a cannibalized electronic device as the first piece of equipment to be run by Oak: an LCD screen from a minitelevision, speakers from Nintendo's Game Boy, a touch screen on the front, the guts of a Sun workstation squeezed into a tiny case, and so on.

Oak was much more than an operating system for consumer electronics, though. It would link everything. All electronic devices could be networked, and Oak could be the electronic glue sticking it all together. Everything electronic, everything digital, could be run by Oak. Sun Microsystems got so excited about Oak that it set up a new company, FirstPerson, Inc., to develop and push the system.

But Oak never quite found a home. Companies that expressed an interest in using it—France Telecom for its Minitel data system, Mitsubishi for its electronic devices, Time Warner for its interactive TV controllers, and so on—never quite came through. The devices were too expensive, or the potential clients ended up buying products from other companies.

Eventually, FirstPerson went back to basics. They decided to forget consumer electronics, but rather to focus on personal computers. However, they were unable to come up with a way to create demand for Sun's workstations, so FirstPerson was eventually scrapped in early 1994.

Oak was revived a few months later, though, by Bill Joy, one of the founders of Sun. He realized that Oak could be useful on the Internet, and he decided that Sun should develop it and give it away. "Let's create a franchise," he said. In other words, give it away, get enough people to use it, and eventually Sun would "own" that particular market. Oak was modified for use on the Internet and, early in 1995, was renamed *Java*.

A special program was developed, *HotJava*, which could actually run programs that were created using Java. Later, of course, a Java interpreter would be incorporated into Netscape Navigator; in other words, Navigator itself could run Java applications—Java *applets*, as they became known—making HotJava unnecessary for Navigator users.

So, What Exactly Is Java?

Java is a programming language, similar in some ways to C++, but intended to be more reliable. Remember, Java was originally designed for the consumer electronics market, which is far less tolerant of unreliability than the consumer software business.

So, Java allows you to create programs, but you need an operating system to run a program. Generally speaking, if you want to create a word processor that runs in DOS and Windows, on the Macintosh computer, and on Sun workstations, you'll have to create four different versions (at least four, maybe more: one for Windows 3.1, one for Windows 95, and so on). But Java is different. The idea behind Java is that a programmer can create a single version of the program, which then runs inside a Java "interpreter," a program such as HotJava or Netscape Navigator. There are different interpreters for different computers and operating systems—there's a Netscape Navigator that runs on the Macintosh, one that runs in Windows 3.1, one for Windows 95, and so on. So a single Java program can run on a number of different operating systems, as long as the user has an interpreter that will run on his or her computer.

These Java interpreters are not true operating systems, though the principle is the same to some degree. An *operating system* is the interface between a computer's hardware and a program. Rather than writing a program that "talks" directly to the computer's hardware—to the keyboard, to the video screen, and so on—a programmer simply has to write a program that talks to the operating system and can enable the operating system to do the routine hardware stuff. A Java interpreter works in a similar way. It sits between the operating system and the Java program. Instead of writing several versions of the program—each of which talks to a different operating system—the programmer writes a single program that can talk to any Java interpreter on any computer system. The Java interpreter then liaises between the Java program and the operating system, in effect translating what each says into something the other can understand.

This is a breakthrough technology, Java proponents claim, because it smashes constraints forced on software by operating systems. "Interpreted" languages have been around for a while, but they haven't been as sophisticated as Java. Java provides a powerful programming language with which very sophisticated programs can be created and then run on a variety of different computers. No longer is a program only a Macintosh program, only a Windows program, or only a UNIX program. Now it's a Java program, and it can run on anything that has an available Java interpreter.

Where Will It Take Us?

It's been predicted by many that Java is the beginning of the end for "shrink-wrapped" software. Eventually, we'll all use programs created using Java, JavaScript, and similar languages. Instead of buying a word processor or spreadsheet and loading it onto our hard disks, we'll log on to an Internet site and run the program from there, paying a per-minute or per-use fee.

There are many problems with this idea, of course. It remains to be seen whether this will come to pass—and if it does, don't expect it to be soon. It will take years before the really fast connections required for such a scenario are cheaply and easily available and before connecting to the Internet is as reliable as "connecting" to your hard disk. (We admit to more than a little skepticism about this scenario, but who knows what the future will bring. As nuclear physicist Niels Bohr said, "making predictions is very difficult, especially about the future.") Still, Java does seem to be the Internet programming language of the moment—even if we never throw our hard-disk applications away; and Java still provides a mechanism for Web site developers to add life to their pages.

Then Came JavaScript

A system like Java is only useful if it's ubiquitous, or close to being so. It has to be everywhere. Here's a classic example of a system that failed because it *wasn't* ubiquitous: OS/2. Many OS/2 users will complain loudly that this IBM operating system is far superior to any version of Microsoft Windows. Maybe, maybe not (we don't want to get into that argument!). But one thing we can be sure of is that relatively few PC users actually use OS/2. Consequently, very few programs are written for OS/2—so few that if OS/2 couldn't run Windows programs, it probably would have died years ago. It's a vicious cycle: few people use OS/2, so few programmers write programs for it, so OS/2's "user base" remains relatively stagnant, so programmers continue to ignore it.

Sun realizes this little software fact of life and wants to make sure that Java becomes *the* system on the Internet—"the DOS of the Internet," as Sun engineer Arthur van Hoff has put it. And they know that Microsoft is hard on their heels, with products such as *VBScript* and *ActiveX*. But there's a problem: Java is a programming language. It's not easy to sit down and create a Java application, unless you happen to be a programmer who understands how to write Java. So Sun says that it will provide ways to make it easier for people to create these Java applications. They plan to provide special toolkits that will allow any nonprogrammer—any Web-site developer, writer, artist, businessperson—to create Java programs.

The first step to simplifying Java is *JavaScript*. Think of JavaScript as Java's little brother. Although Netscape began development of JavaScript independently (it was originally called *LiveScript*), they soon joined in a partnership with Sun, agreeing to make JavaScript a sort of subset of Java. JavaScript is similar in some ways to Java, but is much simpler to use. You don't need a Java development kit, and you don't need to compile Java applications. All you need to do is add a script to your Web pages and, when a JavaScript-enabled browser (currently, only the Netscape browsers and Microsoft Internet Explorer 3 and later) opens the Web page, it reads the script and follows the instructions. And, as you'll see in this book, you can even use JavaScript to interface with Java—use a script written in JavaScript to pass information to a Java applet, for instance.

What Does *Compiled* Mean?

Compiled is the term given to the process of taking code (ASCII text) written by a programmer and converting it into something that a computer can read and very quickly understand, often in the form of an executable (.EXE or .COM) file. JavaScripts are additional statements in HTML files and are never compiled—they remain ASCII text along with the remainder of the file.

Java vs. JavaScript

There are some important differences between Java and JavaScript. Table 1-1 compares the two systems:

Java	JavaScript
Complicated to use.	Relatively easy to use.
You'll need the JDK (Java Developer's Kit), free from Sun Microsystems.	You don't need a developer's kit. All you need is information about how to write scripts (this book is your introduction to that information) and a JavaScript-compatible browser such as Netscape Navigator.
Programs are compiled into executable files. These files are embedded into Web pages using the <APPLET> tag. When a browser opens the Web page and sees the <APPLET> tag, it retrieves and runs the Java applet.	"Programs" are built into the Web page in the form of a script. There is no separate JavaScript program file, so there's no need to compile, download, and interpret a separate file.
On today's Internet, Java applications tend to be a little slow. The compiled file has to be transferred to a user's computer before it can run.	JavaScript tends to run very quickly. The script is built into the Web page—it's just text—and JavaScripts tend to be smaller than Java applets anyway.
Java is more powerful. It's a full-blown programming language.	JavaScript is more appropriate for relatively simple uses. You won't build a word processor using JavaScript!
Java is *object-oriented*. Java applets, to quote the Netscape documentation, "consist of object classes with inheritance." What does that mean? It means that Java uses a fairly complicated system that we don't need to know about in this book. (We don't want to introduce any more programming-speak than we need to.)	JavaScript is *object-based*. "Code uses built-in, extensible objects, but no classes or inheritance." And that means, you'll be pleased to know, that JavaScript is simpler than Java. JavaScript is not a true object-oriented programming language, though you can still work with objects. (Don't worry about the distinction, it doesn't really matter for the nonprogrammer.)
Java has strict rules about how to use *variables*. They must be declared before using them. You'll learn more about variables in Chapter 4, "Variables & Literals—Storing Data."	JavaScript has what's known as loose typing. That is, it's less restrictive about how you create and use variables.
Java uses *static binding*. More programming jargon, meaning that references to objects must exist when the program is compiled.	JavaScript uses *dynamic binding*. References to objects are checked when the script is run. You'll learn more about objects in Chapter 10, "Objects, Properties & Methods," but you don't need to worry about these binding terms right now.

Table 1-1: The Differences between Java and JavaScript.

TIP

There's an important limitation in both Java and JavaScript that you ought to under-stand right away. For security reasons, when used with a browser for displaying Web pages neither Java nor JavaScript can write to the hard disk (except in a very limited way; see the information on cookies *in Chapter 13, "Advanced Topics"). This limita-tion makes them safer, though. Web users can't download a rogue Java or JavaScript applet that can trash their hard disks. However, this limitation is significant because it also restricts what a Java or JavaScript applet can do. The limitation is being addressed in JavaScript 1.2, which uses "signed objects" to allow a user to identify where a script has come from and to decide whether the script should be allowed to write to the hard disk. See Chapter 14 for more information.*

JavaScript is similar to Java, but it's simpler. It's easier to write using Java-Script, and it's easier to incorporate JavaScript applications into your Web sites. There's no need to compile your applications—you simply write the scripts directly into your Web pages, and the browser interprets them along with the other HTML codes.

Programmers love to argue about semantics, and some would argue that JavaScript is not quite a programming language. You see, the program is already written—your JavaScript-compatible browser already has the JavaScript interpreter built into it. JavaScript is simply a way of creating in-structions that tell the browser what to do. You, the Web-page developer, write a series of JavaScript instructions in your HTML documents. The browser reads those instructions and "interprets" them—that is, it carries out your instructions (assuming of course, you've written something that the browser can understand).

In a sense, then, you are not writing a program when you write JavaScript. The script you write is not *compiled* as a real program must be, and it cannot work alone. This sort of "programming" is often called *scripting;* and there's a common belief that because JavaScript is a form of scripting, it's not quite the same as programming. Rather, it's simply a set of instructions and it requires a browser to run—not just any browser, but a browser that has the JavaScript interpreter built in. However, in another sense you most certainly *are* writing a program. While some JavaScripts are very simple and easy to put together (as you'll see in Chapter 2, "A Few Quick JavaScript Tricks"), JavaScript can be very complicated. Just take a look at the Netscape JavaScript documentation. If you're not a programmer, you'll come away dazed and confused by such terms as *objects, methods, functions, expressions, values, literals, statements, event handlers,* and so forth.

The Penguin Dictionary of Computers defines *program* as a set of instructions composed for solving a given problem by a computer, and that is most certainly what JavaScript is and does. It is, however, easier to use than some programming languages (though much harder than others). In fact, JavaScript combined with this book makes a really good first step into programming. If you then move on to Java (and C and C++), you will find that much of the code you write looks very similar to JavaScript.

Where Can You Get JavaScript?

If you want to create C++ or Visual Basic programs, you need a software development "environment," and you need a compiler. But there is no JavaScript software development environment and you never have to compile your scripts, so the only thing you need is the knowledge—which is what this book is all about, of course. The only other thing you'll need is a JavaScript-compatible browser: a World Wide Web browser that can read, interpret, and run the JavaScripts you create. At the time of writing, the only JavaScript-compatible browsers available are the Netscape Navigator family of browsers and Microsoft Internet Explorer 3 and later. JavaScript was introduced in the Navigator 2.0 browsers. At the time of writing, the latest available version of JavaScript was in the Netscape Navigator 4 browser. If you are using an earlier version of Netscape you should upgrade to the latest Netscape. In fact, even if you are running one of the 4.x versions, check to see that you have the very latest version, as it will contain bug fixes and perhaps new JavaScript features (note also that some of the early Version 4 Preview releases did not have full JavaScript support).

Note, however, that it's not always a good idea to write JavaScripts that use features only available in the very latest browser—those features won't work in the browsers that most users are working with (as I'll discuss at the end of this chapter, under "Which JavaScript Should You Use?"). So, you should consider staying a step or two behind. (Give the browser programmers a chance to sort out bugs, too.)

By the way, it's no longer just Web browsers that can work with JavaScript; any program with a built-in JavaScript interpreter can run JavaScripts. For instance, HTML is now coming to e-mail—some e-mail programs are now able to display Web pages. Some programs will eventually be able to handle non-HTML components of Web pages, such as JavaScript and even Java. At the time of writing, the only e-mail program that could work with JavaScript was Netscape Messenger, the program bundled with Netscape Communicator.

This is a handy feature for JavaScript programmers. If you are collaborating on a JavaScript project with another person, you can exchange JavaScript via e-mail and see what the scripts do right there in the e-mail program.

TIP

You can get the latest version of Netscape Navigator from: http://www.netscape.com/ or http://home.netscape.com/.

So What's It Good For?

What, then, can you get JavaScript to do? Well, you can make JavaScript carry out procedures automatically—that is, when a Web page opens or closes (when the user loads a different page). Or you can make JavaScript carry out procedures at a particular event; for example, when the user clicks on a button or link, simply points at a button or link, moves focus from one component of a form to another component of the form, and so on.

These procedures might be simple—the script can write the date that the document was last updated into the Web page or display a message in a dialog box or in the status bar at the bottom of the browser window. Scripts can open new browser windows and display particular HTML files or display a page selected from the browser's history list. Or they might be complicated—a script can check the contents of a form that the user wants to submit and then warn the user if the information is not valid. A script can also search for information in a "mini-database" built into the Web page or perform complicated financial calculations.

JavaScript Examples

You'll find loads of JavaScript examples scattered across the Web. There are reportedly 300,000 pages on the Web that contain some form of JavaScript, from the very simple to the very complicated. Visit some of the Web sites listed in Appendix H, "Finding More Information," or visit our Online Companion (http://www.netscapepress.com/support/javascript 1.2/), and you'll find examples galore.

So rather than our telling you what *can* be done with JavaScript, why don't we take a quick look at what *has* been done with JavaScript already.

Takeaways & Remotes

Here's a nice idea you might think about for your own Web pages, if there's something useful in the pages that people might want to take with them: use JavaScript to create a small secondary window that contains something they can use after they've left your site.

For instance, Netscape's own search page (http://home.netscape.com/home/internet-search.html) lets you take away a small *site sampler* window. You can then continue on your Web journey. If at any time you need to quickly search for something, you can enter a search word into this "takeaway," then click on the Search button—a request is sent to the search engine, and the response is displayed in a new window. You can see this in Figure 1-1.

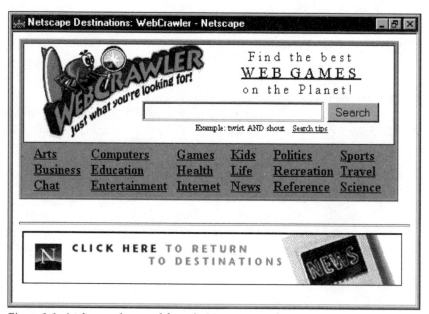

Figure 1-1: A takeaway borrowed from the Netscape search page.

Order Forms

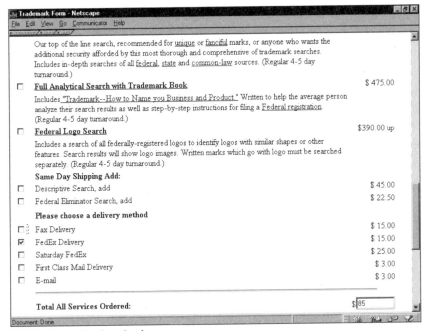

Figure 1-2: A simple order form.

You'll find lots of order forms created using JavaScript. There's a good example at the Seek Information Service site (http://www.ironlight.net/trademark/html/order.html), where you can place an order for a trademark search. This form, which you can see in Figure 1-2, lets a customer select options from a list, and the form keeps a running total at the bottom.

Calculators

A popular demonstration use of JavaScript is to create a calculator. The one in Figure 1-3 is unusual because, instead of using HTML buttons, it uses an image-map picture of a calculator. You can find this at http://www.parallax.co.uk/~rolf/Calculator/.

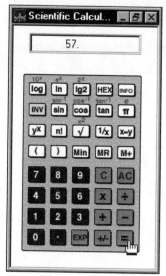

Figure 1-3: An unusual JavaScript calculator.

The 1040EZ Tax Form

The tax form at http://www.homepages.com/fun/1040EZ.html is not provided by the Internal Revenue Service, though it was created from IRS rules and information by a Web- and JavaScript-consulting company. It shows how JavaScript can be used to create forms that carry out calculations. You enter information into the text boxes and when you Tab out of the box or click elsewhere, the form recalculates (see Figure 1-4). When you click on option buttons, the appropriate values are entered into the text boxes, too.

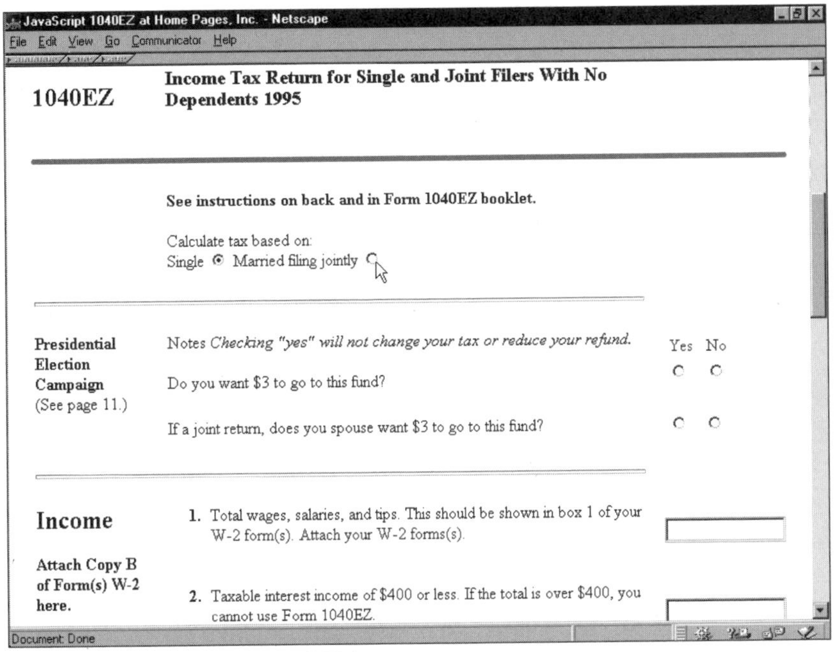

Figure 1-4: The JavaScript 1040EZ form.

The Bozo Filter

Want to block access to your Web page from certain other Web pages? Perhaps a "disreputable" Web site has a link to you and you don't want to be associated with it. Using Alistair Fraser's *Bozo Filter,* you can block access to JavaScript-enabled browsers that come from a specific URL. Or you can display a specific page of information for users that come from that particular URL. You can find more information about this site at http://www.ems.psu.edu/~fraser/Bozo/Bozo.html. (Sounds like this guy has a feud with Mirsky's Worst of the Web. Something to do with an anti-bagpipe bias.)

The Color Coded Resistance Calculator

I like this simple little JavaScript utility (at http://www.ee.upenn.edu/rca/calcjs.html). Select the color bands shown on a resistor, and the JavaScript will tell you the resistor's specifications (see Figure 1-5). There's even a little picture of a resistor at the bottom of the page to show what the resistor you are checking looks like.

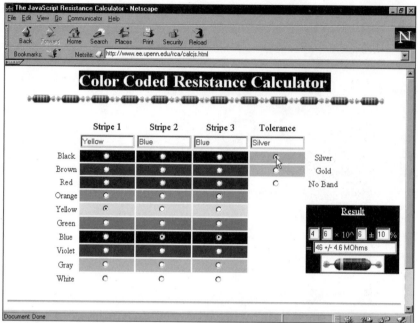

Figure 1-5: The Resistance Calculator.

Webpage Personalizer

Here's another takeaway. This is a little utility for changing window colors. When you visit http://www.geocities.com/SiliconValley/3555/starter.html, a special window opens (see Figure 1-6) that contains color controls. You can now travel around the Web and, in theory, use this window to modify the colors of the Web pages you view.

Figure 1-6: The Webpage Personalizer.

Selecting Where You Want to Go

You can use JavaScript to enable the reader to select from a list of items. For example, when the reader clicks on a button, the information that the reader has selected will be displayed. That information might be another Web page, a picture, a sound, or whatever.

You'll find a good example of this at http://www.tripnet.se/home/brodd/ preview.html (see Figure 1-7). This is a picture viewer; the user can select an entry from a drop-down list box, then click on the Preview Image button. Up pops another window that contains the selected picture and a Close button.

Figure 1-7: A picture viewer.

Measurements Converter

There is a variety of different specialized calculators and converters popping up on the Web—from relocation estimators to runner's calculators to mortgage calculators—and one way to create them is by using JavaScript. There's an excellent set of converters at http://www.mplik.ru/~sg/transl/. Select the type of unit—weight, capacity and volume, length, area, speed, pressure, temperature, circular measure, or time—then enter a unit into the table, click anywhere outside the field into which you typed, and all the conversions are done immediately. You can see the Time Converter in Figure 1-8.

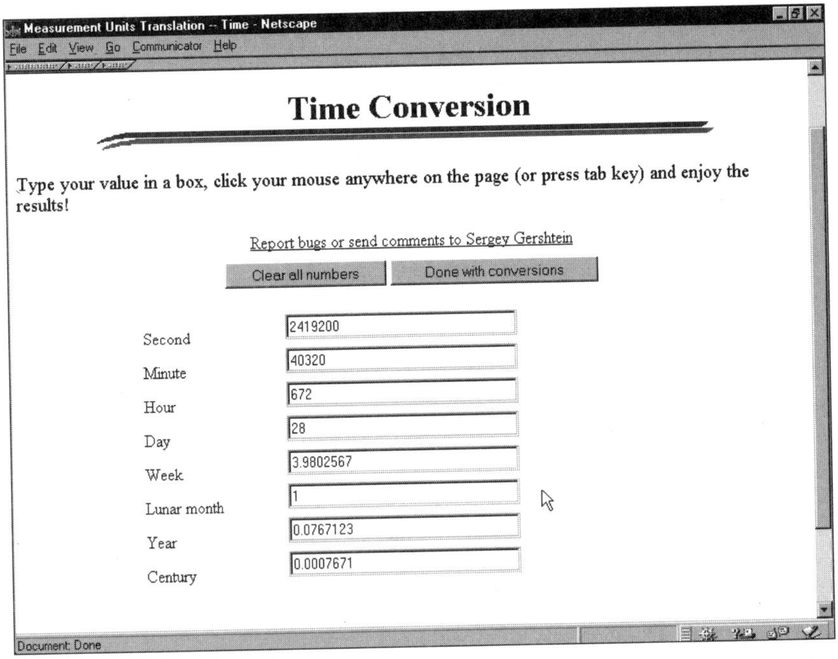

Figure 1-8. A Time Converter.

TIP

If you find neat little utilities that you want to keep, you can simply save the page on your hard disk. You can open the page later, when you need to use the utility. Of course, it's more complicated if these utilities span more than one HTML page, as some of the more sophisticated ones do.

European Capitals

There are a lot of educational Web pages that use JavaScript. In Figure 1-9, you can see an example of one of these, the European Capitals page at http://www.concentric.net/~Kraft/europe/. Click on a country, type the country's name and capital city into the text boxes, then click the Check button. Or click Answer to see the correct answer.

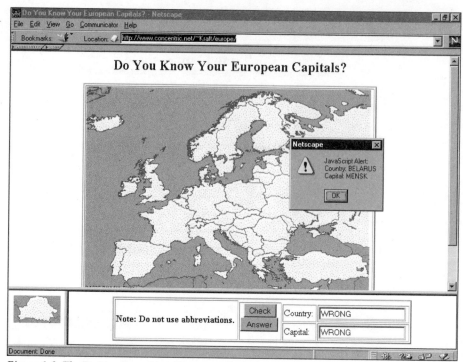

Figure 1-9: The Do You Know Your European Capitals? test page.

Games, Games, Games

True to the spirit of the Internet, much of the energy going into creating JavaScript apps is going into goofing off—you'll find loads of JavaScript games. For instance, there's a Blackjack game at http://www.netzmarkt.de/neu/cas2000e.htm, which you can see in Figure 1-10. You will also find various other card games (Bridge and Five Card Stud, for instance); Rock, Paper, Scissors; a variety of strategy and adventure games; and so on.

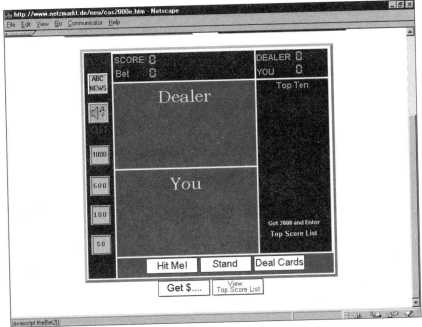

Figure 1-10: A Blackjack game.

An HTML Editor—HTMLjive

More sophisticated programs can be created using JavaScript. An example is HTMLjive (a program that can be used in conjunction with a CGI script), which allows people to create Web pages online and immediately post them. For instance, a professional organization could use such a system to allow its members to post job leads and resumes to its Web site. You can find more information about HTMLjive at http://www.cris.com/~raydaly/ hjdemo.shtml. You can see an example there (see Figure 1-11) and links to the sites that are using the program.

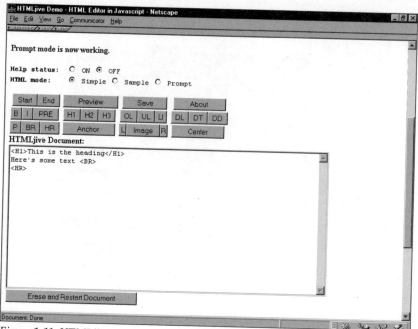

Figure 1-11: HTMLjive.

Remember, though, that JavaScript doesn't let you save anything directly, which is why this editor must be used with a CGI. JavaScript can send the information to the CGI, which can then save it in the correct place. Of course, the completed HTML text can also be highlighted and copied to the clipboard.

Interactive Tables of Contents

JavaScript can be used to manage browser frames. One method is to use JavaScript to create interactive tables of contents. For instance, at http://www.cuesys.com/ you'll find the document shown in Figure 1-12. In the left pane is a table of contents with a small icon before the name of each entry. Click on the icon to "open" a list of subcategories below the name or to close that list.

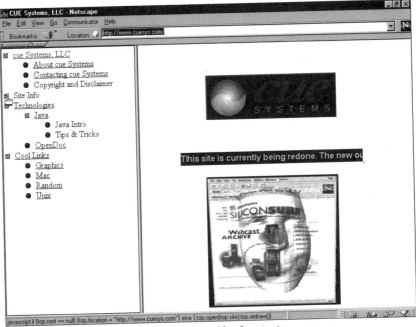

Figure 1-12: The Cue System's interactive table of contents.

Like What You See?

If you like what other people have done, you can often take their scripts. Many of these scripts have been made publicly available by their authors. (We'll be explaining how to incorporate scripts into your Web pages later—see Chapter 20, "Ready-to-Use Scripts.") You can find loads of useful scripts that can be copied from the Internet using Netscape. Simply choose View|Page Source (Navigator 4) or View|Document Source (Navigator 3) to open the document-source window; then copy the text of the Web page (including the script) from the open document-source window, or use File|Save As to save it to a new file. Remember two things, though. First, many scripts are *not* intended for public use. If a script author hasn't specifically stated that you can use the script, then you'd better not use the script in a public Web page, or even in a private Web page on a corporate "intranet." And even if an author says that you can take the script, it doesn't necessarily make it yours. You might not be able to use it commercially—for instance, selling it to other Web developers. However, you can always borrow scripts to see how the author has done something. Then you can take what you've learned and create your own.

Off the Shelf Java

JavaScript provides a way to use Java applets in your documents. Creating Java applets is a time-consuming and skilled job—it's a programmer's job—and if you aren't a programmer, you won't be able to create Java applets. But you *will* be able to take a public domain, shareware, or commercial Java applet and use JavaScript to "connect it" to your Web pages. The JavaScript will send information from the page to the Java applet, and the Java applet can then return something to the Web page. JavaScript will work as a sort of interface between your documents and the Java applet.

We'll look at this feature in Chapter 13, "Advanced Topics." Note, however, that this feature was introduced with Netscape Navigator 3.0 (JavaScript 1.1), and many users are currently working with browsers that don't support this feature.

> **TIP**
>
> *You'll run across the <APPLET> tag now and again in HTML documents. This is used by Java, not JavaScript. It's the tag used to embed Java applets into Web pages.*

Is JavaScript Turned On?

You have a JavaScript browser, but will it work? JavaScript-enabled browsers generally have a setting that allows you to turn JavaScript on or off. If it's off, then none of the JavaScript examples in this book (or any other JavaScripts you run across on the Web) will work. This option is for security reasons; although both Java and JavaScript are designed to be safe, some users want to be completely sure of their security and disable Java or JavaScript apps from running. (Netscape provides the ability to turn off Java and JavaScript independently; some browsers give one setting for both systems.) Many users don't like the idea of a program running automatically when they enter a Web page, regardless of how safe it's supposed to be. And bugs *have* been found in both Java and JavaScript. For instance, in March of 1996 a bug was found that introduced a potential security risk; to quote the Netscape press release, "Through a sophisticated attack, an experienced programmer could potentially write a malicious applet that might exploit this bug and cause a file to be deleted or cause other damage on a user's machine." That bug's been fixed—

that is, more recent versions of Netscape Navigator do not contain the bug. Other bugs are found every now and then, however.

So before we start, make sure that JavaScript is turned on in your browser; if it's not, you won't be able to test our example scripts. In Netscape Navigator 4, choose Edit | Preferences, then click on Advanced in the list on the left side of the Preferences box. In Netscape Navigator 3, choose Options | General Preferences, then click on the Language tab. Make sure that the Enable Java-Script check box has been *checked*. If the check box is clear, any JavaScripts that you try *will not work*.

Internet Explorer currently has no way to disable JavaScript (at the time of writing Explorer was on Version 3). JavaScript will work at all times. Internet Explorer 4 will be released very soon, however, and might be available by the time you read this book. That version might allow the disabling of JavaScript.

Which JavaScript Should You Use?

Which JavaScript? JavaScript is JavaScript, isn't it? Well, not exactly. JavaScript is built into each browser, so each time you install a different browser, you're installing a different version of JavaScript. JavaScript began its life in the beta versions of Netscape Navigator 2. Since that time it's appeared in various beta versions of Navigator 2 and 3 and in the released versions of 3, the preview versions of Navigator 4, and now in the released version of Navigator 4. It's also turned up in beta and released versions of Microsoft Internet Explorer 3 and will soon be in various versions of Internet Explorer 4, too. Also, for each browser version number, there are different platform versions; versions of Internet Explorer running on Windows NT, Windows 95, Windows 3.1, and, perhaps, the Macintosh (the current Macintosh version doesn't support JavaScript). There are versions of Netscape Navigator working on almost 20 different operating systems (loads of different UNIX flavors). All the different platform versions should work just the same . . . but they don't.

So, who is using what browser? That's difficult to know for sure. There are some Web sites that give an idea, though. Each time a browser contacts a Web site it identifies itself, so it's possible to collect statistics on browser use. You can take a look at these sites to get an idea of how many people are using each browser:

- **Web Browser Agent Statistics**—http://www.xmission.com/ ~snowhare/statistics/browsers.html

- **Interse Web Trends**—http://www.interse.com/webtrends/ (this one's handy because it uses graphs to show the trends).

- **WWW Statistics**—http://blueridge.infomkt.ibm.com/knudsen/stats/current.html

- **Webtrends**—http://www.webtrends.com/

- **EWS Browser Statistics**—http://www.cen.uiuc.edu/bstats/latest.html

- **Browser Watch**—http://browserwatch.iworld.com/stats.html

- **Yahoo!—Browser Usage Statistics**—http://www.yahoo.com/Computers_and_Internet/Internet/World_Wide_Web/Browsers/Browser_Usage_Statistics/

In this book, we've identified certain features that were introduced with Netscape Navigator 3 (JavaScript 1.1) and 4 (JavaScript 1.2). The latest version of Navigator has the latest version of JavaScript, because Netscape Communications is developing JavaScript—Microsoft is just following along.

But many visitors to your Web site won't be able to use those features, because many people are using browsers that won't yet have those features built in: Internet Explorer 3, early Navigator 3 betas, Navigator 2, and so on.

For instance, I recently looked at some of the statistics sites I've listed. The EWS Statistics Page showed that 24% of the browsers coming to its site were Microsoft Internet Explorer and 73% were Netscape Navigator (that means 3% weren't either, which means that at least 3% of the browsers have no JavaScript support at all). Of the Netscape browsers, however, a significant portion were *not* Navigator 3; about 23% of the Navigators were Version 2 (about 7% were even earlier), which means that 17% of all the browsers reaching this site were Navigator 2 or earlier.

As for Internet Explorer, 84% were Version 3; that's the version in which Microsoft added JavaScript. So about 20% of all visitors were working with a JavaScript-enabled version of Internet Explorer.

That means that about 37% of all visitors to this site were using a browser that handles an *early* form of JavaScript. Other statistics sites show even higher figures for these "early JavaScript" browsers. The Web Browser Agent Statistics site listed above currently shows only about 45% of visitors using Netscape Navigator 3.0 or later.

However you look at it, a significant number of Web users are working with either no JavaScript or with earlier versions (pre-Navigator 3.0). (These figures, incidentally, are from the first quarter of 1997, months after Navigator 3.0 was released.) Of course these numbers will change—more users will upgrade to Navigator 3.0 or to a later version of Internet Explorer with updated JavaScript . . . but JavaScript will have moved to a later version by then, too. It seems likely that the users working with the very latest version of

JavaScript will always remain in the minority. So it might be a good idea to stay a few steps behind! Sure, learn the latest features, but be aware that many, perhaps most, of the visitors to your site will be using browsers that won't be able to use those features.

You might also consider writing scripts designed for particular browsers. In Chapter 3 you'll see how to use the <SCRIPT> tag to identify the version of JavaScript that you are using, so non compatible browsers will ignore the script.

TIP

To confuse the issue a little, Internet Explorer actually supports some of the JavaScript features that are in Netscape 3 (JavaScript 1.1). We've identified some of these features in this book, but ideally you should test all your scripts with Internet Explorer 3, Netscape Navigator 2, Netscape Navigator 3, and Netscape Navigator 4.

JavaScript Version Numbers

Although you don't often see them, there are actually JavaScript version numbers. Here's what they currently mean:

JavaScript 1	The version in Netscape Navigator 2 and Internet Explorer 3.
JavaScript 1.1	The version in Netscape Navigator 3 and, to some degree, in Internet Explorer 3.
JavaScript 1.2	The version in Netscape Navigator 4, Netscape Messenger, and Netscape Collabra.

You'll also hear the term Jscript. This is what Microsoft is calling its version of JavaScript, built into Internet Explorer 3. It's very similar to JavaScript 1, but with a few slight differences that can sometimes cause problems. Internet Explorer is inconsistent; it supports most of the features in Netscape 2, but also supports *some* that are in Netscape 3.

Also, note that the early versions of Netscape Navigator 4 do not have some of the JavaScript features that are in Netscape Navigator 3. The Netscape Navigator 4 Preview Release 1 version (1/97), for instance, cannot work with the **SRC=** attribute (which we'll see in Chapter 3). So if you're still using any of the preview versions, upgrade to the latest.

Moving On

We've learned what JavaScript is and a little of what can be done with it. Now it's time to do some work. Some of the examples you've seen are quite complicated, but there are things that can be done very quickly and easily—things that you can do to your Web pages to add features with a few keystrokes. For instance, you can add a "modified date" to a Web page in a few seconds. Many other JavaScript tools are very simple to use, too.

So, as a practical introduction to the quick and easy things you can do with JavaScript, we're going to move on to Chapter 2, "A Few Quick JavaScript Tricks."

A Few Quick JavaScript Tricks

Now that you've seen what JavaScript can do, wouldn't it be nice to do something straight away? Well, you can. No, you won't be able to create a sophisticated JavaScript application, but there are a number of simple things you can do immediately.

You might have heard that JavaScript is a simple-to-use scripting language that anyone can use to bring life to Web pages. Well, that's only half true. It's easy when compared to Java. It's not easy when compared to writing a simple word-processing macro, though. It's easy for a programmer—not so easy for a nonprogrammer. Nonprogrammers who want to completely understand Java-Script will have to spend quite a bit of time and effort learning new concepts.

However, having said all that, there *are* a number of things you can do with JavaScript quickly and easily—without really understanding what you are doing! We're going to look at a few of these examples in this chapter. By the time you've finished the chapter—having seen that JavaScript isn't *always* complicated—we're sure you'll have the courage to move on to the trickier stuff.

Remember, we're assuming you understand HTML—at least the basics. We're going to show you how to drop a few simple JavaScript tools into your Web documents. Don't worry about exactly how and why everything works in this chapter; you'll understand more after we examine the detailed explanations later. So, let's start with a simple technique to put a date in your document.

> **TIP**
>
> *All of the examples in this book are in our Online Companion at http://www.netscapepress.com/support/javascript 1.2. (Notice the Online Companion icons in the margins next to the examples—these show you the example number.) You can go to the Online Companion and try each example. Then, you can copy the script directly from the Web page (no need to open the source; we've put a script sample in each document so you can copy straight from the Web page) and paste it into your own Web pages. By the way, you can also copy the entire Online Companion examples—stored in an archive file—back to your hard disk.*
>
> *If you decide to type these scripts for yourself, make sure you type these examples exactly as they appear. If you type anything incorrectly, even typing an uppercase letter where there should be a lowercase letter or vice versa, the script might not work.*

Placing a Modified Date in Your Web Pages

It's often useful to show a date in your Web page indicating the last time that the source document was saved. Readers can quickly see just how old the information is. Well, JavaScript gives you a quick and easy way to do this. Here's what you must do.

> **TIP**
>
> *Writing JavaScript is similar in some ways to writing HTML. It's convenient to have both your HTML editor and Netscape Navigator open at the same time; you can then make changes to your HTML document and script and quickly view the changes in your browser.*

1. Open one of your Web pages in the HTML editor you use and place the cursor exactly where you want to see the Last Modified date.

2. Now, type the following:

Example 2.1

```
<SCRIPT LANGUAGE="JAVASCRIPT">
document.write("This document last modified on: ")
document.write(document.lastModified)
</SCRIPT>
```

3. Save your page. Now take a look at it in any JavaScript-compatible browser. You'll see something like Figure 2-1.

Figure 2-1: Adding a modified date to a document.

Note that you can modify the text if you choose. You might want to see **Last Modified** instead of **This document last modified on**. If so, simply replace the text with the text you prefer.

So, here you have a JavaScript that you can start using right away, even if you don't really understand what it all means.

TIP

If you've been viewing a document in your browser and have just made a change to the JavaScript, remember to save the change in your HTML editor and then click on the browser's Reload button to get the updated JavaScript.

TIP

Important: Some versions of Netscape Navigator have a cache bug. Using the Reload command often does not reload the document. This is a particular problem when creating HTML tags and scripts that incorporate forms; reloading often doesn't properly re-create the form. There are several things you can do to get around the problem. Try pressing the Shift key (or the Option key on the Mac) while clicking on the Reload button—this is supposed to throw out the cached copy and grab a fresh copy of the Web page, even if the page hasn't changed. You can also try using the File | Open File command and opening the page again, or creating a bookmark to the page and using the bookmark to open it. If all else fails, you'll have to close the browser.

Hiding Scripts

There's a problem with the script we've just written, though. Take a look at Figure 2-2. This is Internet Explorer 2.0, which cannot work with JavaScripts. It treats it just like text, so it ends up looking a little funky—like you've screwed something up in your source document. (By the way, you can turn JavaScript off in some JavaScript-compatible browsers. If a user does this, the browser still recognizes JavaScripts—it simply doesn't display the result—so it shouldn't display the garbage you see in Figure 2-2. The garbage is only a problem with non-JavaScript browsers.)

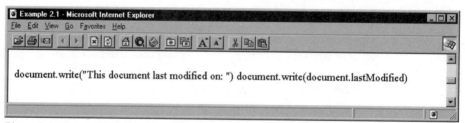

Figure 2-2: The modified date, shown in a non-JavaScript browser.

Example 2.2

You can fix that problem, however, by telling old, non-JavaScript browsers to ignore the script. Modify your previously created script as follows:

```
<SCRIPT LANGUAGE="JAVASCRIPT">
<!--
document.write("This document last modified on: ")
document.write(document.lastModified)
// -->
</SCRIPT>
```

Notice that we've added two lines, **<!--** and **// -->**. These are, of course, the comment tags used in HTML; browsers ignore everything between the comment tags. Well, not all browsers—JavaScript-compatible browsers know that there's a script between the tags, so they look there and read the script.

Once you've added these tags in the correct places (they must be on the line below the **<SCRIPT LANGUAGE="JAVASCRIPT">** tag and the line above the **</SCRIPT>** tag), the script becomes invisible to browsers that don't know what to do with the JavaScript. Take a look at the document with Internet Explorer 2.0, for example, and you won't see anything there. Use Netscape Navigator, though, and you'll see the **This document last modified on** line.

What Page Has the Reader Come From?

If you've moved your Web site recently, you might have left a document at the previous site informing people of the change. You've seen these messages: "Our Web site has moved, please change your bookmarks and inform the owner of the document you've just come from," or something similar. You can add a simple JavaScript to one of these documents to display the URL of the document from which you've just come. For example, type this into your HTML source file:

Example 2.3

```
The URL of the document you are seeking has changed. Please inform the owner
of the document you've just come from
<SCRIPT LANGUAGE="JAVASCRIPT">
<!--
document.write(" (" + document.referrer + ")")
// -->
</SCRIPT>
that this link has changed.
```

Figure 2-3 shows what the user will see when arriving at this document. (Well, something like what the user will see, depending on where he or she has come from. As you can see, the URL in this example is a **file:///** URL, meaning that it's a file on a hard disk.)

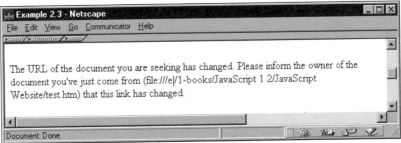

Figure 2-3: Using the URL of the document the user has come from.

As you can see, the document is showing the text as well as, in parentheses, the URL of the document from which the user has just come. What would the user of a non-JavaScript browser see? Because most of the text is outside the comment lines, and because only the **document.referrer** instruction is inside (**referrer** is a *property* of the **document** object, but don't worry about that right now—you'll learn about objects and properties in Chapter 10, "Objects, Properties & Methods"), the reader will see everything but the parenthetical information (the URL of the document). The reader will see something like this:

```
The URL of the document you are seeking has changed. Please inform the owner
of the document you've just come from that this link has changed.
```

By the way, you'll only see a URL between the parentheses if you reach the page through a link in another page. You can't simply load the page by typing a URL into your browser's Location box, or the parentheses will be empty since **document.referrer** will not be defined, so to test your script set up a link in another page, load that page into your browser, then click the link.

Opening Secondary Windows

When the Web first came on the Internet scene, it was a relatively simple hypertext system. Other hypertext systems—such as Windows Help, for example—had a feature that the Web sorely lacked: *secondary windows*. That is, clicking on a link could open another window, leaving the original window open, too. Well, you can use JavaScript to do all sorts of tricks with secondary (or, in Netscape-speak, *targeted*) windows. Here's a simple one you can try. If you want to open another window and place the contents of a particular HTML document in that window, here's how you can do it.

Example 2.4

First, add this information in the head of your HTML document:

```
<head>
<SCRIPT LANGUAGE="JAVASCRIPT">
<!--
function WinOpen() {
 open("window.htm","Window1","toolbar=yes");
}
//-->
</SCRIPT>
</head>
```

TIP

It's a sad truth that JavaScript is not the same on all browsers. A script that runs in one browser might not run in another. The preceding script, for example, would not run on one Solaris version of Netscape Navigator. JavaScript is progressing rapidly, so some incompatibilities are due to the use of scripts on browsers using an earlier version of JavaScript.

This was a bit more complicated, but nothing too bad. You have just declared a *function*. A function is like a little program that you create and store for later use. We've named the function **WinOpen**—when you *call* the function (we'll look at how you call it in a moment), certain things happen, and those things are defined within the braces { and }. What will happen? Well, the **open** instruction will run, opening a window (**open** is actually a special function already built into JavaScript). Inside the parentheses you'll see information about that window. First, it's going to load the **window.htm** file. Next, you'll see the name of the window—in this case **Window1**, but you can call it whatever you like (**Fred**, if you are so inclined). This is simply a name that can be used later in HTML tags to target this particular window.

Next, you'll see some more information about the window. You can see that in this case the window will have a toolbar. If we had put **"toolbar=no"**, or left this information out (by simply leaving **""** in its place), we would not have the toolbar. If we had simply ended with **"Window1")** we would get the toolbar, along with the Location bar and the Directory bar—but that's another story; you can specify other window characteristics, which you will learn about in Chapter 15, "Controlling Windows & Documents With JavaScript."

Okay, now let's run this function. Somewhere further down in your document you can insert the following:

```
<form>
<input type="button" name="WindowButton" value="Secondary Window--Click on
me" onclick="WinOpen()">
</form>
```

If you've created forms in your HTML documents, you'll know that this is HTML, not JavaScript—at least, most of it is. We start with the **<form>** tag, which tells the browser that we are going to create a form; then we use the **<input type=** tag, which tells the browser what sort of form component we want.

We're creating a button (**type="button"**—this is an INPUT element that was introduced with Netscape Navigator 2.0 and JavaScript), and we're calling the button **WindowButton**. Then we are defining the text that will appear on the button: in this case, **Secondary Window--Click on me**.

You then see something a little different: the **onclick=** attribute. This is JavaScript, not HTML; it's one of the JavaScript *event handlers*. We'll look at them in more detail in Chapter 12, "JavaScript Events." All you need to know right now is that **onclick** means "when the user clicks on the item," of course. And what will happen when the user clicks on the item? The **WinOpen** function will run! And what does the **WinOpen** function do? It opens **Window1** and displays the **window.htm** document. Easy. Figure 2-4 shows what you will see after clicking on this button. This window is a bit big, though, for that little text. You will learn about positioning these windows in Chapter 15, "Controlling Windows & Documents With JavaScript."

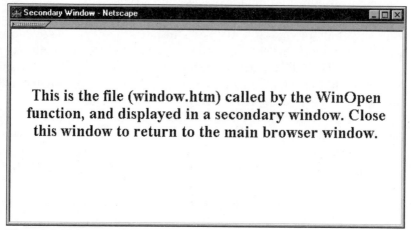

Figure 2-4: We've opened this secondary window by clicking on a button.

By the way, notice that in this figure the toolbar is present, but it's closed; the user can click on the little button in the left side of the window just below the title bar to open it. The manner in which the toolbar is handled varies between browsers. In Navigator 3, the toolbar buttons would be visible—Navigator 3 had only two toolbar states; the toolbar could be shown or hidden. Navigator 4 has three toolbar states: hidden, shown but closed, shown and open.

Navigation Buttons

JavaScript provides a variety of navigation controls. For example, you could add Back and Forward buttons to your documents; these buttons would carry out the same function as the Back and Forward buttons found on the toolbar. Try this:

Example 2.5

```
<form>
<input type="button" value=" <-- 2 Pages " onclick="history.go(-2)">
<input type="button" value="Previous Page" onclick="history.go(-1)">
<input type="button" value=" Next Page " onclick="history.go(1)">
<input type="button" value=" 2 Pages --> " onclick="history.go(2)">
</form>
```

The **onclick** event handlers tell the browser what to do when the user clicks on the button—the browser has to run the **history.go** instruction. This simply takes the user through the browser's history list. You can specify how far, and in which directions, using numbers: **-2** means back two pages, **2** means forward two pages, and so on.

Welcome Messages

How about welcoming readers to your site? You can make their JavaScript-enabled browsers open a dialog box with a special message from you when they arrive at your site. Perhaps a message of the day, important news, or information that changes frequently. Here's what you need to do. Just before the **</HEAD>** tag, enter this text:

Example 2.6

```
<SCRIPT LANGUAGE="JAVASCRIPT">
<!--
alert("Welcome to the World Wide Web\'s Premier slug-farming page. →
Unfortunately we have some bad news. Uncle Albert slipped while walking →
across the pasture last night and will be unable to maintain this site for →
a few days. Don\'t worry though, he\'ll be back just as soon as we can get →
the slime off.")
//-->
</SCRIPT>
```

Unfortunately, there's a bug present in some early JavaScript browsers related to long lines like this—if a line of JavaScript code is 255 characters or more, the browser might "choke" on it. Here's another way to create a message, though:

```
<SCRIPT LANGUAGE="JAVASCRIPT">
<!--
var msg1="Welcome to the World Wide Web\'s Premier slug-farming page. →
Unfortunately we have some bad news. Uncle Albert slipped while →
"var msg2="walking across the pasture last night and will be unable to →
maintain this "var msg3="site for a few days. Don\'t worry though, →
he\'ll be back just as soon as we can get the slime off."
alert(msg1 + msg2 + msg3)
//-->
</SCRIPT>
```

Line Breaks and the → Symbol

Notice the little arrows we've shown in Example 2.6's code? These are *continuation characters*. They simply show you where we've moved the text down a line, even though *you* can't do so when typing your code. There are many cases in which you cannot break lines. For example, when you are entering the alert text you cannot simply press Enter at any point; you should keep all this on one line, even though it's a very long line.

Of course we can't show this as one line in this book, so we have to move parts of the line down. And we've placed these little arrow continuation symbols to show that you can't break the line there.

Where, then, can't you break a line? Avoid breaking a statement. When assigning a value to a variable, do it all on one line. Whenever you are entering text between quotation marks, don't break the line. When using a **document.write** statement, don't break the line. As you can see, we indent text to the right to make the code easier to read (we'll discuss this more in Chapter 8, "Troubleshooting & Avoiding Trouble"). That means that sometimes even short lines are pushed way off to the right, so you might be tempted to press Enter and break the line into two; don't do it.

Later in this book we'll be talking about *event handlers*, which are placed in HTML tags. These also should not be broken between lines, except when you are using multiple statements in an event handler (in which case you can end a statement with **;** then press Enter and type the next one).

How do you deal with this problem of very long lines while you are typing your text? Turn on your text editor's word wrap feature. The text will be wrapped down to the next line where necessary, even though you haven't entered a line break, making it easier to read and work with.

We've created three variables (**msg1**, **msg2**, and **msg3**), then placed the message (in three parts) into those variables. Then we placed those variables into the alert function. (This is more advanced than we really want to explain right now!)

TIP

If you include an apostrophe or quotation marks in your message text, precede the characters with a backward slash (\ ). For example, in the above example we used **Web\'s**, **Don\'t**, *and* **he\'ll**. *For double-quotation marks you'd do the same:* **\"special\"**, *for example. Actually, in some cases you can get away without using the backward slash—in others you can't. It's better to get into the habit of using them all the time.*

Okay, so you don't have to enter this exact message—replace everything between the quotation marks with whatever message you want. We've used a built-in JavaScript function—**alert**—to display our text in a dialog box. As soon as the browser starts loading the document and sees this script, it will run it and display the dialog box. So, what happens when people arrive at your Web page? Before the page even opens, they'll see the dialog box in Figure 2-5. When they click on the OK button, the page will continue loading.

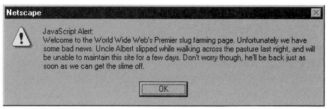

Figure 2-5: Creating Alert messages is very easy.

TIP

This is a very long message. If you were placing a message of this length in an HTML Web document, you would normally break up the lines with carriage returns in your editor—to make it easier to work with. The browser reading the document will ignore the breaks. Don't add breaks in this case, though, when using *the built-in alert function, or your readers will see error messages instead of the dialog box.*

If you prefer to show the message *after* the document has loaded, there's another way to display it: you can use the **onload** event handler. This is placed inside an HTML tag (the **<BODY>** or **<FRAMESET>** tag) and tells the browser to carry out an action as soon as it's finished loading the HTML document or the contents of the last frame. Use this **<BODY>** tag:

Example 2.7

```
<BODY onload="alert('Welcome to the World Wide Web\'s Premier slug-farming →
page. Unfortunately we have some bad news. Uncle Albert slipped while →
walking across the pasture last night and will be unable to maintain this →
site for a few days. Don\'t worry though, he\'ll be back just as soon as we →
can get the slime off.')">
```

This time, the Web document loads and *then* the message box appears.

Departure Messages

You can also display messages when the reader *leaves* a page. Of course, you should be careful how you create these messages, because if the reader moves from the current page to another page he or she will see the message, even though he or she is not actually leaving your site.

Here's how to create a departure message. Instead of using **onload**, this time we use **onunload**:

Example 2.8

```
<BODY onunload="alert('Wait, don\'t go! There\'s lots more! Have you seen→
our slug cuisine section yet?')">
```

TIP

If you see the words **donbt** *and* **therebs** *in the message, you should upgrade your browser. This was a bug in earlier versions of Netscape Navigator 2.0—the browser didn't recognize* **\'** *as an apostrophe.*

Status Bar Messages

Another thing you'll see a lot of—because it's very easy to do—is status bar messages. You'll see messages appear in the status bar when you click on a link, messages in the status bar that appear automatically when you open the document, and even messages that move across the status bar. Be careful with these messages, though. They're the sort of thing that lots of people will use, because they are so easy. But many users will find them irritating. Users who like to glance at the status bar to see the URL of the links they're pointing at won't thank you for making it harder for them to do so. Still, if you want to try it, here's how. Create a link anywhere in your document, like this (link to whatever page you want—it's the **onmouseover** bit that we're interested in):

Example 2.9

```
<a href="slug.htm" onmouseover="window.status='This link takes you to the→
slug-classification page';return true">Slug Fest</a>
```

Simple, eh? We've used another of JavaScript's event handlers—this time, the **onmouseover** event handler, which, not surprisingly, does something when the mouse pointer moves over the link (see Figure 2-6). Make sure that you include the **;return true** part, or it won't work. This is not part of the message, it's part of the **window.status** instruction. You can replace the text between the single quotation marks with anything you want, of course. Note that they must be single quotation marks, however. When you nest quotation marks within other quotation marks (notice the double quotation marks before **window.status** and after **return true**), you must use singles inside.

Notice, also, that when you move away from the link, the message remains in the status bar. Point at another link, though, and the message will be re-placed by the URL of that link. However, when you move the mouse pointer away from the second link, the message reappears. If you pointed at another link that places a message into the status bar, then the new message is used. (There's a way to use a command to clear the status bar, too. You will see that in Chapter 18, "Communicating With the User.")

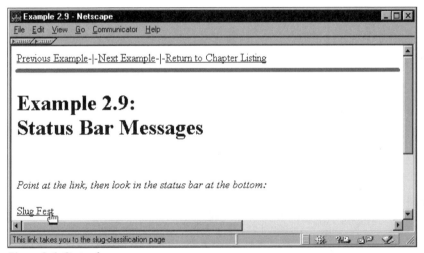

Figure 2-6: Status bar message.

Add Messages to Your Forms

Would you like to add messages to the forms inside your Web pages? You can use these messages to make the forms easier to use. When the reader clicks on an element, for example, or even moves from one element to another, you can display a message providing information about that particular form element. Here's an example. First, in the HEAD of your document, place this script:

Example 2.10

```
<SCRIPT LANGUAGE="JAVASCRIPT">
<!--
function AlertBox1(){
 alert("Remember, if you sign up, we plan to stuff both your e-mail box and→
your snail-mail box with junk mail!")
}
//-->
</SCRIPT>
```

Next, create your form and use the function in the form. We're going to create a check box, like this:

```
<FORM>
<INPUT TYPE="CHECKBOX" NAME="check1" onclick=AlertBox1()> Sign Me Up!
</FORM>
```

In this check box, we've used the **onclick** event handler; so when the user clicks on the check box, something happens. What? The **AlertBox1()** function—which we defined in the HEAD—is called, which in turn calls the built-in **alert** function, which displays our message, as you can see in Figure 2-7.

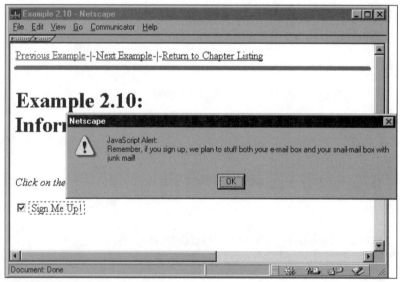

Figure 2-7: Information box.

It would also be nice if we could create a message that appeared when someone moved to or "focused" on an element in any manner—by tabbing into a text box, for example. Unfortunately, JavaScript makes that difficult.

There are some other events you can use: **onblur**, for example, which runs when the focus moves from an element to another, could display a message when the user tabs from one element to the next. It would also display when the user did just about anything, such as moving to another application, using the Back or Forward button, and so on. Then, there's the **onfocus** event handler, which runs when focus moves to an element. It's not very helpful, however, because the browser gets stuck in a loop: focus moves to the element, so the message appears, so you close the message box, so the focus moves to the element, so the message appears. This is not a problem exclusive to JavaScript; the same thing would happen in Visual Basic, for example. But JavaScript has only a small number of events to choose from, so there are fewer ways around the problem. We'll revisit this issue later, in Chapter 12, "JavaScript Events."

Automatically Forwarding Readers

Would you like to automatically forward readers from one page to another? For example, if you've set up a page that uses JavaScript, you can forward people who have JavaScript browsers from your plain old home page to a fancy JavaScript page. Or, if you move locations, you can automatically forward JavaScript-browser users to your new page. Here's an example:

Example 2.11

```
<SCRIPT LANGUAGE="JAVASCRIPT">
<!--
alert("Our URL has changed. Please bookmark the new one when we forward →
you to the new page. And please inform the owner of the page you have →
come from of the change. Thank you.")
//-->
</SCRIPT>
</HEAD>
<BODY onload="location='2-12A.htm'">
```

First, we put an **alert** message in a script at the top of the page. This runs as soon as the browser begins reading the HTML document, so the JavaScript Alert message box opens first. Then, when the user clicks on the message box's OK button, the browser continues reading the HTML until it comes across the <BODY> tag. When it sees the **onload** event handler, it continues loading the page; then, when it's finished, it runs the **onload** instruction. That instruction tells the browser the location of a document that it should load; in this case, the **2-12A.HTM** document. So, the browser automatically loads the next document.

There's a problem with using this technique, though: it messes up the user's history lists to some degree. If someone uses the Back button to go back through the history list, he'll arrive at your document, which will then push him forward again. (He can still use the history list itself, selecting an entry that appears *before* your automatically forwarding document.) There is yet another way to forward people, however—we could use a Confirm dialog box.

Automatic Forwarding— With a Confirm Dialog Box

You can get around the history-list problem by adding a Confirm dialog box. The user will see the message, but will have both the OK and Cancel buttons to choose from. When the user first sees the message, he'll click on OK and will be transferred to your new page. But when he uses the Back button, moving back through the history list, he can simply click on the Cancel button, then on the Back button again. This time he won't be pushed forward again. Here's how to do this:

Example 2.12

```
<SCRIPT LANGUAGE="JAVASCRIPT">
<!--
function redirect() {
        if (confirm ("The Web page has been moved. Please book-mark the→
new page, and ask the owner of the page you've come from to change the→
link. Click on OK to continue to the new page."))   {
                location='2-12A.htm'
        }
}
<!--End-->
</SCRIPT>
</HEAD>
<BODY onload="redirect()">
```

This is a little more complicated. We've created a function called **redirect**, which contains an **if** statement. The **if** statement uses a built-in function called **confirm**, which is very similar to the **alert** function that you have used already —except that it creates a JavaScript Confirm message box, one with an OK and a Cancel button. At the end of the if statement is the **location='2-12A.htm'** instruction. This means, "if the user clicks on OK, display Web document 2-12A.htm."

If this isn't completely clear right now, that's okay—you don't need to understand it to use it; simply type this script into your page, replacing the filename **2-12A.htm** with the correct filename or URL.

You Can't Hide Everything!

JavaScript presents you with a dilemma: it makes it more difficult to create documents that work in a variety of different browsers. Of course, there's already a similar problem on the Web—some browsers won't work with many of the HTML tags you want to use. Many Web-site designers have simply decided they don't care, that they will use all the advanced tags they want (and recommend that users get the latest Netscape Navigator so that all the tags work). Others have created two sets of documents: one for the advanced browsers and one for the not-so-advanced browsers. And others have done their best to develop sites that work reasonably well with both types of browsers. With JavaScript it's more difficult to do that, though. Create one of these special buttons or links, and a non-JavaScript browser won't be able to use it— it might not even display the button correctly. There's not a lot you can do about that. You can hide scripts using the <!-- and --> tags, but it can get complicated trying to provide two ways to access material in the same page, one for JavaScript and one for non-JavaScript browsers. With some of the simple things we've looked at, there's no problem. For example, you can create Welcome messages that will display if the browser can work with JavaScript, but will be completely invisible to the users of non-JavaScript browsers.

Still, most users are now working with JavaScript-enabled browsers (though you'll run into problems with the very latest JavaScript features). Most of the simpler scripts will work in most users' browsers these days.

Moving On

Okay, that's the easy stuff—now it's time for work. As you've seen, JavaScript allows you to do a number of very easy tasks quickly. But you'll only be able to use the real power of JavaScript if you learn more—a lot more—about how to really program with JavaScript. In the next few chapters, we're going to take JavaScript apart, breaking it down component by component and learning what each piece does.

So, move on to Chapter 3, and we'll begin by taking a look at the different places you can put JavaScripts and how to use functions.

First Steps—
Scripts, Functions
& Comments

You've seen how easy JavaScript can be, but we cheated a little. We didn't fully explain what we were doing (though the samples were so simple that in most cases you could probably figure out what was going on). Before we can go any further, you need to understand the basic structure of JavaScript—the various elements of this programming language.

First, we need to explain a little problem in programming. Programmers use all sorts of strange terms to describe their code, and these terms are often imprecise. (Get a group of programmers together and ask exactly what they mean by the term *object*, for example, and you might be forced to listen to a long and confusing argument.)

We're going to use the programming terms as best as we can, but we're not going to delve too deeply into the semantics of programming. Some terms we've ignored, as they are ambiguous and imprecise. We've given simple, down-to-earth descriptions of all the programming terms we are using. It's more important to know how to use each component of this programming language than to get an education in programming terminology.

There's a lot to learn about JavaScript, so we're going to begin with the very basics. Remember, we are assuming that you understand HTML. This is not a book about creating Web pages—it's a book about adding JavaScript to those Web pages, so you'd better understand HTML authoring first. We will explain a little about the HTML tags that we are working with, and you might be able to follow along with limited HTML knowledge; but if you get stumped by the HTML, take a look at an HTML reference for more information about the particular tags or procedures we are using.

Two Ways to Run JavaScript

There are two occasions on which your browser carries out instructions it finds in a JavaScript:

1) Some parts of your JavaScript run as soon as the browser has loaded the Web page.

2) Some parts of your JavaScript run as a result of the user's initiating an action.

There are two types of things you might want to do when the browser loads the page. First, you might want to do something that the user can see immediately. For example, you could display a Welcome message to the user in a Dialog box that pops up over the browser. (You've seen how to do that already, in Chapter 2, "A Few Quick JavaScript Tricks.") Second, you might also want to do something that will not be visible to the user—something that is really preparing things for later. For example, you could define *functions* that you plan to use later—when the user clicks on a button, say. When the browser loads the page, it will read the script, see that you want to define a function, and define the function for you—basically, placing a little bit of information into memory. The user won't notice anything happening. (We'll come back to functions in a few moments.)

As we have two occasions on which scripts are run, we have two ways to write scripts. We can put them between **<SCRIPT>** and **</SCRIPT>** tags, or we can place them inside HTML tags.

The <SCRIPT> Tags

In order to get the browser to carry out a script's instructions automatically, without any input from the user, you must place the script between **<SCRIPT LANGUAGE="JAVASCRIPT">** and **</SCRIPT>** tags, like this:

```
<SCRIPT LANGUAGE="JAVASCRIPT">
The JavaScript goes here
</SCRIPT>
```

Where can you put a script? Anywhere in the HEAD or BODY of your HTML document. (You'll learn as we progress that there are preferred locations for certain scripts, depending on what they are trying to accomplish. As you may have noted, for example, we have been placing functions in the HEAD and the scripts that call the functions in the BODY.) Also, note that you can put multiple scripts in your pages. You don't necessarily need to shove everything into one big script. Rather, you might have a script in the HEAD and a couple of scripts in the BODY.

`<SCRIPT>` Tags

Throughout this book we've used the `<SCRIPT LANGUAGE="JAVASCRIPT">` opening tag. However, the **LANGUAGE="JAVASCRIPT"** piece is actually optional. The scripts will still work if you do this:

```
<SCRIPT>
```
The JavaScript goes here
```
<SCRIPT>
```

It's generally a good idea, though, to use **LANGUAGE="JAVASCRIPT"**. Java-Script is no longer the only scripting language in use on the Web; there's also Microsoft's VBScript, and this language also uses the `<SCRIPT>` tag (**LANGUAGE="VBScript"**). (Though if you omit the language type, browsers will assume the script is JavaScript.)

Also note that you might occasionally see **"LIVESCRIPT"** instead of **"JAVASCRIPT"**. LiveScript was the original, pre-release name for JavaScript; JavaScript-enabled browsers assume that **LIVESCRIPT** means the same as **JAVASCRIPT**. Another attribute has been added to the **`<SCRIPT>`** tag, too; we'll look at the **SRC=** attribute near the end of this chapter.

JavaScript Version Numbers

The `<SCRIPT>` tag can contain a version number along with the script name. At the time of writing there were three ways to refer to JavaScript versions: `<SCRIPT LANGUAGE="JavaScript">` (which refers to JavaScript Version 1, present in Netscape Navigator 2 and Internet Explorer 3), `<SCRIPT LANGUAGE="JavaScript1.1">` (present in Netscape Navigator 3 and, to some extent, in Internet Explorer 3), and `<SCRIPT LANGUAGE="JavaScript1.2">` (present in Netscape Navigator 4 and in Netscape Messenger and Netscape Collabra, the Netscape Communicator e-mail and newsgroup programs). The purpose of providing a version identifier is to allow you to create scripts that will be run only by particular versions of Netscape Navigator. As you'll see as you go through this book, there are many things that will work in one version of Navigator, but will create an error condition in another. It's possible, however, to use the version numbers to identify the script version to the browser and to recognize which browser is being used (via the navigator object), and so avoid errors caused by scripts you know are not compatible with certain versions.

If the browser is not compatible with the specified version of JavaScript, it simply ignores the script following the **<SCRIPT>** tag:

<SCRIPT LANGUAGE="JavaScript">	Scripts preceded by this tag will run in all releases of Netscape Navigator after release 2, and in Messenger and Collabra.
<SCRIPT LANGUAGE="JavaScript1.1">	Scripts preceded by this tag will run in Navigator 3 and later, and in Messenger and Collabra; they will *not* run in Navigator 2.
<SCRIPT LANGUAGE="JavaScript1.2">	Scripts preceded by this tag will run in Navigator 4 and later, and in Messenger and Collabra; they will *not* run in Navigator 2 or 3.

Inside HTML Tags—Using Event Handlers

The other method for placing JavaScripts into your Web pages is to place the script within an HTML tag. This provides a way that the script can respond to things that users do on a page. These scripts are executed only when a user does something like click a button or point at a link. In other words, the scripts are executed in response to *events*, and so they rely on special *event handlers*. This is where the real power of JavaScript comes in. You can make your Java-Script respond to an action the user takes, without communication between the Web server and the user's browser. All the processing is done in the browser.

What events are we talking about? Initially there was **onblur** (when the focus moves away from a form element), **onchange** (when the focus moves away from a form element after the element has been changed by the user), **onclick** (when the user clicks on something), **onfocus** (when focus moves to a form element), **onload** (when the Web page is loaded into the browser), **onmouseover** (when the user points at a link), **onselect** (when the user selects text in a text box or text area), **onsubmit** (when the user clicks on a Submit button), and **onunload** (when the user does something that causes another Web document to load, removing the current one). In Netscape Navigator 3 (JavaScript 1.1) several other event handlers were added: **onabort** (when the user aborts the loading of an image), **onerror** (when a JavaScript or image-loading error occurs), **onmouseout** (when the mouse pointer leaves a link or a hotspot on an image map), and **onreset** (when a form is reset, either because the user clicks the Reset button or because you use the **reset()** method in a script). JavaScript 1.2 added even more events. But don't worry about methods for now, you'll learn all about them later.

We've already used some of these event handlers in Chapter 2, and we'll look at them in more detail in Chapter 12, "JavaScript Events."

Two Simple Scripts

Let's see an example of what we have just discussed. (Remember, you can find all these examples and see exactly how they work in the Online Companion at http://www.netscapepress.com/support/javascript1.2/) We've created a simple HTML document with two scripts inside it. These scripts display the date that the source document was saved, and they display a message box when the user clicks on a button.

First, we placed this script into the BODY of the document, below the <H1> header.

Example 3.1

```
<SCRIPT LANGUAGE="JAVASCRIPT">
<!--
document.write("This document last modified on: ")
document.write(document.lastModified)
//-->
</SCRIPT>
```

Then we created a button in the Web page, like this:

```
<FORM>
<INPUT TYPE="button" NAME="AlertButton" VALUE="Click here" onclick="alert('You
just clicked the button')">
</FORM>
```

What does this look like? You can see both the Web page and the message box that appears when you click on the button in Figure 3-1. Just click on the OK button to remove the box.

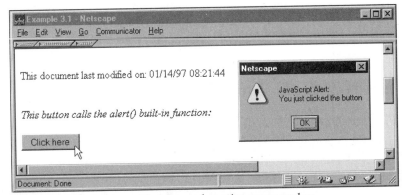

Figure 3-1: Entering a modified date and creating a message box.

Let's take a look at the first script:

```
<SCRIPT LANGUAGE="JAVASCRIPT">
<!--
document.write("This document last modified on: ")
document.write(document.lastModified)
//-->
</SCRIPT>
```

This piece runs as soon as the browser reads it. As you can see from the illustration, it displays the words *This document last modified on:* in the Web page, followed by the date.

The second script is as follows:

```
<INPUT TYPE="button" NAME="AlertButton" VALUE="Click here" onclick="alert →
('You just clicked the button')">
```

In this case, the script is inside an **<INPUT>** tag. We are creating a button, and we're using the **onclick** JavaScript event handler. When the user clicks on the button, the script that appears after **onclick**, the **alert** function, runs. In this case, the command is a *built-in function*. This is a function that is already available to you, but that you don't need to define—in this case a function that is associated with an *object*. We'll learn more about these later, in Chapter 10, "Objects, Properties & Methods."

TIP

> The **TYPE="button"** *is not a standard* **<INPUT>** *attribute, and many browsers currently can't recognize it. It's a new attribute, introduced with Netscape Navigator 2.0 and JavaScript.*

A Quick Look at Functions

The next example shows a JavaScript that is read by the browser as soon as the page is loaded, but causes no actions that the user can see. Try putting the following in the BODY of your document:

Example 3.2

```
<SCRIPT LANGUAGE="JAVASCRIPT">
<!--
function AlertBox(){
   alert("This is the alert box" )
}
```

```
document.write("This document last modified on: ")
document.write(document.lastModified)
//-->
</SCRIPT>
```

This time, you'll see that all you get is the *This document last modified on:* line (along with the actual date), but you don't get a button or anything else. Why? What does the part of the script starting with **function** and ending with } do? Well, this bit of script *defines* a *function*. We will discuss functions in detail in Chapter 7, "More on Functions"; but for now, you can think of a function as a block of script that can be used many times by other scripts within the HTML document. The browser reads the function, loads the function into memory, and then uses the function later, when something *calls* the function. The function then carries out some kind of action—for example, writing some text in a Web page, calling another Web page, carrying out a calculation, or whatever. So this is how a browser can read a script and carry out instructions. It defines the function so it can be used later, even though the action is transparent to the user.

Calling the Function

Of course, in the previous example we haven't called the function, so it won't do anything. So before we move on, let's quickly look at how we can call the function. In the example below we've taken the HTML document from Example 3.2 and added a button that, when clicked, executes the script in the function. That is, it *calls* the function. In the body of the document, we added the following button:

Example 3.3

```
<FORM>
<INPUT TYPE="button" NAME="AlertButton" VALUE="Click here to call the
function" onclick="AlertBox()">
</FORM>
```

When the user clicks on the button, the **onclick** event handler calls the **AlertBox()** function. That function uses **alert** to open the JavaScript Alert message box and display the message shown in parentheses after **alert**.

The <!-- and //--> Comment Tags

In some cases, you might want to hide the JavaScript from other browsers. You can do that by adding HTML comment tags. (In other cases, you might have so much JavaScript in your HTML document that it doesn't really matter—the document will be unusable by any non-JavaScript browser.) Anything between the comment tags will be ignored by the non-JavaScript browsers. Make sure that you place the tags *between* the **<SCRIPT>** and **</SCRIPT>** tags, like this:

Example 3.4

```
<SCRIPT LANGUAGE="JAVASCRIPT">
<!--
The JavaScript goes here
//-->
</SCRIPT>
```

Notice the **//** at the beginning of the line containing the **-->**. This is not normally used within comment tags; but it is required in this case, as it tells the browser that what follows is not part of the script. Some people create comment tags like this:

```
<SCRIPT LANGUAGE="JAVASCRIPT">
<!-- hide script from old browsers
The JavaScript goes here
// end hiding from old browsers -->
</SCRIPT>
```

There's absolutely no need to do this. The practice has probably arisen from the fact that Netscape engineers who created the original public JavaScript documents wanted to show what they were up to. We prefer not to do this—it just adds to the clutter.

JavaScript Comments

As you can see, the HTML comment tags have a limited effect on JavaScript browsers. If the HTML comment tags appear between **<SCRIPT>** and **</SCRIPT>** tags, the JavaScript browser ignores them—it doesn't really treat them as true comment tags, it simply pretends they're not there. So how can you put real comments into your scripts, notes to yourself and others, that the browser will ignore? Use the following characters:

Example 3.4

```
// This is a comment line

/* This is the beginning of a multi-line comment
this is the second line
this is the third line
This is the last line of the multi-line comment */
```

If you want to place a single comment line into your script, start the line with //. In fact, you'll notice that's what we did when entering the last line of the HTML comment: we put // -->, so the // would tell the browser that the --> is not part of the script.

If you want to enter several lines of comments, you can either start each line with // (you'll notice that many JavaScript authors do that), or you can start the first line with /* and finish the last line with */. You can also use // to put comments at the end of script lines, as follows:

```
<SCRIPT LANGUAGE="JAVASCRIPT">
<!--
function AlertBox(){ //I've defined a function here
    alert("This is the alert box" ) //the function runs alert
}
document.write("This document last modified on: ") //now I'm writing text
document.write(document.lastModified) //grabbing the document's modified date

//-->
</SCRIPT>

<FORM>
<INPUT TYPE="button" NAME="AlertButton" VALUE="Click here to call the
function" onclick="AlertBox()"> //this button calls_ the AlertBox function
</FORM>
```

A browser reading this will run the script as normal; but when it gets to the // on each line, it will ignore the text after the //, skipping to the next line. By the way, it's also popular for programmers to add a line like this:

/ /

to set off a block of comment lines, so that they are easy to see while scanning the program. Such lines are also used to split up parts of a script, so you can quickly find your way through it (you might put a line like this above each function you define, for example).

Finally, here's another way to use comments. Some programmers like to do this for multi-line comments:

```
/* This is the beginning of a multi-line comment
* this is the second line
* this is the third line
* This is the last line of the multi-line comment
*/
```

This makes it easier to see the number of lines the comment spans. It's also a method that can be read by an automatic document generator that's provided with the Java Development Kit, so many Java programmers use this method.

These comments are very handy. Often you might want to enter comments to yourself, to remind you what you did in a particular script. In fact, comments are essential, especially for inexperienced programmers, because they help you figure out what a script is doing. Right now, as you write a script, you think you'll remember the script; but come back in six months and try to figure it out, and you'll appreciate having comments to lead the way. Also, remember that if you have colleagues who might need to work with your scripts at some time, they'll be very grateful for any help you can put into your scripts.

Bug Alert—Use HEIGHT & WIDTH Attributes

Many people are reporting problems with their JavaScripts related to inline images. They've found that they run into problems if they don't include the **HEIGHT** and **WIDTH** attributes in the **<IMG>** tag. Of course, the fix is simple: use the **HEIGHT** and **WIDTH** attributes in any documents that contain JavaScript. You can also try placing an empty script (**<SCRIPT> </SCRIPT>**) after the last image tag, though using the **HEIGHT** and **WIDTH** attributes is probably better. It's a good idea to use these attributes even if you *aren't* putting JavaScript into a page, as it improves the manner in which the page loads into a browser.

New in JavaScript 1.1

There were a couple of features introduced in Netscape Navigator 3 (JavaScript 1.1) that we'd like to cover here: the **<NOSCRIPT>** tag and the **SRC=** attribute. The first is similar to the **<NOFRAMES>** tag—it tells a browser what to display if the browser can't work with JavaScript. And the second provides a way to create JavaScript libraries and insert them into a page.

Showing Non-JavaScript Browsers Text: <NOSCRIPT>

You're probably familiar with the **<NOFRAMES></NOFRAMES>** tag pair. These display a message to browsers that are not capable of working with frames. Netscape Navigator 3 (and Internet Explorer 3) can recognize a similar set of tags, the **<NOSCRIPT></NOSCRIPT>** tag pair.

These are very simple to use. In Example 3.5 you can see a tag pair in action:

Example 3.5

```
<NOSCRIPT>You'll only see this text if you are working with a
non-JavaScript-enabled browser or a JavaScript-enabled browser
that does not conform to the Navigator 3.0 level of JavaScript
(JavaScript 1.1), or if your browser has JavaScript turned off in
the Preferences.</NOSCRIPT>
```

That's all there is to it. As you can see in the example at the Online Companion, this text won't appear in the document unless you are working with a non-JavaScript browser, or if you have turned off JavaScript in the browser's preferences.

Using Script Source Files

There's a handy way to manage scripts for your Web pages—or at least, there is if you are writing scripts to be used by Netscape Navigator 3 and later browsers. You can place them in a file separate from the HTML documents, then link to the script file (a text file that contains the script) using an **SRC=** attribute in the **<SCRIPT>** tag. When the browser reads the Web page, it will see the attribute and read the script file as if it were actually written into the HTML document itself. This is particularly useful if you want to create complicated JavaScripts and use them in multiple Web pages. Rather than trying to keep all the scripts in all the HTML files up to date and the same, you only need to maintain one script file, then refer to the file from your source documents.

Here's how to use this feature. As a simple example, let's look at how to embed a script we saw earlier in this chapter. First, create a text file with the following information:

Example 3.6

```
document.write("This document last modified on: ")
document.write(document.lastModified)
```

This is the text from the script in Example 3.1—without the **<SCRIPT>** and **</SCRIPT>** tags, though. Name this file something that ends with **.JS**; **INSERT.JS**, for instance. Now, in your Web page, enter the following **<SCRIPT>** tags:

```
<SCRIPT LANGUAGE="JAVASCRIPT" SRC="INSERT.JS">
</SCRIPT>
```

You can type comments between the tags if you wish. These comments won't be displayed; when the browser sees the **SRC=** attribute it knows that it's supposed to ignore everything between the tags and use the text from the referenced file instead. The effect is the same as if you had written the script directly into the Web page. If you want to include comments, though, make sure you use the // notation before the comment, or browsers that don't recognize the **SRC=** attribute will generate an error message.

However, inserting a file like this won't always work. Make sure that the Web server has been set up to recognize **.JS** files. Ask the system administrator to add a line to the server's configuration identifying the **.JS** MIME type:

```
application/x-javascript .js
```

By the way, note that while this feature works in Netscape Navigator 3.01, it will not work in some of the early Netscape Navigator 4 Preview Releases. Nor will it work in Internet Explorer 3.

TIP

JavaScript 1.2 added two new **<SCRIPT>** *attributes:* **ARCHIVE =** *and* **ID =**. *These are telated to signed scripts, which we'll discuss in Chapter 14, "JavaScript 1.2's Advanced Features."*

Moving On

You've seen where to put your JavaScript scripts, and you've learned how to define functions and use comments. If you tried the examples, you've actually created some JavaScripts—albeit very simple ones. Before you can do anything more complicated, there is plenty more to learn. We're going to move on now to learn about *variables* (little "boxes" that store information for your scripts) and *literals* (the data that you put into those variables).

Variables & Literals—Storing Data

This chapter will explore *variables*. Variables can be thought of as boxes to keep things in that you'll need while running your JavaScript. Perhaps you want to add two numbers together (say, 5 and 7), and you plan to use the result later in your script. Where are you going to store the result? You could put it into a variable in your script:

```
sumresult = 5+7
```

After this piece of code has finished, **sumresult** will contain the number **12** (the result of **5 + 7**). This number is now stored in your document, and you can use the stored number whenever you need it by referring to **sumresult**. You can also put a number directly into the variable. For example, instead of making a calculation and placing the result in the variable, you could simply state that the variable is equal to something, as follows:

```
thisnumber = 2
```

Look, for example, at these scripts:

Example 4.1

```
<SCRIPT LANGUAGE="JAVASCRIPT">
var sumresult = 5+7
var thisnumber = 2
document.write("Here's what's in the sumresult variable: " + sumresult + →
"<P>")
document.write("Here's what's in the thisnumber variable: " + thisnumber)
</SCRIPT>
```

We've created the two variables, **sumresult** and **thisnumber**. We then used the **document.write** command to write the contents of the variables to the Web page. What will you see? The following:

```
Here's what's in the sumresult variable: 12
Here's what's in the thisnumber variable: 2
```

Notice that when we used the **document.write** instruction, we were able to write three different things: text that we wanted displayed in the page (we enclosed this text with the **"** and **"** quotation marks), the variable values (**sumresult** and **thisnumber**, which don't need to be enclosed in quotation marks), and an HTML tag, **<P>**, the tag that starts a new paragraph. (The HTML tag, like the text, must be enclosed in quotation marks.) We joined all these items together using + signs.

> **TIP**
>
> *We put spaces before and after the + sign. You don't have to use spaces (the script still will work), it just makes reading it a little easier.*

It is usual in most programming languages to *declare* variables. This means that before you use a variable, you give it a name. This tells whatever is running the program to put aside appropriate memory for the contents of your variable.

In JavaScript, you declare variables using the **var** keyword:

```
var firstname
```

This declares a variable called **firstname**. You can also put some data into the variable when you declare it. This is called *initializing* a variable. For example:

```
var state = "Colorado"
var salary1 = 50000
```

We've created two variables here: **state** and **salary1**. In each case, we've also placed something into the variable (the variable is, in effect, a "box" that stores the contents of the variable). In the first case, we've stored the word **Colorado**, while in the second case, we've stored a number, **5000**.

> **TIP**
>
> *When you place text into a variable, you enclose the text in quotation marks:* **"** *and* **"**. *We'll discuss this more later in this chapter.*

Actually, what we've done here is not *entirely* necessary—though it's advisable. We've used a somewhat formal method for declaring a variable; but JavaScript allows you to declare one in an informal manner, by simply naming the variable without using the **var** keyword first. We could have done this, for example:

```
state = "Colorado"
salary1 = 50000
```

In this case, we didn't use the **var** keyword; we simply provided a variable name and the contents of the variable. This, in effect, automatically declares the variable. However, it's good programming practice to declare all variables formally, by preceding the name with **var**. Unfortunately, the fact that Java-Script allows variables to be declared informally means that mistakes can be introduced quite easily by simply mistyping. For example, let's say you have declared a variable somewhere, like this:

```
var month
```

and then later placed a value into the variable, like this:

```
months = "June"
```

You mistyped the second name (**months**). What does JavaScript do? Because it allows informal variable declarations, when it sees **months** it assumes that it's a new variable—it declares the **months** variable. Some programming languages won't allow informal declarations, or they provide a way that the programmer can restrict informal declarations if he wishes. In a programming language that doesn't allow informal declarations, **months = "June"** would be regarded as an error, not simply taken as another variable.

Still, although JavaScript does allow informal declarations, there are two things you can do to avoid problems: be very careful when you type variable names, and use the formal method when you intentionally declare variables. It's tidier, and it also helps you find variable declarations in your scripts—you can quickly search on the **var** keyword.

There's another problem with not using **var**, one associated with the *scope* of variables (where the variables are available). As you'll see later in this chapter, there are both *global* and *local* variables; and if you don't use **var**, these can get mixed up. We'll look at that problem later in this chapter, under "Variable Scope—Where Is This Variable Available?"

Naming Variables

You can call a variable almost anything you want, as long as you follow a few simple rules:

- The first character in the name must be a letter (**a–z** or **A–Z**) or an underscore (**_**).

- The rest of the name can be made up of letters (**a–z** or **A–Z**), numbers (**0–9**), or underscores (**_**).

- Don't use spaces inside names. For example, you could use **FirstName** but not **First Name**.

- Avoid the "reserved" words, words that are used for other purposes in JavaScript. For example, you couldn't call a variable **with** or **transient**. You can find a list of reserved words in Appendix E, "Reserved Words."

TIP

It's a good idea also to avoid the names of JavaScript's objects, methods, built-in functions, and so on. In some cases you might be able to use these names and get away with it, in other cases you won't—you'll create a bug in your script. Avoid them—your scripts will be less confusing and less likely to malfunction. You can find lists of these names in the appendices.

5. You must use the same case for your variables whenever you refer to them. If you declare a variable called **state**, don't refer to the variable as **State** or **STATE**.

Here, for example, are some valid variable names:

- **year1999**
- **First_Name**
- **_people**

Here are some invalid names:

- **$1000**
- **1000**
- **&Me**
- **Date&Time**

TIP

You might come across the term identifier; *this is programming-speak for* name. *Variables and functions have* identifiers.

Variable Names Are Case-Sensitive

It's very important to remember that variable names are case-sensitive. In other words, you can't use the variable by typing its name any way other than the way you originally declared the variable, using exactly the same case. Take a look at this little script:

Example 4.2

```
<SCRIPT LANGUAGE="JAVASCRIPT">
<!--
var thetext = "The year is "
var TheText = thetext + "1996"
//-->
</SCRIPT>
```

What does this script do? Well, it begins by defining two variables. First, there's **thetext**. This variable contains the text, **The year is.** The following line declares **TheText**. This variable contains two things: the contents of the **thetext** variable, plus the text **1996**.

You can see this example at work in the Online Companion. You'll see that we added two buttons. Each button uses the **onclick** event handler to use the built-in **alert** function to display the contents of the variables, like this:

```
<I>Clicking on this button shows you the contents of the thetext variable:
</I><BR>
<form>
<input type="button" value="thetext" onclick="alert(thetext)"><BR>
<input type="button" value="TheText" onclick="alert(TheText)">
</form>
```

What happens when you click on the first button? You'll see a dialog box that contains the words *JavaScript Alert: The year is.* It *doesn't* include the text *1996*, though. Why? Because the **thetext** variable only contains the words **The year is;** it doesn't include the year. The year is in the **TheText** variable—the contents of which can be seen when you click on the second button. As you can see, case matters—type the variable in the wrong case, and your script won't work. (By the way, we're not suggesting that it's a good idea to have two variables of the same name, distinguished only by case. You'll only confuse yourself!)

Types of Variables

In most programming languages, you can have different *types* of variables for the different types of data you use. You can have *numeric* variables—that is, variables that hold numbers with which you can then do math. You could also have variables that hold text (text stored in a variable is known as a *string* in programmer babble). You can't use a string variable in math calculations, because the data is held in its own *type* of variable. For example, look at these variables:

```
var number1 = 5
var firstname = "Chuck"
```

The variables have been given types by putting some data into them. The variable **number1** above is a numeric variable, because it has been *initialized* with the number **5**. The variable **firstname** is a string variable, as it contains a string—we know that it's a string, because it's between quotation marks.

JavaScript actually has three types of variables:

- **string variables**—these contain text (the text appears between quotation marks). For example: **var firstname = "Joe"**

- **numeric variables**—these contain numbers. For example: **numberofpeople = 9**

- **Boolean variables**—these contain "logical" statements (**true** or **false**). For example: **Member = true**

TIP

Also, there's a special keyword, **null***, that is treated as an "empty" variable.*

Unlike some programming languages, though, in JavaScript you don't need to specify the type of data that will be held by the variable when you declare it. If you declare a variable without specifying the data type, that variable is classified as *uninitialized*. In fact, if you try to display a variable that has never had data assigned to it, you will get *<undefined>* in your output. For example, take a look at the following script:

Example 4.3

```
<SCRIPT LANGUAGE="JAVASCRIPT">
<!--
var text2
//-->
</SCRIPT>
```

This time we've declared only the **text2** variable, and we haven't placed any data into it. So **text2** is an *undefined*—uninitialized—variable. Later in the script we create the following button:

```
<form>
<input type="button" value="Undefined variable, text2" onclick=alert(text2)>
</form>
```

The built-in function alert calls the **text2** variable. What do we see? We see a message box that says *JavaScript Alert: <undefined>*. (It shouldn't really say *undefined*—it should say *uninitialized*, which is a more accurate term.) This, at least, is how Netscape Navigator 2, 3, and 4 deal with this situation. Remember, though, that each browser might act—*will* act—a little differently when working with JavaScript, just as different browsers display HTML slightly differently. Internet Explorer 3 actually displays a blank message box in this situation.

TIP

There are two types of "faulty" variables. First, there's the uninitialized *variable, which is one that has been declared but has no data; the JavaScript Alert message box will open, as we've just seen. Or, if you try to use the variable somewhere—in a calculation, for example—you'll get an error message. Second, there's the* unde-clared *variable. This is a variable that you have used in a script somewhere—perhaps you refer to it in a button—but you have never declared it. In this case, you'll see an Error message box. (You can see an example of this message box later in this chapter, in Figure 4-1. Note, however, that in both Netscape Navigator and Internet Explorer the message box says that it's an "undefined" variable, though perhaps a better term would be "undeclared.")*

As soon as you put some data into a variable, it becomes one of the three types we mentioned: string, numeric, or Boolean. The very act of placing data into a variable defines the variable's type.

Types Can Change

JavaScript is said to be a *loosely typed* language. That is programmer-speak that means you don't have to be too fussy with how you use your variables. You don't have to specify the type of data that will be held by the variable when you declare it, and a variable type can actually change. For example, you might have this variable at some point in a script:

```
var Member = 5
```

Then, later in the script you might have this:

```
var Member = False
```

The variable started life as a numeric variable, holding the number **5**. Later, it became a Boolean variable, holding **False**. You can think of JavaScript's variables as boxes that can hold different things. They can only hold one type of information at a time: numbers, text, or logical statements. But you can change the content type at any time by replacing one content type with another. In our example, we've replaced a number with a Boolean value; so the variable changed from a numeric to a Boolean variable.

In many programming languages you would have to actually declare what the variable would hold; you would actually state what type of variable you were declaring using a special keyword. In JavaScript you don't need to worry about this—the act of giving the variable data gives the variable its type.

You have to be very careful with changing a variable from one type to another, because you can mess up your scripts if you do something wrong. Look at the following, for example:

```
var text1 = 19
var numb1 = 96
var variable1 = text1 + numb1
```

This gives the result of **115**—19 plus 96 equals **115**. But now look at this:

```
var text1 = "19"
var numb1 = 96
var variable1 = text1 + numb1
```

In this case you are taking a variable containing a string (**"19"**) and adding a number to it (**96**). Instead of getting **115**, you get **1996**. The number in **numb1** is converted to a string, because **text1** is a string, and the value is tacked onto the end of the **text1** value. Thus, **19** "plus" **96** equals **1996**.

+ now numb1 is defined as a string!

> **TIP**
>
> *Don't change variable types! Yes, you can do it if you really want to; but it's a good idea, especially for new programmers, to avoid changing types. Changing types can get you into trouble, so save yourself some headaches and don't do it.*
>
> *However, there's also something called* type conversion, *which refers to the way in which variable types can be mixed in expressions, and how the program will automatically change types for you in some circumstances. We've covered that in Chapter 5, "Expressions & Operators," under "Type Conversion."*

String Variables Hold Text

A string variable is one that holds text. What is text? Well, it can be letters and numbers, and any other characters, such as **!"^%$$*4654654*&**. A string variable can contain a number and still be a string variable (but not a numeric variable). For example:

```
nNumberOfPages = 95
sNumberOfPeople = "95"
```

use n + s to clue for numeric vs. string

The variables above are treated in very different ways by the computer. The variable **NumberOfPages** is numeric, because it has been initialized with the number **95**. This number can be used in calculation. However, **NumberOfPeople** is a string variable, because the number **95** is enclosed in double quotes. You can use this to print the number *95* at some point, but you cannot use it in a calculation. We will see later how string variables and numeric variables are treated differently.

If a JavaScript browser looks at a variable in a script and sees that the data after the = sign is enclosed in quotation marks, it creates a string variable—regardless of what is inside the quotation marks.

Numeric Variables Hold Numbers

Numeric variables hold nothing but numbers. They can hold integers (**4** or **156**, for example) or floating-point numbers (**3.1459**, for example). Integers are whole numbers, and floating-point numbers have a decimal point. In many computer languages you'd need two different types of variables to hold these two different types of numbers. However, in JavaScript there's only one form of numeric variable, and it can contain either of these number types. You can also use scientific notation: **5.1245e21**, for example, or **1.235E-26**.

If a JavaScript browser looks at a variable in a script and sees that the data after the = sign is *not* enclosed in quotation marks, and if it is not the word **true** or **false**, it creates a numeric variable. Actually, it looks a little closer than that, because there are three types of numbers you can use: decimal (base 10, the numbers we are all used to), octal (base 8), and hexadecimal (base 16). If it finds a number with no leading zero, it assumes that it's decimal; if it finds a number with a leading zero, it assumes that it's octal; and if it finds a number with a leading zero followed by **x**, it assumes that it's hexadecimal. However, having said all that, you probably won't need to use octal or hexadecimal often.

By the way, if you try to assign non-numeric data to a variable without putting that text in quotation marks, Navigator won't like it. You'll probably get a "*xxx* is not defined" error message (where *xxx* is the data you were trying to place into the variable).

Boolean Variables Hold True or False

Boolean variables get their name from Boolean algebra, which is a mathematical representation of logical operations. Computers use logic to perform all of their operations, and computer languages use it as well. It's really quite straightforward. A Boolean variable can only contain one of two values: **true** or **false**. Computers operate using 1s and 0s—these can also be represented as **true** or **false**.

Boolean variables are provided in a computer language so that you can write instructions such as:

```
If something is true
    (then do this)
otherwise
    (do this)
```

This is known as a *conditional expression*. It's one of the most powerful instructions you can have in a computer language, because it allows you to put decisions into your program or script—and these decisions are dependent upon Boolean variables. We'll learn more about these conditional expressions in Chapter 6, "Conditionals & Loops—Making Decisions & Controlling Scripts."

Variable Scope—Where Is This Variable Available?

Scope is programmer-speak for "where can I get at the contents of this variable?" Variables can be declared either outside or inside a function, and where they are declared has an effect on the scope:

- **Inside a function.** In the examples that we've just seen, the variables were declared inside functions. The variables are said to be *local* to the function. If you declare a variable inside a function, you can only use it inside the function. Try to use it in some other way—in another function, for example—and it won't work. By the way, this means that you can have a variable declared inside a function and then can use another variable of the same name outside that function, as JavaScript regards the variables as two separate things.

- **Outside a function.** If you declare a variable outside a function, it is said to be *global*. This means that it is available anywhere in the script—inside or outside functions.

Let's take a quick look at the way scope affects variables. In the Online Companion, you'll find a page using this script:

Example 4.4

```
<SCRIPT LANGUAGE="JAVASCRIPT">
<!--
var variable1 = "Contents of variable1 OUTSIDE the functions"

function funcExmpl1() {
   alert(variable1)
}
function funcExmpl2() {
var variable1 = "Contents of variable1 INSIDE the function"
   alert(variable1)
}
function funcExmpl3() {
   alert(variable2)
}
//-->
</SCRIPT>
```

What does this script do? It starts by declaring a variable named **variable1**, and it then places the string **Contents of variable1 OUTSIDE the functions** into that variable. This is a global variable, because we declared it outside a function. Next, it defines a function named **funcExmpl1**, which uses the built-in function **alert** to display the value of **variable1**.

Then we define another function, this time **funcExmpl2**. In this function, though, we've started by declaring a variable called **variable1**. This time we put the following text into the variable: **Contents of variable1 INSIDE the function**. This is a *local* variable, because it's *inside* the function. Finally, the function uses **alert** to display the contents of **variable1**.

Then we define another function, **funcExmpl3**. This simply uses **alert** to display the contents of **variable2**, which hasn't been declared anywhere.

Later in this Web page we've created a few buttons, like this:

```
<FORM>
<INPUT TYPE="button" NAME="ButtonA" VALUE=" Show the global variable1 outside
the functions " onclick="alert(variable1)">
<P>
```

This button uses the **onclick** event handler to call **alert** directly—it's not calling a function that we've created. The **alert** object displays the contents of **variable1**, because it has been "passed" to it inside the brackets (more on this later). Go to the Online Companion and try this; when you click on the button, you'll see a message box showing this: *JavaScript Alert: Contents of variable1 OUTSIDE the functions.*

As you can see, we're viewing the contents of the global variable named **variable1**. We don't see the contents of the local variable named **variable1**, because it's only available to the function in which it is declared. Now, here's the second button:

```
<INPUT TYPE="button" NAME="ButtonB" VALUE=" Show the global variable1 as seen
from function funcExmpl1 " onclick="funcExmpl1()">
<P>
```

This button uses the **onclick** event handler to call the function named **funcExmpl1**. Refer back to the earlier scripts, and you'll see that **funcExmpl1** uses **alert** to display the contents of the *global* variable **variable1**. So this time we see this: *JavaScript Alert: Contents of variable1 OUTSIDE the functions.*

```
<INPUT TYPE="button" NAME="ButtonC" VALUE=" Show the local variable1 as seen
from function funcExmpl2 " onclick="funcExmpl2()">
<P>
```

TIP

The button INPUT TYPE *currently doesn't allow size control, so we added spaces to make all the buttons more or less the same size.*

This button uses the **onclick** event handler to call function **funcExmpl2**, which, as we saw earlier, used **alert** to display the contents of **variable1**. This time, though, we are seeing the *local* **variable1**, because we declared a variable with that name *inside* the function. The local variable is visible to the function in this case. (By the way, the global variable has not been reset in any way; use the previous buttons and you'll still see the contents of the global variable. It's just that when using this particular function, the local variable is used—though see the problem we cover in the next section, "Why You Should Use Var.") We see the following message: *JavaScript Alert: Contents of variable1 INSIDE the functions.*

```
<INPUT TYPE="button" NAME="ButtonD" VALUE="Using a variable
in a function where the variable has not been
declared"onclick="funcExmpl3()">
</FORM>
```

Finally, this button uses the **onclick** event handler to call function **funcExmpl3**, which in turn uses the **alert** object to display the contents of **variable2**—a variable that has not been declared anywhere. This time we see what's shown in Figure 4-1. As we mentioned earlier, if you try to use an undeclared variable, you'll get an error message.

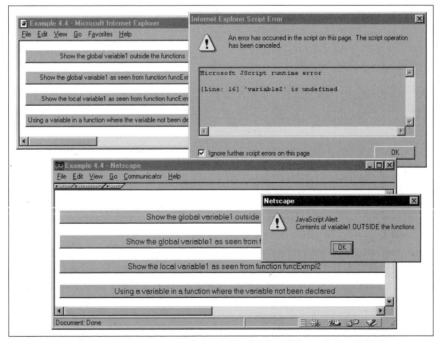

Figure 4-1: Referring to the contents of a variable that hasn't been declared displays an error message; we clicked the last button in the Internet Explorer window. In the Netscape Navigator window we clicked the first button.

Why You Should Use Var

Earlier in this chapter you learned why you should use the **var** keyword when you declare your variables. Well, here's another reason: if you don't, things can get awfully mixed up. For example, take a look at this script:

Example 4.5

```
<SCRIPT LANGUAGE="JAVASCRIPT">
<!--
var func1 = "This is the global variable named func1"
function Display1() {
   alert(func1)
}

function Display2() {
   func1 = "This is local variable named func1"
   alert(func1)
}
//-->
</SCRIPT>
```

We started by declaring a variable called **func1**. This is a global variable, because it's not inside a function. Next we defined a function, **Display1**, which uses the built-in **alert** function to display the contents of the **func1** variable.

Then we defined another function, **Display2**. This time we declared a variable within the function, a *local* variable, again called **func1**. Notice, though, that we didn't use the **var** keyword this time. Next we used **alert** again to display the contents of the **func1** variable.

After this, in the BODY of the Web document, we created a couple of buttons:

```
<FORM>
<INPUT TYPE="button" NAME="ButtonDisplay1" VALUE="Display1"
onclick="Display1()"><BR>
<INPUT TYPE="button" NAME="ButtonDisplay2" VALUE="Display2"
onclick="Display2()">
</FORM>
```

The first button calls the **Display1** function, and the second button calls the **Display2** function. Remember, each function displays the contents of the **func1** variable; but which **func1** variable, the local or the global?

Well, if you go to the Online Companion and try this, make sure that you click on the Display1 button first. You'll see a message box that says this: *Java-Script Alert: this is the global variable named func1*. Now click on the second button, Display2, and you'll see: *JavaScript Alert: this is the local variable named func1*.

Okay so far; everything is working correctly. But now click on the Display1 button again. This time you'll see this: *JavaScript Alert: this is the local variable named func1.* (By the way, we're referring to the Netscape Navigator alert box here; in Internet Explorer there is no *JavaScript Alert:title* within the box, just the message that the script wants to display.) Now we are seeing the text that was set in **Display2**, which we thought was local to that function. Of course it isn't, because we didn't use the **var** keyword. We though we'd be getting the contents of the local variable, but there isn't a local variable—instead, we reset the global variable. It doesn't matter which buttons you click on now, or what order—the text set in the **Display2** function is what you will see; until you reload the document, you won't see the contents set when the global variable was declared.

Example 4.6

What happens if we modify the script, though? In the Online Companion's Example 4.6, we added the word **var** when declaring the local variable. Instead of this:

```
func1 = "This is local variable named func1"
```

we now have this:

```
var func1 = "This is local variable named func1"
```

in the **Display2** function.

Everything else about this example is exactly the same. Try Example 4.6 and you'll find that the buttons now work correctly. The local variable remains local, and the global variable remains global—regardless of whether you've used the **Display2** button or not.

So, *use **var** and save yourself some confusion!* (Of course, you might come across an event in which you want to change the value of a global variable in a function, but be careful not to befuddle yourself.)

> **TIP**
>
> *Here's another case of something you* can *do, but should avoid. You can, if you wish, use a name for a variable inside a function that you've already used for a global function—but save yourself trouble and don't do it.*

What Is a Literal?

Let's discuss *literals* for a moment. You've already used them, and you don't really need to know much more than you've already learned. *Literal* is simply a fancy term for the data that you place into your script—actual numbers and text, rather than calculated values.

A variable can contain a calculated value, or it can contain a number 32, or the word **John**, something that we have *literally* typed into the script. Literals are things that *you* have put into the script, rather than things calculated by the script. For example, look at this variable:

```
numberofpeople = 27
```

Here, **numberofpeople** is the variable and 27 is a literal. The number **27** cannot vary. It is literally **27**. In this case, we are using a *numeric literal*. As we've already seen, a literal can also be a string or piece of text:

```
firstname = "Derek"
```

Here, **firstname** is the variable, and its contents are "set to the literal" **Derek**. This is a string, of course, as it's enclosed in quotation marks. So this is known as a *string literal*. Just because you put a literal into a variable, though, doesn't mean that the variable is stuck with it; you can do something later in the script that will modify the variable, of course. Remember, literal is just a fancy way for saying, "the stuff you entered (when writing the script) rather than the stuff that's calculated."

Special Characters in String Literals

You can use special "codes" in string literals to represent special characters. For example, let's say you want to include quotation marks in the text that you are placing into a string literal. This presents a problem, because quotation marks are characters used by the script itself to identify different parts of the script. As we've seen, they are used (among other things) to identify string literals! Adding more quotation marks will just confuse the script.

So if you want to include quotation marks in a script, you do it like this: \".

TIP

Don't get these slashes mixed up; remember, we're using the backslash here (\), not the normal forward slash (/) used in HTML tags.

If you wanted to add a backslash in a script, you'd do it like this: \\.

The backslash (\) says, in effect, "the following character (the quotation mark or forward slash or whatever) is part of my text, not part of the script." There are other things that you can do in string literals, too. You can use \n to move the text to a new line, for example. You can use \t to enter a Tab character. And you can also include HTML tags (though they don't require a backslash); for example, you can include **
** to place a line break in the text. When you display text from a string literal in a browser window it's treated in just the same way as text in a Web page, so HTML tags work in the normal manner.

Special Characters

There are a few more special characters (\r, \f, and \b), although you are not likely to use them. Here's the current full list of special characters:

Backslash:	\\
Single quotation mark:	\'
Double quotation mark:	\"
Tab:	\t
Carriage return:	\r
Backspace:	\b
Form feed:	\f
New line:	\n

By the way, \r is a little ambiguous. This is old terminal-computing stuff. Traditionally, \r means carriage return, not line feed (\l). The two (return and line feed) can be replaced by \n, which is equivalent to \r\l. (In other words, "move the text to the left and down a line.") But in JavaScript, \r means carriage return and line feed. If you work in other programming languages or plan to move on to other languages, such as C or C++, you might want to use \n instead of \r for compatibility. However, there are also a few idiosyncrasies in the way that JavaScript handles line breaks. For example, when writing text to a text area form element, you must use \r\n if the browser is running in a Microsoft Windows operating system. However, you only use \n if the browser is running in UNIX. We've discussed this problem further in Chapter 11, "More About Built-in Objects," under "Using String Methods With Object Properties."

The characters you use will depend on what you intend to do with the text, because they don't work in all situations. You can include quotation marks in text written to the Web page (using **document.write**, for example) and to Alert boxes. However, you'll find that HTML tags won't work in Alert boxes (though they *will* work when written to the Web page, of course); and most \ characters won't work when written to the Web page (but *will* work in the Alert box!).

Take a look at the following example. We started by declaring these variables:

Example 4.7

```
<SCRIPT LANGUAGE="JAVASCRIPT">
<!--
var twainA = "\"I never write \'metropolis\' for seven cents, because I can →
get the same price for \'city.\' \" Mark Twain."
var twainB = "\"I never write \'metropolis\' for seven cents, \rbecause I →
can get the same price for \'city.\' \" Mark Twain."
```

```
var twainC = "\"I never write \'metropolis\' for seven cents, <BR>because →
I can get the same price for \'city.\' \" Mark Twain."
var twainD = "\"I never write \'metropolis\' for seven cents, \tbecause I →
can get the same price for \'city.\' \" Mark Twain."
//-->
</SCRIPT>
```

You can see that they all have **\"** and **\'** to place double and single quotation marks into the text. We then used **\r**, **
, and **\t, to show the effect of these different codes (carriage return, HTML line-break tag, and Tab).

In our Online Companion example (Example 4.7), we used the **document.write** instruction to write the contents of each variable to the page. And we created four buttons that write the contents to Alert boxes. You can see an example in Figure 4-2. You'll find that in all cases the quotation marks appear, while the **
** tag works in the **document.write** instruction but not in the Alert box. The **\r** and **\t** codes work in the Alert box, but not in the **document.write** instruction.

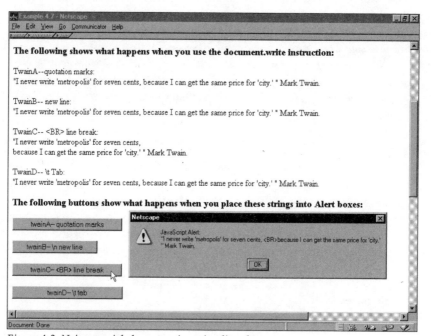

Figure 4-2: Using special characters in string literals.

The 255-character Bug

There's a bug in a number of Netscape browsers (in the 2.0 series and even—in some cases—in the 3.0 beta series) that limits the number of characters you can put on a single line—no more than 255. So it's a good idea never to exceed this limit, even if the browser you are working with does not have this problem; many of the browsers already in use *do*, so if you use long lines, many of your Web site's users can run into problems.

For example, if you want to write a very long message into a variable, don't do it all at once. Instead, write a small portion into several variables, then join them together and place them into the final variable (you'll see how to do that in Chapter 5, "Expressions & Operators").

Make Variable Names Identify the Variables

It's a good idea to choose descriptive names for your variables. Using a variable called **X** might have the advantage of being easy to type; but when you need to make a change to your code in six months you will have to spend time trying to figure out what **X** is. If you had called it **Salary**, then what it represents will be much easier to discern. You will also find it easier to read your programs if you capitalize the first letters in words (**FirstName**, for example).

Because it is easy to forget what type of variable (string, numeric, or Boolean) you are referring to and where it is defined, programmers often prefix the variable name with something that tells them what kind of variable it is and what its scope is. In JavaScript this is easy. Use the **s** prefix to show that a variable is a string, **n** for numeric, and **b** for Boolean. For example, if you wanted to call a variable **Month**, you could prefix the name with **s** for a string variable:

```
var sMonth = "April"
```

Now whenever you see **sMonth** in your script, you will know that it is a string. There is no way that you will get it confused with a variable containing the number of the month as in:

```
var nMonth = 4
```

You might also use the prefix **g** to denote a global variable. This can help avoid the errors that we talked about earlier. For example, a variable **gsMonth** is a global string variable. However, if you plan to change the type of a variable in your program, it might be best not to prefix it with a type. In general, though, using the prefix notation will make things clearer.

Moving On

You've got a good grounding in variables now. The concept of variables is really quite simple: they are little places in which you or the script store information that the script can then use later. We'll learn more about using variables later.

For now, we'll move on to expressions, conditional expressions, and loops—the most powerful part of programming, really. This is often called *program control* or *control flow*, and is all about how you get your programs to do things—how programs make decisions and repeat actions. In effect, you are showing your programs how to interact with the user and the browser.

5

Expressions & Operators— Manipulating Values

You might not realize it, but you already have used *expressions* in the example scripts. An expression is a piece of script that uses variables, literals, and *operators*. An expression takes the values of variables and literals and derives other values from them. Without expressions your programs are nothing more than one-trick ponies; click on this button and the dialog box opens, open this document and a welcome message starts, and so on. To do more, you need to make your programs do some computation and data processing work. Programmers do that by manipulating values in expressions.

So what's an operator? Not surprisingly, an operator enables an action of some kind—doing arithmetic on numbers, adding variables together, and checking to see what a variable contains, for example. The operation produces a result—a value that can then be used elsewhere in the script. As we'll see, the result can be *assigned* to another variable. So let's begin looking at the operators you can use in JavaScript.

Using Operators in Expressions

Take a look at this simple expression:

```
nSum = 4 + 5
```

We are using two operators in this expression. The + is an operator that adds together two literal values and the = puts the result into something, in this case into a variable called **nSum**. Here is another expression:

```
nTax = nCost * nTaxRate
```

This expression is only slightly more complicated. This time we've used the multiplication operator * to multiply the values held by two variables (**nCost** and **nTaxRate**). Again we've used the = operator to take the result and place it into another variable, this time **nTax**.

TIP

*Remember, we're using an identification system for our variables. In this case the **n** in front of the names means that the variables are numeric variables. See Chapter 4, "Variables & Literals—Storing Data," for more information.*

Expressions do their work on the right side and *assign* values to the variable on the left. The = symbol is known as an *assignment operator*, because it assigns values to variables.

The result of an expression is always a single value. You will now be able to clearly see the difference between a variable and a literal in the following:

```
7  =  6 + 7
```

This is gobbledygook. You cannot assign a new value to the number **7**. The number 7 is a *literal*. As we discussed in Chapter 4, "Variables & Literals—Storing Data," you can't change the value of a literal. (You can use it to create another value, but a literal is constant and cannot itself be changed.) The above expression is just plain wrong. You cannot assign new values to literals, you can only assign values to variables. There is, however, nothing wrong with this:

```
nSum = 6 + 7
```

We've carried out the same calculation; we've used the + operator to add two literals together, but this time we've assigned the result to the variable **nSum**.

Expressions, then, take this form:

```
variable = (operators working on variables and literals)
```

In other words, on the left you have a variable to which you'll assign the result of the operation carried out on the right. The operation uses variables, literals, or both variables and literals together to create the result. So this expression is also wrong:

```
nSum = nValue = 6 + 7
```

This is incorrect because it doesn't follow the form we just looked at above; we tried to assign a result to two variables at the same time, and you simply can't do that in JavaScript. Of course you *could* do the following, if you really wanted the same value in both variables for some reason:

```
nValue = 6 + 7
nSum = nValue
```

You have a valid expression on the first line because you've assigned the result to just one variable. Then, on the second line, you've assigned the new value in that variable to the other variable.

Arithmetic Operators

Now, let's look at the operators that JavaScript uses for doing mathematics. This table lists JavaScript operators and describes their uses:

Operator	Use
=	As we've seen, this is used to assign values to variables.
+	Adds two values together.
–	Subtracts one value from another or changes a value to a negative value. (This is known as an *unary negation*—for example, **nValue = – nCost**. In this example we changed the value in **nCost** to a negative value and then assigned the result to **nValue**.)
*	Multiplies two values together.
/	Divides one value by another.
%	The modulus operator shows the remainder left over after dividing one number into another equally.
++	Increments a value (adds 1 to it) in a variable.
––	Decrements a value (subtracts 1 from it) in a variable.

TIP

There are also some other assignment operators (other than =), which we'll discuss later.

Let's look at a few examples of how you can work with these operators.

Adding & Subtracting

Example 5.1

```
var nSum = 0
var nCost = 57
nSum = 25 + nCost + 33
```

This simple script declares two variables and assigns initial values to each. It then adds **25** the value held in **nCost (57)**, and **33** together and assigns the result (**115**) to the **nSum** variable. If you click on the button we've placed in the Example 5.1 page in the Online Companion, you'll see the value of **nSum** in a message box.

Example 5.2

```
var nProfit = 0
var nPrice = 99
var nCosts = 47
nProfit = nPrice - nCosts
```

This time we've declared three variables, used the subtraction operator to subtract one value from another, and then assigned the result to the **nProfit** variable; **99** minus **47** equals **52**.

Multiplying

Example 5.3

```
var nArea = 0
var nWidth = 100
var nLength = 33
nArea = nWidth * nLength
```

In this example, we are using the multiplication operator to multiply a width (the value in **nWidth**) by a length (**nLength**) and then assign the result to the **nArea** variable; **100** x **33** = **3300**.

Dividing

Example 5.4

```
var nPricePerPerson = 0
var nTotalCost = 1500
var nPeople = 40
nPricePerPerson = nTotalCost / nPeople
```

This time we use the division operator to divide the value in **nTotalCost** by the value in **nPeople**; **1500/40 = 37.5**.

Modulus— Remainder After Dividing

Example 5.5

```
var nRoughPrice = 0
var nTotalCost = 1500
var nPeople = 40
nRoughPrice = nTotalCost % nPeople
```

The modulus operator (%) is, in effect, a shortcut for several steps you could carry out using other JavaScript operators. It's used to show what's left over once you divide one number into another, when the second number won't divide equally. For instance, divide 5 into 17, and what's left over? Two. The number 5 divides into 17 three times (5 x 3 = 15), so 2 is left over. This can be calculated like this: **17 % 5**.

In the script example we're dividing **nTotalCost** by **nPeople** (1500/40) which results in **37.5**. In other words, **40** divides into **1500** 37 times, with a bit left over. What's left over? Twenty, because 37 x 40 = 1480, and 1500 - 1480 = 20.

Incrementing & Decrementing Variable Values

The increment and decrement operators are a little different from the others we've looked at. When you add, subtract, divide, or divide and return the remainder, the original value in the variable remains unchanged. For instance, in the last example, the value originally placed in **nTotalCost** is **1500**. What is the value held by **nTotalCost** after the calculation is made? It's still **1500**. We're using the variable as a place to store a value that we can use in a calculation. When we need to make the calculation, the script takes a look in the variable to see what it holds—in this case **1500**—and then uses that value. But it doesn't change what's held by the variable.

The increment and decrement operators *do* modify what's in the variable, though. Take a look at this:

Example 5.6

```
var nY = 6
nY++
```

This uses the increment operator to add 1 to **nY**; we start by declaring **nY** and placing the value of **6** inside; then we use the increment operator to add one, so we end up with **7**. The variable **nY** (as you'll see if you click on the button in our Online Companion) contains the number **7**; so the operator has actually modified the variable itself. We haven't even assigned the value to any other variable in this case.

Using the increment operator like this is, in effect, equivalent to this:

```
var nY = 6
nY = nY + 1
```

The second line might look a bit funny, but it is perfectly okay as far as an expression is concerned. This is like taking the value in **nY** and adding **1** to it and then assigning the result of the calculation back to **nY**.

++?

++ sound familiar? You might recognize the increment operator ++ from somewhere else. You might have heard of the C and C++ programming languages. The name C++ is a pun on the increment operator, as it implies that C++ is an increment (or development) of the C programming language.

Example 5.7

```
var nY = 6
nY--
```

This example uses the decrement (--) operator to make **nY** equal **5**. The decrement operator is like the increment operator, except that you take one away from the variable. This expression is equivalent to this:

```
var nY = 6
nY = nY - 1
```

String Operators

The addition operator + also can be used to put strings together and is called the *concatenation operator* when used this way. (*Concatenate* is a word, little used by nonprogrammers, that means to string or chain together in series.) We've used this operation in earlier examples, but let's take another look:

Example 5.8

```
var sFirstName = "Derek"
var sLastName = "Halfabee"
var sFullName = sFirstName + " " + sLastName
```

The + operator here *concatenates* the strings—that is, it connects them together so the result in variable **sFullName** will equal **Derek Halfabee**. The expression begins by taking the **sFirstName** variable. Then it adds a space. It has performed this operation because we used the + symbol (the concatenation symbol in this case), then enclosed a space between quotation marks: " ". The quotation marks indicate that the space is part of the text. (If you *don't* include this, you'll end up with **DerekHalfabee**, of course.) It then used another + symbol followed by **sLastName**. The result of the operation is assigned to **sFullName**. Remember that **sFirstName** and **sLastName** will not change because the result is assigned to the left side of the expression. (We'll talk more about manipulating strings later.)

Logical Operators

Logical or *Boolean* operators are used often in programming. They are used to get programs to make decisions about what to do next. JavaScript, along with most other programming languages, has two Boolean literals: *true* or *false*. Logical operators are used to create expressions that involve these true or false values. In effect you are creating logical "calculations." Instead of working with numbers, though, you work with states: true or false.

The operators are:

Operator	Meaning
!	Not (tells you what value the variable *doesn't* contain).
&&	And ("adds" two variables together).
‖	Or (this is the "pipe" symbol, usually the shifted \ key. This operator also "adds" variables, but treats the result slightly differently).

These operators are used to make these logical "calculations" by manipulating the contents of a Boolean variable in various ways. The *Not* operator (!) takes a Boolean value and changes it to its opposite value:

```
!true evaluates to false
!false evaluates to true
```

Let's see what this means. Take a look at this example:

Example 5.9

```
var bFirstValue = false
var bCheck = !bFirstValue
```

We've declared a Boolean variable called **bFirstValue**. We've initialized that variable with the Boolean value of **false**. But on the next line we modified that value. We used the *Not* operator by placing it in front of the variable name. This means, in effect, "get the value that is *not* in the **!bFirstValue** variable." **bFirstValue** contains **false**. As there are only two possible Boolean values, the value that is *not* in the **bFirstValue** variable is, of course, **true**. We then used the = assignment operator to place the returned value into the **bCheck** variable. So if you click on the button in this example in our Online Companion, you'll see a dialog box that displays the contents of the **bCheck** variable: **true**.

The *And* (**&&**) and *Or* (**||**) operators are used to combine two Boolean values. The *And* operator combines two values in the following ways:

```
true && true evaluates to true
true && false evaluates to false
false && false evaluates to false
```

We've put these into the following example.

Example 5.10

```
var bFirstValue = true
var bSecondValue = false
var bThirdValue = true
var bFourthValue = false
var bCheck1 = bFirstValue && bSecondValue
var bCheck2 = bFirstValue && bThirdValue
var bCheck3 = bSecondValue && bFourthValue
```

As you can see, in this example we carried out three operations. In the first, in which the result is assigned to **bCheck1**, we added the values of two variables that contain **true** and **false**. In the next case, we added **true** and **true**. And in the last case we added **false** and **false**. In the Online Companion, we added three buttons to the page to display the contents of **bCheck1**, **bCheck2**, and **bCheck3**. You'll see that the first variable contains **false**, the second variable contains **true**, and the third variable contains **false**.

The *Or* operator combines values in a different way. You might think of it like this: "*Either* this one *or* that one must be true in order for the expression to be **true**." So even if only one value is true, it's enough:

```
true || true evaluates to true
true || false evaluates to true
false || false evaluates to false
```

As you can see, the difference is in what happens when you have two values that are not the same. If you are using And, you'll always get **false**. If you are using Or, you'll always get **true**. In the two other cases, you'll get the same result. For instance:

Example 5.11

```
var bFirstValue = true
var bSecondValue = false
var bCheck = bFirstValue || bSecondValue
```

don't put boolean vars in " ", or they're strings

In this case, as you'll see in the Online Companion, the **bCheck** variable contains **true**, not **false**.

We will go into the use of these operators in more detail in the section on conditional expressions.

Other Assignment Operators

The = symbol isn't the only operator that assigns values to variables. There are also other operators that allow you to include the value from the variable to the left of the operator and include it in the operation. Here's what we mean:

Operator	Meaning
=	As we've seen, this takes the result of the operation on the right and places it in the variable to the left of the symbol. For instance, **nPricePerPerson = nTotalCost / nPeople**.
+=	This takes the value in the variable on the left and adds it into the operation on the right, then replaces the original value with the new one from the operation. For instance: **x += y** means add x to y, then place the new number in **x**. This is equivalent to **x = x + y**.
–=	This time the original value is decremented. For instance: **x –= y** means subtract **y** from **x**, then place the new number in x. This is equivalent to **x = x - y**.
*=	This time we are multiplying. For instance: **x *= y** means multiply x times y, then place the new number in **x**. This is equivalent to **x = x * y**.
/=	This divides. For instance: **x /= y** means divide x by y, then place the new number in x. This is equivalent to **x = x /y**.
%=	This is modulus; it divides the number on the left by the number on the right, finds what's left over, then assigns the remainder. For instance, **x %= y** means divide **x** by **y** equally, then take the remainder and assign it to **x**. This is the equivalent of **x = x % y**.

These operators, along with ++ and ––, are known as *shorthand operators* because they provide an abbreviated way to write expressions. If you are just starting to learn programming, you might prefer the long form for these operators. When you feel more confident with the language, you might want to start incorporating them into your scripts.

Bitwise Operators

There are some other JavaScript operators called *bitwise operators* that you might encounter—in the Netscape documentation, for instance. These perform operations on numbers as strings of bits. Computers, of course, think in terms of bits. Although we can write programs using numbers, letters, and a variety of typographical characters, at some point all this must be translated into binary units—*bits*. Bitwise operators allow a programmer to manipulate these bits for a variety of purposes (which we're *not* going to discuss in this book!).

These are advanced operators and are way beyond the scope of this book. In fact, bitwise operations are rather geeky things that are rarely used in programming and *very* rarely used in JavaScript. However, just so that you can recognize bitwise operators if you run across them somewhere, here they are:

Meaning	Operators
shift (various kinds)	<< >> >>> <<= >>= >>>=
and	& &=
xor	^ ^=
or	| |=

Conditional Operators

We haven't looked at all the available operators yet. There are also the *conditional operators*, symbols that are used when creating *conditional expressions*. A conditional expression is one in which you are getting your script to make a decision. For example, you can ask it to compare two variables and carry out a particular operation if the values match, or another operation if the values *don't* match. Conditional expressions are discussed in the next chapter, so we'll cover conditional operators there.

Operator Precedence

When an expression is evaluated, there is a certain order to how it is done. This is known as *operator precedence*. As you will see, this precedence is important to understand, though the details are not so important to remember. Take a look at this expression:

Example 5.12
```
var nCostPerItem = 100
var nNumItems = 5
var nTaxPerItem = 10
var nTotal1 = nCostPerItem * nNumItems + nTaxPerItem * nNumItems
var nTotal2 = nCostPerItem * (nNumItems + nTaxPerItem * nNumItems)
```

Notice that we have two different calculations, one assigning the return to **nTotal1**, the other assigning the return to **nTotal2**. You'll also see that both calculations use the same values, and in the same order. Yet when you click on the buttons in the Online Companion, you'll find that you get *very* different values; **nTotal1** contains 550, while **nTotal2** contains 5500.

Let's examine the first expression:

```
var nTotal1 = nCostPerItem * nNumItems + nTaxPerItem * nNumItems
```

The value returned by this expression is dependent upon the order in which it is evaluated. If it is evaluated simply by going left to right, it will give this:

nCostPerItem * nNumItems	(100 times 5 = 500)
+ nTaxPerItem	(500 plus 10 = 510)
* nNumItems	(510 times 5 = 2550)

But this is *not* the result we get, as you can see in the Online Companion. This is what actually happens when this expression is evaluated:

nCostPerItem * nNumItems	(100 times 5 = 500)
nTaxPerItem * nNumItems	(10 times 5 = 50)
Add the two results	(500 plus 50 = 550)

Expressions are not simply evaluated from left to right, because certain parts are evaluated before others. Higher precedence operators are applied before lower order ones. You can see from the above example that the multiplication operators are applied before the addition operator.

You can force an expression to be evaluated in a particular way using parentheses. For example, look at the last line of the previous example:

```
var nTotal2 = nCostPerItem * (nNumItems + nTaxPerItem * nNumItems)
```

This time the expression has to start by working on the items within the parentheses first. After all, until it calculates a result from within the expression, it has nothing to multiply by **nCostPerItem**. However, note that within the parentheses the order of precedence still holds. In other words, in this case the multiplication operator will be carried out first, then the addition. Finally the result from within the parentheses will be multiplied by the value held by **nCostPerItem**. Here's how it works this time:

nTaxPerItem * nNumItems	(10 times 5 = 50)
nNumItems + 50	(50 plus 5 = 55)
nCostPerItem * 55	(100 times 55 = 5500)

This now evaluates to **5500** (remember within the parentheses the multiplication operator is evaluated first).

Multiplication and division take a higher precedence than addition and subtraction, and that is about all you need to know, really. If you are in any doubt about the order in which an expression is to be evaluated, then use parentheses; the calculations within parentheses must be carried out first, before the result of the parentheses can be used. Programmers often can't remember operator precedence because, well, life is just too short to be wasted learning it. Instead they use parentheses to force calculations to work the way in which they want them to.

If you are in any doubt about how your expression is evaluated it is best to use parentheses. Using parentheses makes it easier to read the program and will save you time because it reduces confusion, especially if you don't know who will be reading your program and what level of knowledge they have. And finally, the biggest bonus is that you won't need to remember a long and uninteresting list of operator precedences.

You can see all the operators in the following table. At the top of the table you'll find the operators that are given the highest precedence (the ones that are used first). At the bottom you'll find the operators with the lowest precedence (the ones carried out last). It looks complicated, but as we stated, few programmers remember all the details of the precedence table used in the language in which they program. Of course we haven't covered all these operators yet, either, so the table will make more sense as we progress. You can see a quick definition of all the symbols in Appendix F, "Symbol Reference."

Operator	JavaScript Symbol
parentheses/member of array/dot operator	( ) [ ] .
negation/increment	! ~ - ++ —
multiply/divide/modulus	* / %
addition/subtraction	+ -
bitwise shift	<< >> >>>
relational	< <= > >=
equality	== !=
bitwise-and	&
bitwise-xor	^
bitwise-or	|
logical-and	&&
logical-or	||
ternary or "shorthand if" operator	?:
assignment	= += -= *= /= %= <<= >>= >>>= &= ^= |=
comma (separates parameters)	,

Type Conversion

Type conversion occurs in expressions in which you use variables of different types. In other words, the program decides what to do with a particular variable and modifies the data in the variable so that it can be used with the other variables. The result, after all, can only be of one type. For example:

Example 5.13

```
var sMonth = "August"
var nYear = 1996
var nDay = 15
var sDate = sMonth + " " + nDay + ", " + nYear
```

The + operator here concatenates the variables and literals into one string and puts it into **sDate**, which is a string variable. Why is it a string variable? Because one of the variables providing data to be concatenated is a string variable; **sMonth** contains the word **August**. And because there's no real way to convert a string to a number, one of JavaScript's type-conversion rules is that if you add a numeric variable to a string variable, the numbers must be converted to strings and the result is a string.

> **TIP**
>
> *Using the concatenation operator (+) to "add" strings to numbers, or numbers to strings, will* always *result in numeric values being converted to strings—even if the strings are numbers. For instance, adding* **"8"** + **1996** + **15** *results in* **8199615**, *not* **2019**.

Because the values in **nYear** and **nDay** are numbers, they are converted to string values before they are concatenated with the other strings. The number **1996** in **nYear** becomes the string **1996**, and the number **15** in **nDay** becomes the string **15**. As we said earlier, numbers and strings are held by the computer in different ways, and during type conversion the way this data is represented internally to the computer changes. You can see that adding the **s** and **n** prefixes to your variable names is important, as it helps you keep all this straight.

At the time of writing the type-conversion rules were not clearly documented, but we can identify a basic rule: If a calculation doesn't make sense, you'll get an error. JavaScript is what's known as *loosely typed*. Other programming languages have much stricter rules about how you can assign a datatype to a variable and how you can convert one type to another. JavaScript, on the other hand, is more tolerant and lets you change types quickly and easily—but you might run into problems when you do so.

For example, if you use an expression that mixes both numeric and string values, JavaScript will convert the numeric value to a string *if it makes sense to do so*. We've just seen an example of how JavaScript converts a number to text when you are using the addition/concatenation operator (+). Whether you add a string to a number, or a number to a string, you'll end up with a string value. This makes sense, and it works.

But this *doesn't* work when you use the subtraction operator (–). Subtract one from another and you'll end up with a numeric value:

Example 5.14

```
var sVariable1 = "555"
var sVariable2 = sVariable1 + 10
var sVariable3 = sVariable1 - 10
```

Here we started with a string variable, with the string value of 555. Then we added **10** to the string and assigned the result to **sVariable2**. This is the same sort of thing we did in the previous example—click on the first button on this page in the Online Companion and you'll see the value held by **sVariable2**: **55510**. The value is a string, not a number.

Then we *subtracted* **10** from **sVariable1** and assigned the result to **sVariable3**. This time, when you click on the associated button, you'll see the number **545**. The result, then, is a numeric value (555 - 10 = 545). This makes sense. Why? Because you can't "subtract" a piece of text from another piece of text, so there's no point trying. Instead JavaScript assumes that you want to do a mathematical calculation, so it converts the text to a number.

The problem arises when you use the subtraction operator between a numeric value and a string value that isn't a number. For instance, take a look at this Online Companion example:

Example 5.15

```
var sVariable1 = "Fred"
var sVariable2 = sVariable1 + 10
```

This is fine; adding **sVariable1** and **10** gives a string value (we'll end up with **Fred10**). But we also created a button that uses the subtraction operator:

```
<input type="button" name="VariableButton" value="sVariable1 - 10: String
with Text - Numeric" onclick="alert(sVariable1 - 10)">
```

You can see that we used **sVariable1 - 10** in the alert instruction. Now, when you click on this button, you'll see two things: an error message saying *sVariable1 is not a numeric variable* and the JavaScript message box, which contains the value *0*. (We put this calculation directly into a button rather than up in the HTML HEAD along with the other stuff, because we didn't want the error message to appear as soon as you opened the Web page, which it would if the variable had been declared in the HEAD.)

But that's okay. The expression is meaningless; what does **Fred** minus **10** mean, after all? Here's another example. What happens when we try to multiply text by a number?

Example 5.16

First, we have the following in the HEAD:

```
var sVariable1 = "Fred"
var sVariable2 = "15"
var nVariable3 = sVariable2 * 2
```

The variable named **nVariable3** has been created by multiplying the contents of **sVariable2** (**15**) by the number **2**. When you click on the associated button, you'll see that we end up with **30**. The script converts the value in the variable to a numeric value and then multiplies it by **2**. It does this because it *can* and because it doesn't make sense to do it any other way.

On the other hand, we also have this button in the page:

```
<form>
<input type="button" name="VariableButton" value="sVariable1 * 10: String
with Text * Numeric" onclick="alert(sVariable1 * 10)">
</form>
```

This button displays the result of multiplying **sVariable1** (**Fred**) by **10**. How can this be done? We don't know, and neither does JavaScript, so it gives us an error message.

Type conversion takes place in a fairly logical manner. If your expression does not make sense, it will probably produce an error. If you are unsure of what might happen, test it by modifying one of the scripts from the Online Companion or try your own.

The typeof operator

JavaScript 1.1 (Netscape Navigator 3) has another operator that you might want to know about but which is a little advanced: **typeof**.

You can use the **typeof** operator to examine an "operand" (a string, variable, method, function, keyword, object, or property). The **typeof** operator will return a string that describes the type of operand. This might be useful if you want to carry out an operation on something, but need to know what that item is before you carry out the operation (so you can select the appropriate operation depending on the type of the operand).

You can see **typeof** in action in the following example. We began by declaring a few variables:

Example 5.17

```
var sSize="big"
var nSize=1
var todayDate=new Date()
```

Then we used **typeof** to write the types of these variables, and a variety of other items, into the page:

```
document.write("sSize = " + typeof sSize + "<BR>")
document.write("nSize = " + typeof nSize + "<BR>")
document.write("todayDate = " + typeof todayDate + "<BR>")
document.write("nothingAtAll = " + typeof nothingAtAll + "<BR>")
document.write("null = " + typeof null + "<BR>")
document.write("false = " + typeof false + "<BR>")
document.write("true = " + typeof true + "<BR>")
document.write("666 = " + typeof 666 + "<BR>")
document.write("A little bit of text = " + typeof 'A little bit of text' →
+ "<BR>")
document.write("document.linkColor = " + typeof document.linkColor + "<BR>")
document.write("document.lastModified = " + typeof document.lastModified →
+ "<BR>")
document.write("document.anchors = " + typeof document.anchors + "<BR>")
document.write("window.history = " + typeof window.history + "<BR>")
document.write("window.length = " + typeof window.length + "<BR>")
document.write("Math.E = " + typeof Math.E + "<BR>")
document.write("blur = " + typeof blur + "<BR>")
document.write("Date = " + typeof Date + "<BR>")
document.write("String = " + typeof String + "<BR>")
```

We ended up with this result displayed in the Web page:

```
sSize = string
nSize = number
todayDate = object
nothingAtAll = undefined
null = object
false = boolean
true = boolean
666 = number
A little bit of text = string
document.linkColor = string
document.lastModified = string
```

```
document.anchors = object
window.history = object
window.length = number
Math.E = number
blur = function
Date = function
String = function
```

You can see that the result of **typeof** depends on what the item contains. For example, the result of **typeof document.lastModifie**d is string, because that's what the property contains. The result of **typeof document.anchors** is object, because the **anchors** array is an object.

Moving On

You've now seen how computers can use expressions and operators to take values and derive other values from them. This is a great start, but there's still something missing. How can a computer take these values and make decisions based on them? That's done with what are known as *conditionals*, special statements that can be used to examine data and carry out operations depending on the value held by the data. Conditionals allow a computer to say, for example, "if this variable contains such and such a value, I'll do this; if it doesn't, I'll do something different."

This is where the real power of programming lies, and that's what we'll be looking at next.

6

Conditionals & Loops— Making Decisions & Controlling Scripts

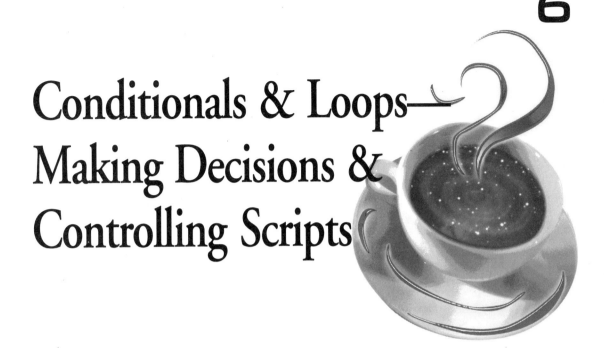

Now, let's move on to the ways in which you can get your program to make decisions and to do things repetitively. Let's look into decision-making first. You can do this by using *conditional* expressions. We all use conditional expressions in everyday speech. For example:

"If your report card is good, I will give you $10."

The first part of this sentence, "If your report card is good," is a conditional expression. It is either true or false. If it is *true*, the second part of the statement will be performed, and the cash will be handed over. If it's *false*—if the report card is bad—the second part of the statement is *not* carried out. Actually, the statement could be a little more complicated:

"If your report card is good, I will give you $10. Otherwise, you'll have to go to summer school."

In this case, something *does* happen if the condition is false. If the report card is not good, then you'll have to go to summer school.

A conditional statement can evaluate to true or false—that is, there are two possible results, true or false. Computers are pretty stupid and cannot handle partly true values, so this expression cannot cope with a situation in which your report card was barely acceptable, but not absolutely awful—you didn't get the $10, but you didn't have to go to summer school either. JavaScript's conditional expression must evaluate to either true or false, and there is no in-between position.

> ## TIP
>
> *That doesn't mean that you can't get a script or program to figure out "shades of gray"; you can do so by using a series of conditional expressions. (As you'll see later in this chapter, under "Shades of Gray: Using Nested if Statements.") But each single conditional expression can only have two possible outcomes.*

The 'if' Statement

One way of writing conditional statements in JavaScript (and in many other programming languages, for that matter) is by using **if** statements. An **if** statement follows this form:

```
if(conditional expression) {
   do something
}
```

The conditional expression goes between the parentheses—( ). If the conditional expression evaluates to true, the expression between the braces { } is performed. If the condition is not true, then the expression between the braces is *not* performed. Let's take a look at an actual example:

Example 6.1

```
var sButton
function function1() {
   if (sButton == "A") {
     alert("You pressed button \'A\'")
   }
}
```

> ## TIP
>
> *Important: You must write **if**, not **IF** or **If**. These last two forms will not work.*
>
> *This creates a function (**function1( )**) that uses an **if** statement to decide what to do. Look at the first line of the **if** statement. Inside the parentheses you see this:* **sButton == "A"**. *This means, "Look at variable **sButton** and see if it is equal to **A**" (that is, if the variable contains the character **A**). If the variable does contain **A**, then the expression evaluates to true. (As we'll see in a moment, **sButton** will contain **A** if you click on Button A. It won't contain **A** if you click on Button B.) It's important to note that the expression within the parentheses after **if** must be true.*
>
> *If it's not true, the instructions within the braces—{ }—will not run.*

> **TIP**
>
> *You'll notice that there are two sets of { } symbols. The first set belongs to the function and encloses its statements, in this case the **if** statement that the function carries out. The second set, which is nested within the first, encloses the instructions that the **if** statement carries out if the condition is true.*

Note that the operator used here is not = but ==, two equals symbols together. There is a difference in meaning between the conditional equals == and the assignment equals =. When you use the assignment symbol (which we talked about in Chapter 5, "Expressions & Operators"), the variable to the left of the = is assigned the value of the expression to the right of the =. However, you don't want to do that in a conditional expression. All we're trying to do is see what is inside the variable to the right of the symbol; we're not trying to actually change anything. In a conditional expression there is no assignment of values—a comparison is done, but variables are not given any new values.

Now, remember that in the case where the expression is true, the line (or lines) of script between the braces is performed. In this case, we have this line: **alert("You pressed button \'A\'")**. In other words, if the condition is true (if the variable contains **A**), then the script will display the Alert message box with the text *You pressed button 'A'*.

There are two buttons in this example, **Button A** and **Button B**:

```
<form>
<input type="button" value=" Button A " onclick="sButton = 'A';function1()">
<input type="button" value=" Button B " onclick="sButton = 'B';function1()">
</form>
```

> **TIP**
>
> *You can see that the **onclick** instruction carries out two tasks: first it sets **sButton**, then it calls **function1( )**. Notice that we've moved the second event down one line and indented it. This is simply to make it easier to read. And there's a semicolon at the end of the first line; this **must** be there.*

We're using the **onclick** event here. When the user clicks on **Button A**, the **sButton** variable is assigned the character **A**. If the user clicks on **Button B**, the **sButton** variable is assigned the character **B**. In both cases, immediately after assigning the value the **onclick** event handler calls **function1( )**, which, as we've just seen, takes a look at what's inside the **sButton** variable.

TIP

Remember to use single quotes for **'A'** *and* **'B'** *when used in the* **onclick** *events, because the instruction after* **onclick** *is within double quotes.*

Don't Mistake = For ==

What happens if you forget the difference between = and ==, and use = in your **if** statement? Take a look:

Example 6.2

```
function function1() {
    if (sButton = "A")    {
     alert("You pressed button \'A\'")
     }
}
```

Example 6.2 is the same as 6.1, except that the equality conditional operator (==) has been replaced with the assignment operator (=). When the page loads, you will get the following message (this is using Navigator—other JavaScript browsers might display a different message):

test for equality (==) mistyped as assignment(=)? Assuming equality test.

The function will load, but Navigator is smart enough to assume that you really wanted to put the conditional ==, and the function will behave in exactly the same way as the previous example. (Internet Explorer doesn't display a message, though as with Navigator it will assume you meant to use the equality operator.) Click on **Button A** to see the message box.

If Statements With Boolean Variables

Look at the **if** line from Example 6.1 again:

```
if (sButton == "A")    {
```

As you've seen, this means "if the stuff inside the parentheses is true, then carry out the instructions beginning after the { symbol." In this case it means "if **sButton** *does* contain **A**, then carry out the instructions."

Note, however, that the contents inside the parentheses can be a single word. For example:

Example 6.3

```
var bStatus = true
function CheckStatus() {
   if (bStatus) {
      alert("The value in bStatus is true")
   }
   else {
      alert("The value in bStatus is false")
   }
}
```

In this script we've declared a Boolean variable named **bStatus** and initial-ized its value to **true**. Then we've created a function called **CheckStatus( )**, which uses an **if** statement to see what value is held by the variable and to display the appropriate Alert box. Notice that the parentheses after **if** contain nothing but the name of the variable. In effect, this means "if the value held by **bStatus** is **true**."

To complete the page, we have two buttons:

```
<form>
<input type="button" value="True" onclick="bStatus = true; CheckStatus()">
<input type="button" value="False" onclick="bStatus = false; CheckStatus()">
</form>
```

The first button sets the value of **bStatus** to **true**, then calls the **CheckStatus( )** function. The second button sets the value of **bStatus** to **false**, then calls **CheckStatus( )**.

The 'else' Clause

As you saw in our report-card analogy, you can create conditional expressions that do something if the condition is **false**. If you didn't get a good report card (a **false** condition), you'd have to go to summer school. This is done by using an **else** clause with the **if** statement, like this:

Example 6.4

```
function function1() {
   if (sButton == "A") {
     alert("You pressed button \'A\'")
   }
   else {
     alert("You pressed button \'B\'")
   }
}
```

We've created **function1( )** in the same way as before, but added three more lines, starting at else {. Again, the instructions that are to be carried out in the false or **else** condition are enclosed within { and }. In this case we display the Alert message box, but with a different message. If the condition is false, **sButton** doesn't contain the value **A**, so we display a message saying *You pressed button 'B'*.

The Use of Braces

In the examples so far, you've used the braces { } to enclose the instructions that are carried out in the true and false conditions. You don't *have* to do this, though we believe it's a good idea to do so. If you don't, only the first expression after the **if** is conditionally executed. In the next example, the braces have been dropped, but the program is not as easy to read:

Example 6.5

```
var sButton
function function1() {
   if (sButton == "A")
     alert("You pressed button \'A\'")
       alert("This is the line after the if statement")
}
```

(Note that the **if** statement itself is still enclosed within { }, which belong to the function; it's just the instructions carried out if the expression is true that are not enclosed.) Try this example and you'll find that if you click on **Button A**, you'll get *two* Alert message boxes—one after the other. Click on **Button B**, and you'll just see the second Alert box, which says *This is the line after the if statement*. So you *can* do this. You might even be able to think of some uses for this situation; but in general it's a good idea to always use the braces—it is too easy to get confused otherwise.

Conditional Operators

There are other conditional operators. If you could only check to see if a value equaled something, you would be rather limited. So we have operators that let us see if a value *doesn't* equal something, if it's greater or less than something, and so on. Here are the conditional operators:

Operator	Meaning
==	Equal to (you have just seen this one in action).
!=	Not equal to; checks to see if the value is *not* something.
>	Greater than; checks to see if something is greater than something else. **x > y** means "check to see if x is greater than y."
<	Less than; checks to see if something is less than something else. **x < y** means "check to see if x is less than y."
>=	Greater than or equal to; checks to see if something is the same as or greater than something else. **x >= y** means "check to see if x is the same as or greater than y."
<=	Less than or equal to; checks to see if something is the same as or less than something else. **x <= y** means "check to see if x is the same as or less than y."
?	Shorthand if operator, often known as the *ternary operator*. It checks a conditional expression to see if it's true, then assigns a value to a variable depending on whether the expression is true or not. **x = (*condition*) ? y : z** means "check to see if the condition is true; if so, place the value of y in x; if not, place the value of z in x."

Not Equal (!=)

Our next example shows the "not equal" operator in use. This **if** statement evaluates to true when the variable **sButton** does *not* contain the value **A**. This example now has three buttons: **A**, **B**, and **C**. Try it.

Example 6.6

```
function function1() {
   if (sButton != "A") {
     alert("The variable is not equal to \'A\' \n It is \'" + sButton + "\'")
   }
}
```

The **if** statement conditional evaluates to true when the variable **sButton** is not equal to **A**. There are three buttons in this example now; the third button assigns the value **C** to **sButton**. When you try this example, you'll see that if you click on **Button A**, nothing happens. Remember, this **if** statement only does something if **sButton** is *not* equal to **A**. If you click on **Button B** or **C**, though, you'll see the Alert message box. This box displays *The variable is not equal to 'A'*; then, on the next line (remember, \n means new line), it displays *It is* ' followed by the value held by **sButton** (**B** or **C**), followed by a space and '.

JavaScript 1.2 Changes

JavaScript 1.2 (Netscape Navigator 4) handles the == and != equality operators a little differently *if* your **<SCRIPT>** tag uses the **LANGUAGE=JavaScript1.2** attribute. (If the attribute is not used, the browser will handle the attributes in the original JavaScript 1.0 and 1.1 manner.) In most cases you'll find no differences, but in some advanced situations you need to understand the changes. In our examples we've been using the equality operators to check the value held by a variable, but you can also use the equality operators to check other *operands* (other items). In such a case you need to know how the operators will work.

In a JavaScript 1.0 or 1.1 browser, or a JavaScript 1.2 browser if you're *not* using the **LANGUAGE=JavaScript1.2** attribute:

- If both operands are objects, the operators compare the object references.

- If either operand is **null**, the operators convert the other operand to an object and then compare references.

- If one operand is a string and the other is an object, the operators convert the object to a string and compare the string characters.

- In other cases the operators convert both operands to numbers and then compare the numbers.

In a JavaScript 1.2 browser if you *are* using the **LANGUAGE=JavaScript1.2** attribute:

- The operators will not attempt to convert operands from one type to another. If necessary you'll have to do the conversions yourself.

- The operators will always compare like-typed operands. If the operands are not the same, they are assumed not to be equal.

Suppose you wrote a bit of programming code like this:

```
var n = 5
var s = "5"

if (n == s) {
  alert("n and s are equal.")
}

var A = 5
var B = 5

if (A == B) {
  alert("A and B are equal.")
}
```

What happens? Are the two values equal or not? The answer depends on the programming language you are using; different languages have different concepts. Some are very flexible, and will gladly concede that the number **5** and the string **"5"** are equal. Other languages are very fussy. They might tell you that **A** does not equal **B**, even though they both contain **5**, just because they are two distinct variables, like two separate copies of the same book.

For Javascript users, this gets a bit more complex, because the early versions used a fairly flexible definition of equality. Browsers were allowed to do type conversion (see Chapter 5, "Expressions & Operators—Manipulating Values") in order to find some sense in which the values were equal, such as converting the number **5** to the string **"5"**. Then, starting with version 1.2, the designers of Javascript decided to use a stricter approach. But they didn't want to lose compatibility with older scripts, so they now allow you to choose either type of comparison by using (or not using) the **LANGUAGE=JavaScript1.2** attribute.

You don't need to worry about this right now, as this is fairly advanced stuff. You can find more information in the JavaScript documentation referenced in Appendix H.

Greater Than (>)

The greater than operator (>) is used, not surprisingly, to see if a value is greater than something else. For example:

```
x > y
```

This means, "see if the value of **x** is greater than the value of **y**." The next example shows the greater than operator in use. This **if** statement conditional evaluates to true when the variable **sButton** is not **A**. This example has three buttons: **A**, **B**, and **C**. Try it.

Example 6.7
```
function function1() {
var dToday = new Date()
var nSeconds = dToday.getSeconds()
    if (nSeconds > 30) {
        alert("We are MORE than halfway through this minute. Seconds=" + →
nSeconds )
    }
    else {
        alert("We are LESS than halfway through this minute. Seconds=" + →
nSeconds )
    }
}
```

What's going on here? Well, we began by defining the function **function1( )** again. This time, though, we've created an *object* called **dToday**. This object contains the current date and time and makes use of the built-in object called **Date**. (Don't worry too much about this right now—all you need to know is that the **dToday** object gets the date and time from the built-in **Date** object.)

On the next line we've declared a variable called **nSeconds**. This gets the seconds from our **dToday** variable. (Again, don't worry about the **dToday.getSeconds( )** instruction; we'll be looking at these built-in objects and how they work in Chapter 11, "More About Built-in Objects." For now all you need to know is that **nSeconds** contains the number of seconds past the current minute.)

TIP

> *These date and time objects derive the date and time from the computer on which the script is running—that is, on the computer on which the browser is running.*

Now, what does the **if** statement do? It takes a look at the value in the **nSeconds** variable—the number of seconds past the current minute. We are using the greater than operator, so we're not looking for an exact value; we just want to know if the value is more than **30**. If it *is*, we display the first Alert message box. If it *isn't*, we display the second Alert message box (after **else**).

Greater Than or Equal To (>=)

You can get even more precise by using the "greater than or equal to" operator. In the last example, you told the **if** statement to determine if the **nSeconds** value was greater than **30**. So what would happen if it were right on 30 seconds when you clicked on the button? Well, 30 isn't greater than 30; so the condition would be false, and the **else** Alert box would appear.

That's okay in many situations, but it's possible to be a little more accurate by getting the **if** statement to check for a value that is the same or more than another. Here's an example:

Example 6.8

```
Welcome to this Web page, and
<SCRIPT LANGUAGE="JavaScript">
<!--
var dToday = new Date()
var nHours = dToday.getHours()
   if (nHours >= 12) {
     document.write("Good Afternoon.")
   }
   else {
     document.write("Good Morning.")
   }
//-->
</SCRIPT>
```

We've actually embedded this little script into the Web page text. As you can see, the text says *Welcome to this Web page, and*. The script determines what appears next, though. Again, we've grabbed the time from the **Date** object. This time, though, we've grabbed the hours (instead of the seconds) and placed the value into the variable named **nHours**. Then we used an **if** statement to see if the value is more than—or the same as—**12**. If it is, it's the afternoon; so we use the **document.write** instruction to write **Good Afternoon.** to the Web page. If it *isn't* (that is, if it's anything less than **12**), we use the **document.write** instruction after **else**, and write **Good Morning.** to the Web page.

Shades of Gray: Using Nested if Statements

In some cases **if** statements are *nested*. That means that one **if** statement is placed within another. You'll remember from earlier in this chapter that conditional statements only allow two choices, so it can't choose from a range of possible decisions. Well, nesting **if** statements provides one way for you to do this. While one **if** statement cannot choose from a range, if you nest a few **if** statements together, the script *can* choose. Your first **if** statement has two options: a final decision or another **if** state^int, or maybe two **if** statements. It's the same for the second **if** statement. It might have a final decision and an **if** statement, or two more **if** statements. You can continue down a *cascade* of **if** statements, each one leading to another.

This is more like the way that people make decisions, isn't it? Rather than saying, "Either we'll go to eat tonight or we'll go to the movies," you make a series of decisions. If you decide to eat, what sort of food do you want to eat? If you decide to eat Indian food, which Indian restaurant will you visit? Will you eat from the buffet or from the menu? If from the menu, what will you choose? Each decision leads to another.

Take a look at this simple example:

Example 6.9

```
<SCRIPT LANGUAGE="JavaScript">
<!--
function function1() {
var dToday = new Date()
var nDay = dToday.getDay()
   if (nDay == 0) {
   alert("It's Sunday")
   }
   else {
       if (nDay <= 5) {
          alert("It's a week day")
       }
          else {
             alert("Hey, it's Saturday")
          }
   }
}
//-->
</SCRIPT>
```

We're using the **Date** object again; this time we're grabbing the actual day, which is a number representing the day of the week, from day **0** (Sunday) to day **6** (Saturday).

TIP

> *When JavaScript uses a range of numbers, it starts at **0**, not **1**. So the last day of the week is **6**, not **7**. Sorry, but that's a geek convention.*

The processing cascades down these **if** statements. If **nDay** is equal to **0** (it's Sunday), the first **alert** line is executed—*It's Sunday*. If it's any other number, though, the **else** part of the statement is executed. Inside the **else** braces is another nested **if** statement. In this **if** statement, we check to see if the day is equal to or less than **5**. (In other words, it must be **1, 2, 3, 4,** or **5**—it can't be **0**. If it was **0**, the script would have executed the first part of the previous **if** statement.) If it is, then the first **alert** line is executed; you'll see the message *It's a weekday*. If it isn't, then there's only one thing it can be—it must be Saturday—so the **else** line is executed.

Unfortunately, nesting **if** statements can get a little complicated. You end up with lots of { } symbols; and you must make sure that you get them paired correctly, or you'll get errors. Remember, for every opening {, you must have a closing } in the correct position. Very deep nesting can look very cluttered, but it's simply a matter of practice to read them and keep it all straight.

TIP

Notice that we've indented the { } symbols to the right and placed the closing } on its own line. You can also use blank lines in places, to help break up each section. This makes it easier to read the scripts. We'll talk a little more about this in Chapter 8, "Troubleshooting & Avoiding Trouble."

Boolean (Logical) Operators in Conditional Expressions

There is a class of operators that we haven't discussed much yet, the *Boolean* operators. Boolean algebra is a way in which logical statements are expressed in a branch of mathematics called *logic*. (It's really not as bad as it sounds.) In fact, as with straightforward conditional expressions, we also use Boolean operators in our everyday speech. For example, how about this one:
*When I've learned HTML **and** I've learned JavaScript, I'm going to take a vacation.*

The two conditional expressions in the first line are linked together with an "and" to form one conditional expression. They both must be true for the whole expression to be true. Unless I've learned HTML *and* JavaScript, I'm not going to take a vacation. So Boolean operators are used to combine conditional expressions together. You can use them to return **true** only if both conditions are true, or if either one or the other is true. These are the Boolean operators you can use:

Operator	Meaning
!	*Not*. Tells you what value the variable *doesn't* contain.
&&	*And*. Condition x *and* condition y must be true.
||	*Or*. (These lines are the "pipe" symbols, usually the Shift \ key). Condition x *or* condition y must be true.

Logical expressions evaluate to true or false, as do conditional expressions. Let's see how these operators are used in conditional expressions.

Example 6.10

```
function function1() {
var dToday = new Date()
var nHours = dToday.getHours()
var nDay = dToday.getDay()
   if ((nDay == 5) && (nHours >= 12)) {
      alert("Thank God it's Friday afternoon"  )
   }
   else {
      if ((nDay == 6) || (nDay == 0) ) {
         alert("Hey, it's the weekend" )
      }
      else {
         alert("Just another day")
      }
   }
}
```

We've used a nested **if** statement here, just as in the previous example. But this time we're also using Boolean conditional expressions. Here's the first one:

```
if ((nDay == 5) && (nHours >= 12))      {
```

This means, "**if nDay** is **5** *and* **nHours** is greater than or equal to **12**, then it's Friday afternoon." If both conditions are **true**, the program executes the code immediately following the first {; you'll see the Alert message box with *Thank God it's Friday afternoon*. If they aren't both true, then the script moves on to the **else** statement, which contains the nested **if** statement, which contains the following line:

```
if ((nDay == 6) || (nDay == 0) )        {
```

This means, "**if nDay** is **6** *or* **nDay** is **0**, then it's Saturday or Sunday." If it's Saturday or Sunday, the program executes the instruction starting after the {, displaying the Alert message box with the message *Hey, it's the weekend*. If neither expression is **true**, then the last Alert box is displayed, *Just another day*.

Note, by the way, that **((nDay == 6) && (nDay == 0))**—which means "if **nDay** is **6** *and* **nDay** is **0**"—is actually meaningless, because **nDay** cannot have two values (it can't be Saturday and Sunday at the same time). You wouldn't get an error message, but the statement would never return **true**—the script would always run the **else** statement.

Note also that the entire conditional expression must be enclosed in parentheses. The following expression,

```
if (nDay == 5) && (nHours >= 12)  {
```

would cause an error when the script loaded. So you must add the parentheses after **if** and before {, like this:

```
if ((nDay == 5) && (nHours >= 12))  {
```

As you can see, you can combine conditional expressions using Boolean operators. You can also use these operators to combine Boolean variables, as you learned in Chapter 5, "Expressions & Operators—Manipulating Values." These expressions can get to be quite complex and difficult to read, so it is best to use parentheses to group logical expressions into understandable units of code. Also note that if you combine many Boolean variables using Boolean operators, it is easy to get confused over what you actually mean!

Boolean Not—What *Doesn't* the Value Contain?

Earlier in this chapter, you saw what the != operator does. This is the *not equal to* operator, and you can use it to tell a script to do something if a variable is not equal to a particular value. You'll remember that we used it like this:

```
function function1() {
   if (sButton != "A")   {
     alert("The variable is not equal to \'A\' \n It is \'" + sButton + "\'")
   }
}
```

If **sButton** does not equal **A**, the Alert is displayed. What if the variable is a Boolean variable, though? You'll remember from Example 6.3 that simply placing the name of the Boolean variable in the parentheses is the same as saying "if this variable contains true." Well, all you need to do is place an exclamation mark immediately before the variable name to say "if this variable does *not* contain true." For example, look at the following:

Example 6.11
```
var bStatus = true
function CheckStatus() {
   if (!bStatus) {
      alert("The value in bStatus is false")
   }
   else {
      alert("The value in bStatus is true")
   }
}
```

This script is the same as the one in Example 6.3 with three changes. We've placed **!** immediately before the variable name (**!bStatus**). In the first **alert** line we changed **true** to **false**, and in the second **alert** line we changed **false** to **true**. Now, if **bStatus** is *not* **true**—that is, if it contains **false**—the first line will be displayed.

Another Form of if Statement

There's another, shorthand way to write an **if** statement, though it's important to note that this expression doesn't just compare values, it also assigns a value to a variable. It looks like this:

```
variable = (condition) ? value1 : value2
```

This expression uses the **?** operator to assign values to a variable that is dependent on a conditional expression. If the **condition** in the parentheses (it could also be a Boolean variable) evaluates to true, then the **variable** is made equal to **value1**. If it is false, then the **variable** is made equal to **value2**.

Here's an example:

Example 6.12
```
function function1() {
var dToday = new Date()
var nSeconds = dToday.getSeconds()
var sText = (nSeconds > 30) ? "MORE" : "LESS"
    alert("We are " + sText + " than halfway through this minute. Seconds=" +
nSeconds )
}
```

This example does exactly the same thing as Example 6.7. If **nSeconds** is greater than **30**, then it makes the variable **sText** equal to **MORE**; if it isn't greater than **30**, it makes **sText** equal to **LESS**. This variable is then used in the Alert box to display a message.

Loops

You've now seen how you can control which statements of your program are executed using the conditional expressions. You've learned, in effect, how to give your scripts decision-making abilities. Now let's look at how to repeat tasks—how to execute lines of your program over and over. As you'll learn, this provides a way for you to make a script carry out an operation over and over until a certain condition is reached, at which point you can make the script do something. These operations are known as *loops*, and we'll start by looking at the **for** loop.

The for Loop

The **for** statement is one way you can write a loop into your program. Look at the next example:

Example 6.13

```
function function1() {
var i
   for (i = 1; i < 4; i++) {
      alert("The value in i is " + i )
   }
   alert("The loop has finished and i is " + i )
}
```

This is a **for** statement. Try it in the Online Companion. This loop counts up to three. Each time it adds one, it executes the line of code within the braces. This code displays an Alert box showing the value of the variable **i**. The Alert box stops the program and waits for you to click the OK button. Then the loop continues.

> ### TIP
> *There's nothing unusual about the action of this Alert box. Whenever a script opens an Alert box, it always stops and waits for the user to click on the OK button.*

Let's look at the format of the **for** statement in more detail:

```
for (initial expression; conditional expression; update expression) {
   code to be run if conditional expression is true
}
```

The first part of the **for** statement, the *initial expression*, is executed the first time the loop is executed—before anything else is done. It is usual to initialize a "counter" here (a variable that will hold a number showing how many times the loop has been executed), and in this example it sets the counter **i** equal to **1**.

The *conditional expression* is evaluated before the loop can be executed. If this expression is true, then the next cycle around the loop is started, and the code within the curly brackets is run (in the example, the Alert box is displayed). If the conditional expression is *not* true, then the code is not executed and the loop ends. The browser moves on to the next line of script immediately after the closing } of the **for** statement (which, in our example, displays an Alert box telling us that the loop has ended). In our example script the conditional expression is **i < 4**, which means "run the loop if the value of **i**—the counter—is less than **4**."

The *update expression* is evaluated each time a cycle of the loop ends. In other words, the code in the curly brackets is executed before the update expression is executed. In our example, this expression increments the value in variable **i** by 1 using the increment operator, **++**. *Update expressions* are usually used to increment the counter, and the counter is used to determine how many times the loop will run.

You might want to play around with the values in the example. Copy the example to your hard disk and change the values to see how it works. Try changing the **for** loop to the following:

```
for (i = 0; i < 4; i++) {
```

The program will now execute the loop four times with **i** = **0, 1, 2**, and **3**, ending with **4**.

Now try changing the conditional expression to

```
for (i = 0; i < 6; i++) {
```

The loop is now executed 6 times with **i** = **0, 1, 2, 3, 4**, and **5**, ending with **5**. Finally, try changing the update expression to

```
for (i = 0; i < 6; i= i + 2) {
```

The counter is now incremented by **2** each time so that the loop is now executed 3 times with **i** = **0, 2**, and **4**. Try playing around with this code to get a good understanding of what is happening.

> **TIP**
>
> *Be careful with the conditional and update expressions. If you get these wrong, you can get the script stuck in a perpetual loop. For example, try dropping the **i=** part from the update expression—use just **i+2** as the update expression, for example. Because this is faulty and doesn't update the counter, the conditional expression is always **true**, so the loop goes on forever. You'll have to crash the browser to get out of it.*

For = Nested if?

Many advanced statements in programming are really created as shortcuts. You don't need to use a **for** statement—you can do the same thing using nested **if** statements. The code in our example is more or less equivalent to this:

Example 6.14

```
function function1() {
var i = 1
  if (i < 4) {
     alert("The value in i is " + i )        // i now equals 2
     if (i < 4) {
        alert("The value in i is " + i )      //i now equals 3
        if (i < 4) {
           alert("The value in i is " + i )   //i now equals 4
           if (i < 4) {              //i is not less than 4 so this is false
              alert("The value in i is " + i )
              i++
           }
        }
     }
  }
}
```

This is a series of nested **if** statements that do the same thing. Clearly the **for** statement is much easier to create and understand. Also, it would be very difficult to replace a long and complicated **for** statement with nested **if** statements.

The while Loop

Another way to create a loop is by using a **while** statement. You can perform exactly the same function as in Example 6.13 with the following statement:

Example 6.15

```
function function1() {
var i = 1
  while (i < 4) {
     alert("The value in i is " + i )
     i++
  }
  alert("The loop has finished and i is " + i )
}
```

The loop executes *while* the conditional expression in the parentheses is true. Once **i = 4** and the condition evaluates to **false**, the loop no longer executes and the program goes to the next line, which is the last Alert box.

Here's the basic format of the **while** loop:

```
while (conditional expression) {
   code to run while conditional expression is true
}
```

As you can see, the **while** statement has a conditional expression. If the expression is true (in the prior example, if **i < 4**), then the code between the braces is run. If it is not true, then the browser moves on to the next line of the script. In this case, it displays an Alert box telling us that the loop has finished. We still have a counter in this example, but the counter is now placed in the code between the braces; **while** statements have no *update expression*.

Lets try another **while** loop, but this time without a counter:

Example 6.16

```
function function1() {
var sWord =""
  while (sWord != "Aardvark") {
    sWord = prompt("Input the word \'Aardvark\' in order to stop the loop","")
  }
  alert("The loop has finished")
}
```

This example uses a new element of JavaScript that we have not seen yet: the Prompt dialog box (see Figure 6-1). The **prompt** box "collects" something a user types into it. In this case it displays the message *Input the word 'Aardvark' in order to stop the loop*, and whatever the user types in will be put into the **sWord** variable when the user clicks on the OK button. This **while** loop will go around and around until **sWord** contains the word **Aardvark**. In the previous example, you used a counter as the condition on which the **while** statement depended. In this case you are using the contents of **sWord** as the condition. (We've actually told the **while** statement to continue as long as **sWord** *does not contain* **Aardvark**.) So until the user types in the correct text, the **while** loop will continue and will display another prompt box.

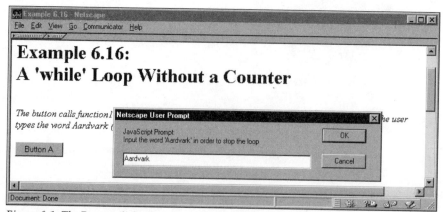

Figure 6-1: The Prompt dialog box.

do while Loops

Another common form of loop is the **do while** loop. This type of loop is important because it guarantees that the instructions will be carried out at least once, by placing the conditional expression *after* the instructions that must be carried out. (With other loops the conditional expression is checked first, so in some cases the instructions are never carried out.)

There are two ways to create **do while** loops. There is no true **do while** loop in JavaScript 1.0 and JavaScript 1.1. You can, however, simulate one, as you'll see in a moment. If you're writing scripts for JavaScript 1.2 (Netscape 4), you can use the new built-in **do while** loop. Here's the basic **do while** format:

```
do {
    code to carry out
}
while (conditional expression)
```

You can simulate a **do while** loop in some cases by repeating the code you want carried out. For instance, look at this example:

Example 6.17

```
function function1() {
var sWord ="Aardvark"
   sWord = prompt("Input the word \'Aardvark\' in order to  stop the loop","")
   while (sWord != "Aardvark") {
     sWord = prompt("Input the word \'Aardvark\' in order  to stop the loop","")
   }
   alert("The loop has finished")
}
```

Remember, the purpose of the **do while** is to make something run even if the **while** condition is false. So we started by initializing **sWord** with **Aardvark**. In this case the **while** loop wouldn't normally run at all, because the condition is **false**; **sWord** *does* contain **Aardvark**. So we simply put the same code that is inside the **while** loop just above the **while** loop. Now, even though **sWord** already contains **Aardvark**, the Prompt dialog box will open. Then, if the user doesn't type **Aardvark**, the **while** loop kicks in. (If the user clicks on OK without typing anything into the Prompt dialog box, **sWord** will be cleared.)

Another way to handle it (a more elegant way, perhaps) would be this:

```
while(true) {
    code to carry out
    if (!condition)
    break
}
```

By putting **true** in parentheses you are ensuring that the **while** loop at least begins. Then the **if** statement determines whether the loop should continue or not.

If you want to use JavaScript 1.2 **do while** loops, you can do so like this:

Example 6.18

```
function function1() {
var sWord =""
   do   {
     sWord = prompt("Input the word \'Aardvark\' in order to stop the loop","")
   }
   while (sWord != "Aardvark")
   alert("The loop has finished")
}
```

In this example you can see that the **do while** statement begins by displaying the Prompt dialog box (even if **sWord** already contained **Aardvark** the Prompt dialog box would open). The data from the dialog box is placed into **sWord**. Next you see **while** followed by a conditional expression in parentheses. If this expression is true—that is, if the value in **sWord** does not equal **Aardvark**—the program loops back up to the **do** line. If it's false (once **sWord** *does* equal **Aardvark**), the browser skips down to the next line and displays the Alert box.

Breaking Out of a Loop—break

In order to stop a loop from inside you can use the **break** statement. This statement makes the program skip to the line after the loop. There are times when using the conditional expression to stop a loop is not enough, and you want your program to decide what to do from within the loop. You can use **break** from within **for** and **while** statements. Look at the following example to see what we mean. We've allowed the user to execute a **break** by clicking on the Cancel button of a dialog box:

Example 6.19

```
function function1() {
var bResult
   for (i = 1; i < 4; i++) {
   bResult = confirm("i = " + i + "\nClick cancel to execute a \'break\'
statement","")
       if (bResult == false) {
          break;
       }
```

```
     }
     alert("The loop has finished\ni = " + i)
}
```

The example is a **for** statement that will loop until **i** is equal to **4**. The loop displays a Confirm dialog box, as seen in Figure 6-2. You have seen how these work before, in Example 2.12. When the user clicks on a button, a Boolean value is returned—**true** if he clicks on OK, **false** if he clicks on Cancel. That value is placed in the **bResult** variable.

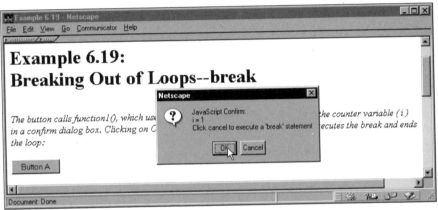

Figure 6-2: The Confirm dialog box.

The next instruction that is executed, immediately after the Confirm dialog box has closed, is an **if** statement. This statement checks the value in **bResult**; if the value is **false**, the conditional expression is true, so the instruction within the next braces is run. That instruction is the **break**. And **break** simply means, "don't go back to the top of the **for** instruction; instead, go to the next line of the script, after the loop." The final line uses **alert** to display a dialog box to tell us that the loop has finished.

JavaScript 1.2 (Navigator 4) improves the **break** a little. Loops can now contain labeled statements, and a **break** can use the label to define which part of the loop is being broken out of. For instance, we've modified the previous example:

Example 6.20

```
<SCRIPT LANGUAGE="JavaScript">
<!--
function function1() {
var bResult
var bResult2
```

```
external :
   for (i = 1; i < 4; i++) {
        bResult = confirm("i = " + i + "\nClick cancel to execute a→
\'break\' statement","")
        if (bResult == false) {
             bResult2 = confirm("Are you sure? Click OK to break completely→
out of the loop. Press Cancel to break just the internal part of the loop.")
internal :
                 if (bResult2 == true)  {
                     break  external;
                 }
                 else {
                     break  internal;
                 }
alert("You broke internal")
        }
    }
   alert("You broke external")
}
//-->
</SCRIPT>
```

We have labeled two parts of this script: **main :** and **internal :** . And we've
modified the script a little, so that when you click on the confirm box's
Cancel button you'll see another dialog box, which asks if you want to break
completely out of the loop or if you simply want to break out of the internal
part of the loop.

As you can see, the **break** statements specify one of the labels (**break external;** and **break internal;**). If you click on OK the **break external;** statement is
used, and you break all the way out to the alert box that says *You broke external*.
Click on Cancel, though, and you only break to **internal**, so you'll see the alert
box that says *You broke internal*, then the script loops around again.

Returning to the Top of the Loop—continue

As with **break**, **continue** is a way of controlling **for** or **while** loops, except that
the loop is not terminated. Instead the **continue** statement returns processing
immediately back to the top of the loop, and the next cycle starts. In other
words, **continue** provides a way to stop the processing of the rest of the lines
of code within the loop.

When the **continue** statement is executed, processing goes back to the conditional expression in a **while** loop, or the update expression in a **for** loop. Take a look at this **while** loop to see what we mean:

Example 6.21

```
var bResult
var i = 0
    while (i < 4) {
        bResult = confirm("i = " + i + "\nClick cancel to execute a
\'continue\' statement","")
        if (bResult == false) {
            continue;
        }
        i++
    }
    alert("The loop has finished\ni = " + i)
}
```

The example is a **while** statement that will loop until **i** is equal to **4**. The loop displays a Confirm box. Again, the result from the Confirm dialog box (**true** for OK, **false** for Cancel) is placed in the **bResult** variable.

The **if** statement takes a look at **bResult**. If **bResult** contains **false**—that is, if the user clicked on the Cancel button—the conditional expression is true, so the instruction immediately after { is run. That's the **continue** statement, which returns processing to the beginning of the **while** statement without running the **i++** operation. If **bResult** contains **true**—that is, if the user clicked on the OK button—the conditional expression is not true, so the instruction within the curly brackets is not run. Instead, the **i++** operation runs and *then* returns to the top of the **while** statement.

So if you continually click on the OK button the loop runs completely until the process has finished. If you click on the Cancel button, you will not get anywhere. You are simply stuck, because the value in **i** is never incremented. In fact the only way to get out of the loop is by completing it. At some point you must click on the OK button several times to finish.

As with the **break**, JavaScript 1.2 (Navigator 4) improved the **continue** a little. The **continue** can also contain labels. You use the labels in the same way as with **break** to tell the script where to go when it continues.

The switch Statement

JavaScript 1.2 (Navigator 4) also introduces the **switch** statement. This is used to allow you to pick a statement by matching an expression with a **case** label. For example, the **switch** can look in a variable, compare the contents with a series of **case** labels, then carry out the statement defined by the matching **case** label. If the value doesn't match any of the **case** labels, a default statement can be used instead. It works like this:

```
switch (expression){
        case label :
                statement;
                break;
        case label :
                statement;
                break;
        case label :
                statement;
                break;
        case label :
                statement;
                break;
        case label :
                statement;
                break;
        default : statement;
}
```

The switch looks at the **expression**, then compares the result with the first **case** label. If it matches, it runs the statement below that **case** label; then the **break** moves the program down to the statement immediately following the **switch**. If a match isn't found, the next **case** label is checked for a match, and so on. If there are *no* matches, it runs the **default** statement. (If there's no **default** statement, it moves on to the next item after the **switch** without doing anything.) You can include as many **case** labels as you wish. If you really wish, you can omit the **break**s, though this is uncommon; programmers almost always include **break**s in switch statements. Still, you *could* do it, and you should understand what happens if you do. So, for instance, you could do this:

```
switch (expression){
        case label :
                statement;
        case label :
                statement;
        case label :
                statement;
        case label :
                statement;
        case label :
                statement;
        default : statement;
}
```

If you *don't* use the **break**, something unexpected will happen: All the statements following the matching **case** label will be run, even though they appear below **case** labels that *don't* match.

Here's an example of a **switch** statement (with **break**s) in action:.

Example 6.22

```
function runSwitch()  {
var sColor = prompt("Type Red, White, Green, or Blue (or type something
else)")
switch (sColor) {
   case "Red" :
     alert("Your Favorite Color is Red");
     break;
   case "White" :
     alert("Your Favorite Color is White");
     break;
   case "Green" :
     alert("Your Favorite Color is Green");
     break;
   case "Blue" :
     alert("Your Favorite Color is Blue");
     break;
   default :
     alert("You didn't type one of the four colors.");
   }
 alert("That's all, folks.");
 }
```

The labels are enclosed in quotation marks: **case "Blue" :**, for example. As you can see in the Online Companion, when you click the button that calls the **runSwitch( )** function, a prompt dialog box opens. You must type something and click OK. If you type one of the four colors, the **switch** will match the color to the label and display the appropriate alert box. If you type something completely different—another color, for example—the **default** statement is run, so you'll see the *You didn't type one of the four colors* message. And whatever you do, you'll see the *That's all, folks* message when the **switch** finishes.

Moving On

You've learned how to control the flow of a program. Conditional expressions and loops are very powerful. Without them programs would not accomplish much. With them programs can apply logical thought to problems.

Now it's time to find out more about functions. You already have seen a little basic information about functions—how to get functions to store little scripts that can be called and executed later. But there are a couple of things we haven't looked at yet: how to pass parameters to functions and how to work with values that are returned by functions. And that's just what we'll look at in the following chapter.

7

More on Functions

We have already had a quick look at functions in Chapter 3, "First Steps—Scripts, Functions & Comments," and have used them in many of our examples, but we need to discuss them a little more, as there are a number of features of functions that we haven't looked at yet. We need to see where functions can be defined, how they can return values that can be used by other parts of the script, and how to pass information from other parts of the scripts to the functions.

Let's start again from the beginning, to make sure that we all get this straight. Let's take a look at how to define functions.

Defining a Function

Defining a function is the process by which we state the function name and explain what it does. It is always in this format:

```
function functionname() {
    the instructions that the function carries out
}
```

A function definition always starts with the keyword **function** so that when the browser loads the page it knows which bits of script are functions. We have called a lot of the functions in our examples **function1,** but it is a good idea to give your functions meaningful names like **DisplayMessage** or **GetText**. This will help you keep all those functions straight, and help you and others identify the purposes of those functions when you read through a script later. The lines of script between the outermost braces (the { }) define what the function will do when it is called or used.

When your browser loads the page it will read in the function and hold it in the computer's memory ready for use, so that when the function is *called* by another piece of JavaScript—an actual script or an event handler—the browser can find it in memory and execute the instructions contained in it.

Where You Put Your Function Is Important

We have been putting our function definitions into the HEAD section of our HTML pages in the examples because it is the first part of the document to be loaded. (There's no danger of functions being called by a piece of JavaScript later in the document before the functions have been loaded into memory.) You can define functions anywhere in a Web page, but you must take care to define them before you call them. This is not as straightforward as it sounds, so let's use some examples to see how JavaScript works with functions.

Example 7.1

```
<SCRIPT LANGUAGE="JavaScript">
<!--
function1()
function function1() {
  alert("This is function1 running.")
}
//-->
</SCRIPT>
```

You don't have to do anything on this page; there are no buttons to click. When the page is loaded into the browser, the function is executed and all it does is display an alert box with the text *This is function1 running*. Take a close look at this piece of code, though. The function call—the point at which the function is used—actually comes before the function definition, but the code works okay. This tells us that all of the code within the <SCRIPT> and <\SCRIPT> tags is read into memory before it is executed, so it doesn't matter in what order you put your functions within those tags.

Also note that the browser stops loading the Web page at this point; the page is not displayed until you click the OK button on the Alert box (when you put an **alert** in a script like this you are, in effect, pausing the script while the Alert box is displayed), so the script in the HEAD section is not only loaded first, but it is also executed (if there is anything to execute) before the rest of the page is displayed. Now look at this example:

Example 7.2

```
<SCRIPT LANGUAGE="JavaScript">
<!--
function1()
//-->
</SCRIPT>
<SCRIPT LANGUAGE="JavaScript">
<!--
function function1() {
  alert("This is function1 running.")
}
//-->
</SCRIPT>
```

This is, in some respects, the same as the first example. The instructions are exactly the same, but we've split the instructions into two separate scripts. However, this example produces a load-time error and the error alert box is displayed with the message "function1 is not defined."

TIP

A load-time error occurs when the script is first loaded into memory. You'll learn more about this in Chapter 8, "Troubleshooting & Avoiding Trouble."

This is because the function is called from a block of script that is read before the block that contains the function definition. Although the call and the definition are in the same order, they are now in two completely different scripts. In the next example, we have swapped the two blocks of script and now it works fine.

Example 7.3

```
<SCRIPT LANGUAGE="JavaScript">
<!--
function function1() {
  alert("This is function1 running.")
}
//-->
</SCRIPT>
<SCRIPT LANGUAGE="JavaScript">
<!--
function1()
//-->
</SCRIPT>
```

These are the same scripts as before, but in a different order. So it looks like the browser will read in everything between a **<SCRIPT>** and **<\SCRIPT>** tag pair and then execute it. It then reads and executes the next block of script and so on. To make your life simpler, it is always best to define your functions in the HEAD section before anything else. That way you can be sure that your functions will have loaded before they are used.

Functions Can Return Values

We've used functions in a fairly simple way so far. Just to complicate the issue, though, we'd like to explain that functions can *return* values. This means that they can be used to assign values to variables by putting the function calls in the following format:

```
variable = functionname()
```

In the following example you can see how a function returns the text that has been typed into a prompt box. First, we define the following function in the HEAD, which uses the **prompt** method to open a Prompt dialog box.

Example 7.4
```
<SCRIPT LANGUAGE="JavaScript">
<!--
function function1() {
    var sTypedText
    sTypedText = prompt("Type some text in, then click on OK", "")
    return sTypedText
}
//-->
</SCRIPT>
```

This script defines a function (**function1( )**). The function declares a variable named **sTypedText**. **sTypedText** will contain a string. Where does the string come from? We've used the **prompt** built-in function to get the string from the user. We'll learn more about built-in functions in Chapters 10 and 11. All you need to understand right now is that when you use the **prompt** function in this manner, the text that appears within parentheses and quotation marks will appear as an instruction within a Prompt dialog box (see Figure 7-1). When the user clicks on the OK button in the Prompt dialog box, the text that has been typed is made available to the script. On the next line of the script we've used the **return** keyword to tell the script that we want the function to return something. What? The text currently held by **sTypedText**, of course.

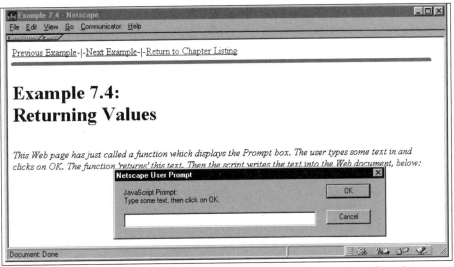

Figure 7-1: The Prompt dialog box collects text from the user and returns it to the script.

Later in the document we've used this script:

```
<SCRIPT LANGUAGE="JavaScript">
<!--
var sText
sText = function1()
document.write("You just typed: <P><H3>" + sText + "</H3><P>")
//-->
</SCRIPT>
```

This script starts by declaring a variable named **sText**. Then we "initialize" the variable—that is, place data into it by assigning **function1( )** to the variable. What data does **function1( )** contain? It contains the text that we told the function to return. Finally, we used **document.write** to write some text into the Web page: *You just typed:*, followed by a new paragraph (**<P>**), and the text held by the **sText** variable. (We formatted that text, and ended the paragraph after the text, using the **<H3>**, **</H3>**, and **<P>** HTML tags.)

Where did we call **function1( )** from? We called it by assigning it to **sText**. Because we used the **return** keyword when we defined the function, **function1( )** returns a value to the line that called it—dropping it into the **sText** variable.

What happens if the user clicks on Cancel? The value **null** *is returned (try it and see). What if the user clicks on the OK button without typing anything? An empty string is returned. Yes, there is a difference. In the first case, you'll see* **null** *written into the Web page. In the second case, nothing is written into the Web page.*

You *must* use the **return** keyword to use this system. If you didn't use the **return sTypedText** line in the first script, what would happen? The Prompt dialog box would appear, but the text returned from **prompt** would not be stored anywhere, as you can see in the following example:

Example 7.5

```
<SCRIPT LANGUAGE="JavaScript">
<!--
function function1() {
    var sTypedText
    sTypedText = prompt("Type some text in, then click on OK", "")
}
//-->
</SCRIPT>
```

We removed the **return sTypedText** line from this script (compare to Example 7.4). Try it in our Online Companion, and you'll see that the text is not written to the page.

It's interesting to consider that the text is actually being returned twice. First, we get the text from this:

```
sTypedText = prompt("Type some text in, then click on OK", "")
```

Remember, **prompt** is a built-in function, one that you don't have to define because it's already defined for you and built into JavaScript. The **prompt** function automatically returns the text from the Prompt dialog box (we don't have to tell it to do so). This return value is then assigned to the **sTypedText** variable. Then we use the following line:

```
return sTypedText
```

It tells **function1( )** to return a value and that the value it returns should be the value held by **sTypedText**. Finally, we get the text the second time from this line:

```
sText = function1()
```

This time **function1( )** returns a value and assigns it to **sText**.

What would have happened if we hadn't assigned the returned value to anything? If, instead of this line:

```
sText = function1()
```

we had this line:

```
function1()
```

The function would still have worked. We would see the Prompt dialog box—but we wouldn't receive the returned value for any further use inside our program. The text typed by the user would be unused by our script.

Multiple Returns

You can have more than one **return** statement in your function so that you can return different things depending upon what has happened within the function. The following example illustrates this using another built-in function called **confirm**. This displays a dialog box with two buttons: OK and Cancel. If the user clicks on OK the **confirm** function returns **true**. If the user clicks on the Cancel button **confirm** returns **false**.

Example 7.6

```
<SCRIPT LANGUAGE="JavaScript">
<!--
function function1()   {
var bResultReturned
    bResultReturned = confirm("Click OK or cancel.")
    if (bResultReturned)   {
       return "You pressed the OK button"
    }
    else   {
       return "You pressed the Cancel button"
    }
}
//-->
</SCRIPT>
```

This is very similar to the example we looked at earlier, in which the **return** keyword is used to tell the function to return something. This time, though, we haven't told the script to return text typed by the user. We can't do that, because the user doesn't type anything into a Confirm dialog box (see Figure 7-2). Instead, the **confirm** built-in function returns one of two values, a Boolean **true** or a Boolean **false**. So we've told the script to return a string literal, a line of text we've typed into the script. And we've used an **if** statement to determine *which* line of text should be used. You saw what

if (bResultReturned) means in Chapter 6, "Conditionals & Loops—Making Decisions & Controlling Scripts." It means, "if the Boolean variable **bResultReturned** contains the value **true**, carry out the instruction following. If not, go to the **else** statement and carry out the instruction following that." In each case the instruction is to return some text.

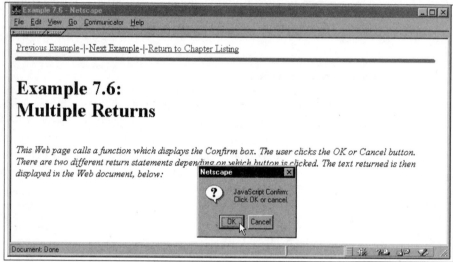

*Figure 7-2: The Confirm dialog box returns **true** or **false**.*

Later in the Web document, we used the script from Example 7.4 to write the return value into the Web document. So if the **confirm** function returns **true**—that is, if the user clicked on OK—the script writes **You pressed the OK button** into the document.

Passing Values to Functions

You might have wondered why empty parentheses are always placed after function names. They are there to hold *arguments* or parameters. By putting values into the brackets, you can pass data into a function when you call it. In order to do this you must have already defined the function with variables in the brackets where it will receive the data, as in the following example:

Example 7.7

```
<SCRIPT LANGUAGE="JavaScript">
<!--
```

```
function function1(sText) {
    alert(sText)
}
//-->
</SCRIPT>
```

Notice that we've added **(sText)** after the function name. (We finally used those parentheses.) This means that the function will expect data to be passed to it, and this data will be made available to the function in the variable **sText**. We say that **sText** is an *argument* of the function **function1**. The function then displays the data from **sText** in an Alert box. Later in our example Web page, we call this function with this simple script:

```
function1("Text that is passed to the function")
```

We've used the parentheses again. This time we've placed a string literal into the parentheses. When the interpreter (the browser) runs this line it looks inside the parentheses; it will take this text and place the text into the **sText** variable inside the function. The function then uses **alert** to display the contents of the variable.

Why not just use a global variable? Well, using global variables can get confusing, and programmers try to use them as little as possible to pass data to functions. If you have a global variable that is used and updated by many functions, it is difficult to know what has happened to it and where. This makes debugging more difficult. If you eliminate the need for global variables by passing your data to a function and receiving data back from it by "return," your program has a more solid structure and is easier to read, and your functions are modular. You can easily use them from different places in your program without having to worry about the effect on other parts of the program through changes to the global variables.

Passing Multiple Values

You can pass many values into your function by separating the arguments with commas, as in the following example:

Example 7.8

```
<SCRIPT LANGUAGE="JavaScript">
<!--
function Percentage(nNum, nPerc) {
    return nNum * (nPerc/100)
}
//-->
</SCRIPT>
```

We've created a function that carries out a calculation. It has two arguments (or two parameters): **nNum** and **nPerc**. Each represents a numeric variable, the value for which will be passed to the function when we call it. The function takes those values and carries out a calculation; first it divides the value in **nPerc** by **100**, then it multiplies the result by the value in **nNum**. Then the function returns the result of this calculation.

Later in the script the function is called like this:

```
<SCRIPT LANGUAGE="JavaScript">
<!--
var nValue1 = prompt("Type in a number","")
var nValue2 = prompt("Type in the percentage you wish to calculate","")
var nPercent = Percentage(nValue1, nValue2)
document.write("<H3>" + nValue2 + " percent of " + nValue1 + " = " +→
nPercent + "</H3>" )
//-->
</SCRIPT>
```

We've started by declaring two variables, **nValue1** and **nValue2**. In each case we've assigned a value to the variable using the **prompt** built-in function. In other words, a Prompt dialog box opens (the text within the quotation marks and parentheses is displayed in the box), then the user types something into the box and clicks on OK. When he does so, the number that was typed is returned from the **prompt** function and placed into the variable.

The next line, **var nPercent = Percentage(nValue1, nValue2)**, declares another variable, **nPercent**. This time, though, we've assigned a value to the variable by calling the **Percentage** function that we defined earlier. You'll notice that we are passing two values to the function, **nValue1** and **nValue2**— the values returned by the Prompt boxes. The browser takes those values and, as we've just seen, places them in **nNum** and **nPerc**, where the function uses them to perform the calculation and returns the result, which is assigned to the **nPercent** variable in the current script. Finally we've used **document.write** to write the result of the calculation to the Web page.

Note that the variable names we used when calling the function (**nValue1** and **nValue2**) are different from the names used within the function (**nNum** and **nPerc**). They don't *have* to be, though; we could have used the same names, as we'll see next.

TIP

This example will only work if numbers are put into the text boxes. If you put in non-numerics or click on OK without typing anything, you will get an error. A program should really be able to process inputs in a sensible manner, but we've left out the error checking because this is just an example. We'll learn about error checking in Chapter 17, "Forms & JavaScript."

Call by Value

JavaScript uses a convention known as *call by value* when it calls functions.
This means that the arguments a function receives are the same *value* as what
was in the calling statement—but not *actually* the same *variable*. The received
arguments are copies of the originals. In our last example, when the function is
called the variables **nValue1** and **nValue2** are copied into temporary variables
nNum and **nPerc,** which are separate from **nValue1** and **nValue2**. Both **nNum**
and **nPerc** are said to be *local* to the function. The next example illustrates that
if the function changes the values of the local variables **nNum** and **nPerc**, this
has no effect on the values of **nValue1** and **nValue2**. In fact to make this quite
clear, we've even changed the names of **nNum** and **nPerc** to **nValue1** and
nValue2, respectively. In other words, the names of the original variables are
now the same as the names of the variables in the function to which the values
are being passed.

Example 7.9

```
<SCRIPT LANGUAGE="JavaScript">
<!--
function Percentage(nValue1, nValue2) {
  var nResult = nValue1 * (nValue2/100)
  nValue1 = 0
  nValue2 = 0
  return nResult
}
//-->
</SCRIPT>
```

This example is the same as the previous example, except that after carrying
out the calculation the script resets the values of **nValue1** and **nValue2** to **0**.
We added buttons to the page so you can view the values held by **nValue1**
and **nValue2**; you'll see that they remain the same as the values you typed.

Working With Functions

Functions are useful for several reasons:

- When you have a piece of code that you might want to use from several
  places in your script, you can use a function so that you do not have to
  repeat the same code in several places.

- Functions are especially useful in JavaScript when used by *event handlers*.
  You can have lots of code in the event-handlers part of an object (a text
  box or button) on an HTML form, but it can easily become a mess. It's

much clearer if you create a function instead, then call the function from the event handler. (We'll learn more about event handlers in Chapter 12, "JavaScript Events—When Are Actions Carried Out?").

■ Functions can be used to make your program more readable and tidier. You can split your program up into manageable chunks that are easier to understand than one mass of code.

Let's look at another version of the percentage calculator we just created:

Example 7.10

```
<SCRIPT LANGUAGE="JavaScript">
<!--
function GetNumbers(form) {
    var sNumber = form.txtNumber.value
    var sPercentage = form.txtPercent.value
    form.txtResult.value= Percentage(sNumber, sPercentage)
}
function Percentage(sNum, sPerc) {
    var nResult = sNum * (sPerc/100)
    return nResult
}
//-->
</SCRIPT>
```

We've created two functions in this script, so you can see how creating multiple functions lets you break your complicated scripts into smaller blocks. First we've created **GetNumbers(form)**.

What is being passed to **GetNumbers** in parentheses? The **form** variable? No, this is the **form** *object*. Now, this is a little advanced and we'll be looking at some of these things later, in Chapter 10, "Objects, Properties & Methods." But what you need to understand here is that the **form** object contains information about the form held in the page (which we'll look at in a moment). The **form** object contains information about its components, **txtNumber** and **txtPercent** (we'll see these in a moment, too). This information is passed to the variables **sNumber** and **sPercentage** by naming the information like this: **form.txtNumber.value** and **form.txtPercent.value** (in other words, the value held by the **txtNumber** box in the **form** and held by the **txtPercent** box in the **form**).

Now, look at this line:

```
form.txtResult.value= Percentage(sNumber, sPercentage)
```

This line means, "place the value returned from the **Percentage** function into **form.txtResult.value**." In other words, this function is also writing to an object in the form. As you'll see in a moment, **txtResult** is the Result text box.

This value comes from the **Percentage** function. As you can see, we're passing the variables **sNumber** and **sPercentage** to the **Percentage** function, which you can see lower in the script. This function is the same as the functions we've seen earlier in this chapter—it calculates the percentage, then returns the result (which goes to **form.txtResult.value**).

Later in the Web page we've created this form, which you can see in Figure 7-3:

```
<FORM>
Enter a number: <INPUT TYPE="text" NAME="txtNumber"  SIZE=6><BR>
Enter the percentage you want: <INPUT TYPE="text" NAME="txtPercent"
SIZE=6><P>
<INPUT TYPE="button" VALUE="Result" onclick="GetNumbers(this.form)">
<INPUT TYPE="text" NAME="txtResult" SIZE=10>
</FORM>
```

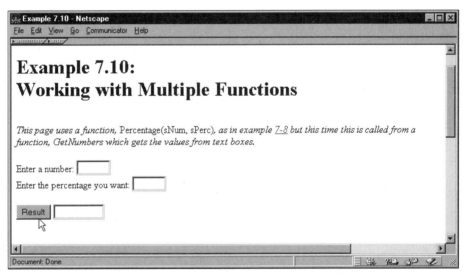

Figure 7-3: We created this form and called a function from the Result button.

The form has three text boxes: **txtNumber**, **txtPercent**, and **txtResult**. It also has a button, which calls the **GetNumbers** function using the **onclick** event handler. Notice that we've passed the values from the form to the function using **(this.form)**. That means "pass a reference to the form through to the function." The function then uses the reference to get at the individual objects in the form with the dot notation (more on this in Chapter 17, "Forms & JavaScript").

So what happens when the user clicks on the button? The form reference is passed to the **GetNumbers** function, which then gets the values from the

txtNumber and **txtPercent** boxes and passes them to the **Percentage** function, which returns the result of the calculation to **GetNumbers**, which passes the value back to the **txtResult** box.

Now, we could have done this all in the **onclick** event handler if we'd wished, but it would be a mess. Not only is it clearer this way, but it makes it easier to reuse bits of code, too. The **Percentage** function is like a tool that can be used in many places for many reasons. We just have to call it to use it, rather than rewriting it each time we need it. So we can actually use this function from several places within the script. You can create libraries of code like this, too—pieces that you can just plug into any of your scripts where required.

Built-in Functions

As well as being able to make your own functions, there are several that come as part of JavaScript and are called *built-in* functions. In other words, you don't need to define these functions; they are automatically there, waiting for you to use them from any point in your script. These are the built-in functions available to you:

Function	Description
eval	Returns a number from an operation containing a string.
parseInt	Evaluates a string and returns an integer.
parseFloat	Evaluates a string and returns a floating-point number.
escape	Returns the ASCII-encoded value of a character.
unescape	Returns a character represented by the ASCII encoding; the opposite of escape.
isNaN	Tells you whether a value is **NaN** (not a number). This only works in the UNIX versions of Netscape Navigator in JavaScript 1.0, but works on all operating systems in JavaScript 1.1 (Navigator 3).
taint	This (and the following) was added in JavaScript 1.1 (Navigator 3). It's used to "mark" data as tainted so it can't be passed to another Web server. (In JavaScript 1.0 data can never be passed; in JavaScript 1.1 data can be passed if it's not tainted.) See http://home.netscape.com/eng/mozilla/3.0/handbook/javascript/advtopic.htm#1009533 for detailed information about this advanced subject. However, note that data tainting is no longer being developed, having been replaced by a more advanced security system, digitally "signed" scripts. See Chapter 14, "JavaScript 1.2's Advanced Features," for more information about this system.
untaint	This removes tainting from data, so it can be forwarded to other servers.

Eval(string)

The **eval** function requires a string of some kind. This string is usually a mathematical expression, but it can be any JavaScript statement or expression,
including variables and the properties of objects. (We'll look at objects in
Chapter 10, "Objects, Properties & Methods.") This function is especially
useful when working with forms, because the data typed into a form is always
a string, though a numerical value is often desired. For example, look at this
script:

Example 7.11

```
function GetNumbers(form) {
    form.txtResult.value= eval(form.txtCalc.value)
}
```

This is taking the value held by the **txtCalc** field in the form, carrying out
the calculation in the form, and returning the result—a floating-point number—to the **txtResult** field. If you look at this example in the Online Companion (or see Figure 7-4), you can see that you can type an equation into the text
box.

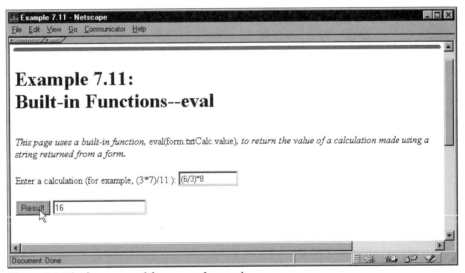

*Figure 7-4: The form we used for our **eval** example.*

The value from **txtCalc** is a string value. Form values are always strings.
But this string contains more than numbers; in the example suggested in the
Web page, you would have this: **(3*7)/11**. Without **eval** it would be very diffi-
cult to calculate this, as it's a mixture of numbers and special characters.

Why, then, did the previous examples work in which we took the results from form fields and carried out a calculation? Because those fields contained nothing but numbers and, as we saw in Chapter 5, "Expressions & Operators—Manipulating Values," JavaScript tries to "do the right thing" and carry out a calculation if it can. In the case of **(3*7)/11**, though, it needs a special function, **eval**, to help it with the calculation.

The **eval** function can be used for more than evaluating numerical expressions, however. Its argument string can also include object references and JavaScript statements—for resetting initial values of data variables, for example.

parseInt(string, radix)

The word *parse* is used in programming to mean the process by which a computer examines a set of instructions and tries to make sense of it. JavaScript has a couple of "parse" functions: **parseInt** and **parseFloat**. Regardless of the name's origin, though, these are really functions that are used to get numbers out of strings before you use them in calculations. (Use a string in a calculation and you'll probably get a strange result.) All text entered into a form is regarded by JavaScript as a string—so if you have a form that collects numerical data, you need some way to ensure that the string represents a number.

The **parseInt** function examines a string and tries to return a decimal integer. You must specify what "radix" (base) the number within the string is in: binary, octal, decimal, or hexadecimal. The **parseInt** function looks at the string, does its best to extract a number from it in the specified base, then converts that number to decimal.

We've created an example to show **parseInt** at work, but note that in some early versions of JavaScript parseInt will work differently. In JavaScript 1.1 and 1.2 **parseInt** returns **NaN** ("not a number") if it's unable to extract a number from the string, while in earlier JavaScript versions it would return **NaN** on Solaris and Irix versions of Netscape Navigator and return **0** on all other versions.

Example 7.12

```
function GetInteger(form) {
var nBase
    if (form.cmbRadix.selectedIndex == 0)nBase = 2;
    if (form.cmbRadix.selectedIndex == 1)nBase = 8;
    if (form.cmbRadix.selectedIndex == 2)nBase = 10;
    if (form.cmbRadix.selectedIndex == 3)nBase = 16;
    form.txtInteger.value= parseInt(form.txtNum.value, nBase)
}
```

We start with a series of **if** statements. This series looks at the selection box named **cmbRadix** and checks to see what is selected. (We'll learn more about this in Chapter 17, "Forms & JavaScript.") We are referring to the **selectedIndex** property of the selection box named **cmbRadix**. The **selectedIndex** is the position in the box of the selected item, starting at **0**—that is, if the user clicks on the first item in the box, the **selectedIndex** value is **0**; if he clicks on the second, the value is 1, and so on (**form.cmbRadix.selectedIndex** means "the **selectedIndex** position in the **cmbRadix** form element, in the **form**").

This tells us which base the user has selected (we'll see the selection box in a moment). So, this series of **if** statements figures out what value to place in the **nBase** variable. For example, if the second item in the selection box has been selected, then **nBase** will be **8** (in other words, the user has chosen octal).

TIP

*Okay, so we broke our rule. In Chapter 6, "Conditionals & Loops—Making Decisions & Controlling Scripts," we told you that it's not a good idea to write **if** statements like this, that it's better to use all the brackets correctly. Well, sometimes rules are made to be broken, and this is one case where creating **if** statements without brackets just seemed clearer.*

Once that's been figured out, we use **parseInt** to look at the number in the **txtNum** field of the form (**form.txtNum.value** means "use the **value** in the **txtNum** field of the **form**"). It uses the **nBase** variable to determine what base the number within the string is in. It then extracts the number and converts it to decimal. The returned value—a decimal integer—is then placed into the **txtInteger** field. (**form.txtInteger.value** means "the value in the **txtInteger** field in the form," and as we are using the assignment operator, this value is placed into the text box.)

Now, here's the form we've used:

```
<FORM>
Select a radix (base) you want to convert to--10 (decimal), 2 (binary), 8
(octal), 16 (hexadecimal):
<select name="cmbRadix" size="4">
<option>Binary (Base 2)
<option>Octal (Base 8)
<option selected value>Decimal (Base 10)
<option>Hex (Base 16)
</select><BR>
Type a number: <INPUT TYPE="text" NAME="txtNum" SIZE=12><BR>
```

```
<INPUT TYPE="button" VALUE="Result"  onclick="GetInteger(this.form)">
<INPUT TYPE="text" NAME="txtInteger" SIZE=20>
</FORM>
```

As you can see, we've created a selection box, two text boxes, and a button. You can select the base in which you have typed the number in the string from the **cmbRadix** selection box (or simply leave **Decimal** selected, as that's the default value). Then type a number into the **txtNum** box and click on the **Result** button to use the **onclick** event handler to call the **GetInteger** function. The result from that function is passed to the **txtInteger** box, as you can see in Figure 7-5.

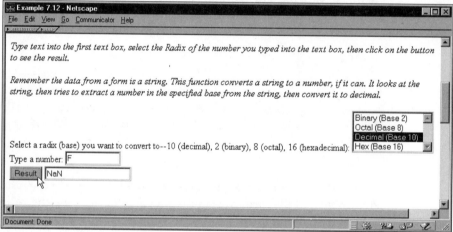

Figure 7-5: The **parseInt** function at work.

Try this in the Online Companion and see what happens. The **parseInt** function takes the value in the text box—which is a string, remember—and tries to convert it to a number the best it can. It will remove any portion of the number to the right of a decimal place (it doesn't round the number, it simply discards everything to the right of the decimal place). If it encounters a character that is not a number in the selected base (for example, a letter if you are using decimal or any letter other than A to F if using hexadecimal), **parseInt** will use all the digits up to the first character that it can't recognize and then discard the rest. If it doesn't recognize the first character, it simply returns **NaN** (in JavaScript 1.0 it will only return **NaN** on Solaris and Irix browsers; on all others it returns 0). For example, assuming we are using base 10:

If you type this...	You'll get this...
23	23
23&	23
&23	0 or NaN (depending on the JavaScript version and operating system)
23.9875634	23

If you use the same numbers with Binary (base 2), all will return **NaN**, because binary doesn't use any of the characters (it only works with 1 and 0, of course). Use Hex (base 16), and you'll get this:

If you type this...	You'll get this...
23	35
23&	35
&23	0 or NaN (depending on the JavaScript version and operating system)
23.9875634	35

Why? Because **23** in hexadecimal is **35** in decimal. Try **1F** and you'll get **31**, because **1F** in hexadecimal is **31** in decimal. Try **G1** and you'll get **NaN**, because **G** is not used in hexadecimal.

parseFloat(string)

This function is almost the same as **parseInt**, except that it returns a floating point number—it won't discard the portion to the right of the decimal place, and you are not specifying a radix to be used. Take a look at this example:

Example 7.13

```
function GetFloat(form) {
    form.txtFloat.value= parseFloat(form.txtNum.value)
}
```

We haven't worried about the **if** statements this time, as we don't have to select a base. All the user does is enter a number and click on a button. The text entered into the form is passed to **parseFloat** (**form.txtNum.value**, the **value** in the **txtNum** box). The **parseFloat** function then returns the floating-point number evaluated from the string, placing it into the **txtFloat** text box.

Here's the simple form we used:

```
<FORM>
Type a number: <INPUT TYPE="text" NAME="txtNum" SIZE=12><P>
<INPUT TYPE="button" VALUE="Result" onclick="GetFloat(this.form)"> <INPUT
TYPE="text"  NAME="txtFloat" SIZE=30>
</FORM>
```

The **parseFloat** function will not truncate the digits after the decimal point. It will also understand exponential values and the - and + signs. For example:

If you type this...	You'll get this...
23	23
23&	23
&23	0
23.9875634	23.9875634
-23	-23
+23	23
99e2	0.98999999999999999
99e-55	9.9000000000000004e-054

You can see an example in Figure 7-6.

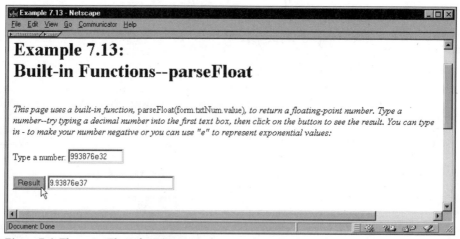

Figure 7-6: The **parseFloat** function at work.

escape(character)

The **escape** function is used to return the ASCII encoding value of a character in the ISO Latin-1 character set. Use **escape** to evaluate **?** (for instance (**escape(?)**) and **%3F** will be returned). Try **escape(?>)** and **%3F%3E** is returned. For instance, in the following example, we started with this function:

Example 7.14
```
function ConvertASCII(form) {
    form.txtASCII.value= escape(form.txtCharacter.value)
}
```

This is a simple function that takes the value in the **textCharacter** field of the form and evaluates it with the **escape** function. The result is then placed in the **txtASCII** field of the form. Here's the form:

```
<FORM>
Type any character: <INPUT TYPE="text" NAME="txtCharacter"  SIZE=12><P>
<INPUT TYPE="button" VALUE="ASCII Value"  onclick="ConvertASCII(this.form)">
<INPUT TYPE="text"  NAME="txtASCII" SIZE=20>
</FORM>
```

Type a character into the **txtCharacter** text box, click on the **ASCII Value** button, and the value from **txtCharacter** is sent to the **ConvertASCII** function, where it is evaluated using **escape** and returned to the form. Try it in the example and see. Note, however, that you can only use non-alphanumeric characters—no letters or numbers. If you type **D**, for example, **escape** will return **D**. And some non-alphanumeric characters won't work either: @, _, +, -, ., and /.

unescape

This function is the exact opposite of **escape**. It takes an ASCII encoding value and returns the character that the value represents. In the following example we've used the same script as in the previous example, except that we've replaced **escape** with **unescape**.

Example 7.15
```
function ConvertASCII(form) {
    form.txtASCII.value= unescape(form.txtCharacter.value)
}
```

As you can see, this is the same as in the previous example, except that we used **unescape** instead of **escape**. Try typing **%3F** or **%27** and clicking on the button to see the character that the value represents.

TRAP

You might see **unEscape** *in some documentation. You must type* **unescape** *all in lowercase, though, or it won't work.*

isNaN(number)

This built-in function is only used on UNIX systems in JavaScript 1.0, but works on all platforms in JavaScript 1.1. It's used to evaluate an argument to see if it's **NaN** (not a number): the function returns **true** (it is not a number) or **false** (it is a number).

When you use the **parseInt** and **parseFloat** functions, if they evaluate a string that is not a number, they return **NaN**. (As explained earlier, some JavaScript 1.0 browsers will return 0 instead of **NaN**.)

For example, you might use **isNaN** in an **if** statement, like this:

```
if (isNaN(FloatValue)) {
  RunThis()
} else {
  OrThis()
}
```

In this **if** statement we use **isNaN** to look at the value held by the **FloatValue** variable, which holds the value returned by the **parseFloat** function earlier. If the value held by **FloatValue** *is* **NaN** (that is, it's not a number), then the **RunThis** function is called. If the value is not **NaN**, the **OrThis** function is called—this function presumably does something with the number in **FloatValue**. For instance, take a look at this script that has been modified from example 7.12.

Example 7.16
```
function GetInteger(form) {
var nBase
var nCheck
    if (form.cmbRadix.selectedIndex == 0)nBase = 2;
    if (form.cmbRadix.selectedIndex == 1)nBase = 8;
    if (form.cmbRadix.selectedIndex == 2)nBase = 10;
    if (form.cmbRadix.selectedIndex == 3)nBase = 16;
    nCheck = parseInt(form.txtNum.value, nBase)
    form.txtInteger.value = nCheck
```

```
        if (isNaN(nCheck) ){
            alert("Nope, not a number!")
        }
        else {
            alert("Yep, it's a number!")
        }
    }
```

This is very similar to Example 7.12, with two exceptions. First, we put the value from **parseInt** into a variable called **nCheck**. Then we used **nCheck** in an **if** statement containing the **isNaN** function. Now, as you'll see if you use this example at the Online Companion, when **parseInt** returns **NaN** (for instance, type X into the first text box and click the button) you'll see the *Nope, not a number!* message. If **parseInt** returns a number, though (type in 1 and click the button), **isNaN** is false, so you'll see the second message (*Yep, it's a number!*).

The Function Object

JavaScript 1.1 (Netscape Navigator 3) has an object called **Function**. This object allows you to build your own functions. In other words, you can take a string of JavaScript code, place it inside a function, then call the function whenever you need to run that bit of code. Here's a very simple example:

Example 7.17
```
var FuncObj = new Function("location='7-17b.htm';")
```

We'll be looking at objects in detail in Chapters 10 and 11. For now all you need to know is that to create one of these Function objects you must create a variable (**var FuncObj**, or whatever you wish to call it; **FuncObj** will be the name of your newly created object). You then assign to this variable the script by using the **new** keyword, followed by the word **Function** (that's the name of the **Function** object "class," and as you'll learn later you use an object class—in this case **Function**—to create an object "instance"—in this case **FuncObj**). In parentheses after the word **Function** you place the script you want to place in the new function. In this case, calling the **FuncObj( )** function runs **location='7-17b.htm';**. In other words, when the new **FuncObj** function is called the browser loads page **7-17b.htm**. In our example we simply called **FuncObj( )** by putting it in a button:

```
<INPUT TYPE="button" VALUE="Run function" onClick="FuncObj()">
```

You can also assign functions to event handlers; instead of declaring a variable and then using **new Function**, you assign **new Function** to an event like this:

Example 7.18

```
document.Form01.txtBox.focus()
document.Form01.txtBox.onblur  = new Function("alert('Select a title')")
document.Form01.DisplayMsg.onclick = new Function("alert('Completed name')")
```

These new functions have been assigned to the **onblur** and **onclick** event handlers in **Form01**. When you Tab out of **txtBox** the **onblur** event handler runs the function that displays the *Select a title* message. And when you click on the **DisplayMsg** button the **onclick** handler displays the *Completed name* message. By the way, these have to appear in the body of the Web page *after* the form has been created, or the new functions can't be assigned to the form objects.

You can pass parameters—arguments—to the new function in most cases (not when assigning to an event, though) and have the function return a value. Here's an example:

Example 7.19

```
var FuncObj = new Function("x","x=x/2;return(x)")
function Func1() {
var x= document.Form01.txtInteger.value
x = FuncObj(x);
alert(x);
}
```

Notice that we begin by creating the new function, **FuncObj( )**, and state that an argument will be passed to the function when it's called; **"x"** is the argument, **"x=x/2;return(x)"** is the actual script that will act on the value stored in **x**. We then have a function called **Func1( )**, which takes the value typed into a text box (**document.Form01.txtInteger.value**) and places it in a variable named **x**, then passes **x** to **FuncObj( )**. **FuncObj( )** divides the value in **x**, then returns **x** back to **Func1( )**, which displays the value of **x** in an **alert** box.

TIP

There are other built-in functions. The ones we've just looked at, though, work independently; they are not linked to any object. The other built-in functions (and there are quite a few) are "methods" related to "objects." They are used in a different manner, so we're not going to look at them right now. We'll come back to them in Chapter 10, "Objects, Properties & Methods."

Moving On

We're going to take a break from programming for a while and look at the problems you can run into while creating your script. In the next chapter we'll find out how good programming practices can help you avoid some problems in the first place and how—when you *do* run into trouble (and you will, regardless of how careful you are)—you can track down the source of your problems.

We'll explain how you can save a great deal of trouble by simply taking care in the way you write your scripts by declaring variables correctly, by using sensible names, by using parentheses in calculations, and so on. You can also space your scripts in such a manner that they are easier to read. We'll also look at how to use Alert boxes to help you "debug" your scripts.

8

Troubleshooting & Avoiding Trouble

Don't expect to write bug-free programs. There's no such thing as a sophisticated bug-free program, because there's no such thing as a perfect programmer. While very simple programs or scripts—the sort of things that take up a line or two of code—can be made bug free, the more complicated your script the more likely it will contain bugs. So in this chapter you can take a break from learning about the different elements of JavaScript and instead learn how to figure out your mistakes and how to avoid problems in the first place.

Not Just Your Bugs

There are two types of bugs you'll have to watch for: yours and those in the JavaScript browsers. In other words, you might introduce bugs into the scripts you write, but you will also run into situations in which JavaScript just doesn't seem to work correctly whatever you do—because JavaScript is new and has bugs. Most of the JavaScript bugs will be removed with future versions of Netscape Navigator, but no product is completely bug free.

For example, some versions of Netscape Navigator have a 255-character-line bug. This is present in the 2.0 versions of Navigator and even in some of the beta 3.0 versions, and limits the number of characters that you can place on a single line in a script. If you create a line that is more than 255 characters long, your script might work fine with your browser . . . but it won't work if the user is using one of the browsers that contain this bug. There are ways around this problem, of course—when writing a very long message into a variable, for example, you'll have to do it step by step, placing portions into two or more variables, then concatenating the variables (with the + operator) into the final variable. (We talk more about this problem in Chapter 19, because we ran into it while creating our Area Code application—see under *The Line Break Problem*.)   To further complicate these bugs, they vary between platforms. A bug that appears in a JavaScript browser that runs on a Macintosh might not appear in the same version-number browser running in UNIX or Windows.

There's not much you can do about these bugs, except try to keep informed. You'll find information about these bugs in the JavaScript newsgroups, mailing lists, and Web pages. In particular, at the time of writing the JavaScript FAQ Web page is a good source for information about bugs: http://www.freqgrafx.com/411/jsfaq.html. See Appendix H, "Finding More Information," for more sources of information about JavaScript.

Avoiding Trouble

Better to avoid bugs in the first place than to track them down once they've found their way into your scripts. You can do this by following a few rules:

- Build your scripts a piece at a time and test each piece before moving on to the next piece. It's easier to find a bug in 10 or 20 lines of script than in a few hundred.

- Use lots of comment lines to remind you what each piece is for, what data the variables contain, what functions do, and so on.

- Don't change variable types. As you saw in Chapter 4, "Variables & Literals—Storing Data," you can change variable types if you wish, but you'll probably get confused if you do and end up using a variable in the wrong way.

- Use good naming conventions. If you use logical variable names that help you to identify the data held by the variable, and the datatype (string, numeric, Boolean), you'll find it easier to read your scripts and keep everything straight.

- Declare variables explicitly. As you saw in Chapter 4, if you don't declare variables correctly by using the **var** keyword, you can run into problems in which the wrong variable is used.

- Don't use a name for a variable that is inside a function if you've already declared the name globally to refer to something else. This is related to the previous suggestion; if you start mixing names and not declaring variables explicitly, you might find a variable being used at the wrong time. Mixing names like this is simply confusing.

■ Be careful how you pass parameters. As you saw in Chapter 7, "More on Functions," you should try to change passed variables only, not global variables.

■ Many, though not all, JavaScript names and keywords are case sensitive, so be very careful about how you type your scripts.

■ Variable and function names are case sensitive. Naming your functions and variables in a consistent manner will help you avoid declaring a variable or defining a function, and then calling or referring to it later using the wrong case.

■ As you saw in Chapter 6, "Conditionals & Loops—Making Decisions & Controlling Scripts," in some circumstances you can omit the { } braces in **if** statements. This might save time now, but can lead to problems later— especially if you are creating nested **if** statements. Without the braces, **if** statements can be ambiguous and might not function in the intended manner. However, in some instances not using braces can actually make the script clearer—use your judgment.

■ Put parentheses into logical expressions. Logical expressions can be very confusing. They can look like they do one thing, when in fact they actually do something quite different. By using parentheses you can be sure that your logical expressions do exactly what they are meant to do.

■ Define functions and global variables in the HEAD. That way you can be sure that they will be created before the rest of the document loads. The user won't be able to do anything that uses the function or variable before it is available.

Watch the Layout

As you've seen so far, scripts have been "spread" over several lines. For instance, take a look at this example that was used in Chapter 6, "Conditionals & Loops—Making Decisions & Controlling Scripts":

```
<SCRIPT LANGUAGE="JavaScript">
<!--
function function1() {
var dToday = new Date()
var nHours = dToday.getHours()
var nDay = dToday.getDay()
```

```
                if ((nDay == 5) && (nHours >= 12))        {
                        alert("Thank God it's Friday afternoon"  )
                }
                else     {
                        if ((nDay == 6) || (nDay == 0) )          {
                                alert("Hey, it's the weekend" )
                        }

                        else     {
                                alert("Just another day")
                        }
                }
        }
//-->
</SCRIPT>
```

The script above is exactly the same as the following script:

```
<SCRIPT LANGUAGE="JavaScript">
<!--
function function1() {
var dToday = new Date()
var nHours = dToday.getHours()
var nDay = dToday.getDay()
if ((nDay == 5) && (nHours >= 12))
{alert("Thank God it's Friday afternoon")}
else{if ((nDay == 6) || (nDay == 0) )
{alert("Hey, it's the weekend" )}
else{alert("Just another day")}}}
//-->
</SCRIPT>
```

In fact, you can remove most of the spaces in this script and string out this entire script into one block of text, like this:

Example 8.1

```
<SCRIPT LANGUAGE="JavaScript">
<--
function function1(){var dToday=new Date();var nHours=dToday.getHours();→
var nDay=dToday.getDay();if((nDay==5)&&(nHours>=12)){alert("Thank God it's→
Friday afternoon")}else{if((nDay==6)||(nDay==0)){alert("Hey, it's the→
weekend" )}else{alert("Just another day")}}}
//-->
</SCRIPT>
```

Note that this is not *exactly* the same as the original example. We had to add three semi-colons—after each statement—to make sure it worked in Navigator 4 (which is a bit fussier than Navigator 2 and 3). The semi-colon makes quite clear that a new statement is beginning. You'll see the semi-colons we added after **Date();, getHours();,** and **getDay();.**

This example is confusing, though. Better to write your scripts with lots of spaces and line breaks. As you can see in the first example, we've done several things to make the script clearer:

- We've placed each variable declaration on a new line. (We didn't have to, but it makes it much easier to find them!)

- When we placed an opening brace ({), we moved it to the right a bit—it's easier to see.

- After the opening {, we moved down a line and indented the instruction that is within the brackets. This makes it easier to see the instruction.

- When we placed a closing brace (}), we placed it on its own line and directly below the starting point (directly below the first letter of **function, if,** or **else,** for example). As we said before, you must make sure that for every opening { you have a closing }. This is one way to make it easy to count the braces.

- We indented the contents of **if** statements. The **if** and its corresponding **else** are at the same level. When we nested an **if** statement, we indented the **if** and **else** to the right of the **if** and **else** in which they were nested. Indenting means, in effect, "this bit of code is linked in some way to the bit of code under which it's indented."

- Although most (though not all) spaces are "unnecessary," we included spaces all over the place. We have spaces between variables, operators, and values, for example (**nHours >= 12**), though we don't need them. They just make it easier to read the script.

- Another thing you can do—though we haven't—is place a semicolon at the end of each line. Some JavaScript programmers do this out of habit; you have to in C. In JavaScript it's generally optional, with a notable exception being when putting multiple statements within an event handler (we'll look at event handlers in Chapter 12, "JavaScript Events—When Are Actions Carried Out?").

We've done all these things for one reason—to make our scripts easier to work with and read. The clearer your scripts, the less likely you are to introduce mistakes. And the clearer your scripts, the easier it will be to track down problems.

TIP

Don't Type, Copy! You can be the world's most careful programmer and still introduce bugs into your scripts by mistyping something. Typos are probably the most common source of program errors, so it's a good idea to type as little as possible. Whenever possible, copy a piece of script that you've already used somewhere else (and know to be good) and paste it into the script on which you are working. You can also use your text or HTML editor's tools to build "libraries" of scripts. And if you're creating JavaScript 1.1 scripts you can use the <SCRIPT> tag's SRC attribute to call existing scripts from source files.

A Word About Spaces

How many spaces can you use? In general, as many as you want. You might want to simply press the Tab key to indent items—press several times if necessary. There's no limit to the number of spaces you can use. You also can enter extra blank lines here and there to spread things out; but, as discussed in Chapter 2, don't use line breaks *inside* statements. The JavaScript interpreter simply ignores all these extra spaces and line breaks.

However, you will find a few situations in which you *must not* use spaces. In Chapter 15, "Controlling Windows & Documents With JavaScript," for example, we'll examine how to open secondary windows, using *window features* to define what window components should be used and the window size. For example, the following instruction opens a window and includes the location bar and toolbar and allows the user to resize the window:

```
open("window.htm","Window1","location,resize,height=250,width=450,toolbar")
```

You'll notice that there are no spaces between the window features starting at **location**. Each feature is separated with a comma, but if you use a comma followed by a space you will actually turn off all subsequent features. Because window features is really one parameter—though it has several different parts—you cannot place spaces within it.

TIP

Adding a space somewhere it's not allowed is actually a good diagnostic tool. You can use it to "turn off" things while you check for a script problem in a particular case.

Tracking Down Problems

However carefully you write your scripts, you are bound to introduce mistakes. Eventually you'll find you have a script that doesn't work quite correctly, and you will have to figure out why. Eventually? Well, okay, soon—probably your first and every subsequent script. In fact troubleshooting is an integral part of programming, in the same way that editing is an integral part of writing. You will almost *always* have to troubleshoot unless you've written a very tiny script. So let's see what you can do to track down problems.

There are basically two types of bugs:

- **Load-time bugs**. These bugs appear as soon as your Web page loads in the browser, and are caused by problems in the scripts that are read by the browser as soon as it opens the Web page. These are often bugs in scripts that declare variables and define functions; there can also be bugs in scripts designed to write information into the Web page. Generally you'll see an error message when these errors occur. This type of bug occurs because there is something wrong with the script—it doesn't make sense to your browser.

- **Run-time bugs**. These are bugs that appear later—when an event handler runs the script. For example, the bugs might not appear until the user clicks on a button or, if you are using the **onunload** event handler, until the user loads a different page. These bugs *may* or *may not* display an error message. (If there's a run-time bug in a script using the **onload** event handler, the bug will appear immediately after the page has loaded.)

Why do some bugs cause error messages to appear, while some don't? Quite simply, some bugs, such as syntax errors, can be recognized by the JavaScript interpreter (the browser), while others can't. When the browser reads the JavaScript it tries to make sense of it. If it can't, it displays an error message. For example, if you have missed a closing }, or if you haven't used quotation marks when you should have, or if you used double-quotation marks when you should have used singles, or used the = assignment operator when you should have used the == conditional operator, or called a function that doesn't exist, the browser will get "confused." It can't understand your script, so it displays an error message telling you that you've got a problem.

On the other hand, the script might work perfectly as far as the interpreter is concerned. But that doesn't mean it does what you want it to do. For example, in a calculation you might have used one numeric variable instead of another one, the one you really should have used. The browser can still make the calculation, as you've given it a numeric value. As far as you are concerned, the answer is wrong because the script uses the wrong value. But the browser has no way to know that, so it has to assume the script is good.

Finding Load-time Bugs

Let's start by looking at load-time bugs. Say, for example, that you've created a script and the script just loaded in your browser for the first time. Up pops an error message—the one in Figure 8-1, for instance. (This is the error message that appears when you use Example 6.2.)

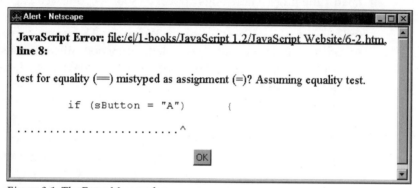

Figure 8-1: The Error Message box.

Some load-time errors can occur without an error message appearing when the page first loads. You might have made a mistake in the HEAD that the browser doesn't recognize as a mistake, so it doesn't display an error message. However, this mistake won't become apparent until an event runs the script. (We'll be looking at problems in the HEAD again in a few moments, when we look at run-time errors.)

What do you do? You read the error message, of course. In this case you can quickly see what you did wrong. The message says *test for equality (==) mistyped as assignment (=)? Assuming equality test.* The browser has found a situation in which it thinks that you probably want to check a variable to see if it matches a value, yet you used the = assignment operator instead of the == conditional operator. (It actually uses == instead of =, but warns you so that you can fix the error. This is a Netscape Navigator error message, by the way;

Internet Explorer doesn't bother to display a message in such a condition, it just goes ahead and uses the == operator.) You'll also see that below the message is the line in which the problem occurred:

```
if (sButton = "A") {
```

And, indeed, you can see that = was used instead of ==. The browser will also try to provide more information. You'll notice that the message box tells you the line number on which the script error occurs. It also tells you the file in which the problem occurs. You might think that would be obvious, but if you are loading several documents into frames, this will help you not only identify in which document the problem lies, but even go directly to that document; the document name is a link, so click on it to load that document into the browser.

Notice that under the line of code is a series of periods and a caret (^) pointing up at the code. Also, notice that part of the code is colored red. These are indicators that are supposed to point directly at the part of the code that has a problem, though as you can see they're not always accurate. Still, they usually point in the general direction of the problem.

In this case the fix is quick and easy; simply replace the = with ==, save, and click the Restore button in the browser.

In Figure 8-2 you'll see an example of another problem.

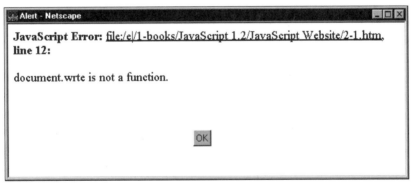

Figure 8-2: A simple typo caused this problem.

In this case you've got a typo; instead of typing **document.write**, you typed **document.wrte**. The browser thinks you are trying to use a function, but finds that you haven't defined that function anywhere. Again, the solution is simple—find **document.wrte** and correct the spelling. Error messages are not always as easy to figure out. Sometimes the browser won't really understand what you've done wrong, but will tell you what *appears* to be wrong. For instance, we took Example 4.7 and removed one of the \ symbols preceding the quotation mark in the Mark Twain quote. We ended up with four error messages, one after another. Here are the messages we saw:

```
missing operator in expression
var twainA = ""I never write \'metropolis\' for seven cents
.................^
```

```
twainB is not defined
```

```
twainC is not defined
```

```
twainD is not defined
```

Although you'll end up with four separate message boxes, with the last message box on top, you should look at the box that appeared first. (The others might be caused by the problem addressed by the original message, so fix that first problem and you might not need to worry about the others.)

Now, in this case we're told that there's a missing operator in the expression. The browser hasn't realized that the second quotation mark is supposed to be part of the string literal, so it assumes it's part of the script itself. Still, if you look carefully at the message, you can quickly see what you did wrong. Replace the \ and save, close all of the message boxes, reload, and all the error messages will go away.

> **TIP**
>
> *Why did we get the* twainB, twainC, and twainD is not defined *messages? The actual error messages come from later in the script, where we're using* **document.write** *commands to write the contents of these variables into the Web page. But the source of the problem is in the first script—these variables weren't declared properly in that script. Because the browser got confused in the first line of the first script, it was unable to finish the script properly.*

Finding Run-time Bugs

Run-time bugs are problems that only appear when a script actually runs— when some kind of action occurs. As we said before, you won't always see error messages with these, because the browser might not consider the problem to be an error. While an error message helps you pinpoint the problem— by showing you the line number and even pointing at the error (or close to the error) in the line—you can still figure out bugs that don't cause messages to appear. You'll simply have to review your script carefully.

The first step is to figure out what ran the script. If, for example, the problem lies in something being written into the Web page, you need to find where in your script you are writing to the page. If something strange happens as soon as the page has finished loading, take a look at the **onload** event handler in the Web page's **<BODY>** tag. If something goes wrong when you click on a button, find that button in the script. Then work your way back from there. If the event handler names a variable, check to see that it names the correct variable.

What about bugs that cause erroneous results, though the program seems to run correctly? Perhaps the most likely problem in a bug that doesn't display an error message is a variable with the wrong data. Find where the variable was declared and look at all the places in the script where the variable has had data assigned to it. More important, look at the last point at which the variable had data placed into it. Carefully examine all the way back to the origins of that data: Is it coming from the right place, is it being calculated correctly? What data will the variable have when you click on the button?

Your Own Debugger—Checking Values With Alerts

There's a problem with tracking down bugs in JavaScript—there's no *debugger*. A debugger is a special tool used by programmers to help them remove bugs. It runs through the program line by line, showing the programmer the status of the program as it proceeds. For example, it will show the programmer what values are held by the variables as the program runs. In effect the debugger can look "inside" the program as it runs and confirm that each piece of the program works correctly.

In JavaScript you are on your own. There is currently no debugging tool, so you must do all the work for yourself. There is a good way to *duplicate* the actions of a debugger, though, using the Alert dialog box. When programmers debug code, they are basically looking at variable values inside their programs as they run. Using the Alert dialog box method allows you to do just that.

You can place lines of code (or code *stubs,* as they're known to programmers) in your scripts to open Alert dialog boxes. These boxes display the contents of a variable at each point in the script. In fact we did this in earlier examples. Take a look at Example 6.13, for instance:

```
function function1() {
var i
        for (i = 1; i < 4; i++) {
                    alert("The value in i is " + i )
        }
        alert("The loop has finished and i is " + i )
}
```

We put an **alert** into a loop. The alert displays the value of the variable **i** each time the loop runs. When an Alert box opens, the browser stops at that line in the script. You can then read the value held by the variable to confirm that it's correct, then click on the OK button to continue the script. If you are debugging a loop that goes around many times, you can insert an **if** statement to limit the conditions under which you get the Alert box.

TIP

Remember to take out your code stubs when you have finished debugging the program!

Common Errors

Here are some common mistakes you should watch out for:

- You created a conditional expression using the = assignment operator instead of the == conditional operator.

- You used a variable that you haven't yet declared.

- You used a variable that you've declared, but it hasn't been initialized— that is, it has no value.

- You forgot to include parentheses in the correct places or didn't include the correct number (there must be an equal number; each opening (must have a closing)).

- You forgot to include braces or didn't include the correct number (again, there must be an equal number; each opening { must have a closing }).

- You declared a variable inside a function, then tried to use it globally— that is, *outside* the function.

- You forgot to include ( ) immediately after a function name.

- You didn't put quotation marks in the correct places, enclosing string literals, for example.

- You used double quotation marks (" ") instead of single quotation marks (' '). Remember, if you are placing something that must be enclosed in quotation marks and it's nested within something else enclosed between double quotation marks, then you must use single quotation marks.

■ You haven't explicitly declared a variable (using **var**) within a function, and when you tried to use it you ended up setting the value of a global variable of the same name. (See Example 4.5.) This demonstrates why you should not design programs to use local variables with the same name as global variables, and why you should always declare variables using **var**.

■ You mistyped a name or keyword or typed it in the wrong case.

■ You accidentally changed a variable's type and ended up using the variable in the wrong situation for its current type.

■ You created a Boolean expression that you didn't fully understand, and it works differently from the way you thought it would. Combinations of many Boolean variables and Boolean operators have different meanings, depending on where you put the parentheses.

■ You created a calculation that doesn't work the way you think it should. Again, the calculation will vary according to operator precedence and where you put the parentheses.

■ You referred to something (a day of the week or an entry in an array) using its position number, but counted from 1, not 0. Remember that programmers often count from 0, not from 1. So in many cases when you have to specify a number—an item's position in a selection list, for example—you must call the first item 0, the second 1, and so on.

■ You have multiple statements in an event handler (see Chapter 12, "Java-Script Events—When Are Actions Carried Out?") and haven't placed a semicolon after each expression.

Moving On

Back to work. In our next chapter we're going to take a look at arrays. These provide a way for you to store many related values. You can think of an array as a multivalue variable; in fact, that's exactly what it is.

Arrays are very useful things. You can use two or more arrays in conjunction to link related data. One array might contain first names, the next second names, the next e-mail addresses, for example. You can then search one array and display the corresponding data from one of the other arrays. So turn to the next chapter and we'll show you how to do just that.

Building Arrays

What is an *array*? A very useful thing, that's what. It's a collection of data, and it's an essential programming tool. Later you'll see just how useful an array can be when we create our area-code program in Chapter 19. We'll be using examples from that application in this chapter as we examine how to create arrays.

As you already know, you can create variables that hold information. However, a variable can hold only one thing at a time. What if you want to store 10, or 100, or 500 items at once? And what if all these items are all similar (such as information related to a telephone area code)? Well, you could create 10, 100, or 500 variables, but this would be very clumsy. Better to create an array to hold all this information. In fact, an array can be thought of as a multidata variable. Use one name for this array (rather than 10, 100, or 500 variable names), then place all the information into the array.

Some programming languages have built-in array systems. JavaScript does, too, but it wasn't added until recently. Starting with Netscape Navigator 3 (JavaScript 1.1) a true **Array** object was introduced. So JavaScript has two ways to create arrays: a "simulated" array that must be used if you want to be compatible with all versions of JavaScript, and a true **Array** object that will work with Netscape Navigator 3 and later.

We'll look at the new **Array** object, introduced with Netscape Navigator 3.0, at the end of this chapter. Because Netscape 2.0 can't use the **Array** object, we'll first look at how to create an array *without* it.

Creating an Array

If you want to use an array that will work with Netscape Navigator 2.0, you will need to "simulate" one. You can create an array in three steps:

1. First create a new object class by writing a special function.

2. Call the function.

3. Then enter the data into the array.

Step 1: Creating the Array Object

Let's start by seeing the "official" way to "simulate" an array. Then we'll discuss a much quicker "shortcut" method for simulating an array.

The first step is to create a new *object class*. (You'll learn more about objects in Chapter 10, "Objects, Properties & Methods.") An object is simply a thing that describes something: the **document** object is a description of the document, a **form** object is a description of the form, and so on. JavaScript has objects that are already created for you, and you can also create your own objects. Creating an object is a little advanced; we'll discuss it in Chapter 13, "Advanced Topics," but even there we won't go into too much detail. It doesn't matter too much if you don't understand the full capabilities of object creation. As long as you can see how we use the object to create the array, that's enough.

In order to create an array, you must first create an object that describes the array. You can do that by defining a special type of function, like this example:

```
function makeArray(n) {
    this.length = n
    for (var i=1; i <= n; i++) {
        this[i] = null;
    }
    return this
}
```

We've created a function called **makeArray**. Notice that we are going to pass the value **n** to this function in the parentheses when we call it.

What does **this.length = n** mean? It simply means "place the value **n** into the **length** property of this object." Objects contain properties; a property contains information about the object. In this case, **length** is a keyword to represent the number of items that will be stored in the array. So the value stored by the length property is **n**, which will be passed to the function when it is called (as you'll see in a few moments). In other words, when we call this function to create our array, we're going to tell the function how many items will be stored in the array.

Next we have a **for** statement. This statement declares a variable, **i**. It initializes **i** with the value **1**. Then it uses the conditional expression (go back to Chapter 6, "Conditionals & Loops—Making Decisions & Controlling Scripts," if you can't remember this stuff) to compare **i** with the value held in **n**; as long as **i** is equal to or less than **n**, the instructions within the { } are run: **this[i] = null**. This sets the value at the position **i** in the array to **null**.

> **TIP**
>
> *We've initialized to* **null**—*that is, we've put the value* **null** *into the array positions. You can also initialize to other values: to* **0**, *for example, which might be more appropriate in some scripts.*

Then the *update expression* is run (**i++**); this increases the value held in **i** by one. The loop then continues. When the value in **i** is greater than the value of **n** (the number of items in the array), the **for** loop ends, and the last instruction is run. The instruction **return this** means "return the object that's been created."

So, we've created a function that describes the array object we want. But in order to use an object you need to create an *instance* of the object (the function is merely the "blueprint"). So to do that, we have to call the function.

Step 2: Call the Function

We create our array object instance by declaring a variable in a special way, as in this example:

```
var arrayname = new functionname(n)
```

For instance:

```
var area = new makeArray(187)
```

This creates an array called **area**. Notice that we are passing the number **187** to the **makeArray** function. That's because this array will contain 187 items. So, what do we have now? A special variable that can contain 187 items. Now we can put data into the array.

TIP

*Okay, we've broken one of our rules, or a suggestion anyway. We suggested that you place a letter before a variable name to indicate the variable type (**sArea**, for example, instead of **area**). However, in this case we didn't bother, for two reasons. First, we wanted to use a small name, because we're going to be using it many times. Second, because we're using it so often in the script, we're not likely to forget what type of data it holds.*

Step 3: Placing Data Into the Array

If we were assigning a value to a normal variable called **area**, we'd simply do this:

```
area = "Alabama          "
```

We've placed the string **Alabama** (plus a number of spaces afterward) into the variable **area**. But we want to put 187 items into this special variable, the **area** array. So we need to number each one, like this:

```
area[1] = "Alabama          "
area[2] = "Alabama          "
area[3] = "Alaska           "
area[4] = "Alberta          "
area[5] = "Antigua          "
area[6] = "Arizona          "
area[7] = "Arizona          "
area[8] = "Arkansas         "
area[9] = "Bahamas          "
area[10] = "Barbados         "
area[11] = "Bermuda          "
area[12] = "British Columbia "
area[13] = "British Columbia "
```

Each time that we placed an item into the variable, we gave it a number, so that the items are indexed. We can ask our script, "what's in position 9?," and we'll get the result **Bahamas**. (You'll learn more about this in a few moments.)

TIP

We've entered spaces to make the variables the same size. That's a simple way to make sure that when the program displays the results, they line up properly. In Chapter 19, you can see a way to insert spaces when the text is displayed, rather than adding the spaces to the variables.

Now, why do we have multiple occurrences in some instances (two **Arizonas** and two **Alabamas**, for example)? Well, this comes from our Area Code example. This is an application that allows you to search for a state, province, or country in North America and get a list of the associated telephone area codes. There are multiple area codes in some of these places, so we needed more than one entry. In fact, we've created multiple arrays that are "parallel" to each other. For example, there's another array called **cde**, which contains the actual area-code numbers. Here's how we created both **area** and **cde** together:

```
var cde = new makeArray(187)
var area = new makeArray(187)
area[1] = "Alabama        "; cde[1] = 205
area[2] = "Alabama        "; cde[2] = 334
area[3] = "Alaska         "; cde[3] = 907
area[4] = "Alberta        "; cde[4] = 403
area[5] = "Antigua        "; cde[5] = 268
area[6] = "Arizona        "; cde[6] = 520
area[7] = "Arizona        "; cde[7] = 602
area[8] = "Arkansas       "; cde[8] = 501
area[9] = "Bahamas        "; cde[9] = 242
area[10] = "Barbados       "; cde[10] = 246
area[11] = "Bermuda        "; cde[11] = 441
area[12] = "British Columbia "; cde[12] = 250
area[13] = "British Columbia "; cde[13] = 604
```

First we created both arrays: **var cde = new makeArray(187)** and **var area = new makeArray(187)**. Then we entered all the data in the same way. On each line we entered data into the same positions in both arrays. The **;** symbol means that an entry into one array has ended, and the entry into the other array has started. We don't have to do it this way. We could simply create one array, fill the array, then create and fill the next array below the first one. But doing them together like this helps us read the script and figure out what is happening. We can quickly see, for example, that the area code for Bermuda is **441**.

TIP

Some browsers (some of the Netscape Navigator 3.0 betas and earlier) have a bug that limits line length to 255 characters or less in some cases. If you run into this problem, you might not be able to put multiple array entries on one line. Instead create each array separately, or simply move long variable assignments down to the next line.

0 or 1?

Elsewhere in this book you have learned that when you number a list of items in JavaScript you start from 0, and in most cases that's true. However, when you create an array in this manner (as a function), you should start numbering from 1. In JavaScript 1.0 (the JavaScript in Netscape Navigator), the 0 position contains the property length, a number that indicates the theoretical size of the array. (In other words, it's the number passed to the function in parentheses, which is not necessarily the same as the number of values that are stored in the array, of course. In the earlier example, the value was 187.)

Note, however, that in most programming languages the entries in the array would begin at position 0. And in fact they *do* start at 0, if you create a script that's to be read by a JavaScript 1.1 browser (Netscape Navigator 3). So what should you do? If you're building an array using this method (using a function), never refer to the length of the array using **area[0]**, because in some browsers this will get you the array length, while in others it will get you the first array element. Instead refer to the array length using **arrayname.length**. Also, never place any information into position **[0]**, because in some browsers this will be taken as the length, in others as an element. Simply leave **[0]** empty and start at **[1]**.

Note also that *real* array objects count up from 0. As you'll see in Chapter 10, "Objects, Properties & Methods," JavaScript has a series of array objects created for special purposes. The frames array lists all the frames in the document, the options array lists all the options in a selection box, and so on. These arrays work in the normal manner, counting from 0. And the new JavaScript 1.1 **Array** object also starts counting from 0.

Grabbing Data From an Array

How can we get data out of our array? Well, think about how we could get data out of a normal variable. We could, for example, do this:

```
alert(normv)
```

That would simply open an Alert box and display the value held in the **normv** variable. You've probably already figured out how to get a value out of an array. You could do this:

```
alert(area[6])
```

That would open the Alert box and display the value held in position **6** of the **area** array.

Take a look at the following example. We've created two small arrays:

Example 9.1

```
<HEAD>
<SCRIPT LANGUAGE="JAVASCRIPT">
<!--
function makeArray(n) {
    this.length = n
    for (var i=1; i <= n; i++){
        this[i] = null;
    }
    return this
}

var acode = new makeArray(187)
var area = new makeArray(187)
area[1] = "Alabama          "; acode[1] = 205
area[2] = "Alabama          "; acode[2] = 334
area[3] = "Alaska           "; acode[3] = 907
area[4] = "Alberta          "; acode[4] = 403
area[5] = "Antigua          "; acode[5] = 268
area[6] = "Arizona          "; acode[6] = 520
area[7] = "Arizona          "; acode[7] = 602
area[8] = "Arkansas         "; acode[8] = 501
area[9] = "Bahamas          "; acode[9] = 242
area[10] = "Barbados         "; acode[10] = 246
area[11] = "Bermuda          "; acode[11] = 441
area[12] = "British Columbia "; acode[12] = 250
area[13] = "British Columbia "; acode[13] = 604
//-->
</SCRIPT>
</HEAD>
```

As you can see, we began by creating the array objects, then we put 13 entries into each array. (We still passed the number **187** to the array, meaning that the array will be 187 entries long. But that's okay. You'll see in a moment what happens if you try to get an entry from a position that has not been filled.) Then we created these buttons:

```
<FORM>

<Compu<INPUT TYPE="BUTTON" VALUE="What's in area Position 12?"
onclick="alert(area[12])"><P>
<INPUT TYPE="BUTTON" VALUE="What's in acode Position 12?"
onclick="alert(acode[12])"><P>
<INPUT TYPE="BUTTON" VALUE="What's in area Position 110?"
```

```
onclick="alert(area[110])"><P>
<INPUT TYPE="BUTTON" VALUE="What's in area Position 500?"
onclick="alert(area[500])"><P>
<INPUT TYPE="BUTTON" VALUE="What's in area Position 0?"
onclick="alert(area[0])"><P>
<INPUT TYPE="BUTTON" VALUE="What's the area length (area.length)?"
onclick="alert(area.length)"><P>
</FORM>
```

Try the Online Companion example and you'll see that the first button displays *British Columbia* in the Alert box, the value stored in position **12** of **area**. The second shows *250*, the value stored in position **12** of **cde**. The third and fourth buttons, though, display *null*, because in both cases they are positions that haven't been filled (and we initialized it to **null**, remember).

TIP

*In the second case—the fourth button—not only is the position empty, but we're also trying to find a value from an entry larger than the number (**187**), which we told the function would be held by the array. Actually, thanks to the rather informal way in which JavaScript works with arrays, this doesn't matter much. You'll learn more about that under "The Shortcuts," later in this chapter.*

Notice also that the last two buttons display **area[0]** and **area.length**. In Netscape Navigator 2, those are exactly the same thing. Clicking both buttons displays the number **187**, the length of the array we defined. But in Netscape Navigator 3 and Internet Explorer 3, clicking the second-to-last button displays **null**, because in JavaScript 1.1 the first element does *not* hold the array length, and we haven't defined any data for that element.

We've put the same arrays in another example in our Online Companion. This time we've added a function in the HEAD to figure out the position:

Example 9.2

```
function GetArray(form) {
var nBase
    if (form.array.selectedIndex == 0) sArray = area;
    if (form.array.selectedIndex == 1) sArray = cde;
    form.returninfo.value = sArray[form.arraypos.selectedIndex]
}
```

You saw a script similar to this in Chapter 7, "More on Functions." The reference to the form is passed to the function (you'll see the form in a moment). The selection position from the array selection box (**form.array.selectedIndex**) is checked; if the position is **0**, the **sArray** variable is set to **area**. If it's **1**, it's set to **cde**. (You'll learn more about referring to a form element in this manner in Chapter 17, "Forms & JavaScript.") Then we find the value in the array. The statement **sArray[form.arraypos.selectedIndex]** means "find the selected item in the selection box called **arraypos**; this is the position in the array named in **sArray**." The information held in that position is then passed back to the form: **form.returninfo.value**, which means "place this information in the **returninfo** text box."

Here's the form that was used:

```
<FORM>
Select array you want to check: <select name="array" size="2">
<option selected value>area
<option>cde
</select><P>
Select an array position you want to check: <select name="arraypos"
size="2">
<option>
<option selected value>1
<option>2
<option>3
<option>4
<option>5
<option>6
<option>7
<option>8
<option>9
<option>10
<option>11
<option>12
<option>13
<option>14
</select><P>
<INPUT TYPE="button" VALUE="What's in this position?"
onclick="GetArray(this.form)"><P>
Here's the information in that position: <INPUT TYPE="TEXT"
NAME="returninfo">
</FORM>
```

We have two selection boxes: one in which you can select the array name, the other in which you select the position. When you click on the button, the function you just saw is called, and the information from the array position is placed into the text box, as you can see in Figure 9-1.

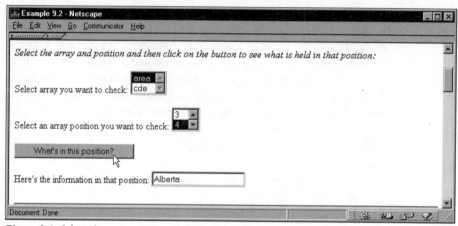

Figure 9-1: Select the array name and the position, then click on the button to see the value held there.

Matching Arrays

A powerful feature of arrays is the ability to match values; position *a* in array *x* represents position *a* in array *y*, for instance. In our example, position **1** in the area array represents position **1** in the **cde** array, position **2** represents position **2**, and so forth.

In this way you can refer to a position in one array and see the information in that array and the associated array (or associated *arrays*, as you might have multiple arrays). For instance, in the following example you can select an area from a selection box and see the corresponding area code. In other words, you are specifying a value in one array, and the script is displaying the corresponding value in the other array.

Example 9.3

```
<FORM>
Select the area for which you want to retrieve the area code: <select
name="area" size="14">
<option >
<option selected option>Alabama 1
<option> Alabama 2
<option> Alaska
<option> Alberta
<option> Antigua
```

```
<option> Arizona 1
<option> Arizona 2
<option> Arkansas
<option> Bahamas
<option> Barbados
<option> Bermuda
<option> British Columbia 1
<option> British Columbia 2
</select><BR>
<INPUT TYPE="button" VALUE="What's the area code?"
onclick="form.returninfo.value=cde[form.area.selectedIndex]"> <INPUT
TYPE="TEXT" NAME="returninfo">
</FORM>
```

We built a form with a selection box in it. In the box we have a list of all the areas in our array. Notice, by the way, that there is a blank space at the top of the list. (There was a blank space in one of the selection boxes in the previous example, too.) The problem is that while arrays count from **1** up, selection boxes count from **0** up! If we put **Alabama 1** in the first position, when we use the **selectedIndex** property (as you'll see in a moment), we would get the index value **0**. **Alabama** is position **1** in the array, not **0**. We could have converted the selection-box positions to array positions, as we did with the **if** statements in the **array** selection box in the last example. However, we added a blank option at the top to shift the entries down into their correct positions as a quick fix.

Now, what happens when you click on the button? Here's the **onclick** instruction again:

```
onclick="form.returninfo.value=cde[form.area.selectedIndex]"
```

As you can see, this time we are looking at the **cde** array; you selected an entry from the **area** array, but what we want is the matching position in **cde**. We then take the position number and place it between the [ ] brackets; **form.area.selectedIndex** means "look in the **area** selection box and find the **selectedIndex** position (the position of the selected item)." So if you selected the blank space at the top, we would have, in effect, this:

```
cde[0]
```

If you selected the fifth position, you'd get this:

```
cde[4]
```

and so on.

So, we find the information in the appropriate **cde** position and then place that information into the **returninfo** text box. You select something in one array, but get an associated value from another array, as you can see in Figure 9-2. Simple.

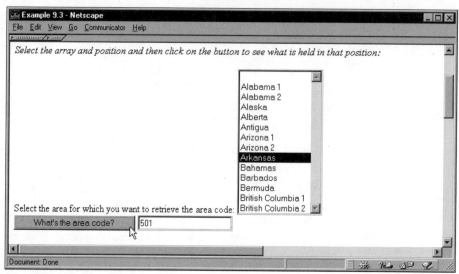

Figure 9-2: You select from one array (area) and get a value from another array (cde).

Actually there is a better way around the problem of the array index not being the same as the option index. You can use **selectedIndex +1** to index the array, like this:

```
onclick="form.returninfo.value=cde[form.area.selectedIndex + 1]"
```

The Shortcuts

As we mentioned before, there's a quicker way to create an array. You see, JavaScript has what might be termed "loosely defined" arrays. In some programming languages, such as C, you have to define an array very carefully and specifically. The method for creating an **array** object shown above is a formal method for doing so:

```
function makeArray(n) {
    this.length = n
    for (var i=1; i <= n; i++){
        this[i] = null;
    }
    return this
}
```

We've named the array, set the array length, set all the array position values to null, and returned the **array** object. But JavaScript's rather loose array definition allows you to create this **array** object with just one line of script. You can see an example in the Online Companion. We've simply taken the first example from this chapter and removed most of the lines from where the function was defined, leaving nothing but this:

Example 9.4

```
function makeArray(n) {
}
```

Try this page, and you'll find that almost all of it works exactly the same as in the first example (when we created the array more formally). Click on the buttons and you'll see the same information, with one exception, this button:

```
<INPUT TYPE="BUTTON" VALUE="What's the area length (area.length)?"
onclick="alert(area.length)">
```

This button displays the area array's **length** property. But because we took out the **this.length = n** line, that property is no longer being set. So when you click on that button, you'll see *undefined* in the Alert box.

Let's see something else about this **length** property. In the next example, we've copied the first example again, and retained the formal method for creating the array. However, we have also done the following:

Example 9.5

```
var acode = new makeArray(3)
var area = new makeArray(3)
area[1] = "Alabama        "; acode[1] = 205
area[2] = "Alabama        "; acode[2] = 334
area[3] = "Alaska         "; acode[3] = 907
area[4] = "Alberta        "; acode[4] = 403
area[5] = "Antigua        "; acode[5] = 268
area[6] = "Arizona        "; acode[6] = 520
```

Notice that this time we've passed the number **3** to the function. In other words, we are saying, "this array will contain three items." But we've put more than that in there (in fact the Online Companion example has 13, not the 6 shown here—we didn't want to repeat that stuff).

Try the example. What happens? All the buttons work correctly. Even though we are asking for information in position **11**—a position larger than the number we've told the function the array will contain—we still get the information. Note, however, the last button. When we ask for the **area.length** value we get **3**, not **13**. We get the value that we told the function the array would contain, not what it actually contains.

So, do we need to specify the **length**? The array works even if we don't set the **length** parameter; it doesn't seem to use it. In fact, we don't have to bother passing a number to the function and it will still work okay.

Well, it's a good idea to specify the length. Why? You might want to create a script that needs to know how long the array is. In Chapter 19, "The Area Code & Telephone Directory Applications," you'll learn how you can search an array—and you must be able to tell the search script when to stop.

When creating an array in this manner (using a function), **length** is just an object property. You have to set it and make sure that it is correct if you wish to use it. As we will see in Chapter 13, "Advanced Topics," you can create an object's property simply by assigning it. This is similar to the way that you can create variables. In fact, assigning a value to an array element is actually the same as creating a new property for the object. How about the rest of the formal array creation, though? Take a look at these pieces:

```
for (var i=1; i <= n; i++){
        this[i] = null;
}
return this
```

You can generally do without these. The **for** loop is used to set all the positions in the array to **null** or **0**. But if you are about to place data into all those positions anyway (and you probably are), you need not do this. And the last piece, **return this**, is also unnecessary, as the array will be returned without it.

True Array Objects in JavaScript 1.1

Starting with Netscape Navigator 3 (JavaScript 1.1) there's a true **Array** object that you can use to build arrays. This is a built-in object, one that's already there, waiting for you to use; it saves you the first step of array creation—you no longer have to create an object class. Now you just go straight to the second step and create an *instance* of the object. (Remember, the *class* is the blueprint, the *instance* is the actual usable object. We'll learn more about this in the following chapter.)

In the example we looked at earlier, we could create an array called **area** like this:

```
var area = new Array()
```

We've used the **new** keyword; as you'll learn in Chapter 11, you use the **new** keyword to create an instance of an object. So we've created a variable called **area**, and we've used **new Array()** to make **area** an instance of an **Array** object. Then we could begin placing data into the array in the way we did before:

```
area[0] = "Alabama       "
area[1] = "Alabama       "
area[2] = "Alaska        "
area[3] = "Alberta       "
```

Note one important difference with the **Array** object: it starts with element **0** instead of **1**. In the old-style arrays created using a function, element **0** is used to store the array length. When you create an **Array** object, its length is stored as a property of the object. It can be referenced in your script, as shown in the following example. First we'll create an array, like this:

Example 9.6

```
var info = new Array(3)
info[0] = 123
info[1] = 456
info[2] = 789
```

Then we'll create a function that will show the contents of the array:

```
function showArray(a) {
    var l = a.length
    var i
    document.write("<BR>Array length is " + l + ".<BR>")
    for (i = 0; i < l; i++) {
        document.write("Item " + i + " is " + a[i] + ".<BR>")
    }
}
```

As you can see, the **showArray** function accepts an array that it calls **a**, and it uses the expression **a.length** to find out how many elements the array has. So we can tell this function to show us the contents of any array we care to name. And that's just what we'll do later in the Web page, by calling **showArray()** and telling it to work with the **info** array:

```
showArray(info)
```

You can see the result of this script in Figure 9-3.

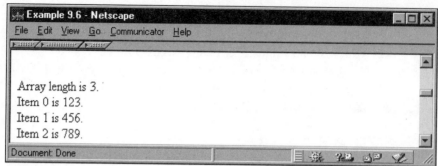

*Figure 9-3: This page uses **showArray(info)** to display the length and contents of the **info** array.*

*You can see that in the above example (Example 9.6), after setting the array length to 3, the last element is numbered **2**, not **3**. For any **Array** object, if the length is **n**, the last element is numbered **n - 1**. Remember this. It's easy to forget, which makes it a common source of mistakes, for experienced programmers as well as beginners. If counting from zero seems awkward, you can usually just skip it and start with element **1**; but the conditions at the other end of the array remain the same. That is, the last element number will still be **n-1**.*

Now let's try adding these statements:

Example 9.7

```
info[9] = "the end"
showArray(info)
```

Although the array was declared to have a length of **3** (so the last element is numbered **2**), we just tried to assign something (the words **the end**) to element **9**, which would require the length to be at least **10**. What happens? JavaScript automatically extends the array to make room for element **9**, as well as **3** through **8**, though items **3** through **8** are **null** since you have not assigned any value to them. This time, calling **showArray** gives the result you can see in Figure 9-4.

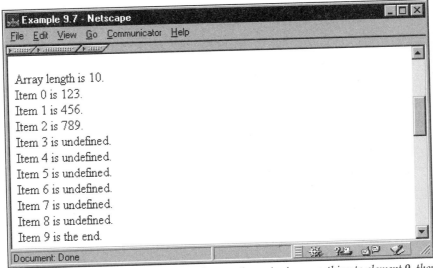

Figure 9-4: *This time we extended the **info** array by assigning something to element **9**, then used **showArray(info)** to display the length and contents of the array.*

Another nice feature of the **Array** object is that there's an easy way to initialize the array. Instead of writing this:

```
var info = new Array(3)
info[0] = 123
info[1] = 456
info[2] = 789
```

we could have written this:

Example 9.8

```
var info = new Array(123, 456, 789)
```

Simply put the initial values into the parentheses, and the **Array** object will automatically set them into the appropriate positions. This can sometimes save you quite a bit of typing.

There's another way to store data in **Array** objects. Instead of numbers, you can use string values in place of the index numbers (the *subscripts*, as they're often known). For example, you can write this:

Example 9.9

```
var house = new Array(0)
house["color"] = "white"
house["style"] = "ranch"
```

```
house["bedrooms"] = 3
house["baths"] = 2
```

Note that this time we declared the array to have a length of **0**. Then we created several elements, but instead of using index numbers we used index "names": **house["color"]** instead of **house[0]**, for example.

This can be handy in some situations, and it will work fine, with one major difference. Elements with string indexes are stored differently from those with numeric indexes. They actually become properties of the object; so **house["color"]** is equivalent to **house.color** in the above example. In fact, the **house** array still has a length of **0**, even after we stored data in it (as you can see if you use this example at the Online Companion). Properties are really not elements of an array, even though they can be referenced with square brackets. (You'll be learning more about properties in the next chapter.) The array will appear to have no length, but it's still storing data for you.

Multidimensional Arrays

What happens if the elements of an **Array** object are arrays themselves? The result is an array of arrays, also called a *2-dimensional array*. This nesting of arrays within arrays can go on for three, four, or more dimensions.

A 2-dimensional array could, for example, be used to store sales statistics for three regions in four different months:

Example 9.10

```
var monthName = new Array("Jan.", "Feb.", "Mar.", "Apr.")
var regionName = new Array("North", "Central", "South")

var jan = new Array(100, 120, 180)
var feb = new Array(110, 90, 150)
var mar = new Array(100, 115, 190)
var apr = new Array(105, 115, 175)

var sales = new Array(jan, feb, mar, apr)
```

We assigned the month and region titles to the two arrays—**monthName** and **regionName**—using the shorthand method of assigning data to arrays. Then we created four more arrays—**jan**, **feb**, **mar**, and **apr**, each containing three sales numbers, one for each region—and finally combined all four into a single array called **sales**. The following script will write all the data in the form of an HTML table:

```
var r, m

document.write("<TABLE><TR><TH> Month </TH>")
for (r = 0; r < 3; r++) {
    document.write("<TH>" + regionName[r] + "</TH>")
}
document.write("</TR>")
```

This begins by declaring two variables, **r** and **m**; we'll see those in use in a moment. (In most of our examples we've declared each variable on a separate line; the above example shows how you can declare multiple variables on one line, by separating them with commas.) Then it writes the word **Month** in the first cell of the table, followed by the three region names (see Figure 9-5). We've used a **for** loop to loop around and display the contents of the **regionName** array, one element in each cell of the top row. Then we do this:

```
for (m = 0; m < 4; m++) {
    document.write("<TR><TH>" + monthName[m] + "</TH>")
    for (r = 0; r < 3; r++) {
        document.write("<TD>" + sales[m][r] + "</TD>") // two-dimensional
    }
    document.write("</TR>")
}
document.write("</TABLE>")
```

This uses two nested **for** loops. The outer loop uses the variable **m** to step through all the months, writing the month names—stored in the **monthName** array—in the first column. The inner loop uses the variable **r** to enter the data from the **sales** array into the appropriate rows. Note this statement:

```
document.write("<TD>" + sales[m][r] + "</TD>") // two-dimensional
```

This contains the expression **sales[m][r]**, which represents the **r**'th element of the **m**'th element of **sales**. The double index (**[m][r]**) is how JavaScript accesses an element of an element. For example, where **m** represents **0** and **r** represents **3**, JavaScript looks at the first array stored in **sales** (the **jan** array), then looks at the third element stored within that array (**180**).

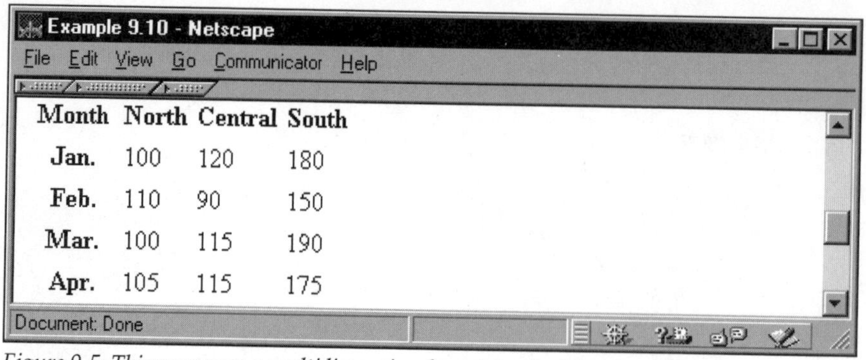

Figure 9-5: This page uses a multidimensional array to display sales figures.

The **Array** object has some other benefits over the "simulated" array (one defined using a function) we saw earlier. It has several methods that can be very handy:

Method	Description
join(sep)	Returns a string containing all the elements of the array, with the value of **sep** as a separator between elements.
reverse( )	Reverses the order of the elements of an array.
sort( )	Sorts the elements of an array.

Moving On

Arrays are really quite simple. The next subject we want to look at is a little more complicated, though. We're going to explain how to work with objects. Objects are "things" that can be described and manipulated using properties and methods. For example, there's a **document** object, which describes the currently open document. This has a range of properties (such as **lastModified**, which we've used before and which is the date that the document was saved) and methods (such as **clear**, which clears the window, and **write**, which we've used a number of times as well).

We're going to learn about the different objects available to you, the way they are linked together in a hierarchical system, about object classes and object instances, and more in the following chapter.

Objects, Properties & Methods

So far we have tried to avoid talking about objects as much as possible, because they can get a little complicated. But the time has come to deal with them. You might have heard of *Object Orientation* (OO) and wondered what all the fuss was about. Object Orientation provides a way to build a program that "reflects" or models the real world more closely than can be done using a non-object-oriented programming language. Programs are built using objects that have properties or data associated with them, and also have behavior or methods that belong to them.

For example, let's consider an object in the real world—a house. It has properties, such as the number of rooms, number of windows, and so on. It also has behaviors associated with it—things that you can do to it and with it:

- People can *live* in the house.
- The house can be *painted*.
- The house can be *sold*.
- The house can be *rented*.

If you owned many houses you might want a program that could help you manage them. The program would have "house" objects in it, one such object for each house you wanted to manage. For each house there would be values for each of its properties: the number of rooms, the rental value, the house's dimensions, and so on. You would probably want to create forms for the input of each house's properties. You could also have functions or *methods* associated with each house object, which would represent behavior associated with that particular house. You might have a method that lists materials needed to paint the house or a method that calculates the rent to be collected.

There is much more to full object-oriented programming (OOP) than this, but JavaScript is not full OOP. JavaScript provides various objects for you to use and even allows you to create your own objects, but it does not implement more complicated OO concepts. (This is just as well, because OOP can get very complicated, especially for people with little or no programming experience. In fact, many *programmers* don't understand OOP, either.)

So, in summary, an object has a collection of *properties* and *methods* associated with it.

The Object	The House
The Object's Properties	Rooms, doors, windows, fireplaces, etc.
Methods (which are types of functions)—behaviors associated with the object itself and with the object's properties	You can sell the house. You can rent the house. You can paint the house (and the rooms, doors, etc.). You can clean the house (and the windows, floors, etc.).

JavaScript provides a number of objects for you to use. We have already used the **document** object a few times earlier in this book, for example. The **document** object is the Web page that your HTML and JavaScript produces. There are other objects, such as the **window** object and the **form** object.

Properties—Variables Belonging to Objects

The properties of an object are variables belonging to the object. They are specified using the dot notation (.) in the following way:

```
objectname.propertyname
```

where **objectname** is simply the name of the object and **propertyname** is, yes, you've guessed it, the name of the property. For instance, in our house example, if we wanted to refer to the house's basement we could call it this:

```
house.basement
```

Simple, eh? We're going to look at the **navigator** object now. This object is used to describe the browser viewing the Web document that contains the script. It is a simple object in that it currently has only four properties. The following example displays each of the properties:

Example 10.1

```
<SCRIPT LANGUAGE="JavaScript">
<!--
function DisplayProperties() {
    document.write("<P><B>navigator.appCodeName =</B> " + navigator.appCodeName)
    document.write("<P><B>navigator.appName =</B> " + navigator.appName)
    document.write("<P><B>navigator.appVersion =</B> " + navigator.appVersion)
    document.write("<P><B>navigator.userAgent =</B> " + navigator.userAgent)
    document.write("<P>The following are JavaScript 1.1 properties, which →
won't appear in Navigator 2.")
    document.write("<P><B>navigator.mimeTypes[0].type =</B> " + →
navigator.mimeTypes[0].type)
    document.write("<P><B>navigator.plugins[0].name =</B> " + →
navigator.plugins[0].name)
    document.write("<P>The following are JavaScript 1.2 properties, which →
won't appear in Navigator 2 or 3.")
    document.write("<P><B>navigator.language =</B> " + navigator.language)
    document.write("<P><B>navigator.platform =</B> " + navigator.platform)
}
//-->
</SCRIPT>
```

This is a fairly simple script. We created a function, called **DisplayProperties**, which is called later in the source document (the script above is in the HEAD). The **DisplayProperties** function writes several lines to the Web page, using the **document.write** method. (A method is simply a function associated with a particular object.) In this case the **write** method is associated with the **document** object and is used to write text to the Web page. The example does this for all the **navigator** properties, one after another. First it uses HTML tags to start a new line and begin bold text, then it writes the name of the property followed by = (notice that all the HTML tags, the name, and the = are enclosed in quotation marks), and then it writes the property name.

Later in the source document the function is called from this simple script:

```
<SCRIPT LANGUAGE="JavaScript">
<!--
DisplayProperties()
//-->
</SCRIPT>
```

You can see the result in Figure 10-1 (your output might look different—this is from the Windows 95/NT Netscape 4.0 Preview Release 2). Note that if you're using Netscape Navigator 2 or Internet Explorer 3 you won't see the last two properties (and in fact you'll see an error message before the page displays).

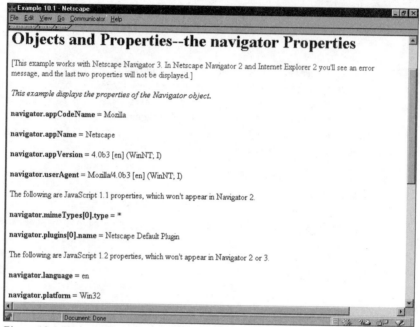

Figure 10-1: We've written the contents of the navigator properties to the Web page.

What are all these properties? Let's see:

Property	Description
navigator.appCodeName	The browser's code name. **Mozilla** is the code name given to the Netscape Navigator family of browsers.
navigator.appName	The browser's application name. The Netscape Navigator family of browsers identifies itself by providing the word **Netscape** as the **appName**. If you're using Internet Explorer you'll see **Microsoft Internet Explorer** instead.

Property	Description
navigator.appVersion	This is information that identifies the browser version number, in this format: **releaseNumber (platform;country)**. For example, you might see something like **4.0b2 (WinNT; I)**—that's beta 2 of Version 4; it's the Windows NT version; and it's an International release (if there'd been a U rather than an I, it would have been a U.S. release). Unfortunately there's currently some inconsistency over this information—you might see **2.01 (Win95; I; 32bit)**, for example, which means Version 2.01, Windows 95 version, International release, 32-bit program. If you are using Internet Explorer you might even see something like this: **2.0 (compatible; MSIE 3.01; Windows NT)**, which presumably means that the browser is Netscape Navigator 2 compatible; it's Internet Explorer 3.01; and it's running on Windows NT.
navigator.appUserAgent	This is the information sent from the browser to the server in the user-agent header when the browser requests a Web page from the server. In some cases it's a combination of the **appCodeName** and the **appVersion** (though it doesn't have to be). For example, you might see this: **Mozilla/4.0b2 (WinNT; I)** or **Mozilla/2.0 (compatible; MSIE 3.01; Windows NT)**.
navigator.mimeTypes[0].type	**mimeTypes** refers to the **mimeTypes** array, which is a list of **MimeType** objects; these are objects in their own right. In other words, a **MimeType** object has properties of its own (we'll be discussing this concept in a moment). So as an example we've looked at the **type** property of the first **MimeType** object (**mimeTypes[0]** means "the first **MimeType** object"). The result in the illustration shows **audio/x-liveaudio**, meaning that the first **MimeType** object is the LiveAudio data type. This property of the **navigator** object was added in JavaScript 1.1 (Netscape Navigator 3).
navigator.plugins[0].name	**plugins** refers to the **plugins** array, which is a list of **Plugin** objects; these are also objects in their own right. That is, a **Plugin** object has properties of its own. So as an example we've looked at the name property of the first **Plugin** object (**plugins[0]** means "the first **Plugin** object"). The result in the illustration shows **Netscape Media Player, Audio Streaming Plugin, v.1.0.1402**, meaning that the first Plugin object is the Netscape Media Player plugin. This property of the **navigator** object was also added JavaScript 1.1.

Property	Description
navigator.language	The language version of the browser. For instance, **en** means the browser is using English. This property was added in JavaScript 1.2 (Navigator 4).
navigator.platform	The operating system the browser is running in. For instance, **Win32** means a 32-bit Windows operating system (currently Windows 95 or NT). This property was added in JavaScript 1.2 (Navigator 4).

TIP

To learn more about the **mimeTypes** *and* **plugins** *arrays (and the associated* **MimeType** *and* **Plugin** *objects, see Chapter 13, "Advanced Topics."*

Navigator or Browser?

For a while, the only JavaScript browsers were the Netscape Navigator family of browsers. So the Netscape developers had a lead on other browser companies and have defined the future of JavaScript. Netscape Communications calls its browsers "navigators," which is why this is the **navigator** object rather than the browser object. But remember that this is really referring to the browser—any JavaScript-compatible browser. Another company must use the **navigator** object to provide information about its browser, even if it doesn't refer to its browser as a "navigator" (which must amuse the Netscape developers, if only a little). Microsoft, for example, has been forced to use the **navigator** object—using the name chosen for a browser by its major browser rival—in order to identify the Internet Explorer browser to JavaScripts.

You've seen how you can write the value held by an object's property directly by naming the property. But you can also get an object's properties by assigning them to variables, like this:

```
variable = objectname.propertyname
```

We could have assigned the property values to a variable in the previous example and then placed the variable name into the **document.write** instruction, for instance. In some cases, you can also set a property's value, like this:

```
objectname.propertyname = value
```

The next example uses the **document** object to illustrate this. Every Web page has a **document** object—in the same way that our "house" object contained all the information about our house, the **document** object contains all the information about the page.

The **document** object can be used to change how that page is displayed. The following example sets the background color (**bgColor**) property of the document to indigo, but then the user can select red, green, blue, or white by using the buttons.

Example 10.2

```
<SCRIPT LANGUAGE="JavaScript">
<!--
document.bgColor = "indigo"
//-->
</SCRIPT>
```

This first script is in the HEAD and immediately sets the color of the page to **indigo**. Notice that we have the property name (**document.bgColor**), the assignment operator (=), and the value we want to assign to the property (**indigo**). There's a huge list of colors you can choose from; you can find this list in Appendix G, "Color Values"; you can also read more about document colors in Chapter 15, "Controlling Windows & Documents With JavaScript," and use the Color Chart in the Online Companion to view the colors.

In the BODY, we've created these buttons:

```
<FORM>
<INPUT TYPE="button" VALUE="Red" onclick="document.bgColor = 'red'">
<INPUT TYPE="button" VALUE="Blue" onclick="document.bgColor = 'blue'">
<INPUT TYPE="button" VALUE="Green" onclick="document.bgColor = 'green'">
<INPUT TYPE="button" VALUE="White" onclick="document.bgColor = 'white'">
</FORM>
```

As you can see, the buttons use the **onclick** event handler to set the **document.bgColor** property to the specified color. Click on the buttons and see; the color of the document changes each time you click (see Figure 10-2).

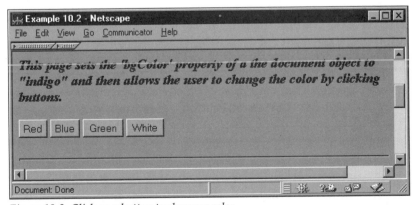

Figure 10-2: Click on a button to change a color.

TIP

> *Note that some properties of objects are read-only. You can't change the* **navigator** *object's properties, for example.*

Methods—Functions Belonging to Objects

Methods are functions that are associated with objects. Remember our house example? The house is the *object*. Cleaning the house would be the *method*. Methods are simply another class of function. In Chapter 7, "More on Functions," we looked at two classes of functions: those you create yourself and the built-in functions. Well, methods are the third class of functions. They are also built-in—you don't have to define them, they are just there waiting for you to use—but they are dependent on objects, while the built-in functions we saw in Chapter 7 are independent of objects.

We used a method in the last example when writing to the Web page:

```
document.write("<P><B>navigator.appCodeName =</B> " + navigator.appCodeName)
```

This line uses the **write( )** method of the **document** object to write to the page. The parameters for the **write( )** method go in the brackets and, in this case, the method needs one string as its argument—the text that is being written. The general format for using a method is:

```
objectname.methodname(parameters for method)
```

TIP

> *As with the other functions we've looked at (see Chapter 7), methods can return values.*

String Variables Are Objects

We've worked a lot with **string** variables already, and because **string** variables are actually objects, **string** objects have properties (well, one property to be precise; the length of the **string** variable is its only property) and methods. (Well, okay, starting with JavaScript 1.1—Netscape Navigator 3—there are actually *two* properties, *if* you create the string using the new **String** object; that's discussed in Chapter 11.) We can, therefore, use one of the **string** methods to convert between upper- and lowercase as we did in the following example:

Example 10.3

```
<SCRIPT LANGUAGE="JavaScript">
<!--
var sText
var sUpper
sText = prompt("Input a string in lower case","")
sUpper = sText.toUpperCase()
document.write("The string in Upper case is: <P><H3>" + sUpper + "</H3>")
//-->
</SCRIPT>
```

We declared two variables, **sText** and **sUpper**. Then we initialized **sText** using the **prompt( )** method (**prompt( )** is actually a method of the **window** object, though in this case we don't need to say **window.prompt( )**, just **prompt( )** will do). We've used this method before—the user types something in the Prompt dialog box, and when he clicks on OK that text is returned and assigned to **sText**.

TIP

Here's another method we used a lot earlier in this book: the **alert( )** *method. Again, this is really* **window.alert( )**, *but you don't need to include the* **window**. *piece— it's assumed (unless you are putting the script in an event handler, in which case you must include it—see Chapter 12, "JavaScript Events—When Are Actions Carried Out?"). Another method we've used is* **window.confirm( )**.

Next we used the **sText.toUpperCase( )** method. (Note that we are using the parentheses at the end of the method name because a method is a type of function, and functions always end with parentheses; and, as we saw in Chapter 7, we can pass information to functions using these parentheses.) **sText** is our string variable—but as we've said, string variables are objects, and string objects can use the **toUpperCase( )** method. So this method simply takes the text from the **sText** variable and converts it to uppercase, then returns the result to the **sUpper** variable. The final line uses the **document.write( )** method to write the contents of **sUpper** to the Web page.

Object Hierarchy—The document Object

This object and property thing can get a little confusing, because properties can actually be objects in their own right, with their own properties. Which brings us to what's known as the *object hierarchy*, a system by which all this fits together hierarchically: one thing sitting below another. For example, let's look at the **document** object's properties:

Property	Description
alinkColor	The color of the text used in a document to display an active link—a link that the user has clicked on, but the user has not yet released the mouse button (the HTML **ALINK** attribute).
Anchor	Each anchor in the document (the **<NAME=** tags) is a property of the **document** object, though each anchor has its own properties, so they are also objects.
anchors array	This is an *array* (we learned about arrays in Chapter 9, "Building Arrays") that lists all of the **Anchor** objects in the document.
Applet	A Java applet embedded into the document using the **<APPLET>** tag. Each **Applet** has its own properties, so it's also an object in its own right. This was added in JavaScript 1.1 (Netscape Navigator 3).
applets array	Another array, this time listing all the **Applets** in the document. Also added in JavaScript 1.1.
Area	This property is a special form of **Link** object, added in JavaScript 1.1 (Netscape Navigator 3). It's a link that is created by putting a hotspot on an image (the **<AREA>** tag, used within the **<MAP>** tag). This property is also an object in its own right. See the **Link** property, below.
bgColor	The color of the document background (the **BGCOLOR** attribute).
classes	A property added in JavaScript 1.2 (Navigator 4), used within the **<STYLE>** tags to set the style of multiple HTML text elements.
cookie	A piece of text related to this page stored in the cookie.txt file. You'll learn about cookies in Chapter 13, "Advanced Topics."
domain	The domain name of the server that sent the document. Introduced with JavaScript 1.1 (Navigator 3).
Embed	A currently undocumented object; a file type embedded into a Web page using the **<EMBED>** tags.
embeds array	An array listing all the **Embed** objects in a document.
fgColor	The color of the document's text (the **TEXT** attribute).
Form	Each form (the **<FORM>** tags) in the object is a property of the object. Again, as each form contains its own properties, each form is also an object.
forms array	This is an array that lists all of the **Form** objects in the document.
ids	A property added in JavaScript 1.2, used within the **<STYLE>** tags to modify the style of text that would otherwise be set using the **classes** property.

Property	Description
Image	Each **<IMG>** tag is an object within the document object. You can also create your own **Image** objects. This is a new object, added to JavaScript 1.1 (Netscape Navigator 3).
images array	This is an array that lists all the **image** objects in the document.
lastModified	The date that the document was last modified (based on the host computer's date setting).
Layer	A movable segment of a document that sits above the main Web page but can sit above or below other layers or be hidden. Created using the **<LAYER>** and **<ILAYER>** tags. Added in JavaScript 1.2.
layers array	A list of all the **Layers** in the document.
Link	Each link (the **<A HREF=** tags) in the document is a property and, as with each form and anchor, an object.
linkColor	The color of the text used in this document to display a link to a document that the user has not yet viewed (the **LINK** attribute).
links array	This is an array that lists all of the **Link** and **Area** objects in the **document.**
location	The complete (absolute) URL of the document. Note, however, because of the confusion between **document.location** and **window.location**, this property is no longer documented; Netscape prefers that people use **document.URL** (see below) in the place of **document.location**; the property will continue to work, though.
referrer	The URL of the document containing a link that the user clicked on to get to this document. If the user didn't get to this document via a link, this is empty.
tags	A property added in JavaScript 1.2, used within the **<STYLE>** tags to set the style of a particular HTML text element.
title	The text between the document's **<TITLE>** and **</TITLE>** tags.
URL	A string containing the document's complete URL. Although this property was in JavaScript 1.0 (Navigator 2), it wasn't documented, and perhaps for that reason won't work in Internet Explorer 3.
vlinkColor	The color of the text used in this document to display a link to a document that the user has already viewed (the **VLINK** attribute).

Are These *Really* Properties?

Are the **Anchor**, **Applet**, **Area**, **Form**, **Image**, and **Link** objects really properties of the document object? Strictly speaking, some might claim that no, they're not! We could tell you that while these objects are *descendants* of the **document** object, they are not *properties* of the object. We'd then have to discuss two different hierarchical systems. We've chosen to simplify the situation and regard these objects as properties.

Why? Because they are indeed descended from the **document** object, and you will refer to them using the same sort of notation. For example, to refer to the **title** property you would refer to **document.title**. To refer to a form named **formB** you would refer to **document.formB**. We have done the same elsewhere. When we talk about the **radio** object, for example, we treat it as a property of a **Form** object. It's descended from the **Form**, after all, and is referred to in the same way. We believe that it's simpler to regard these things as properties and to list them as properties in various tables—as a beginning programmer you don't need to worry about the distinction between a property and an object that is a descendant but not a property.

Each of these properties contains information about the Web document currently displayed in the browsers. We've seen the **lastModified** property before—it's the date that the document was last saved. The fgColor property is the color of the text in the document (the **TEXT** attribute in the <BODY> tag). The **title** property is the document's title (<TITLE>).

But how about the **forms** property? This is a special property, because it's also a list (or an array) of objects. The array lists each **Form** object in the document, so it contains its own properties. But each individual **Form** is also an object, because each **Form** object contains its own properties. In fact each individual **Form** object has a property called the **elements** array. This array contains a list of the elements contained by the form: buttons, text boxes, and so on.

Objects having properties that are objects is what the object hierarchy is all about. The object that is a property of another object is said to be a *descendant* of the first object. The **document** is said to be a **Form** object's *parent* or *ancestor*. The **Form** object can be said to be the *child* or *descendant* of the **document**. When you read the Objects reference in Netscape's "JavaScript Authoring Guide" (see Appendix H, "Finding More Information"), you'll notice that for each object there's a *Property* section—a listing all the properties of that object—but there's also a *Property of* section that states the name of the parent of the object, which is the name of the object from which the current object is descended (that is, of which it is a property).

This part of the object hierarchy can be shown like this:

```
Object        Properties       Properties         Properties
  |           of               of the             of a
  |           window           document object    Form object
  |             |                |                  |
  V             V                V                  V
window----> closed
            defaultStatus
            document----------> alinkColor
            Frame               Anchor
            frames array        anchors array
            history             Applet
            innerHeight         applets array
            innerWidth          Area
            length              bgColor
            location            classes
            locationbar         cookie
            menubar             domain
            name                Embed
            opener              embeds array
            outerHeight         fgColor
            outerWidth          Form ------------>    action
            parent              forms array           Button
            personalbar         ids                   Checkbox
            self                Image                 elements array
            scrollbars          images array          encoding
            status              lastModified          FileUpload
            statusbar           Layer                 Hidden
            toolbar             layers array          length
            top                 Link                  method
            window              linkColor             name
                                links array           Password
                                location              Radio
                                referrer              Reset
                                tags                  Select
                                title                 Submit
                                URL                   target
                                vlinkColor            Text
                                                      Textarea
```

As you can see from this hierarchy, **document** is a property of **window**. But because it has its own properties, it's also an object. A **Form** is a property of a **document**, but it also has a number of properties of its own. The **Form** property, then, is an object in its own right. Notice also the arrays. The arrays are lists. The **forms** array lists each **Form** in the document. The **elements** array is a list of all the elements in the **Form**. The **frames** array lists all the **Frame** objects in a window, and so on. (We'll come back to arrays in a little while.)

The elements in a form might be text boxes, select boxes, buttons, and so on—depending on what you've created. For example, if you have a radio button in a form, then you have a **Radio** object, which is a property of the **Form** object, which is a property of the **document** object, which is a property of the **window** object. (Remember our sidebar earlier; we are using the term *property* loosely, to mean any property of an object or any object descended from an object.)

If you wish to refer to a property or a method belonging to an object, you must specify the complete path through the object hierarchy (with the exception of the **window** object, which is assumed and can be left out in most cases). In the following example there is a **Form** object called **Customer** (its **name** property is **Customer**), and it has a text box object called **Lastname**. In order to refer to a property of the **Lastname** object, we must specify the entire path through the hierarchy, like this:

```
document.Customer.Lastname.propertyname
```

In the following example the **value** property of the **Lastname** text box is set to Smith when the button is clicked:

Example 10.4

```
<SCRIPT LANGUAGE="JAVASCRIPT">
<!--
function ChangeText() {
  document.Customer.Lastname.value = "Smith"
}
//-->
</script>
```

This function simply places the text **Smith** into the **value** property of the **Lastname** form element (in the **Customer** form). Later in the page we have the form:

```
<FORM NAME="Customer">
<INPUT TYPE="button" NAME="But1" value="Change the text box's value
property" onclick="ChangeText()">
<INPUT TYPE="text" NAME="Lastname" value="">
</FORM>
```

When you click on the button the **ChangeText( )** function is called. The text box **value**—that is, the contents of the text box—is then changed.

You can see from the example above that we specify the name of the object using the object hierarchy by first putting **document**, then the form name (**Customer**), and then the element object's name (**Lastname**).

Note that you do not need to specify the **window** in the object reference even though it is at the top of the hierarchy. Generally you don't need to use the window object's name unless you are referring to another window.

Using Arrays

You can also refer to an object by its array position—if it's one of the objects that is listed in an array. An array is a property of an object that contains a list of descendent objects. For example, you can refer to a form using the **forms** array. This array contains a list of all of the **Form** objects contained by the document. Similarly, the **elements** property of a **Form**—the **elements** array— can be used to refer to an element object in the **form**. The following example has two functions that loop around, incrementing a variable i, which is used as the index to the **elements** array.

Example 10.5

```
<SCRIPT LANGUAGE="JAVASCRIPT">
<!--
function DisplayElementNames() {
        for (i=0; i<4; i++)  {
            alert("The element[" + i + "] name is " + →
document.Customer.elements[i].name)
        }
}
function DisplayElementContents() {
    for (i=0; i<4; i++)  {
        alert("The element[" + i + "] value is \'" + →
document.Customer.elements[i].value + "\'")
    }
}
//-->
</script>
```

We've started with the **DisplayElementNames** function. This uses a **for** statement to loop around, displaying an Alert box for each element. Notice that we have a variable called **i**, which is initialized to the value **0**. The first element in the form has the number **0** (remember, we count up from 0, not from 1). As long as the value in **i** is less than **4**, the loop continues, and each time the loop goes around it increments the value in **i** (that's what **i++** means, remember?; see Chapter 6, "Conditionals & Loops—Making Decisions & Controlling Scripts," for information about for loops). Now, what happens during each pass through the loop? The **alert( )** method is used to display the Alert dialog box. In that box we have some text, but we also included the array number of the element (**i**) and, more important, we included the contents of the **name** property. The **name** property is, not surprisingly, the **name** of the form element; whatever appears after **NAME=** in the HTML tag.

Now, how have we referred to this **name** property? See the following:

```
document.Customer.elements[i].name
```

This means the **name** property of element **i** in the **elements** array, in the form named **Customer**, in the **document**. As you can see, we used the object hierarchy and the **elements** array to specify exactly the element we are talking about. (Of course we've used the **i** variable to specify the element number, because as we pass through the loop over and over again, the value in **i** goes from **0** to **1** to **2** to **3** and then stops, because we've told the **for** statement to stop as soon as **i** is no longer less than **4**.)

The second function (**DisplayElementContents( )**) works in exactly the same way, using a **for** loop to display the contents of the elements one by one. What do we mean by contents? The value held by the element. Here's how we referred to the value:

```
document.Customer.elements[i].value
```

Again, this means the **value** property of element **i** in the **elements** array, in the form named **Customer**, in the **document**. This time **value** means either the text that appears after **VALUE=** in the HTML tag, or the actual value typed by the user into the text box.

Later in the page we have this form:

```
<FORM NAME="Customer">
<INPUT TYPE="button" NAME="But1" value="Display the elements names"
onClick="DisplayElementNames()">
<INPUT TYPE="button" NAME="But2" value="Display the elements
contents(Value)" onClick="DisplayElementContents()"><p>
Lastname: <INPUT TYPE="text" NAME="Lastname"><p>
Firstname: <INPUT TYPE="text" NAME="Firstname">
</FORM>
```

This form has four elements. You can type text into the two text boxes. When you click on the first button, the **DisplayElementNames( )** function runs. As you've seen, that function displays the name of each element in

the form, one after the other. If you click on the second button, the
DisplayElementContents( ) function runs, so you'll see the **value** property of
the elements, one after the other (in the case of the text boxes, whatever you
typed in; in the case of the buttons, you'll see what appears after **value=**).

Arrays & Objects

Don't get confused between the arrays and objects, between the **elements**
array and an **element** object, for example. Both are properties. The elements
array is a property of a **Form** object and is an array—a list—of the element
objects that the **Form** contains. An element object is also a property of a **Form**
object, but it is an individual element: a button, selection box, or whatever.
There is a similar distinction between the **forms** array and a **Form** object.
When a property has a plural name, then it contains an array of objects. When
it has a singular name, then it's a single item. If we talk of **forms**, we are talking about an array; if we talk of **Form**, we are talking about a single object. You
might think of the hierarchy like this:

```
document--------- forms array [form1]--------    elements array[element1]
                                                               [element2]
                                                               [element3]
                                                               [element4]
                             [form2]--------    elements array[element1]
                                                               [element2]
                                                               [element3]
                             [form3]--------    elements array[element1]
                                                               [element2]
```

The **form***n* and **element***n* listings are the individual objects, as listed in the
forms and **elements** array.

Here's another example: the **anchors** property in a **document**. This is an
array of anchor objects. The hierarchy looks like this:

```
document---------- anchors array [anchor1]
                                 [anchor2]
                                 [anchor3]
                                 [anchor4]
```

This structure is used for any case in which a parent can have more than
one child of a particular type. A **document** can have many **forms**; a form can
have many **elements**. Note, then, that there are two ways to name an object

that is listed in an array. Let's say you have a form called **secondForm**, and it's, well, the second form in the HTML document (counting down from the top). You want to refer to the **length** property (the number of elements in the form). You can refer to the form like this:

Example 10.6

```
document.forms[1].length
```

. . . or like this:

```
document.secondForm.length
```

The first method uses the array; **forms[1]** means the second form in the array. (Remember, we start counting at 0.) The second method uses the form's name. The example in the Online Companion shows that, whichever method you use, you get the same result.

Similarly, we can refer to elements within a form by name or by element array position. Here's how we might grab the value from a text box called **Lname** in a form called **secondForm**:

Example 10.7

```
document.secondForm.Lname.value
```

We refer to the element's value—that is, the property that contains the actual text displayed in the text box.

> **TIP**
>
> *The full hierarchy would be* **window.document.secondForm.Lname.value**. *However, you can omit the* **window.** *bit (although if you are referring to another window, you would need to use the window name).*

We could also refer to the element like this:

```
document.secondForm.elements[3].value
```

assuming that the text box is the fourth element in the form.

We could even refer to it in this way:

```
document.forms[1].elements[3].value
```

TIP

The elements *array is different from the* **anchors, forms, frames, links,** *and* **options** *arrays. While all these other arrays have objects of the same name (minus the* s: **anchor, form, frame, link, option***), there is no* **element** *object. Rather, there are several different objects—the* **button, checkbox, hidden, password, radio, reset, select, submit, text,** *and* **textarea** *objects—which are listed in the* elements *array.*

Object Classes & Instances

You need to understand the difference between object *classes* and object *instances*. An object *class* is the definition of an object. The **document** object is a class; the **string** object is a class; the **Date** object is a class, and so on. A class is like a blueprint for something. But you can't use a blueprint—you have to use the blueprint to create something first. So before you can use an object, an *instance* must be created.

Let's go back to the house analogy we used earlier in this chapter. Remember that we were using a house object. The blueprint for a four-bedroom house can be thought of as an object class. We can talk about our four-bedroom-house object class—a type of house that we'd like to live in. Before you can live in your four-bedroom house you (or someone else) have to create an actual house—an *instance* of the house—from the object *class*. The class is the blueprint, the instance is the one you actually own and live in.

So although JavaScript has all sorts of objects available to you, these objects cannot be used until an instance is created. There are two ways to create an instance. In most cases, the instance is created for you automatically under certain conditions. For example, when you open a Web document the browser automatically creates a **document** object instance. If there are links in the document (**<A HREF=>**), it also creates a **Link** object instance for each link, and a **links** array, too.

However, in some cases the instance is not created automatically. For example, if you want to use the **Date** object, you must create the instance yourself (as we'll see, that's done using the **new** keyword).

TIP

It's important to understand the distinction between an object class and an object instance. But also understand that when people talk about "using an object" in their scripts, they are, of course, generally talking about using the object instance.

Let's take a quick look at all the objects, their purpose, and whether the object instances are automatically created or must be created by you.

Object name	The object contains information about...	How is the instance created?
Anchor	An anchor in the document (**<A HREF=>** and **<A NAME=>**).	Automatically, if the document loaded contains anchors.
anchors array	A list of all the anchors in a document.	Automatically, if the document loaded contains anchors.
Applet	A Java applet embedded into a page using the **<APPLET>** tag. Introduced in JavaScript 1.1 (Netscape Navigator 3).	Automatically if the document loaded contains Java applets.
applets array	A list of all the **Applet** objects in the document.	Automatically if the document loaded contains Java applets.
Area	An HTML tag (**<AREA>**), within the **<MAP>** tag, used to create an image map from an image. This object was added in JavaScript 1.1.	Automatically if the document contains image maps.
arguments array	A list of the arguments in a function. This is a property of any **Function** object or user-created function. This object was added in JavaScript 1.2.	Automatically if a function is created.
Array( )	An object introduced in JavaScript 1.1, used to create arrays. See Chapter 9, "Building Arrays," for more information.	Using the **new** keyword. A built-in object that is not a property of any other object.
Boolean( )	Used to work with Boolean values. Added to JavaScript 1.1.	Using the **new** keyword. A built-in object that is not a property of any other object.

Object name	The object contains information about...	How is the instance created?
Button	A button in a form (**<INPUT TYPE="BUTTON"**).	Automatically if the document contains a button.
Checkbox	A checkbox in a form (**<INPUT TYPE="CHECKBOX"**).	Automatically if the document contains a checkbox form element.
Date( )	The date.	Using the new keyword. A built-in object that is not a property of any other object.
document	The currently displayed document.	Automatically when the document is loaded.
elements array	A list of all the elements in a form (the **button**, **checkbox**, **hidden**, **password**, **radio**, **reset**, **select**, **submit**, **text**, and **textarea** objects).	Automatically if the document contains forms.
Embed	A currently undocumented object; a file type embedded into a Web page using the **<EMBED>** tags.	Automatically when the document is loaded, if the document contains **<EMBED>** tags.
embeds array	An array listing all the **Embed** objects in a document.	Automatically if the document contains embedded **<EMBED>** tags.
event	An object that is created when an event-handler's event occurs. The object can then be queried to determine information about the event. Added in JavaScript 1.2 (Navigator 4).	Automatically when an event occurs.
FileUpload	An HTML tag (**<INPUT TYPE="FILE">**) used to create a file-upload element in a form.	Automatically if the document contains an **<INPUT TYPE="FILE">** tag.
Form	A form in a document.	Automatically if the document contains a form.
forms array	A list of all the forms in a document.	Automatically if the document contains a form.

Object name	The object contains information about...	How is the instance created?
Frame	A window frame.	Automatically when the window opens.
frames array	A list of all the frames in the window.	Automatically when the window opens.
Function	The **Function** object is a function that has been created by compiling a string of JavaScript into the object using the **new Function( )** statement. This is a built-in function and is not a property of any other object. This object was added in JavaScript 1.1 (Navigator 3).	Using the **new** keyword.
Hidden	A hidden text object in a form (**<INPUT TYPE="HIDDEN"**).	Automatically if the document contains a hidden form element.
history	The browser's history list.	Automatically when the document loads.
history array	A list of the entries in the history entries stored by the browser window (that is, in the history object).	Automatically when the document loads.
Image( )	An image embedded into a document with the **<IMG>** tag. Or an image created using the new keyword (**imagename = new Image( )**). This is a new object, introduced with JavaScript 1.1.	Automatically if the document contains **<IMG>** tags, or with the new keyword.
images array	A list of all the **Image** objects in the document.	Automatically if the document contains images, or when you use the new keyword to create an **Image( )** object.
Layer	A movable segment of a document that sits above the main Web page but can sit above or below other layers or be hidden. Created using the **<LAYER>** and **<ILAYER>** tags. Added in JavaScript 1.2.	Automatically if the document contains layers.
layers array	A list of all the layers in the document.	Automatically if the document contains layers.

Object name	The object contains information about...	How is the instance created?
Link	A link (**<A HREF=>**).	Automatically if the document contains a link.
links array	A list of all the Link and Area objects in the document.	Automatically if the document contains links or image maps.
location	The URL of the current document.	Automatically when the document opens.
Math	Mathematical constants and functions.	Automatically. A built-in object that is not a property of any other object.
MimeType	A MIME type (Multipurpose Internet Mail Extension) supported by the browser. Added to JavaScript 1.1.	Automatically when the document loads.
mimeTypes array	A list of all the MIME types supported by the browser. Added to JavaScript 1.1.	Automatically when the document loads.
locationbar	The window's location bar. This was added in JavaScript 1.2.	Automatically when the document loads.
menubar	The window's menu bar. This was added in JavaScript 1.2.	Automatically when the document loads.
navigator	The browser viewing the Web page.	Automatically when the page loads into the browser.
Number( )	An object used to work with numbers. Added to JavaScript 1.1.	Automatically. Built in.
Option( )	An option that can be added to a selection list (**<SELECT>**). Added to JavaScript 1.1.	Created using the **new** keyword.
options array	A list of all the options in a select element.	Automatically if the document contains a selection list.
Password	A password text field in a form (**<INPUT TYPE="PASSWORD"**).	Automatically if the document contains a password field.
personalbar	The window's personal bar (the new customizable button bar in Navigator 4). This was added in JavaScript 1.2.	Automatically when the document loads.
Plugin	A plug-in installed in the browser. Added to JavaScript 1.1.	Automatically if the browser has installed plug-ins.
plugins array	A list of all the **Plugin** objects. Added to JavaScript 1.1.	Automatically if the browser has installed plug-ins. ➡

Object name	The object contains information about...	How is the instance created?
Radio	A set of radio buttons in a form (**<INPUT TYPE="RADIO"**).	Automatically if the document contains a radio button.
RegExp	An object used to create new regular expressions. (Regular expressions are patterns that are used to match combinations of characters in strings.) This object was added in JavaScript 1.2.	This is a built-in object.
Reset	A reset button in a form (**<INPUT TYPE="RESET"**).	Automatically if the document contains a reset button.
screen	An object containing information about the screen in which the browser is running. This was added in JavaScript 1.2.	Automatically when the document loads.
scrollbars	The window's scroll bars. This was added in JavaScript 1.2.	Automatically when the document loads.
Select	A selection list in a form (**<SELECT>**).	Automatically if the document contains a selection list.
statusbar	The window's status bar. This was added in JavaScript 1.2.	Automatically when the document loads.
String ( )	A string. Starting with JavaScript 1.1 you can create a **String( )** object using the **new** keyword.	Automatically when you create a string. Or using the **new** keyword.
Submit	A submit button in a form (**<INPUT TYPE="SUBMIT"**).	Automatically if the document contains a submit button.
Text	A text box in a form (**<INPUT TYPE="TEXT"**).	Automatically if the document contains a text box.
Textarea	A textarea in a form (**<TEXTAREA>**).	Automatically if the document contains a textarea box.
toolbar	The window's toolbar. This was added in JavaScript 1.2.	Automatically when the document loads.
window	The current window or a window you have created. The **window** object is the top-level object in the hierarchy for **document**, **location**, and **history** objects.	Automatically when the window opens.

As you can see from this table, the object hierarchy is dependent on the circumstances. Many of these objects only appear if certain conditions are present in the document. If the document has no forms, for example, there will be no instances of the **Button**, **Checkbox**, **Form**, **Hidden**, **Password**, **Radio**, **Reset**, **Select**, **Submit**, **Text**, or **Textarea** objects.

What's a Built-in Object?

You might run across the term *built-in object* now and again. So what's a built-in object? The term "built-in" is used ambiguously to mean different things. Some JavaScript documentation uses it to mean objects that are not created by you (as you'll see in Chapter 13, "Advanced Topics," you can create your own objects). But it's mainly used to refer to the **Array( )**, **Boolean( )**, **Date( )**, **Function( )**, **Math( )**, **Number( )**, **RegExp**, and **String** objects, which are built-in to JavaScript in the sense that they are not dependent on a particular document or window. They are not properties of another object and are either created automatically or created with the use of the **new** keyword.

A Confusing Case—location

There are a few confusing names in this hierarchy, because they appear more than once in the hierarchy. First, there's **location**. This is both a property of the **document** object (**document.location**) and a property of the window object (**window.location**). To make things really confusing, both contain similar information. The **document.location** property contains the URL of the current document (the location of the document).

Note, however, that you don't have to use **document.location**. There's another property, which is exactly the same, named **document.URL**. The **document.location** property has been used in the past because, although the URL property was present in JavaScript 1.0, it wasn't documented. The **document.location** property is no longer documented, as Netscape is encouraging people to use **document.URL** instead. However, **document.location** will still work, as you can see from the following example, which was in the first edition of this book.

The **window.location** property also contains a URL. But while **document.location** cannot be changed—in the same way that the document title is fixed, so is the document location—you *can* change the properties of the **window.location** object.

The **window.location** object is used to modify the contents of the window, loading a different Web page. This is also an object, as it has several properties, such as **href**, **protocol**, and **host**. The **document.location** (or, now, the **document.URL**) property is used to tell you what is currently loaded. Here's an example that demonstrates the difference:

Example 10.8

```
function WinOpen() {
    NewWindow  = open("2 1.htm","Window1","toolbar=yes,height=250,→
width=450,");
}
```

We started with this simple script in the HEAD. The function **WinOpen** creates a new window (using the **open** method). (We've looked at how to open windows before, and we'll return to the subject in Chapter 15, "Controlling Windows & Documents With JavaScript.") **NewWindow** is the name we gave the new window (so is **Window1**, but **Window1** is intended to be used when referring to the window as a target in HTML tags; when we refer to the window in our scripts we use the name preceding the = assignment operator, as you'll see in a moment). The file **2-1.HTM** is loaded into this window. Then we have a form with these four buttons:

```
<FORM>
<FORM>
<I>Click on this button to create a new window:</I><BR>
<input type="button" name="WindowButton" value="Create Secondary Window and
place Example 2.1 in the window" onclick="WinOpen()">
<P>
<I>Click on this button to view the value held by the
</I>document.location<I> property:</I><BR>
<input type="button" name="Button3" value="Show secondary document.location
property" onclick="alert('document.location = ' + →
NewWindow.document.location)")"><P>
Click on this button to view the value held by the </I>window.location<I>
property:</I><BR>
<input type="button" name="Button3" value="Show secondary
window.location.href property" onclick="alert('window.location.href = ' + →
NewWindow.location.href)")"><P>
<I>Change the </I>window.location<I> object's </I>href<I> property:</I><BR>
<input type="button" name="Button2" value="Change the secondary
window.location object to example 2-2" onclick="NewWindow.location.href = →
'2-2.htm'")"><P>
<I>Try changing the </I>document.location<I> property (it won't work):</
I><BR>
```

```
<input type="button" name="Button2" value="Change the secondary window's
document.location object to example 2-3"
onclick="NewWindow.document.location = '2-3.htm'")
</form>
```

Click on the first button to run the **WinOpen** function. The new window opens and loads file **2-1.htm**. The second button opens an Alert box that shows you the **NewWindow.document.location** property. The third button opens an Alert box showing you the **NewWindow.location.href** property. Click on these and you'll see that the URL shown is the same in both cases; in fact they are always the same.

TIP

Remember that earlier in this chapter we told you that there's no need to use the **window**. *part of a hierarchical name. Here's a case when you* must *use the window name* **NewWindow.location.href***, for example. We're referring to another window, not the window holding the buttons, so we have to name it.*

The fourth button lets you change the contents of the window. It modifies the **href** property of the **window.location** object (**NewWindow. location.href**). You can go to the secondary window to see that the contents have changed. Use the two previous buttons to see that the **document.location** and **window.location.href** properties have changed.

Finally, the last button tries to change the **NewWindow.document.location** property. Try it, and you'll find that it doesn't do anything—you can't change that property. (Nor can you change its equivalent, the **document.URL** property.)

As we stated, you can use document.URL instead of **document.location**— it's exactly the same thing, and it's been around for a while (it's in the Navigator 2 browsers). However, **document.URL** was not documented before Navigator 3 was released, so Microsoft, basing its version of JavaScript on the documentation available with Navigator 3, hasn't added it to Internet Explorer 3. Thus, while **document.URL** will work with all JavaScript-enabled versions of Navigator, it won't work with Internet Explorer 3 (the current version). So you might want to continue using **document.location** for a while.

TIP

There's another confusing property: the **window.window** *property. We'll cover this in the next chapter.*

Summary

Before we move on, let's just go over this stuff to make sure that we have it straight.

An *object* is a thing: a house, or a **document**, or a **Form**. An object has *properties*, other things associated with the object. The house has rooms; the **document** has forms; the **Form** has buttons and text boxes.

Properties may be objects, too. A **Form** is a property of a **document**. But a Form is also an object, because it has its own properties.

Objects have *methods* associated with them. A method is simply another type of function. The **document.write( )** and **window.alert( )** functions we've used so often are methods.

In most cases you can forget the **window.** part of an object name, as **window.** is assumed to mean the window in which you are working. You only need to name the window when referring to a different window or when writing a script in an event handler.

An *array* is a list of objects. The **forms** array lists all the forms in the document, for example. You can refer to an object by its actual name or by its position in the array.

An *object class* is a description of an object—a sort of blueprint. An *object instance* is an actual object that has been created and can be used in your scripts.

Moving On

Objects provide a very powerful programming tool, as you'll find out in the next chapter. In this chapter we explained the basic structure and purpose of objects and arrays. Now we need to look at a number of particular objects in more detail. We're going to start by looking at the **Date( )**, **Math( )**, and **String( )** objects in the next chapter. Then, later in the book, we'll cover other objects in more detail.

More About Built-in Objects

Now that you've learned the basics about working with objects—properties, the object hierarchy, arrays, and so on—let's take a look at a different breed of objects, the ones that are often described as *built-in* objects. The built-in objects are **Array( )**, **Boolean( )**, **Date( )**, **Function( )**, **Math( )**, **Number( )**, **RegExp( )**, and **String( )** objects. The **navigator** and **screen** objects are also built-in objects, in the sense that they are not part of the object hierarchy and they're always present. However, there's a difference between the first group of built-in objects we've just listed and the **navigator** and **screen** objects. The first group of built-in objects are like libraries of information, waiting to be used if you need them. They're object classes that don't exist until you create an object instance, as we discussed in Chapter 11. On the other hand, the **navigator** and **screen** objects are always present, holding information about the browser and the video resolution in which the browser is running. You can have only one **navigator** object, and one **screen** object, while you can have multiple instances of the other objects.

We've already seen **Function( )** in Chapter 7, and **Array( )** in Chapter 9, and we'll look at **RegExp( )** in Chapter 14. (You'll find information about **screen** in Chapter 15, and we discussed **navigator** in Chapter 10.) In this chapter we'll look at the others, starting with the **Date( )** object.

The Date( ) Object

The **Date( )** object enables you to work with dates and times. In order to work with the **Date( )** object, you must begin by creating an object instance (as we discussed in Chapter 10, "Objects, Properties & Methods"). You use the **new** keyword to do this. For example, you could create a **Date( )** object instance called **TodaysDate** like this:

```
TodaysDate = new Date()
```

Notice that the **Date** object ends with parentheses. This is so we can pass information to the object. That means that when we create the **Date( )** object, we can do one of two things: grab the current date and time (that's what we've just done), or create an object instance that holds a particular date and time. We can do that in three different ways:

```
name = new Date("month, day, year hours:minutes:seconds")
name = new Date(year, month, day)
name = new Date(year, month, day, hours, minutes, seconds)
```

Notice that the first method is creating a string (we've put the information between quotation marks). The other methods use numeric values, as shown in the following example:

Example 11.1

```
LaunchDate1 = new Date("aug, 15, 1997 12:02:00")
LaunchDate1 = new Date("15, aug, 1997 12:02:00")
LaunchDate2 = new Date(1997, 7, 15)
LaunchDate3 = new Date(1997, 7, 15, 14, 02, 02)
```

TIP

*Notice that in the last two methods, the month counts forward from **0**. January is month **0**, February is month **1**, and so on. Luckily, the days don't count from 0!*

You can see these dates in the example in the Online Companion. We've created buttons that display the values held by the **Date( )** objects. Different JavaScript versions work a little differently. In JavaScript 1.1 and later, you'll get the time zone displayed along with the time. For example, in JavaScript 1.0 **TodaysDate** shows something like this:

```
Mon Aug 07 09:21:09 1997
```

In JavaScript 1.1 or 1.2, you'll see something like this:

```
Mon Aug 07 09:21:09 Mountain Daylight Time 1997
```

Date Methods

Now let's see what methods (functions) are available for the **Date( )** object.

Object	Function
eval	Starting with JavaScript 1.1 (Navigator 3) all objects have this method. Used to evaluate a string of JavaScript code, it processes any statements it finds in relation to the object.
getDate( )	Looks in the **Date( )** object and returns the day of the month.
getDay( )	Returns the day of the week.
getHours( )	Returns the hours.
getMinutes( )	Returns the minutes.
getMonth( )	Returns the month.
getSeconds( )	Returns the seconds.
getTime( )	Returns the complete time.
getTimeZoneOffset( )	Returns the time-zone offset (the number of hours' difference between Greenwich Mean Time and the time zone set in the computer running the script).
getYear( )	Returns the year.
parse( )	Returns the number of milliseconds between the stated date and January 1, 1970 00:00:00 (the Date object stores times and dates in the form of milliseconds since this date).
setDate( )	Changes the **Date( )** object's day of month.
setHours( )	Changes the hours.
setMinutes( )	Changes the minutes.
setMonth( )	Changes the month.
setSeconds( )	Changes the seconds.
setTime( )	Changes the complete time.
setYear( )	Changes the year.
toGMTString( )	Converts the **Date( )** object's date (a numeric value) to a string in GMT time, returning something like the following: Weds, 15 June 1997 14:02:02 GMT (the exact format varies depending on the operating system running on the computer).
toLocaleString( )	Converts the **Date( )** object's date (a numeric value) to a string, using the particular date format the computer is configured to use.
toString	All objects have this method. Used to convert an object to a string.
UTC( )	Use **Date UTC(year, month, day, hrs, min, sec)** to return that date in the form of the number of milliseconds since January 1, 1970 00:00:00 (the hrs, min, and sec are optional).
valueOf	Starting with JavaScript 1.1 (Navigator 3) all objects have this method. Used to convert an object to a primitive value.

As you can see, you can both retrieve and set different portions of the **Date( )** object that you've created. You also have several special methods for manipulating dates. Remember that you refer to a method in this form:

```
objectname.methodname( )
```

For example, look at this script:

```
TodaysDate.getMonth( )
```

Here's an example. First we created a **Date** object called **TodaysDate**:

Example 11.2

```
TodaysDate = new Date( )
```

Then we created these buttons:

```
<FORM>
<INPUT TYPE=BUTTON VALUE="Get the hour held by TodaysDate"
onclick="alert(TodaysDate.getHours())"><P>
<INPUT TYPE=BUTTON VALUE="Get the year held by TodaysDate"
onclick="alert(TodaysDate.getYear())"><P>
<INPUT TYPE=BUTTON VALUE="Set the year held by TodaysDate to 99"
onclick="TodaysDate.setYear(99)"><P>
<INPUT TYPE=BUTTON VALUE="Get Greenwich Mean Time"
onclick="alert(TodaysDate.toGMTString())">
</FORM>
```

As you can see, we've used the methods to see the hour held by the object (**TodaysDate.getHours( )**); to get the year held by the object (**TodaysDate.getYear( )**); to set the year to a different value (**TodaysDate.setYear(99)**); and to convert the date held by the object to Greenwich Mean Time (**TodaysDate.toGMTString( )**). (So, if your computer is not set to the Greenwich Mean Time zone, you'll see a different time in the Alert box.)

The Math( ) Object

The **Math( )** object provides properties and methods that are used to carry out mathematical calculations. The object's properties are mathematical constants (pi, Euler's constant, the base 10 logarithm of e, and so on). Its methods are mathematical procedures: functions used to round numbers, to check for the largest number, to calculate cosines, to calculate a square root, and so on. Of course, we've already seen how to carry out mathematical operations using the math operators: +, -, /, and others. But the **Math( )** object is more advanced, providing many mathematical "shortcuts."

Here are the **Math( )** properties. They contain constants that are useful for people who like to mess with this sort of thing (if that includes you, then you already know what they are and what they are for).

Properties	Value
E	The base of natural logarithms, Euler's constant (approximately 2.718).
LN2	The natural logarithm of two (approximately 0.693).
LN10	The natural logarithm of 10 (approximately 2.302).
LOG2E	The base 2 logarithm of e (approximately 1.442).
LOG10E	The base 10 logarithm of e (approximately 0.434).
PI	The ratio of the circumference of a circle to its diameter (approximately 3.14159).
SQRT1_2	The square root of one-half (approximately 0.707).
SQRT2	The square root of two (approximately 1.414).

Here are the methods you can work with:

Methods	Result
eval	Starting with JavaScript 1.1 (Navigator 3) all objects have this method. Used to evaluate a string of JavaScript code, it processes any statements it finds in relation to the object.
abs( )	Returns a number's absolute value (its "distance from zero"; for example, both 2 and −2 have absolute values of 2).
acos( )	Returns the arc cosine of a number (in radians).
asin( )	Returns the arc sine of a number (in radians).
atan( )	Returns the arc tangent of a number (in radians).
ceil( )	Returns an integer equal to or immediately above a number (**ceil(-22.22)** would return **-22**; **ceil(22.22)** would return **23**; and **ceil(22)** would return **22**).
cos( )	Returns the cosine of a number (in radians).
exp( )	Returns e^{number}.
floor( )	The opposite of ceil. (**floor(-22.22)** would return **-23**; **floor(22.22)** would return **22**; and **floor(22)** would return **22**.)
log( )	Returns the natural logarithm (base e) of a number.
max( )	Returns the greater of two numbers.

Methods	Result
min( )	Returns the lesser of two numbers.
pow( )	Returns base^{exponent}.
random( )	Returns a pseudo-random number between zero and one. (Only works on UNIX versions of Netscape Navigator in JavaScript 1.0. Starting with JavaScript 1.1—Navigator 3—it works on all operating systems.)
round( )	Returns a number rounded to the nearest integer.
sin( )	Returns the sine of a number (in radians).
sqrt( )	Returns the square root of a number.
toString	All objects have this method. Used to convert an object to a string.
tan( )	Returns the tangent of a number.
valueOf	Starting with JavaScript 1.1 (Navigator 3) all objects have this method. Used to convert an object to a primitive value.

Here are a couple of simple examples:

Example 11.3

```
<FORM>
Type two numbers:
<INPUT TYPE="text" NAME="num1">
<INPUT TYPE="text" NAME="num2"><P>
<INPUT TYPE="button" VALUE="Find the largest number"
onclick="form.result.value = Math.max(form.num1.value,form. num2.value)">
<INPUT TYPE="text" NAME="result">
</FORM>
```

You type numbers into **num1** and **num2**. Then, when you click on the button, the **Math.max(form.num1.value,form.num2.value)** methods are used to compare the values in the **num1** and **num2** fields. The maximum value is then placed into the text box, **result**.

TIP

We could also have written **Math.max(this.form.num1.value, this.form.num2.value).** *We've referred to the text boxes,* **num1** *and* **num2**; **this.form** *means "the information in* this *form, the same form the button is in." However,* **form.num1.value** *is a sort of shorthand; we can drop the* **this.** *bit if we want.*

Example 11.4

```
<FORM>
Enter the radius of a circle: <INPUT TYPE="text" NAME="num1"><P>
<INPUT TYPE="button" VALUE="Find the circumference"
onclick="form.result.value = 2*Math.PI*form.num1.value"> <INPUT
TYPE="text" NAME="result"><P>
<INPUT TYPE="button" VALUE="Find the square root of the
first number" onclick="form.result2.value =  Math.sqrt(form.num1.value)">
<INPUT TYPE="text" NAME="result2">
</FORM>
```

We're doing two things here. First, we are calculating the circumference of a circle, which is based on the radius that the user types into the first text box: **2*Math.PI*form.num1.value**, which is the same as multiply 2 by pi, by the value in the text box **num1**.

The second calculation simply finds the square root of the value in the first text box: **Math.sqrt(form.num1.value)**, which means return the square root of the value in the text box **num1**. You can see an example in Figure 11-1.

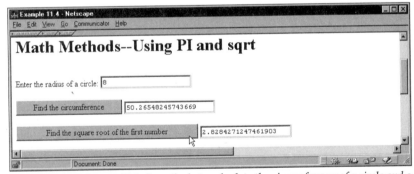

Figure 11-1: We've used Math methods to calculate the circumference of a circle and a square root.

The String( ) Object

Each string in a script is an object, as we saw in Chapter 10, "Objects, Properties & Methods." Starting with JavaScript 1.1 (Netscape Navigator 3), you can create strings with **new**, like this:

```
var s = new String("This is the value of s.")
```

However, this actually has the same effect as writing this:

```
var s = "This is the value of s."
```

Of course, the big difference with the **new** method is that although it has just the same effect as simply declaring the variable . . . it won't work with all browsers! So, you might want to avoid this object in some cases. However, creating a **String,** object using **new** also provides another benefit. You can use the **prototype** property—which we'll discuss in Chapter 13—to add other properties to the object.

A **String( )** object has only two properties: **length,** which is the number of characters within the **String( ),** and **prototype.** There are a number of methods related to **String** objects, however, providing lots of ways to manipulate your strings.

TIP

The **length** *properties are always related to an object's size, even though the size is not always what you'd think of as a length in plain English;* **anchors.length** *is the number of anchors in a document;* **links.length** *is the number of links in a document; and* **select.length** *is the number of options in a selection box, and so on.*

Methods	Result
eval	Starting with JavaScript 1.1 (Navigator 3) all objects have this method. Used to evaluate a string of JavaScript code, it processes any statements it finds in relation to the object.
anchor(*Name***)**	Used to turn the string into an HTML anchor tag (**<A NAME=**), using *Name* as the anchor name.
big( )	Changes the text in the string to a big font (**<BIG>**).
blink( )	Changes the text in the string to a blinking font (**<BLINK>**).
bold( )	Changes the text in the string to a bold font (**<B>**).
charAt(*index***)**	Finds the character in the string at the *index* position (0 is the first character, 1 is the next character, and so on).
fixed( )	Changes the text in the string to a fixed-pitch font (**<TT>**).
fontcolor(*color***)**	Changes the text in the string to a color (**<FONT COLOR=***color***>**).
fontsize(*size***)**	Changes the text in the string to a specified size (**<FONTSIZE=***size***>**).
indexOf (character, returns *from*)	Used to search the string for a particular character, and then the index position of that character (the first character is index position 1). You can specify the index position *from* which you should begin the search.

Methods	Result
italics( )	Changes the text in the string to italics (<I>).
lastIndexOf (character, *from*)	Like indexOf, but searches backward to find the last occurrence of the character. The *from* position is the number of characters from the end.
link(*href*)	Used to turn the string into an HTML link tag (**<A HREF=**), using *href* as the anchor name.
small( )	Changes the text in the string to a small font (**<SMALL>**).
split(*sep*)	Returns an array created by splitting the string into separate sections at each occurrence of the separator string *sep*. This method was added in JavaScript 1.1 (Netscape Navigator 3).
strike( )	Changes the text in the string to a strikethrough font (**<STRIKE>**).
sub( )	Changes the text in the string to a subscript font (**<SUB>**).
substring (*indexA,indexB*)	Returns a portion of the string—a subset—starting with the character at *indexA* and finishing with the character at *indexB*.
sup( )	Changes the text in the string to a superscript font (**<SUP>**).
toLowerCase( )	Changes the text in the string to lowercase.
toUpperCase( )	Changes the text in the string to uppercase.
toString	All objects have this method. Used to convert an object to a string.
valueOf	Starting with JavaScript 1.1 (Navigator 3) all objects have this method. Used to convert an object to a primitive value.

Using String Methods

How, then, do we refer to a **String( )** object? By the name of the variable holding the string; or, if you used the **new** keyword, by the name you gave to the **String( )** object. Take a look at this example. We started by creating these functions:

Example 11.5

```
function GetLength(form) {
var stextLength = form.string1.value
        form.result.value= stextLength.length
}
function Position(form) {
var sPos = form.string1.value
        form.result2.value= sPos.charAt(5)
}
```

The **GetLength** function takes the value from a text box called **string1** and places it in a variable called **stextLength**. Then, it finds how many characters are in the string using the length property: **stextLength.length**. Then, it returns that value to the **result** text box in the form.

The **Position** function takes the same value, placing it in the **sPos** variable. Then, it uses the **charAt** method to find out which character is at position **5** (the sixth character in the string). Then, it returns that value to the **result2** text box in the form.

As you can see in the Online Companion, we have two buttons in the form. The first takes the text that you typed and counts the number of characters in the string. The second finds out what character is at position **5**, as you can see in Figure 11-2.

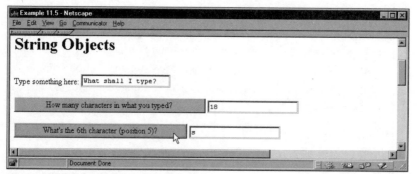

Figure 11-2: We've counted the number of characters and checked a position, using the **length** *property and the* **charAt** *method.*

Of course, these string methods are mostly used for modifying how text is written to a page. So, let's have a quick look at what can be accomplished:

Example 11.6

```
function function1() {
var sTypedText
    sTypedText  = prompt("Type some text, then click on OK.", "")
    return sTypedText
}
```

This is a function we've used before. When **function1( )** is called, a Prompt dialog box opens. When the user types in some text and clicks on OK, the text is assigned to the **sTypedText** variable. The value in **sTypedText** is returned by the function.

```
<SCRIPT LANGUAGE="JavaScript">
<! --
var sText
    sText  = function1()
    document.write("You just typed: <P>" + sText)
    document.write("<BR> This is big: " + sText.big())
    document.write("<BR> This is a link: " + sText.link ("11-6.htm"))
    document.write("<BR> This is blinking text: " +  sText.blink())
    document.write("<BR> This is bold: " + sText.bold())
    document.write("<BR> This is colored: " +  sText.fontcolor("green"))
    document.write("<BR> This is italics: " +  sText.italics())
    document.write("<BR> This is small: " + sText.small())
    document.write("<BR> This is strikethrough: " +  sText.strike())
    document.write("<BR> This is subscript: " + sText.sub())
    document.write("<BR> This is superscript: " +  sText.sup())
    document.write("<BR> This is lowercase: " +  sText.toLowerCase())
    document.write("<BR> This is uppercase: " +  sText.toUpperCase())
// -->
</SCRIPT>
```

When this script runs a variable, **sText** is declared. Then, we use the **document.write** instruction to write the text in **sText** to the Web page. But notice that after each occurrence of **sText**, you will find a method name: **big( )**, **blink( )**, **sub( )**, and so on. You can see the effect of all this in Figure 11-3.

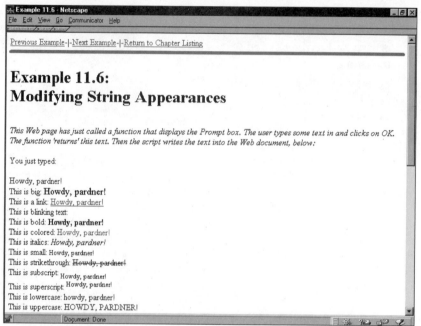

Figure 11-3: We've used the string methods to write the text from the Prompt dialog box in a variety of ways.

Using String Methods With Object Properties

It's worth noting that many object properties are actually strings. That means that you can use these string methods with those properties. Here's an example. There are a few features in JavaScript that vary between the different operating systems. If you want to place several lines of text into a textarea box, the code you must use to break the lines depends on the type of computer on which the browser is running. If it's a Windows browser you must use **\r\n**. If it's a UNIX browser you should use **\n**, and for the Macintosh you must use **\r.**

Well, there's a special property that we've seen before, **navigator.appVersion**, which tells us the application version of the browser **appVersion** is a string, so we can apply any of the string methods we want to this property.

What we need to do, then, is find out which browser is being used, and then pick the newline character accordingly. We can apply the **lastIndexOf** method to the **appVersion** to do this. The **lastIndexOf** method searches a string for some specified text. For example: **navigator.appVersion.lastIndexOf('Win')**

This simply means, "start at the end of the **appVersion** string, and look for **Win**." If it finds it, it will return the position of the text within the string. But if it can't find it in the string, it returns **-1**. So, we can create a little routine like this:

```
var nl=null
    if (navigator.appVersion.lastIndexOf('Win') != -1) {
        nl = "\r\n"
    }
    else {
        if (navigator.appVersion.lastIndexOf('Mac') != -1) {
            nl = "\r"
        }
        else {
            nl = "\n"
        }
    }
```

We've declared a variable called **nl**. Then, we have an **if** statement. The statement uses **lastIndexOf** to see if **Win** is in the string. If it is, it returns some number. If it isn't, it returns **-1**. Then we compare this result to **-1**. The **!= -1** piece means, "not equal to **-1**." If the letters **Win** appear in the **appVersion** string, we get a number—but not **-1**, so the next line is executed and we place **\r\n** into the **nl** variable. If the letters **Win** *don't* appear in the string, we get **-1**; so, the **else** line is executed. The **else** contains a nested **if**. This time, we're checking to see if we can find the letters **Mac** in the string; if we can, we place **\r** into **nl**. If we can't, the browser must be a UNIX browser, so we go onto the next **else** and place **\n** into **nl**.

We've created an example of how this works:

Example 11.7

```
<SCRIPT LANGUAGE="JAVASCRIPT">
<! --
var nl=null
        if (navigator.appVersion.lastIndexOf('Win') != -1) {
            nl = "\r\n"
        }
        else {
            if (navigator.appVersion.lastIndexOf('Mac') != -1) {
                nl = "\r"
            }
            else {
                nl = "\n"
            }
```

```
    }

function placeText()  {
var text1=prompt("Type over this line if you wish", "This is the default →
first line of text")
var text2=prompt("Type over this line if you wish", "This is the default →
second line of text")
var text3=prompt("Type over this line if you wish", "This is the default →
third line of text")
var text4=prompt("Type over this line if you wish", "This is the default →
fourth line of text")
var text5=prompt("Type over this line if you wish", "This is the default →
fifth line of text")
document.text.codes.value= text1 + nl + text2 + nl + text3 + nl + text4 + nl →
+ text5
}
// -->
</SCRIPT>
</HEAD>
<BODY onload=placeText()>
```

We started with the **nl** variable we've just seen, placing the appropriate code into the variable depending on what's in the **appVersion** string. Then, we created a function that runs when the document loads (notice the **onload** event handler calling the function from the last line; we'll learn more about the event handlers in the following chapter).

This function displays five prompt boxes and takes the text you typed (or the default text, if you haven't typed anything) and places it into five variables, **text1** through **text5**. Finally, it writes the text to the **codes** textarea (**document.text.codes.value** means "the **value** held by the **codes** element in the **form** in this **document**"). Notice that it intersperses the **textn** variables with the **nl** variable, to place the line-break code that will make the lines "stack" rather than chain together into one long line.

So remember, many properties are strings and can have the string methods applied to them.

Boolean( ) & Number( )

JavaScript 1.1 (Netscape Navigator 3) added two more built-in objects, **Boolean( )** and **Number( )**. (It also added the **Array( )** object, but see Chapter 9 for information about that one.)

The **Boolean( )** object can be used to convert non-Boolean data to Boolean data, and is created like this:

```
objectname = new Boolean(data)
```

The format of the data with which you initialize the object defines whether the object will contain **true** or **false**. It follows these rules:

- If you create a **Boolean( )** object without providing data, the new object automatically contains **false**.

- If you provide **0**, **null**, the word **false** not in quotation marks, quotation marks that don't enclose anything, or an empty string, it contains **false**.

- If you provide the word **true** (not in quotation marks) or any text within quotation marks, it contains **true**.

You can see a few examples of this in the following example:

Example 11.8

```
<script language="JAVASCRIPT">
<!--
var sBool1 = "any old text"
var sBool2
bBool1 = new Boolean(sBool1)
bBool2 = new Boolean(sBool2)
bBoolEmpty = new Boolean()
bBoolEmptyString = new Boolean("")
bBoolNull = new Boolean(null)
bBoolFalse = new Boolean(false)
bBoolTrue = new Boolean(true)
bBoolFalseString = new Boolean("false")
bBoolZero = new Boolean(0)
bBoolFive = new Boolean(5)


document.write("This object comes from a variable that contains text: <b>" + →
bBool1 + "</b><br>")
document.write("This object comes from a variable with nothing in it: <b>" + →
bBool2 + "</b><br>")
document.write("This object was not given data when created: <b>" + →
bBoolEmpty + "</b><br>")
document.write("This object was given quotation marks with nothing between →
them: <b>" + bBoolEmptyString + "</b><br>")
document.write("This object was given null: <b>" + bBoolNull + "</b><br>") →
document.write("This object was given the word false, not in quotation →
marks: <b>" + bBoolFalse + "</b><br>")
```

```
document.write("This object was given the word true, not in quotation marks: →
<b>" + bBoolTrue+ "</b><br>")
document.write("This object was given the word false, in quotation marks: →
<b>" + bBoolFalseString + "</b><br>")
document.write("This object was given the number 0: <b>" + bBoolZero + " →
</b><br>")
document.write("This object was given the number 5: <b>" + bBoolFive + " →
</b><br>")

//-->
</script>
```

Take a look at the Online Companion, where you'll see the words **true** and **false** displayed according to the type of data you provided. The **Number( )** object, according to the developers, is one that you'll probably rarely need. However, it might come in useful now and again. You could use the **Number ( )** object to store a number, and associate other information with the number using the **prototype** property to create another property of the object (see Chapter 13 for information about **prototype**). You could give the number a name, for example, describing what the number is. Refer to the JavaScript Guide for more information (see Appendix H).

Moving On

Way back in Chapter 3, "First Steps—Scripts, Functions & Comments," you learned about how you get a script to run. Since then, we've been looking at *what* happens when a script runs, but now it's time to return to the *when* question. In the next chapter, we're going to examine the event handlers again. We've used a few of them throughout the book—most notably the **onclick** handler. We want to look at the others, though, and learn a little more about the ones we've used before.

JavaScript Events—
When Are Actions
Carried Out?

How do you make something happen in a JavaScript? We've made a lot happen already, so you know that you can drop a script straight into HTML document to be run as soon as the browser reads it. You also know how to use *event handlers* to run scripts at a particular time. Up to this point, we've mostly used the onclick event handler, which runs a script when the user clicks on a button. In this chapter we're going to look more closely at all the event handlers.

By an *event* we mean something that happens when the user does something: opens or closes the Web document, moves the mouse pointer over something, clicks on something, presses the Tab key, and so on. In some cases events are automatic, such as when a page loads or unloads—that is, when a page is replaced by another Web page.

You'll place event handlers into HTML tags—the tags used to create links and form elements, for instance. You'll use the following basic syntax:

```
<TAG tagattributes eventHandler="JavaScript Code">
```

TAG represents the HTML tag name, while **tagattributes** represents the normal attributes used to create the item. The **eventHandler** is, of course, the name of the JavaScript event handler you want to use. **JavaScript Code** is the JavaScript instruction that you want to carry out when this event occurs.

Each event handler is designed for a specific HTML tag. For instance, the **onload** and **onunload** event handlers are placed into the **<BODY>** tag (you can also place them in the **<IMG>** tag if you are writing scripts for Netscape Navigator 3.0 or later). There's no point putting them elsewhere. Similarly, the **onclick** event handler will only work with the **button**, **checkbox**, **radio**,

reset, and **submit** form elements and with links (**<A HREF=>**). There's no point trying to use the **onclick** event handler with a **text** or **textarea** form element, for instance.

TIP

We've written all event handlers in lowercase: **onclick, onblur, onmouseover,** *and so on. You'll often see these in mixed case:* **onClick, onBlur, onMouseOver.** *You can use whatever case you want when putting an event handler into an HTML tag, as HTML is not case sensitive. However, a new JavaScript feature (added to Netscape Navigator 3.0 (JavaScript 1.1)) allows you to modify event handlers from scripts. As JavaScript is case sensitive, you have to use the correct case when naming event handlers in scripts—and the correct case is all lowercase . . . at least for scripts that will run in Navigator 3. This changed again with JavaScript 1.2, though; now you can use mixed case. By mixed case we mean you could write, for example,* **onclick** *or* **onClick.** *You could not, however, use something like* **OnClick** *or* **Onclick** *or* **OnCliCK.**

Should you use mixed case, though? Probably not. If you use mixed case the handlers will work fine in Navigator 4, but won't work in Navigator 3, so it's a good idea to stick with lowercase event handlers.

The Event Handlers

There are nine event handlers available to you. Here are their names and the event that sets off each one:

- **onblur**   When focus moves away from a form element.
- **onchange**   When focus moves away from a form element, after the contents of the element have changed.
- **onclick**   When the user clicks on a form element or link.
- **onfocus**   When focus moves to a form element.
- **onload**   When the Web page loads (or when an image loads, if using Netscape Navigator 3.0 or later—JavaScript 1.1).
- **onmouseover**   When the user points at a link with the mouse pointer.
- **onselect**   When the user selects something in a form element.
- **onsubmit**   When the user submits a form.
- **onunload**   When the current Web page is replaced with another (or, with Netscape 3.0 or later, when an image loads).

Four new event handlers were added to JavaScript 1.1 (Navigator 3):

- **onabort**   When the user aborts an image load.

- **onerror**   When an image is unable to load.

- **onmouseout**   When the mouse pointer moves away from an area of an image map or from a link.

- **onreset**   When the user clicks on a Reset button in a form.

More were added to JavaScript 1.2 (Navigator 4):

- **ondragdrop**   The JavaScript is executed when the user drops something (a file, for instance), onto the Navigator window.

- **onkeydown**   The JavaScript is executed when the user presses a key.

- **onkeypress**   The JavaScript is executed when the user holds down a key (this event is always preceded by an **onkeydown** event).

- **onkeyup**   The JavaScript is executed when the user releases a key.

- **onmousedown**   The JavaScript is executed when the user presses a mouse button.

- **onmousemove**   The JavaScript is executed when the user moves the mouse cursor.

- **onmouseup**   The JavaScript is executed when the user releases a mouse button.

- **onmove**   The JavaScript is executed when the user or a JavaScript moves a window or frame.

- **onresize**   The JavaScript is executed when the user or a JavaScript resizes a window or frame.

Now let's take a detailed look at the different event handlers available to you.

onblur

This event handler is used to carry out an event on a *blur*. A blur is the event in which the *focus* moves away from the form element using the event handler. In other words, when the user does something to move away from the form element onto another by clicking on another form element—or even simply clicking outside the form somewhere—or by pressing Tab.

The **onblur** event handler works with the selection list (**<SELECT>**), multi-line text input (**<TEXTAREA>**), and text input (**<INPUT TYPE="TEXT">**) components. You might use **onblur** to confirm that the user has placed the correct information into a form. For instance, look at the following example, which is in two parts, a function definition in the HEAD and a function call in the BODY. First the function:

Example 12.1

```
function testAge(form) {
var nAge = form.ageBox.value;
    if (nAge >= 18)  {
          if (nAge >=100)  {
               alert("You entered an age of " + nAge +". Are you sure  →
this is correct?")
          }
    }
    else  {
          alert("You entered an age of " + nAge + ". You must be 18 or  →
over to use this service!")
      }
}
```

As you can see, the function is called **testAge**. We are passing information to it from a form. We take **form.ageBox**—the value typed into the text box in the form—and place it into the **nAge** variable. Then we use an **if** statement to check the value held by the variable (the age originally typed into the form, as you'll see in a moment). If the number is **18** or over, we check to see if it's **100** or over. If it is, we display an Alert box that asks the user if the age is correct. If it isn't **100** or over, we do nothing; the age must be okay. If the number is less than **18**, though, we run the second **else** instruction, displaying an Alert box warning the user that he must be 18 or over (see Figure 12-1).

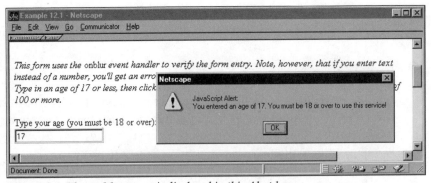

Figure 12-1: The **onblur** *event is displayed in this Alert box.*

> **TIP**
>
> *There's a problem with **onblur**. If the user swaps to another application, then swaps back, the focus changes so the user may see a message at an inappropriate time.*

In the body of the document we created this form:

```
<FORM>
Type your age (you must be 18 or over): <BR>
<INPUT TYPE="text" NAME="ageBox" onblur="testAge(this.form)">
</FORM>
```

As you can see, this form only has one element, a text box. The user types something into the box. Notice the **onblur** event handler. When the user moves the focus away from this element, the **onblur** instruction runs, passing the contents of the form to the **testAge** function. Anything the user does to move focus sets off the **onblur** event handler: pressing the Tab or Enter keys, clicking elsewhere in the Web document, using the Back or Forward commands, using the history list or bookmarks, or clicking on a toolbar button or in the Location box.

> **TIP**
>
> *Pressing the Tab key only sets off an event handler if there is more than one form element. If there's no element to Tab into, the event handler won't work. Other ways of setting off the event handler will work, though.*

Try this example at the Online Companion. You'll see that if you enter an age below 18 or above 99 and then click somewhere out of the text box, an Alert message appears. Type anything from 18 to 99, though, and nothing happens when you click outside the box.

> **TIP**
>
> *There's a problem with this script. If the user enters text instead of a number, an error message appears. We can fix the problem using the **parseFloat** function (or **parseInt** in a later version of JavaScript—it's not functioning correctly in Netscape Navigator 3.0 or earlier. You can see an example of how we used **parseFloat** later in this chapter (Example 12.3) and when we discuss form validation in Chapter 17, "Forms & JavaScript."*

onchange

The **onchange** event handler is similar to **onblur**, except that something must have changed in the form element before the user moves focus from the element—the user must have selected something different from the selection list, or must have entered or modified text in the text box or textarea elements. If you use **onchange** and the user moves from the element without changing anything, nothing happens.

Again, this event handler will work with the selection list (**<SELECT>**), multi-line text input (**<TEXTAREA>**), and text input (**<INPUT TYPE="TEXT">**) components.

Here's a simple illustration. We've modified the previous function call by placing a default value representing an age of 25 in the **ageBox**. And we added a line in the function itself to display an Alert message, even if you change the age from 25 to another valid one of 18 to 99.

Example 12.2

```
<FORM>
Type your age (you must be 18 or over): <BR>
<INPUT TYPE="text" NAME="ageBox" VALUE="25" onchange="testAge(this.form)">
</FORM>
```

As you can see, we've placed a value in the text box (**25**), and we've used the **onchange** event handler instead of the **onblur** to call **testAge**.

You'll find, when you use this example, that if you click inside the text box and then outside the text box nothing happens. But if you click inside, change the number to something under 18 or over 100, then click outside, an Alert box will appear.

> **TIP**
>
> *In some browsers **onchange** might work a little prematurely. It might be set off as soon as you select something in a selection box, rather than after you move focus from the selection box. You can't rely on this as a feature, though, because in some browsers the user must still move focus away from the selection box.*

onclick

The **onclick** event handler can be used to execute JavaScript when the user clicks on something: a button (**<INPUT TYPE="BUTTON">**), a check box

(**<INPUT TYPE="CHECKBOX">**), an option (radio) button (**<INPUT TYPE="RADIO">**), a link (**<A HREF=>**), a Reset button (**<INPUT TYPE="RESET">**), or a Submit button (**<INPUT TYPE="SUBMIT">**). We've used dozens of **onclick** examples throughout this book, so we won't look at a basic onclick example. However, starting with Netscape Navigator 3.0 (Java-Script 1.1) you can add confirmations to onclick handlers. For instance:

Example 12.3

```
<A HREF="adult2.htm" onclick="return confirm('Remember, this page is for  →
adults only. If you are under 18 or living in an area where such images are  →
illegal, please do not continue. Click on Cancel to stop the transfer, or OK  →
to go to the page.')">The Naughty Bits</a>
```

If the user clicks on this link, a **confirm** box opens. If the user clicks OK, the link will work; if he clicks Cancel, the link *won't* work. Notice that you must place **return** and a space before **confirm( )**.

onfocus

The **onfocus** event handler is the exact opposite of **onblur**. It carries out an action when the focus is moving *to* the element, not away from it. It works with the same form elements: the selection list (**<SELECT>**), multi-line text input (**<TEXTAREA>**), and text input (**<INPUT TYPE="TEXT">**) components. How do you move focus to an element? There are only two ways: by pressing the Tab key or by clicking inside the element.

There's a problem with using **onfocus**, though. You can get stuck in a loop. Here's how. You click on the element and the script associated with the **onfocus** event handler runs. If that script does something that moves the focus from the form element, then after the script has finished and focus moves back to the element, the **onfocus** event handler runs again, and you are in a loop. The script runs again, finishes, and returns focus, so the script runs again. And so on.

You have to be very careful about using **onfocus**. Only use it if you are absolutely sure that you have a script that cannot go wrong. Test it repeatedly for everything that could possibly go wrong: the user enters something too long or too short, text is entered instead of a number, the user switches programs and then returns to the previous program, and so on. If you create a program that has an error-message-producing bug at an **onfocus** event handler, you'll have some very unhappy users. The error message will appear; the user will click on OK; the focus will move back to the form element, so the error message will reappear . . . here's our loop!

So you can only use **onfocus** to do something that doesn't change focus away from the element, and you can only use it with a script that can't go wrong. You'll often find it's easier to use **onblur** to carry out an event when the focus is moving away from the previous element onto this one—although that only works if the user is working through the form in the correct order, of course, which cannot usually be assumed.

Here's one example of an **onfocus** script:

Example 12.4

```
function runTotal(form) {
    var nNum1 = parseFloat(form.num1.value)
    var nNum2 = parseFloat(form.num2.value)
    form.total.value = nNum1 + nNum2
}
```

We've used this script to place the sum of two values into a text box. The **runTotal** function is passed information from the **form**. We've created two variables, **nNum1** and **nNum2**. We used the **parseFloat** built-in function (which we looked at in Chapter 6, "Conditionals & Loops—Making Decisions & Controlling Scripts") to convert the values from the forms into numbers. Remember, anything entered into a form is regarded as a string. The **parseFloat** function will take that string and, if possible, convert it to a numerical format—so **nNum1** and **nNum2** are numerical, even though the values in **num1** and **num2** are strings.

Then we add **nNum1** to **nNum2** and place the result into the form's **total** field.

Here's the form we used:

```
<FORM>
Type number 1: <INPUT TYPE="text" NAME="num1" VALUE="0"><BR>
Type number 2: <INPUT TYPE="text" NAME="num2" VALUE="0"><BR>
Click in this box to see the total: <INPUT TYPE="text" NAME="total"
onfocus="runTotal(this.form)">
</FORM>
```

The user enters numbers into the first two text boxes. Then he tabs to the last box (the **total** text box) or clicks inside it. The **onfocus** event handler calls the **runTotal** function, passing the information from the form to the function. The function then replaces the contents of the **total** box with the result of the addition, as you can see in Figure 12-2.

Figure 12-2: Simply tabbing into the last text box causes the **onfocus** event handler to add the numbers.

onload

Using the **onload** event handler causes the browser to execute the script when the page is loaded into the browser (specifically, once the browser has finished loading the page and any frames). This event handler can only be placed into the **<BODY>** or **<FRAMESET>** tags in this format:

```
<BODY onload="the script you want to run">
```

A common use for this event handler is to display an opening message, such as this:

Example 12.5

```
<SCRIPT LANGUAGE="JavaScript">
<!--
function confirmEntry( ) {
    if (confirm("As you have a JavaScript browser, you can go to our →
JavaScript enabled site. Click on OK to do so, or click on Cancel to →
remain at this (non-JavaScript) page.")){
            location='12-5a.htm'
            }
}
//-->
</SCRIPT>
</HEAD>
<BODY onload="confirmEntry( )">
```

We've created a function called **confirmEntry( )**. This function uses an **if** statement to display the Confirm dialog box. If the user clicks on the OK button, the first statement after the { is run (**location='12-5a.htm'**). In other words, if the user clicks on OK, the browser is redirected to another Web page. If the user clicks on Cancel, though, no action is taken.

Then notice how we call the function—using the **onload** event handler in the **<BODY>** tag (you can put it anywhere in the tag, before or after other attributes). Notice also that the instructions after = must be in quotation marks.

More recent versions of JavaScript—Netscape Navigator 3.0 and later (JavaScript 1.1)—also allow you to place the **onload** event handler in the **<IMG>** tag, so you can do something when an image loads.

TIP

*There's another way to get a script to run when the page loads, of course—simply place the script in the HEAD. Unlike the **onload** event, though—which loads the entire page and frames and* then *runs the script—any script in the HEAD will run* before *the Web document is loaded, which may be useful in some cases.*

onmouseover

Simply pointing at a link that contains the **onmouseover** event handler runs the script. This is commonly used to display messages in the status bar. However, as with **onfocus**, there are significant problems with **onmouseover**.

First, many people find those cute little status-bar messages rather irritating. Unfortunately they block the view of the URL, and many Web users *want* to see the URL when they point at a link. It often gives them information that helps them decide whether or not to click on the link. If you block their view, they might not be too happy.

TIP

There might be times when you want *to hide a link from users. I've just seen a site that has a series of multiple-choice questions. Each possible answer has a link to another page—the wrong answers link to a document called **wrong.html** . . . which means that the user can quickly see which answers are wrong! JavaScript could be used to hide this fact.*

The other problem is that, although you can run any script you want from an **onmouseover** event, it might not be a good idea to do so. The user might not realize that the mouse pointer was over the link and, when something happens unexpectedly, might wonder what on earth is happening. For instance, let's say that you've used **onmouseover** on a link to open a Prompt dialog box. The user isn't at your Web page right now, but was a few minutes ago. The user employs the keyboard shortcut for the Back command to move back through the history list, eventually arriving at your site—where the mouse pointer just happens to be sitting over the link with an **onmouseover** event built in. The Prompt dialog box opens automatically, and the user thinks, "What did I do?"

Still, here's an example of using the **onmouseover** event. We've already gone through an example that uses status bar messages (see Example 2.9 from Chapter 2), so we'll do just what we said you should beware of doing: we'll use the **onmouseover** event handler to open an Alert box.

Example 12.6

```
<SCRIPT LANGUAGE="JavaScript">
<!--
function confirmMove( ) {
    if (confirm("Are you sure you want to use this link? I really don't →
think you should. Well, if you insist, click on OK and I'll take you to →
the referenced page. Otherwise click on Cancel and leave the link alone!"))
    {
        location='12-6a.htm'
        }
}
//-->
</SCRIPT>
```

First, we created a function called **confirmMove( )**. This is very similar to the previous example. It uses an **if** statement which uses the built-in function **confirm** to decide whether to display another page (**12-6a.htm**) or do nothing, returning the user to the current page. Next we created this link:

```
<A HREF="12-6A.HTM" onmouseover="confirmMove( )">Click right here. <I>Not!
</I></A>
```

The **onmouseover** event handler runs the **confirmMove( )** function. So, when the user points at the link, the Alert box opens (as you can see in Figure 12-3). If the user clicks on OK, the browser loads **12-6a.htm**. If the user clicks on Cancel, the box closes and the user returns to the current document.

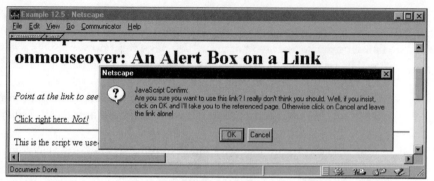

Figure 12-3: Simply pointing at the link displays this Alert box. Clicking on OK takes the user to another page.

You should note, however, another problem with **onmouseover**: You can get into the same sort of loop that you can get into with the **onfocus** event handler. You might try this for yourself. Copy the page containing this example to your hard disk. *Don't* copy the file to which the **confirm** function forwards you. Then try pointing at the link. You'll find that the Alert box opens, but when you click on the OK button it opens again . . . and keeps opening over and over. Your only way out is by clicking on Cancel several times. So you'd better make sure that the document you are linking to is always available!

onselect

The **onselect** event handler makes the browser execute the JavaScript when the user selects text in a text (**<INPUT TYPE="TEXT">**) or textarea (**<TEXTAREA>**) form element. This is probably a fairly limited use. The problem is that right now there's no way for a script to grab the text that the user selected.

Here's a very quick and simple example that shows the handler at work, though:

Example 12.7

```
<FORM>
<INPUT TYPE="TEXT" VALUE="Select part of this text. Select part of this
text. Select part of this text." SIZE="50" onselect="alert('That\'s it, you
highlighted something.')">
</FORM>
```

In theory when the user selects any of the text, an Alert box will open. Right now, though, **onselect** is still in development and probably won't work on your browser.

onsubmit

The **onsubmit** event handler executes the script when the user clicks on a Submit button to submit a form. This is typically used for form validation. The event handler isn't placed in the Submit tag, though, it's placed in the **<FORM>** tag, like this:

```
<FORM NAME="formname" onsubmit="instructions">
```

When the user clicks on the Submit button, the **onsubmit** instructions run. For instance, here's how you could display an Alert box when submitting a form:

Example 12.8

```
<FORM NAME="submittest" onsubmit="alert('Thanks for your information; →
remember to check back with us next week.')">
Type your age (you must be 18 or over): <BR>
<INPUT TYPE="text" NAME="ageBox"><P><BR>
<INPUT TYPE="SUBMIT">
</FORM>
```

That's simple; the **onsubmit** event handler simply calls the **alert** function when the Submit button is clicked (**<INPUT TYPE="SUBMIT">**).

But the **onsubmit** event handler can be used for more than this; it's also a handy way to verify a form's input. You can use it to send the information from the form to a function, which can then verify that the information has been entered correctly. Then, if the data is not correct, the form will *not* submit the information.

For instance, remember the **onblur** event handler we used earlier in this chapter when we validated the input of a text box? Let's do the same thing, using the **onsubmit** event handler:

Example 12.9

```
function testAge( ) {
var nAge = document.age.ageBox.value;
     if (nAge >= 18) {
         if (nAge >=100) {
              alert("You entered an age of " + nAge +". Enter an age from
18 to 99.")
```

```
                        return false
           }
           else {
              return true
           }
      }
      else {
         alert("You entered an age of " + nAge + ". You must be 18 or over →
to use this service!")
         return false
      }
```

This is very similar to the **onblur** example we used, except that we are using **return false** and **return true**—if the user enters an incorrect age, we return **false**; if the age is okay, we return **true**.

Then we have this form:

```
<FORM NAME="age" onsubmit="return testAge( )">
Type your age (you must be 18 or over): <BR>
<INPUT TYPE="text" NAME="ageBox"><P>
<INPUT TYPE="Submit" NAME="Submit">
</FORM>
```

You can see that the **onsubmit** instructions are **"return testAge( )"**. This means, "call the **testAge** function, and return a value." Either **true** or **false** is returned. If **false** is returned the form is not submitted.

Although this isn't connected to an actual CGI script in our Online Companion, you can still see it at work (see Figure 12-4). Notice that if you enter an incorrect number, you see an Alert box. When you click on the OK button, the number in the text box remains. But if you enter a correct number, the page "flashes" and the number is removed—it's been submitted.

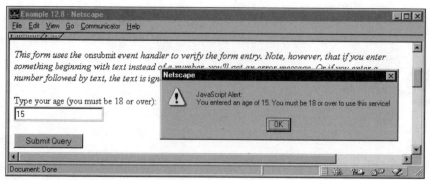

Figure 12-4: We used the **onsubmit** *event handler to call a function that verifies the form input; if the input's incorrect, the form is not submitted.*

onunload

The **onunload** event handler runs when the user does something to load another page into the browser—that is, when he unloads the current page. The user can click on a link to load a new page, enter a URL into the Location text bar and press Enter, use the Back and Forward commands, or select a page from the history list or bookmarks, for instance. Anything that replaces the current page with another page will cause the **onunload** event handler to run.

The **onunload** handler is placed in the **<BODY>** or **<FRAMESET>** tags, just as with the **onload** event handler. The only difference is that the script for **onunload** is placed in memory and does not run until the page is unloaded. However, there are currently limits to what can be accomplished with **onunload**. You can open another window, for instance, but you can't put anything into it. In fact, if you try to do so, you might crash your browser.

The **onunload** event handler currently has a lot of problems, and is really only useful for displaying the sort of goodbye message we saw in Example 2.8 in Chapter 2. This event simply can't do much—you can't use objects and, in fact, trying to do so can make the browser crash.

> **TIP**
>
> *Remember also that when the user reloads a document, the current document is unloaded, so the* **onunload** *event handler runs.*

Here's an example of this **onunload** weirdness:

Example 12.10

```
<SCRIPT LANGUAGE="JavaScript">
<!--
function Bye( ) {
var sAname = document.AccountForm.account.value
    alert("Please make a note of your account name (" + sAname + "), and →
remember to bookmark this Web page");
}
//-->
</SCRIPT>
</HEAD>
<BODY onunload="Bye( )">
```

This is a simple little function. The value held in the **account** text box of the **AccountForm** is placed into the **sAname** variable. Then an Alert box opens and displays a message, including the value in **sAname**. Notice also that the **onunload** event handler should run the **Bye( )** function when you load a different page.

Now, here's the text box and a button:

```
<FORM NAME="AccountForm">
Type your account name: <INPUT TYPE="TEXT" NAME="account">
<INPUT TYPE="BUTTON" NAME="TEST" VALUE="TEST" onclick="Bye( )">
</FORM>
```

You can see the text box named account (the value of which we refer to as **document.AccountForm.account.value** in the **Bye( )** function). The button also calls the **Bye( )** function. Why? Well, try this in the Online Companion. Open the page, then type something into the text box. Don't click on the button, though. Open another page—click on the Back button, for instance. The Alert box might not appear (if you are using Netscape Navigator 3.0 or later it probably will; in earlier versions it won't). In fact, your browser might actually crash.

Now return to the page and click on the button. This time the Alert box *will* appear. Now leave the document. Again, the Alert box appears, with the text from the text box included in the message.

What has happened? Clicking on the button sets the value in the **sAname** variable, so when you unloaded the **Bye( )** function it already had the value. On the other hand, when you *didn't* click on the button, the objects had been destroyed, so **Bye( )** was unable to get past the first line of the script. As you can see, the **onunload** event handler has problems that can really limit what you can do with it. Certain **onunload** bugs have been fixed in more recent versions of Netscape Navigator.

The New Event Handlers

A number of event handlers were added to JavaScript with Netscape Navigator 3.0 (JavaScript 1.1), and a few modifications were made:

- **onabort** The JavaScript is executed if the user stops an image from loading (by clicking on the Stop button or a link, for instance). This works with the **<IMG>** tag.

- **onblur** This event handler now works with windows and framesets. For instance, you can run scripts when a particular window or frame loses focus. It also works with **button, checkbox, fileupload, radio, reset,** and **submit** objects.

- **onclick**   This event handler now allows you to add a **confirm** box; the action is not carried out unless the user clicks a Confirmation box's OK button. (This won't work for buttons, but should work for links, check boxes, and radio buttons.)

- **onerror**   The JavaScript is executed if an image can not be loaded correctly, perhaps because it's corrupted or the URL specifying the image is incorrect, or if the loading of a document creates a JavaScript error. This event handler works with the **<IMG>** tag. It can also be used in a script to associate it with the **window** object.

- **onfocus**   As with **onblur**, this event handler now works with windows, framesets, and the **button, checkbox, fileupload, radio, reset**, and **submit** objects.

- **onload**   This now works with the **<IMG>** tag. You can run scripts when an image loads.

- **onmouseout**   This event handler occurs when the mouse pointer is moved away from a hotspot on an image map or from a link.

- **onmouseover**   This has been modified; you can now add an onmouseover event handler to the **<AREA>** tag, to define what happens when the user points at a hotspot on an image map.

- **onreset**   This works when the user clicks a form's Reset button or when you use the form's **reset( )** method.

Should you use these? Perhaps not immediately. Remember, you are writing scripts that will be used by visitors to your site. Until most people are using a version of browser that has these event handlers, they won't do you much good.

onabort

The **onabort** event handler operates if the user aborts the loading of an image, either by clicking the browser's Stop button or by taking some other kind of action to load another page (clicking a link, clicking the Back or Forward button, using the history list, and so on). For instance, in Example 12.11 we've added **onabort** to this image tag:

Example 12.11

```
<IMG SRC="bell.gif" WIDTH=144 HEIGHT=119 onabort="doNotGo( )">
```

If you load this page, but click the Stop button before the image has had time to completely load, the **doNotGo( )** function runs:

```
function doNotGo( ) {
    if (confirm("'Ere, 'ang on, you haven't seen everything yet! Why not let
the image finish loading before you leave! Click OK to continue loading."))
{
        history.go(0)
        }
}
```

This function displays a message and then, if the user clicks the **confirm** box's OK button, uses the **history.go(0)** method to reload the page.

onerror

The **onerror** event handler doesn't handle all types of errors, only errors related to images (corrupted or missing images) and JavaScript errors. It has no effect on most browser errors. It can be used in a couple of ways: within the **<IMG>** tag or in a script.

In Example 12.12 we use **onerror** to display an **alert** box. As you can see, the **<IMG>** tag refers to a file named **null.gif**, but **null.gif** does not exist:

Example 12.12

```
<img src="null.gif" onerror="alert('Oops, the picture is no longer
there.')">
```

This displays an **alert** box. If the image *were* there, but in some way damaged so that the browser couldn't load it, the event handler would also run.

You can also attach the **onerror** event handler to the window itself, so that it runs when the browser generates a JavaScript error. In Example 12.13 we've intentionally created an error condition by calling a nonexistent function from a button, but if you use this example (in a compatible browser, that is) you won't see an error message. That's because we have this simple script in the **HEAD**:

Example 12.13

```
<SCRIPT>
window.onerror=null
</SCRIPT>
```

We've assigned **null** to **onerror**, which tells the browser to suppress error messages. (Notice that **null** does not have quotation marks around it.) This might be useful if you'd like to make sure that visitors to your site who are using old versions of JavaScript browsers don't see error messages caused by your more recent JavaScripts.

In Example 12.14 we have both suppressed the normal error messages—using a different technique this time—and added a message of our own:

Example 12.14

```
<SCRIPT>
window.onerror=runError
function runError( )    {
        alert("Uh, oh, you've encountered a JavaScript error. Do you have →
the latest version of Netscape Navigator? If not go to http:// →
www.netscape.com/ and download it.")
        return true
}
</SCRIPT>
```

You can see that we've started with **window.onerror=runError**. This is defining a function named **runError** and associating it with the **onerror** event handler. On the next line we then fully define the function; it displays an **alert** box. Finally, we have **return true**. This is what suppresses the normal (ugly) error-message boxes.

You could use **onerror** to set up your own error-handling system, grabbing error data and formatting it into an error report. The Netscape JavaScript documentation has an example of this.

onmouseout

The **onmouseout** event handler can be used with links and client-side image maps. It goes in either the **<A HREF=>** tag or the **<AREA>** tag. Here's an example in which we make something happen when the user moves the mouse pointer away from a hotspot on an image:

Example 12.15

```
<img src="bell.gif" usemap="#imagemap" alt="Image Map" height=119 width=144
border=0>
<map name="imagemap">
<area shape=rect coords="1,  1, 73,  119" href="nowhere1.htm"
onmouseout="alert('You have just missed a hotspot--go back if you want to go
to the nowhere1.htm file.')">
```

```
<area shape=rect coords="72, 3, 142, 119" href="nowhere2.htm" →
onmouseout="alert('You have just missed a hotspot-go back if you want to go
to the nowhere2.htm file')">
</map>
```

We actually have two hotspots on this image (if you've created client-side image maps you'll know that the **<AREA>** tag is used to define the area covered by the hotspot). Each hotspot has an **onmouseout** event handler in it. As you'll see when you use the example, if you point at a hotspot and then move the mouse away, the message box opens.

onreset

The new **onreset** event handler runs when the user clicks a form's Reset button, though the event handler is placed inside the **<FORM>** tag, not in the Reset button's tag. Here's a simple example of **onreset** in action.

Example 12.16

```
<form onreset="alert('The form has been cleared and returned to its →
original state.')">
<input type="text" value="Here's the text" size="20">
<input type="reset">
```

When the user clicks on the Reset button the **onreset** handler displays the alert box, informing the user that the form has been reset. Wouldn't it be nice if you could add a confirmation message, though, to make sure that the user really wants to reset the form? Well, you can't do that directly, because once the Reset button has been clicked there's no way to abort the Reset action. However, you could fake a Reset button, like this:

Example 12.17

```
<form onreset="alert('The form has been cleared and returned to its →
original state.')">
<input type="text" value="Here's the text" size="20">
<input type="button" value="Reset" onclick="confirmReset( )">
</form>
```

You can see that this is not a real Reset button; we've used **<input type="button">** instead of **<input type="reset">**. It's just an ordinary button, but we've made it work by adding an **onclick** event handler: **onclick="confirmReset( )">**. This calls the **confirmReset( )** function:

```
<SCRIPT LANGUAGE="JAVASCRIPT">
function confirmReset( )        {
        if (confirm("Are you sure you want to clear this form?"))    {
        document.forms[0].reset( )
           }
}
</SCRIPT>
```

This function displays a confirm box asking the user if he wants to reset the form. If the user clicks OK, the script uses **document.forms[0].reset( )**. That is, it uses the form's **reset( )** method to reset the form. The **reset( )** method is a way that you can use JavaScript to simulate a click on a Reset button. Note, by the way, that this example still uses the **onreset** event handler. Look back at the form and you'll see

```
<form onreset="alert('The form has been cleared and returned to its original
state.')">.
```

The **onreset** event handler is activated by the **reset( )** method, just as it would be if a Reset button had been clicked.

Resetting Event Handlers

Netscape Navigator 3.0 (JavaScript 1.1) also allows you to reset event handlers from scripts. You can, for instance, have several functions that you want to use from an **onclick** event handler. You can use a script to assign a particular function to that event handler in a particular situation: **document.Form1.Button1.onclick = function3** means "assign **function3** to the **onclick** event handler in **Button1**, in **Form1**." Notice by the way that we have **function3**, not **function3( )**. If we used **function3( )** at this point in the script the browser would try to actually call **function3( )**; all we want to do is assign **function3( )** to the event handler, so we drop the parentheses.

Let's look at an example that is based on Example 12.3. This example has a form that can be reset and a "fake" Reset button. But we have two different messages that can be displayed. First, remember that the fake button uses an **onclick** event, like this:

Example 12.18

```
<input name="resetButton" type="button" value="Reset" onclick="confirmReset(
)">
```

This button uses onclick to call **confirmReset( )**. But we can change that **onclick** handler to call a different function. We've added these two buttons:

```
<input type="button" value="Change Message to Snotty"
onclick="document.forms[0].resetButton.onclick=confirmReset2"><br>
<input type="button" value="Change Message to Polite"
onclick="document.forms[0].resetButton.onclick=confirmReset">
```

If you click the top button, the **onclick** handler in the button named **resetButton** is reset to call the **confirmReset2( )** function (remember, we left off the **( )** because we're not calling the function, we're just assigning it to **resetButton**'s **onclick** handler). If you click the lower button the **onclick** event handler is set back to **confirmReset( )**.

The event Object

Starting with version 1.2 (Navigator 4), Javascript provides **event** objects to give event handlers more power and a more systematic design. The **event** object is very specialized; in fact, the only place where you can even refer to it is in the event-handler strings that you attach to links and other HTML objects. For example:

Example 12.19

```
<A HREF="Javascript:void(null)" onclick="alert('You clicked at ' + event.x +
', ' + event.y)"> This is a basic onclick link. </A>
```

This simple link generates an alert message using two properties of the event object, **event.x** and **event.y**. The **x** and **y** properties give the horizontal and vertical position at which the mouse was positioned when you clicked on the link.

Obviously, you can't put very much Javascript code into a link tag, so the most common way to use **event** is to immediately pass it to some function. This function becomes your custom event handler. So, tags such as these . . .

Example 12.20

```
<FORM>
<INPUT TYPE="button" VALUE="Open Window" onclick="handle(event)">
</FORM>

<A HREF="Javascript:void(null)" onmouseover="handle(event)"> This is an
onmouseover link. Point anywhere in this link and the event information will
be passed to the function. Point anywhere in this link and the event
information will be passed to the function. Point anywhere in this link and
the event information will be passed to the function.</A>
```

. . . can grab **event** object information and pass it to a handler function. Note that **handle(event)** means "pass the **event** information to the **handle** function. You could then have a function like this:

Example 12.20

```
function handle(e)  {
    propwin =
window.open("","win","width=350,height=400,scrollbars=1,resizable=1,alwaysRaised")
    propwin.focus( )
    propwin.document.open( )
    propwin.document.write("<form><input type='button' Value='Close this
Window' onclick='self.close( )'></form>")
    propwin.document.write("The event handler received this type of
event:<BR><B>" + e.type + "</B><P>")
    var prop;
    for(prop in e) {
      propwin.document.writeln("  " + prop + " = " + e[prop] +
"<BR>" );
    }
}
```

This example takes the information from the **event** object, and passes it to the handle function. The function creates a window with a button at the top (it also puts focus on the window (**propwin.focus( )**), in case information is written to the window when it's already open. It opens the "document stream" to the window (**propwin.document.open( )**), then begins writing information to the window. (Don't worry about these window techniques right now; we'll be covering them in Chapter 15.) The function uses the **document.write( )** method to write the **type** property of the event object to the window: **e.type** means, "the **type** property of **e**," and we've specified that **e** holds the **event** object (**function handle(e)**).

The function then creates a variable called **prop**, and uses a **for** loop to go through each of the properties in **e** (the **event** object) and write them to the page: **for(prop in e)** is a specialized form of the **for** loop, intended for use in finding out the properties of an object. The use of the word **in** means that it will get each of the properties of the object. Then **+ prop + " = " + e[prop]** means that it will write the property name followed by = followed by the value held by that property.

Note that one function can be used to handle many different events. The **type** property allows the function to find out what kind of event has occurred.

The **event** object has quite a number of properties:

Property	Description
data	An array of strings representing URLs passed by the **ondragdrop** event handler.
height	The height of a window or frame.
layerX	A number that usually specifies the cursor's horizontal position in pixels, relative to the document layer in which the event occured. For a resize event, this number specifies the width of the resized object.
layerY	A number that usually specifies the cursor's vertical position in pixels, relative to the document layer in which the event occured. For a resize event, this number specifies the height of the resized object.
modifiers	A number containing bit values that indicate whether keys such as Alt or Shift were pressed (see "Mask Values," below).
pageX	A number that specifies the cursor's horizontal position in pixels, relative to the Web page in which the event occured.
pageY	A number that specifies the cursor's vertical position in pixels, relative to the Web page in which the event occured.
screenX	A number that specifies the cursor's horizontal position in pixels, relative to the top left corner of the computer screen.
screenY	A number that specifies the cursor's vertical position in pixels, relative to the top left corner of the computer screen.
target	A link's target if the event is run from a hypertext link.
type	A string that identifies the type of event.
which	For keyboard events, a number giving the ASCII code for the pressed key. For mouse events, this property is **1** for the left button, or **3** for the right button.
width	The width of a window or frame.
x	Provided for compatibility with earlier versions; use **screenX (onmove)** or **width (onresize)** instead.
y	Provided for compatibility with earlier versions; use **screenY (onmove)** or **height (onresize)** instead.

Note, however, that not all properYWes are useful for every type of event. For example, when an **onkeypress** event is passed to your program, its **x** and **y** parameters will always be the location of the upper-left corner of the input field; they do not show the actual location of the cursor. Your handler function can always check the **type** property to find out what kind of event it is handling; then it will know which properties are useful. The properties used for each event type are listed below. (At the time of publication this doesn't all work quite correctly; either bugs will be fixed, or this table may change.)

Event type	Properties used
onclick	layerX, layerY, pageX, pageY, screenX, screenY, which
ondragdrop	data
onkeydown onkeypress onkeyup onmousedown onmouseup onmousemove onmouseout	layerX, layerY, pageX, pageY, screenX, screenY, which, modifiers
onmouseover	layerX, layerY, pageX, pageY, screenX, screenY
onmove	screenX, screenY (x and y in earlier versions)
onresize	width, height (x and y in earlier versions)
Note: all events have the **type** property.	

Mask Values

Besides **type**, the **modifiers** property also provides some important information about the event. To work with this property you will use a set of *mask values*, values that are provided as properties of the **Event** object. Note the upper case **E**: **event** and **Event** are two different objects. **Event** is a holder for a number of mask values, as listed below:

Name	Meaning
ALT_MASK	For keyboard events, this indicates that the Alt key was held by the user.
CONTROL_MASK	For keyboard events, this indicates that the Ctrl key was held by the user.
SHIFT-MASK	For keyboard events, this indicates that the Shift key was held by the user.
META_MASK	For keyboard events, this indicates that the Meta key was held by the user.
Note that the mask names are all uppercase.	

To use a mask you test the modifiers value with what's known as a *bitwise-and* operation (using **&**, the ampersand character). For example, in a handler for keyboard events you could do this:

```
function getKey(e) {                              // e is the event object
    if (e.modifiers & Event.SHIFT_MASK)  {
      alert("You pressed a Shift-key.")
    }
}
```

The **getKey( )** function is taking the information from the **event** object, and using an **if** statement to determine whether the **alert** box should be displayed. The information inside the **if** parentheses—**e.modifiers & Event.SHIFT_MASK**—is a little complicated, and is based on rather confusing binary arithmetic. Just remember that **if (e.modifiers & Event.SHIFT_MASK)** means "return **true** if the Shift key was held by the user." You could also say, for instance, **if (e.modifiers & Event.ALT_MASK)**, meaning "return **true** if the Alt key was held by the user."

Event Capturing

Another new feature in Navigator 4 is event capturing, a feature that gives you lots of flexibility in handling events. Event capturing is managed by four methods that are available for **window** and **document** objects:

Method	Description
captureEvents( )	Enables capturing of events.
releaseEvents( )	Disables capturing of events.
routeEvent( )	Allows an event to be passed to any other assigned handlers.
handleEvent( )	Passes an event to a specific handler.

This is a rather advanced operation. For casual users, the thing it's handy for is to get control of events that are not normally passed to a script. For example, you might want to have your script do something when the user presses the right mouse button, which in Navigator normally pops up a menu. For instance, this statement . . .

```
document.captureEvents(Event.CLICK)
```

. . . allows the **document** object to receive all click events. Note that we have used the **Event** object again. The mask value, in this case **CLICK**, specifies which event is to be captured (again, the mask value must be uppercase). If you wanted to capture more types of events, you could write:

```
document.captureEvents(Event.CLICK | Event.MOUSEUP | Event.MOUSEDOWN)
```

In this case several mask values have been combined by the *bitwise-or* operation (| , the vertical bar character). The possible mask values are **MOUSEDOWN, MOUSEUP, MOUSEOVER, MOUSEOUT, MOUSEMOVE, CLICK, KEYDOWN, KEYUP, KEYPRESS, DRAGDROP, MOVE,** and **RESIZE** (which, of course, correspond with the event-handler names: **onmousedown, onmouseup, onmouseover,** and so on).

In order to capture the events, you also need to specify an event handler, with a statement like this:

```
document.onclick = myHandler
```

myHandler would be the name of the function you have written to handle the event. Note that in this statement, we wrote the name of the function without any arguments or parentheses after it. That's because we're not calling or defining the function here; we're just making a reference to it. Similar statements could be used for **document.mouseup** and **document.mousedown,** or any other event types we wanted to capture.

To capture only right-button events, for instance, we could write a handler like this:

```
function myHandler(e) {                         // e is the event object
    if (e.modifiers == 3) {
       alert("Right mouse button detected.")
    }
    else {
       routeEvent (e)
    }
```

This function checks the **modifiers** property to see if the right button was pressed (remember, **3** refers to the right button). If it wasn't, the function calls **routeEvent** to pass the event on to wherever it would have gone if capturing was not in effect.

Moving On

You've learned about the basics of the JavaScript language. But there's a lot more than the basics. There are all sorts of complicated things that you can do with JavaScript. This book is an introduction to JavaScript, not an attempt to turn you into a master programmer. Still, we are going to cover a few advanced subjects in the following chapter.

You'll learn how to create your own objects, properties, and methods, work with *cookies,* and test and optimize your scripts. And once that chapter's over, we'll move on to the next part of the book and look at some more practical examples of how to put JavaScript to work.

Advanced Topics

You have now seen all the basic features of the JavaScript programming language—but there's plenty more. What we've squeezed into this chapter are the fairly advanced techniques—things you might want to try once you are more comfortable with the basics of the language.

We're going to look at how to create your own objects—that's right, not only does JavaScript provide you with a slew of ready-to-use objects, but you can create more as needed. We'll also talk a little about a new JavaScript feature, the capability to link JavaScripts to Java applications; we'll examine the use of *cookies*, bits of data that are stored on the user's hard disk in a file called **cookies.txt;** and we'll look at how JavaScript works with plug-ins and MIME types. We will also discuss how to make your scripts smaller (by breaking programming rules), and we'll talk a little about testing your programs.

Creating Your Own Objects

Let's begin by learning how to create objects. You have actually done this before, back in Chapter 9, "Building Arrays." You'll remember that in the first method we looked at we created an object that we used to hold the array, and it's that object-creation method that we're going to look at in more detail here.

Objects are created in two steps:

1. First define your object class by writing a *constructor* function. This function will have the same name as the object you are creating.

2. Create an instance of the object using the **new** keyword.

The constructor function defines the object class. (You can review classes and instances in Chapter 10, "Objects, Properties & Methods.") A class is not an actual object—it's the "blueprint" for that object. We then use the class to create the actual object instance.

You use the constructor function to create properties for your new object. You use the **this** keyword, which refers to the current object, in order to give it properties. For example, take a look at this constructor function:

Example 13.1

```
function product(nam, p) {
    this.name = nam
    this.price = p
}
```

This code by itself has not created any objects. In effect the function has created the object class. In this case, we created an object class called **product**. This object has two properties: **name** and **price**. Where will the information for these properties come from? You can see that the information will be passed to the object in the parentheses when we call this object-creating function; **nam** will be the first value passed in the parentheses, and the function will put this into the **name** property; and **p** will be the second value passed in the parentheses, which will be put into the **price** property. In other words, **this.name = nam** means "give **this** object instance a property called **name**, and give **name** the value passed to the function as **nam**."

Remember that a function does not do anything until it is *called*. So you haven't created an object instance until you call the constructor function. But we have to call the function in a slightly different way. In earlier chapters you saw how to call a function by simply naming it (making sure that you include the parentheses after the name). When we call a function that we are using to create an object instance, though, we use the **new** keyword. But we are also creating an object variable of sorts. We actually create a variable, then assign the object function to the variable. So in this case we create object instances of the **product** object like this:

```
var product1 = new product("TimeSaver", "$23")
var product2 = new product("MoneySaver", "$11")
var product3 = new product("Time n'MoneySaver", "$99")
```

We now have three new object instances, **product1**, **product2**, and **product3**. Yes, they are variables, but special ones that contain more than one piece of information. You can see the **name** and **price** properties we are passing to the products, too. The **name** property of **product1** is **TimeSaver**, while its **price** is **$23**, for example.

Viewing Object Properties

You can now get at the object's properties by specifying its property names using the dot notation we've already seen. The following example writes the values of these properties to the page:

Example 13.1

```
document.write(product1.name + " " + product1.price + "<BR>")
document.write(product2.name + " " + product2.price + "<BR>")
document.write(product3.name + " " + product3.price + "<BR>")
```

Creating an Object Hierarchy— Properties Can Be Objects

As with some of the JavaScript objects we've looked at before, you can create objects whose properties can themselves be objects. We begin our next example with two object classes, **product** and **order**. The **order** class has a property called **ProductType**, which is used to hold an object of the class **product**.

Example 13.2

```
function product(nam, p)  {
    this.name = nam
    this.price = p
}
function order(custname, prod, numbof)  {
    this.customer = custname
    this.ProductType = prod
    this.quantity = numbof
    this.OrderDate = new Date()
}
```

We've just created the two object classes, **product** and **order**. The **product** class is exactly the same as before, but our new **order** class has four different properties. However, note that we are only passing three values to the function: **custname, prod,** and **numbof.** The fourth property, **OrderDate,** is being created from one of the built-in JavaScript objects, the **Date** object; **new Date()** means "create a new **Date** object instance." In effect, when we call this function it creates a property from another object.

Now let's create the object instances:

```
var product1 = new product("TimeSaver", "$23")
var product2 = new product("MoneySaver", "$11")
var product3 = new product("Time n'MoneySaver", "$99")
```

```
var order1 = new order("Mr Brainless", product2, 5)
var order2 = new order("Mr Bonkers", product3, 22)
var order3 = new order("Mr Bozo", product1, 1)
```

First we created the **product1**, **product2**, and **product3** instances—exactly as before. Then we created the **order1**, **order2**, and **order3** object instances. Notice that when we created **order1, product2** was passed as the second value, the **prod** value. In other words, another of **order1**'s properties is also an object; not only is the **OrderDate** an object in its own right, but **ProductType** is also an object—this time one that we created. As you can see, in this manner we can create our own object hierarchy.

We can reference properties lower down in this hierarchy in the same manner we've already used. For example, if we want to see the price of the product in **order1**, we would refer to **order1. ProductType.price**. No, not **order1.ProductType.product2.price**, as you might imagine. In effect **product2** *is* **ProductType**; when we passed the values from **product2** to **ProductType** it loses its original name.

We could write out information from our objects like this:

Example 13.2 (continued)

```
document.write("NAME: " + order1.customer + "<BR>QUANTITY: " + →
order1.quantity + " ")
document.write("<BR>DATE: " + order1.OrderDate)
document.write("<BR>PRODUCT TYPE: " + order1.ProductType.name + "<BR>PRICE: →
" + order1.ProductType.price + "<P>")
document.write("NAME: " + order2.customer + "<BR>QUANTITY: " + →
order2.quantity + " ")
document.write("<BR>DATE: " + order2.OrderDate)
document.write("<BR>PRODUCT TYPE: " + order2.ProductType.name + "<BR>PRICE: →
" + order2.ProductType.price + "<P>")
document.write("NAME: " + order3.customer + "<BR>QUANTITY: " +order3.quantity + " ")
document.write("<BR>DATE: " + order3.OrderDate)
document.write("<BR>PRODUCT TYPE: " + order3.ProductType.name + "<BR>PRICE: →
" + order3.ProductType.price + "<P>")
```

You can see what this looks like in Figure 13-1.

Figure 13-1: We've written all the values from our objects and their associated properties.

Creating Methods for Your Objects

As you've already learned, objects have methods in addition to properties. You can create methods for your objects by creating yet another function and referring to it in the constructor function, in a manner similar to the way in which we created object properties:

```
objectname.methodname = functionname
```

Of course a method *is* a function, as you'll remember from our earlier chapters; it's simply a function associated with a particular object. You can then use the method in this manner:

```
objectname.methodname(function parameters)
```

For example, let's create a method called **OrderAmount**. First, we have to define a function called **OrderAmount**:

Example 13.3

```
function OrderAmount() {
    return (this.quantity * this.ProductType.price)
}
```

Notice that this function will **return** a value. When we call the function we want it to send something back to us. And again, we've used the **this** keyword to refer to the current object; **this.quantity** means "the **quantity** property of **this** object—the object that has called the method." So what's the method doing? It's taking the **quantity** and **price** properties, multiplying them, and returning the result.

Next, we associate this method with the **order** object in the last line of the **order** object's constructor function:

```
function order(custname, prod, numbof) {
    this.customer = custname
    this.ProductType = prod
    this.quantity = numbof
    this.OrderDate = new Date()
    this.OrderAmount = OrderAmount
}
```

Notice that we haven't passed another value to the function. We've simply added the **this.OrderAmount = OrderAmount** line, which means "create a method based on the **OrderAmount** function."

This method is then used like any other method, by calling it:

```
order1.OrderAmount()
```

We added the following line to our example to display the total cost for each product:

```
document.write("TOTALCOST = " + order1.OrderAmount() + "<BR>")
```

In other words, **order1.OrderAmount()** means the value obtained when you use the **OrderAmount()** method of **order1**.

> **TIP**
>
> *Okay, so we cheated a little. We used integers rather than floating-point numbers. We could have used prices like **22.99**, **10.99**, and so on. However, some versions of Netscape Navigator, including the 3.0 betas and earlier, have problems working with numbers such as these—instead of seeing **22.99** you'd see **23.989999999999998** or something similar.*

Object Prototypes

JavaScript 1.1 (Netscape Navigator 3) introduced a new property to objects called **prototype**. This can be used to add properties and methods to objects. The new property or method is added to an entire class of object, not just to a single instance. The **prototype** can be used on any object class, even built-in ones like strings and arrays.

For example, suppose you are creating an application that requires writing a lot of text in different colors. You decide that it would be convenient if all string variables had a **color** property, as well as a **colored()** method that could be used like the **bold()** and **italics()** methods that JavaScript already provides. Adding the new property is as simple as this:

Example 13.4

```
var txt = new String("Here is some sample text.")
String.prototype.color = "gray"
```

Actually, it's even simpler than that. The first statement above just creates a variable to help with our demonstration. The second statement is the one creating the new property, called **color**, for all **String** objects. The default value of **color** is **gray**; this is the color that will be initially assigned to a **String** object's **color** property whenever a **String** object is created with **new**. (Starting with Navigator 3 **String** objects can be created using the **new** keyword; see Chapter 11 for more information.)

To display strings in color, we can create a function that adds the required HTML tags:

```
function textColor() {
    return "<FONT color='" + this.color + "'>" + this + "</FONT>"
}
```

The reference to **this.color** allows this method to find the **color** of any string on which the method is used (**this** means the string to which the function is referring, of course). To make this function available as a method for strings, we use **prototype** again, to create a method called **colored**:

```
String.prototype.colored = textColor
```

Why is this a method and not a property? Because we've assigned the function to the item we've just created; remember, a method is a type of function, a function that belongs to an object. So when we assign a function to a new item that we are creating using the **prototype** property, it must be a method that we're creating.

Now we can try out our new method and property. We'll write the string stored in the variable **txt** in the normal manner, without color information. Then we'll write it in its default color, and then a couple of other colors as well:

```
document.write(txt + " (no color)<BR>")
```

The statement above is a simple **document.write** statement that you've seen a number of times. We're writing the text stored in **txt**, then we're writing **(no color)**, then we write an HTML line break:

```
document.write(txt.colored() + " (default property color)<BR>")
```

This time we used the colored method to write the text; **txt.colored( )** means "apply the **colored( )** method to the text in the **txt** variable." What color is used? Remember that **colored( )** simply grabs the color from the **color** property and places that inside the **<FONT color=>** tag. So we'll be using gray, because gray is the default color:

```
txt.color = "red"
document.write(txt.colored() + " (red)<BR>")
```

This time we did something a little different. We started by assigning a color to the **txt.color** property; we assigned **red**. So when we use the **colored()** method the word **red** is placed into the **<FONT color=>** tag, and the text is displayed in red:

```
txt.color = "blue"
document.write(txt.colored() + " (blue)<BR>")
```

This is the same as before, except that this time we used **blue**, by assigning blue to the **txt.color** property.

Note, by the way, that our new property and method will work even though the **txt** variable was created before the new property and method were defined.

Finally, note that properties and methods created in this manner work not just for **String** objects created with the **new** keyword, but for literals, too—**String** objects created by simply entering the text into a script. For example:

```
document.write("This also works with literals.".colored() + "<BR>")
```

We've told the **document.write** statement to type the words. As you can see, right at the end of the string we've added **.colored()** to use the **colored()** method.

Using Cookies

JavaScript is currently limited in the way that it can save information to the user's client computer hard disk. (JavaScript will soon be able to write to the hard disk and use other system resources, as you'll learn in Chapter 14 when you read about signed scripts.) This is for security reasons. If JavaScripts were allowed to write to the hard disk it would make the work of those busy virus writers too easy. Scripts could be set up to destroy important files as soon as someone opened a Web page. This is a serious limitation, however, reducing JavaScript's capabilities. So right from the start JavaScript did have *one* way you could write to the hard disk: by writing to a special text file (called **cookies.txt** in many cases). This is actually something that was in use before JavaScript (CGI scripts can write to **cookies.txt**, too). The cookie file is stored on your hard disk in one of these directories:

Version	Directory
Netscape Navigator Windows versions	..\Netscape\cookies.txt or, in Netscape 4, within the individual user directories.
Netscape Navigator Macintosh versions	System Folder:Preferences:Netscape f: MagicCookie
Netscape Navigator UNIX versions	~/.netscape/cookies
Internet Explorer Windows versions	Cookies are stored as individual text files within the Cookies subdirectory of the main Windows directory.
Internet Explorer Macintosh versions	System Folder:Preferences:Explorer:Explorer Cache:cookies.txt

When you write to a cookie file you are creating a *cookie.* You might have already seen scripts that do this. In fact many, many Web pages now set cookies, though unless you have your browser set to notify you, you might not have realized what was happening. Turn on cookie notification, then move around on the World Wide Web and it won't be long before you see the dialog box shown in Figure 13-2. (A good place to find cookies is in the Netscape General Store; when you add something to your "shopping basket" the server sends you a cookie.)

TIP

Your browser might be set to accept cookies without notifying you. To see the notification in Netscape Navigator 4, select Edit | Preferences, click on Advanced, and check the Warn Me Before Accepting a Cookie *checkbox. In Netscape Navigator 3, select Options | Network Preferences, click the Protocols tab, and check the* Accepting a Cookie *checkbox. In Internet Explorer select View | Options, click the Advanced tab, and check the* Warn Before Accepting "Cookies" *checkbox.*

For example, if you go to the Netscape Create Your Personal Workspace page (http://personal.netscape.com/custom/page/show_page.html) and begin creating a customized home page you might see the dialog box in Figure 13-2. This is to warn you that a cookie is being sent, and the message asks you if that's okay. If it is, the information setting up your customized page will be stored as a cookie.

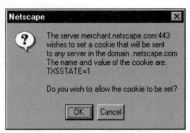

Figure 13-2: You are being sent a cookie and have the option to not receive it.

Because the cookie is saved in a text file (and because its size is limited) it can't do any harm. Text files are not executable files, so they can't run programs. Actually cookies are not always saved on your hard disk. When Netscape Navigator initially stores a cookie it stores it temporarily in memory, not in a text file. Then, when you close the browser, it stores it in the text file *if* an expiration date has been set for the cookie. If not, it just throws it away. So cookies can be used to store data for a single session, or over long periods so that the next time a user comes to your site that information will still be available on the user's machine. It's very easy to do this, as the **document** object has a **cookie** property, which is a string that holds cookie data for that document.

There are some restrictions on cookies. The browser is not allowed to create more than 300 cookies, each 4KB, so the cookie files are restricted to 1200KB. Also, no one Web site may have more than 20 cookies.

Let's set and display a cookie:

Example 13.5

```
function SetCookie(name, form) {
    document.cookie = name + form.txtCookie.value + ";"
    form.txtCookie.value = ""
}


function ShowCookie(form) {
    form.txtCookie.value = document.cookie
}
```

The first function, **SetCookie()**, takes the **name** and information from the **form** that is passed to it when it is called. It then sets the **document.cookie** property, placing the **name** value inside it plus the text that the user types into the **form.txtCookie.value** text box, followed by a semicolon (**;**). Then it clears the **form.txtCookie.value** text box.

The second function, **ShowCookie()**, simply takes the text from the **document.cookie** property and places it into the text box.

Here's the form we are using:

```
<FORM>
<INPUT TYPE="Text" NAME="txtCookie" size=50 ROWS=10 COLS=73></TEXT><P>
<I>Now click on this button to copy the text into the cookies.txt file:
</I><BR>
<INPUT TYPE="button" VALUE="Create Cookie" NAME="butSet"
onclick="SetCookie('Cookie1', this.form);"><P>
<I>Now click on this button to copy that cookie from the cookies.txt file
back into the text box.</I><BR>
<INPUT TYPE="button" VALUE="Display Cookie" NAME="butDisplay"
onclick="ShowCookie(this.form);">
</FORM>
```

Type some text into the **txtCookie** text box, then click on the first button to call the **SetCookie()** function. Notice that we pass **Cookie1** (the name of the cookie) and **this.form** (information from the form) to the function. When you click on this button you'll see the dialog box in Figure 13-3. This dialog box is asking if it's okay to save something to the cookie. Click on OK and that information is saved. Then click on the last button, to call **ShowCookie( )**. The information is grabbed from the **document.cookie** property—which in turn has to look in **cookies.txt** to find it. It is then displayed, along with the cookie name in the text box.

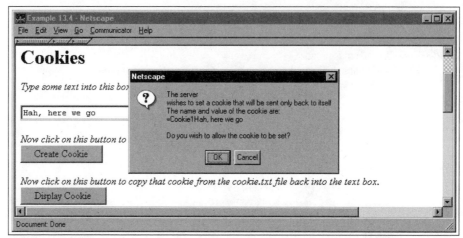

Figure 13-3: Setting a cookie is as easy as placing a value in the document.cookie property.

If you'd like to know more about working with cookies, see the "Netscape Authoring Guide" and go to http://www.netscape.com/newsref/std/cookie_spec.html. Also, check the JavaScript pages listed in Appendix H, "Finding More Information," for public domain cookie functions that you can use.

Properties Are Array Elements of Objects

We learned about arrays in Chapter 9, "Building Arrays." You might not have realized then that the properties of an object in JavaScript can be considered to be items in an array. Because objects are also arrays, you can access an individual property using an index, (as in **object[i]**), provided you know the right index to use. For example, if we displayed the value of **Math[0]**, we'd see **2.7182818284590451**, the value of **E**, the first **Math** property.

We created a little program so you could see this at work. We used the
for...in statement which can be used to access all the properties of an object. In
this example, you can select one of several different objects to look at, and the
for..in statement loops around to display each property in the object:

Example 13.6

```
function show_properties(form, obj, obj_name) {
var sDisplay = ""
var i = 0
    for(i in obj){
        sDisplay = sDisplay + obj_name + "." + i + " = " + obj[i] + nl
    }
    form.txtObjectList.value = sDisplay
}
```

Notice that we are referring to the object property that we want to see using
obj[i], where **i** is the index value. You can see this program in use in Figure 13-4.
Try it for yourself: select the object you want to look at, then click on the button
to see that object's properties in the textarea. (Note that this script won't work in
Internet Explorer 3 and some versions of Navigator earlier than version 3.)

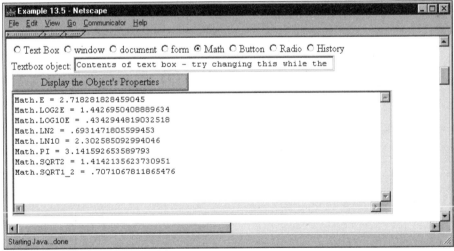

*Figure 13-4: This little program lets you view object properties using the array method of
addressing the property.*

LiveConnect—Using Java Applets With JavaScript

A feature called *LiveConnect* was introduced with JavaScript 1.1 (Netscape Navigator 3). This system allows you to connect JavaScripts and Java applets together. This means that complicated applets can be built by Java experts and then made available for those using JavaScript. The JavaScript programmer will write the code that sends information to the Java applet, and the Java applet can then return information back to the JavaScript.

A Java applet is a program that has been created in a form that can be easily used by many different types of computers—the same program can be run on Windows, Macintosh, and UNIX computers, as long as it has a Java interpreter available. Netscape Navigator and Internet Explorer both have Java interpreters. LiveConnect allows JavaScripts to work together with Java applets, letting JavaScript programmers extend the power of JavaScript by accessing the features of a more advanced language. JavaScript can also be the "glue" that sticks Java objects together. This is a path now taken in many areas of software development, where objects are written using a language that requires a high level of programming knowledge, and these objects are then made available to users in a language that is simpler to work with. This is similar to the Visual BASIC/C++ system where VBXs and OCXs are built in C++ by one set of programmers and used in Visual BASIC by another set.

JavaScript is able to access variables and methods of applets in an HTML document like this:

```
document.appletName
```

where **appletName** is the name of the Java applet. The Java applet is embedded into an HTML page using the **<APPLET>** tag, like this:

```
<APPLET CODE=animate.class NAME=appAnimate WIDTH=10 HEIGHT=10>
</APPLET>
```

In this example, the **appAnimate** Java applet, your JavaScript will be able to access it using this:

```
document.appAnimate
```

In LiveConnect, Netscape plug-ins, JavaScript, and Java are all related and can work with each other (we'll be talking more about plug-ins in a moment). JavaScript is able to access Java variables, methods, packages, classes, and objects. Java can access JavaScript methods and properties, too.

A detailed explanation of LiveConnect is beyond the scope of this book, since it requires an understanding of the Java language. However, we'll give you a quick look at how to communicate with Java and a couple of simple examples. As you might expect, Java is very similar to JavaScript, so you have a bit of a head start on learning Java. Both languages use a similar system of objects, methods, and properties. LiveConnect allows both languages to read and write each other's data and to call each other's functions and methods. We'll show a simple example, in which JavaScript calls a function in an applet, and vice versa.

In Example 13.7 an applet is loaded into a Web page by the HTML **<APPLET>** tag:

Example 13.7

```
<APPLET NAME="ticket" CODE="ticket.class"  WIDTH=300 HEIGHT=200 MAYSCRIPT>
```

The **NAME** attribute specifies the name that will be used by JavaScript to refer to the applet. The **CODE** attribute gives the name of the file containing the applet. The **WIDTH** and **HEIGHT** values set the size of the applet's space on the screen. The **MAYSCRIPT** attribute is needed to allow the applet to access JavaScript. This is a security feature. If you don't include **MAYSCRIPT**, the applet will not be allowed to access JavaScript, giving you protection against unknown applets snooping around in your browser.

Applets become properties of the **document** in which they are placed. Since the applet has been named **ticket**, we can now refer to its objects and methods by writing them into our JavaScript code as **document.ticket.***name*. JavaScript includes an **applets** array that contains all the applets in the document. The first applet defined in a document can be referred to either as **document.appletName** or as **document.applets[0]**. The property **document.applets.length** equals the number of applets in the document.

Our example includes an HTML form in which you type the number of tickets you want for the Kludge Kowboys concert. The form has a button that calls the **setTicketQuantity** function in the applet. When you click the button, the number that you typed appears in the applet's window. Here's what the form looks like:

```
<FORM NAME="myform">
<INPUT TYPE="text" SIZE="10" NAME="numTickets">
<INPUT TYPE="button" VALUE="Click to Order"
onclick="document.ticket.setTicketQuantity(document.myform.numTickets.value)">
</FORM>
```

As you can see, we've used **onclick** to take the value in the **numTickets** text box and send it to the **setTicketQuantity** function that's built into the Java applet named **ticket**.

The Java applet has a Sold Out button that sends a message back to the JavaScript code. In the HEAD of this Web page we have a function called **message**:

```
function message(msg1, msg2) {
    alert(msg1 + msg2)
}
```

There's nothing in this Web page itself—no JavaScript—that calls the message function. Rather, the Java applet calls it; LiveConnect allows the applet to call **message** directly.

The Java Console

Most of the power of LiveConnect is only available if you know Java programming. But there is one Java feature that might be helpful to you and is quite easy to use: the Java Console. This is a special window that can be used for reading and writing simple text, without worrying about any HTML formatting or object references. If you are working with Java, sending messages from JavaScript to Java applets, you can use the console to check that you are sending the correct information. To open it, select Options | Show Java Console (in Navigator 3) or Communicator | Java Console (Navigator 4). (There is no Java Console in Internet Explorer 3.)

In Java the console is called **System.out**, and the method **System.out.println(msg)** writes the string **msg** to the window. In JavaScript, you need to write **java.lang.System.out.println(msg)**. We have provided a simple example that allows you to type some text into a form and sends it to the Java Console when you click a button. This is the function that's called when you click the button:

Example 13.8

```
function writeConsole(s) {
    java.lang.System.out.println(s)
}
```

The button simply uses an **onclick** event handler to send the text to the **writeConsole** function, passing the text to the function as **s**. The function then uses **java.lang.System.out.println(s)** to "print" that text to the Java Console.

Has Java Been Enabled?

All this is very nice, but what happens if the browser doesn't work with Java or if it *can* work with Java, but Java has been disabled by the user? You can check for these conditions and then run a script accordingly. You can use the JavaScript 1.1 (Netscape Navigator 3) **navigator.javaEnabled( )** method. This returns **true** if the browser has Java enabled, **false** if it doesn't. For example, you can use an **if** statement to run one of two different functions according to whether Java has been enabled, like this:

```
if (navigator.javaEnabled()) {
    function1()
}
else function2()
```

Here's an actual example. We've taken our earlier Java example page and modified the page so that JavaScript will check to see if the browser has Java enabled. If it has, it displays the page as normal. If it hasn't, it displays an alert box, then finishes displaying the page but *without* the Java applet. We put this in the Web page:

Example 13.9

```
Kludge Kowboys in Concert, only $50.00 per ticket.<BR>
Please enter number of tickets desired:
<script language="JAVASCRIPT">
<!--
    if (navigator.javaEnabled()) {
        javaYes()
    }
    else javaNo()
//-->
</script>
```

If Java is enabled, we run the **javaYes( )** function. If it isn't, we run the **javaNo( )** function. Here are those functions from the HEAD:

```
var sAddJava = "<FORM NAME='myform'><INPUT TYPE='text' SIZE='10' →
NAME='numTickets'><INPUT TYPE='button' VALUE='Click to Order' →
onclick='document.ticket.setTicketQuantity(document.myform.numTickets.value)'>→
</FORM></td><td><APPLET NAME='ticket' CODE='ticket.class' WIDTH=300 →
HEIGHT=200 mayscript></APPLET>"
```

```
function javaYes()  {
    document.write(sAddJava)
}

function javaNo()   {
      alert("Your browser doesn't have Java enabled, so you can't run the →
Java app associated with this page. Either you have a non-Java browser, or →
Java is disabled in your browser's properties.)")
      document.write("<b>[The form and Java applet go here in a Java-enabled→
browser.]</b>")
}
```

We began by creating a variable called **sAddJava**, which contains all the text and HTML tags required to add the form and Java applet to the Web page. The **javaYes()** function simply uses the **document.write** method to write all the text in the **sAddJava** variable to the Web page. In other words, if the browser is Java-enabled, everything is written to the Web page as normal. If we run **javaNo()**, though, we begin by displaying an alert box informing the user that the browser can't work with Java, and suggesting two reasons why. Then we use document.write to add a note to the Web page itself showing where the Java applet would go.

Note that this won't work in Internet Explorer 3, and it won't work in some of the Netscape Navigator 4 preview versions; for example, when Navigator 4b3 checks **navigator.javaEnabled()** it always returns **true**, regardless of the actual condition of the browser.

Checking for Plug-ins & Viewers

Another feature of LiveConnect is the ability to check to see what file types can be handled by the browser—which plug-ins and viewers have been installed. There are four objects and arrays you can use to do this:

- **Plugin**—a plug-in that has been installed in the browser.
- **plugins**—an array listing the **Plugin** objects.
- **MimeType**—a MIME (Multipart Internet Mail Extension) file format recognized by the browser.
- **mimeTypes**—an array of **MimeType** objects; **mimeTypes** is a property of both the navigator and **Plugin** objects.

There are three ways that a browser can handle data files transmitted to it:

- **Display it internally.** Browsers support HTML and text files, of course, along with several image formats (XBM, JPEG, and GIF), and also have a variety of other formats that they can handle without "assistance." Netscape Navigator can also work with WAV, AU, and SND files.

- **Display it in an external viewer.** A viewer is another program to which the browser sends the file if it can't handle it itself.

- **Display it in a plug-in.** A plug-in is really an internal viewer. It's a software module that has been added to the browser for the purpose of handling particular file formats.

JavaScript can be used to see what files can be handled by the browser, so you can use a script to decide what to display to the browser. You can use **mimeTypes** and **MimeType** to find out which MIME file formats the browser is configured to use internally or with an external viewer, and use **Plugin** and **plugins** to find out which plug-ins have been installed. You can also use **mimeTypes** and **MimeType** to find out which MIME types those plug-ins can handle.

The following example shows you how you can find out what is enabled in the browser:

Example 13.10

```
<h3>These are the MIME Types:</h3>
<script language="JAVASCRIPT">
<!--
for (i=0; i < navigator.mimeTypes.length; i++) {
    document.write("<B>" + i + ": " + navigator.mimeTypes[i].type + ": →
</B><BR>" + navigator.mimeTypes[i].description + "<BR>>" + →
navigator.mimeTypes[i].suffixes + "<BR>" + →
navigator.mimeTypes[i].enabledPlugin + "<P>")
}
//-->
</script>
<h3>These are the plug-ins:</h3>
<script language="JAVASCRIPT">
<!--
for (i=0; i < navigator.plugins.length; i++) {
    document.write("<B>" + i + ": " + navigator.plugins[i].name + ": →
</B><BR>" + navigator.plugins[i].filename + "<BR>" + →
navigator.plugins[i].description + "<BR>" + navigator.plugins[i].length + "<P>")
}
//-->
</script>
```

These two scripts use **for** loops to show all the information held by the **plugins** and **mimeTypes** arrays. The **length** property is the number of **Plugin** objects (for the **plugins** array) and **MimeType** objects (for the **mimeTypes** array). For each of the arrays we display the properties of each object held by the array. For example, for each **MimeType** object we see something like this displayed in the Web page:

```
1: audio/x-liveaudio:
Streaming Audio Metafiles
>lam
[object Plugin]
```

These are the **type**, **description**, **suffixes**, and **enabledPlugin** properties:

- **type**—shows the MIME type, in this case audio/x-liveaudio. In some cases the browser will have information about file types that it can handle for which it has no corresponding MIME type, in which case you'll see x-unknown-content-type-.

- **description**—a description, if the browser has a description in its MIME configuration information. You'll find that many of the MIME types don't have descriptions.

- **suffixes**—the file extensions used for this file type.

- **enabledPlugin**—indicates whether there's a plug-in that can handle this file type. If so you'll see [object Plugin]. If not you'll see null.

For each **Plugin** object we see something like this:

```
3: QuickTime Plug-In:
H:\Program Files\Netscape\Communicator\Program\plugins\NPQTW32.DLL
QuickTime Plug-In for Win32 v.1.1.0
1
```

This shows the **name**, **filename**, **description**, and **length** properties of each **Plugin** object:

- **name**—the plug-in name, in this case the QuickTime plug-in.

- **filename**—the path and filename of the file that runs the plug-in.

- **description**—a description of the plug-in.

- **length**—the number of MIME file types that the plug-in can handle.

Now, you've just seen that if there's a plug-in for a particular MIME type you see **[object Plugin]** for **navigator.mimeTypes[i].enabledPlugin**. This means that the information from the **Plugin** object is being passed to the **mimeType** object. You can use these objects and properties to decide what to show the visitor to your site according to what his browser is capable of displaying. Take a look at this example:

Example 13.11

```
<script language="JAVASCRIPT">
<!--
checkMIME = navigator.mimeTypes["audio/x-midi"]
if (checkMIME) {
    document.write("<b>MIME description:</b> " + checkMIME.description + →
"<BR>")
    usePlugin = checkMIME.enabledPlugin
        if (usePlugin)  {
            document.write("<b>Plug-in name:</b> " + →
checkMIME.enabledPlugin.name + "<BR>")
        }
      else {
          document.write("No plug-in available for this MIME type.")
      }
}
else {
    document.write("This MIME type not recognized by the browser.")
}
//-->
</script>
```

Our Online Companion actually has three of these little scripts; the first checks for audio/x-midi, the second for text/html, and the third for text/x-bingbong. We chose the audio/x-midi example because this MIME type is supported in all Navigator 3 and 4 versions using the LiveAudio plug-in. The text/html example shows what happens when you have a MIME type that the browser can handle, but for which there is no plug-in (in this case text/html is, of course, the basic HTML document format, so the browser handles it itself, but it can also handle a non-plug-in format using an external viewer). And the last format is an example of what happens when the browser doesn't recognize a MIME type; we're pretty sure your browser doesn't recognize the text/x-bingbong format because we made it up. You can see the result of these scripts in Figure 13.5.

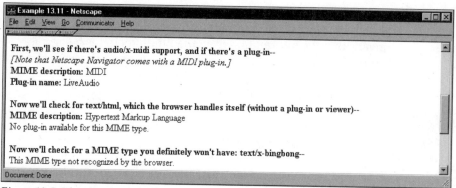

Figure 13-5: It's quite simple to check the MIME type and feed the appropriate format of file to the browser.

This simple script allows you to first figure out if the MIME type of a file you want to send is recognized. If not, the browser won't be able to do anything with the file. If the browser can handle the file type, you have two basic options. You can embed the file into the document using the **<EMBED>** tag, but this requires a plug-in. Or you can create a link to the file so the user can click on the file and transfer it to an external viewer. The script allows you to check to see if there's a plug-in and add **<EMBED>** or an external link accordingly. Or if the MIME type isn't recognized, you can display something else, instead. Of course our example simply writes information to the page telling you what you've found, but it's a simple enough task to modify the script to write an HTML tag instead.

JavaScript & HTML Tags

Starting with JavaScript 1.1 (Netscape Navigator 3) you can use JavaScript within HTML tag attributes. You've always been able to use the event handler attributes within HTML tags, of course, but this new feature takes this a step further.

The new feature introduces *JavaScript entities*, which work in a similar way to character entities. In HTML, character entities allow you to place special characters into the page, in some cases characters that HTML normally reserves for special purposes. For example, if you wanted to show **<B>** in a Web page, you'd have trouble because that's an HTML tag. But you can use character entities to show the < and > characters, like this:

```
&LT;B&GT;
```

< represents <, and **>** represents >; the character entities are identified by the leading **&** and the ending **;**. JavaScript entities are identified in the same way, by leading with an ampersand and ending with a semicolon (though they only work within HTML tags, while character entities work within the Web page's text). The JavaScript expression is placed between these characters and within braces, like this:

```
&{javascript expression};
```

This system allows you to more easily modify the look of your page using JavaScript. For example, you could modify text color according to a value held in a variable, like this:

Example 13.12
```
<script language="JAVASCRIPT">
<!--
var sBgColor = prompt("Type the background color you want to use.")
var sTextColor = prompt("Type the text color you want to use.")
//-->
</script>
</HEAD>
<body text="&{sTextColor};" bgColor="&{sBgColor};">
```

We've created two variables, containing the colors you type into the prompt boxes. Then we used the JavaScript entities to replace the attribute values and change the text and page colors.

There's another way to use JavaScript in tags: you can create JavaScript URLs, like this:

```
<A HREF="javascript:statement">Link text</A>
```

JavaScript URLs are used to carry out JavaScript instructions rather than loading a page; in effect they convert a text link into a JavaScript activator. (In a non-JavaScript browser clicking on the link will probably do nothing, though it might display an error.) Clicking the link carries out whatever JavaScript statement you have placed in the tag, such as running a specified function. In fact if the statement that you've placed after **javascript:** is an expression that returns a URL, the browser will load the page referenced by that URL.

You can ensure that the statement does not return anything by preceding the statement with **void()**. The statement will be carried out, but if the statement would normally return a value that value will not be sent to the browser as a URL. You can, using this method, make links carry out actions other than loading Web pages. (If a user clicks on the link in non-JavaScript browser nothing will happen.)

Performance

JavaScript is unlike most other programming languages in that it is not compiled. When a program is compiled all of the comments are stripped out and are not included in the executable file (the .EXE files), and the variable names are replaced with numbers that point to their location. Comments and long variable names are of use only to programmers and are found only in the source code. This means that it doesn't matter how long your variable names are or how much commented text you put into your program, the .EXE file is unaffected by these things.

JavaScript, however, is different. JavaScript must be transmitted over the Internet and then transferred to the user's computer, comments and all. This means that comments and large variable names in JavaScript have a cost, in that they increase the amount of text to be transmitted. For the most part, users of your Web page will not want to read comments in your code, yet those comments will increase the time it takes to transmit the page. For small bits of code this won't be significant, but for applications like our Area Code program (see Chapter 18), it can affect the time it takes to load the page.

If you build a large application you might like to keep your variable names and comments to a minimum. We have not because our programs have been designed as part of a tutorial. There are other ways to reduce the size of your script. For example, you can use the ?: conditional operator and some of the assignment operators, such as += or *=, operators that are shorthand techniques.

Also, if you need to reduce the size of your scripts, you might want to consider breaking all or many of the rules that we have given you for making your code easier to read. It's probably not a good idea to do so when you are first learning JavaScript. However, if it becomes essential to cut the size of a script, you can do so by leaving out unnecessary spaces, removing blank lines, not indenting lines, and so on—all things that make the code harder to read, but quicker to transmit.

Testing Your Scripts

Although programmers don't like testing, good ones know that it is an integral part of the development of programs. It is the inherent nature of programming that when you write code—because you are human and not a computer yourself—you will inadvertently put bugs into your program. Programs more than a few lines are just too complex to comprehend in their entirety. So when you change something in one part of the program, under certain circumstances you might be causing unexpected things to happen in another part of the program. You must, therefore, test your programs. Test them while developing them. Test them once they are complete, and test them as fully as you can if you make changes. And when JavaScript editors appear on the scene, as they surely will, find one you like and use it. You'll still have to understand JavaScript, but the program will help automate certain tasks, making errors less likely. (About the time we were going to print, Visual JavaScript was released by Netscape.) JavaScript tools have been added to HTML editors, too. Using them can help you to avoid syntax errors.

Unfortunately the different JavaScript interpreters don't all work in exactly the same way, so programs should be tested with as many different browsers as possible. Although Java and JavaScript are said to be portable, there are differences between how the different platforms (Windows 3.1, Windows 95, Macintosh, and various flavors of UNIX) work. Situations can arise where the code you have written will need to take into account the platform on which it is running, as the code's behavior might be different for each. If you need complete confidence in your code, you should test it on different platforms.

Web pages containing JavaScript might well be read by users who have non-JavaScript browsers as well. It would be a good idea to test your scripts with these types of browsers. Another approach is to set up your Web site so that you can steer non-JavaScript users away from your JavaScript pages. (If you are doing anything fancy with JavaScript, there's just no way to make the page useful for non-JavaScript browsers at the same time.)

Finally, as we've said elsewhere in this book, stay a few steps behind, not ahead. It might be fun playing with the very latest JavaScript features, but most of your audience will be using older browsers.

Moving On

We haven't finished with the advanced topics yet. JavaScript 1.2 (Netscape Navigator 4) introduced some significant new advanced features, such as layers, JavaScript style sheets, regular expressions, and signed objects and scripts. We'll look at these things in the following chapter.

JavaScript 1.2's Advanced Features

JavaScript 1.2—the version that functions in Netscape Navigator 4— introduced several significant new features. These are features that, at the time of writing, you wouldn't want to use in most cases. At present few people are working with Navigator 4 (the version of Netscape Navigator that is included with Netscape Communicator), so these features won't work in most people's browsers. As more people upgrade to Navigator 4, though, it will become more practical to introduce these features into your scripts.

Here are the new advanced features introduced in JavaScript 1.2:

- Layers
- JavaScript style sheets
- Regular Expressions
- Signed scripts and objects

Working With Layers

Netscape has introduced a new HTML tag, the **<LAYER>** tag. Starting with Netscape Navigator version 4 (JavaScript version 1.2), a document can consist of two or more layers. The easiest way to explain how layers work is by analogy. Without layers, a document is like a single piece of paper. With layers, a document is like a piece of paper with several pieces of transparent film laid on top of it, each piece of film a separate document that can contain text and images.

Layers are useful in a number of ways:

- You can position graphics and text by specific horizontal and vertical locations. If you want to be creative with your Web page design, this might be much easier than using tables or other tricks to get everything aligned just the way you want.

- You can easily move a layer around and make all or part of it disappear, to provide animation or to interact with the user.

- You can position one layer so that it overlaps another, and control which one is "on top"; that is, which one overwrites the other.

Layers are easy to use, but a bit hard to explain with words, since they are very visual in nature. You might want to go immediately to the Online Companion and take a look at this chapter's examples; you'll soon see what we mean. Or, take a look at Figures 14-1 and 14-2.

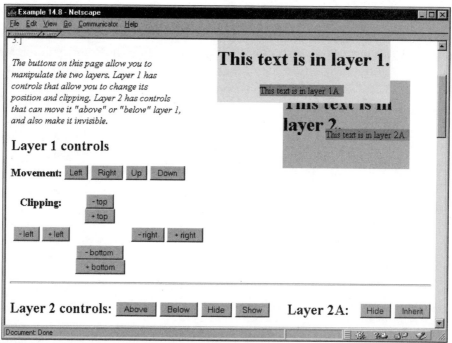

Figure 14-1: Here's a layers example. Click the buttons . . .

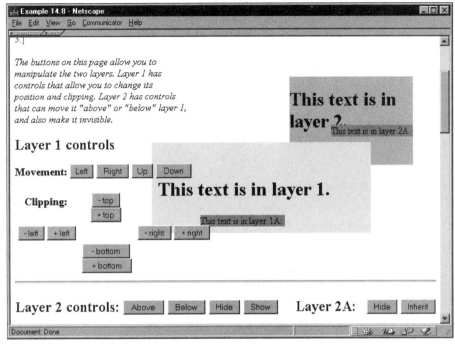

Figure 14-2: . . . and the layers move.

In HTML, a section of a document is turned into a layer when it is enclosed by the **<LAYER>** and **</LAYER>** tags. Here's an example of how layers might be used:

Example 14.1

```
<LAYER NAME="titleLayer" WIDTH=400 LEFT=250 TOP=10BGCOLOR="orange">
<H1> This heading is in a layer. </H1>
This text is in the layer, too.
</LAYER>
<P>Here is some text in body of the document.</P>
```

You can probably guess that this creates a layer named **titleLayer**, with a width of **400** pixels and a background color of **orange**. The **TOP** and **LEFT** attributes are used to control the location of the layer. **LEFT=250** means that the left edge of the layer will be positioned 250 pixels over from the left side of the window. **TOP=10** means that the top edge of the layer will be positioned 10 pixels down from the top of the window. It doesn't really matter where in an HTML document you place the **<LAYER></LAYER>** tags, as the position of the information held between the tags is determined by the **LEFT=** and **TOP=** attributes, not by the position of the text within the source document.

However, there's an associated set of tags, the **<ILAYER>** and **</ILAYER>** tags, which are "inflow" and "inline" layer tags. They sit on the same line as any other text or image in the HTML document and are positioned in the rendered Web page according to the position at which the tags appear within the HTML source document. (For our examples, we'll be sticking with the **<LAYER>** and **</LAYER>** tags.)

TIP

For detailed information on working with HTML layers, see the Creating Multiple Layers of Content document (http://developer.netscape.com/library/documentation/ communicator/layers/index.htm).

If you load the above HTML code (Example 14.1), you will note that the text in the layer appears directly on top of the text in the body of the document. Even more important is the fact that the layer can be moved around after it is created. For example, take a look at this JavaScript statement:

```
layers.titleLayer.top = 200
```

This would instantly move the layer to a new position 200 pixels down from the top of the window. How does this work? In JavaScript 1.2, there is an object called **layers** that holds all the layers created in the HTML. Each layer that you create becomes a property of the **layers** object. You can reference a layer object by the name assigned in the **<LAYER>** tag, which in this case is **titleLayer**; so the complete reference is **layers.titleLayer**. Each **layer** object has properties of its own; the **top** property is the one that controls the vertical position of the layer.

In Example 14.1, you can see this at work. We've added the following button, which contains the statement above controlled by an **onclick** event handler:

```
<INPUT TYPE="button" VALUE=" Down " onclick="layers.titleLayer.top = 200">
```

In other words, click the Down button and the top edge of the layer named **titleLayer** moves down until it's 200 pixels from the top of the window.

Layers, like many other JavaScript objects, are stored as an array. So, we can refer to layer positions using array positions, as you've seen with other arrays. For example, **titleLayer** could be referred to in JavaScript as any of these:

```
layers.titleLayer
layers[0]
layers["titleLayer"]
```

Layer objects have a number of useful properties. Many of these are related to the attributes of the **<LAYER>** tag; so, let's quickly take a look at those attributes:

<LAYER> tag attribute	Equivalent JavaScript property	Can it be modified by JavaScript?	Meaning
NAME	**name**	No	The layer name assigned in HTML.
LEFT	**left**	Yes	Horizontal position or layer, measured in pixels from left side of window.
TOP	**top**	Yes	Vertical position or layer, measured in pixels from top of window.
WIDTH	No equivalent	—	Layer width in pixels.
VISIBILITY	**visibility**	Yes	Layer visibility control: a string variable whose value may be "hide" or "inherit."
CLIP= "left, top, right, bottom"	**clip.left clip.top clip.right clip.bottom**	Yes	Boundaries of clipping for the layer.
No Equivalent	**clip.width clip.height**	Yes	Space between left/right and top/bottom clipping boundaries.
ABOVE	**siblingAbove**	No	This attribute names the layer immediately above the one being created with the tag.
BELOW	**siblingBelow**	No	Names the layer immediately below the one being created.
Z-INDEX	No equivalent, but use **moveAbove( )** and **moveBelow( )** methods		A number is used to define the layer's position in relation to other layers.
BGCOLOR	No equivalent	—	Background color of the layer.
BACKGROUND	No equivalent	—	Background image file for the layer.

Let's discuss some features of layers in more detail.

How Are Layers Displayed?

As we mentioned, layers act like pieces of transparent film that are placed on top of the main document. Actually, though, a layer does not have to be transparent. The **<LAYER>** tag can include a background color (with the **BGCOLOR** attribute) or image (with the **BACKGROUND** attribute). If neither of these is specified, the layer will be transparent. (Of course, even if the layer is transparent, any text or images that it contains will still be displayed in their normal colors.)

Transparency is important when two or more layers overlap. The browser keeps track of which layers are on top of which. Even when layers don't overlap, the browser keeps track of their "height" above the document. The height is called the Z-index. The **LAYER** tag has a **Z-INDEX** attribute that allows you to explicitly set the order of layers in your HTML code. Or, you can use the **ABOVE** and **BELOW** attributes to specify a layer's immediate neighbors. JavaScript includes two methods, **moveAbove( )** and **moveBelow( )**, that can be used to change the Z index of a layer after the page is loaded.

If no **Z-INDEX** attribute is used in your layers, the layers will be positioned according to which appears first in the HTML source: the first will be the first layer, the second will be above that, the third will be above that, and so on. If you do use the **Z-INDEX** attribute, however, you can tell the browser how to position the layers. (This can get a little confusing, though, because the **Z-INDEX** only affects the layers in which the **Z-INDEX** appears, adjusting their positions relative to other **Z-INDEX**ed layers.) For example, take a look at these layers:

Example 14.2

```
<LAYER NAME="Layer1" WIDTH=400 LEFT=250 TOP=10 BGCOLOR="orange" Z-INDEX=2>
<H1>This is Layer 1</H1>
With a little text.
</LAYER>
<LAYER NAME="Layer2" WIDTH=400 LEFT=350 TOP=50 BGCOLOR="blue" Z-INDEX=1>
<H1>This is Layer 2</H1>
With a little text.
</LAYER>
```

We've reversed the normal position of these layers. Without the **Z-INDEX**, **Layer1** would appear below **Layer2**, because **Layer1** was created first. However, we've used **Z-INDEX=1** for **Layer2**, and **Z-INDEX=2** for **Layer1**; as the higher Z-INDEX number goes *above* a lower one, **Layer2** appears on top of **Layer1**. (Note, however, that if **Layer1** didn't *have* a Z-INDEX, **Layer2**'s Z-INDEX would be irrelevant, and **Layer1** would still appear below **Layer2**; a Z-INDEX only works in relation to other Z-INDEXes.)

Well, that's all HTML, not JavaScript, but we've added a couple of buttons to Example 14.2 that you can use to adjust the relative positions of these layers:

```
<form>
<INPUT TYPE="button" VALUE="Layer2 on Top"
onclick="layers.Layer2.moveAbove(layers.Layer1)"><P>
<INPUT TYPE="button" VALUE="Layer1 on Top"
onclick="layers.Layer1.moveAbove(layers.Layer2)">
</form>
```

As you can see, we've used **layers.Layer2.moveAbove(layers.Layer1)** to move **Layer2** on top of **Layer1**; this quite simply uses the **layers** object's **moveAbove( )** method; you can see that you must specify, within the parentheses, *which* layer the layer in question must be moved above.

Relations Between Layers

Layers can be organized in hierarchical parent-child relationships by nesting their definitions. For example:

```
<LAYER NAME="A">

   ... parent layer text ...

   <LAYER NAME="B">
     ... child layer 1 text ...
   </LAYER>

   <LAYER NAME="C">
     ... child layer 2 text ...
   </LAYER>

</LAYER>
```

In this example, the layer named **A** is the parent, and **B** and **C** are its children. Many operations that you apply to a layer, such as changing its position or visibility, will automatically apply to all of its children. When a layer has children, it has its own **layers** array to hold them. So, for example, to reference layer **B** above, you would write **layers.A.layers.B** in your script.

Objects in Layers

Every **layer** object contains a property called **document**, in the same way that a window contains a **document** property. This is an object, of course, and serves as a container for any arrays, such as **forms** and **links,** which may be

needed to access items in the layer. For instance, if you create a layer named
Layer4, and its HTML text includes several forms, you can reference them in
scripts like this: **layers.Layer4.document.forms[0]**,
layers.Layer4.document.forms[1], and so on.

Positioning Layers

The **<LAYER>** tag's **TOP** and **LEFT** attributes determine where a layer is
placed on its document. The layer object has corresponding properties, also
called **top** and **left**. JavaScript statements can change the values of **top** and **left**
to move a layer around on a page. If you change these properties in small
rapid steps, you can create smooth motion of an animated object. Also, layers
have two methods, **offset( )** and **moveTo( )**, that can be used to change a
layer's location with one statement.

In Example 14.3, you can see how to move layers. First, we created a layer
with a child layer within it, like this:

Example 14.3

```
<LAYER NAME="layer1" LEFT=360 TOP=176 BGCOLOR="#ffff00"><BR>
<H1>This text is in layer 1.</H1><BR>
<LAYER NAME="layer1A" LEFT=72 TOP=80 VISIBILITY=show BGCOLOR="#8888ff">
This text is in layer 1A.
</LAYER>
</LAYER>
```

Then, we created buttons that move the layers like this:

```
<FORM NAME="layerForm">
<B>Movement:</B>
<INPUT TYPE="button" VALUE=" Left " onclick="layers.layer1.left -= 10">
<INPUT TYPE="button" VALUE=" Right " onclick="layers.layer1.left += 10">
<INPUT TYPE="button" VALUE=" Up " onclick="layers.layer1.top -= 10">
<INPUT TYPE="button" VALUE=" Down " onclick="layers.layer1.top += 10">
</FORM>
```

When you click on a button, the **left** and **top** properties are modified. For
example, **layers.layer1.left -= 10** means "move the left edge 10 pixels 'negative' (to the left)," while **layers.layer1.left += 10** means "move the left edge 10
pixels 'positive' (to the right)."

As for moving a layer with **offset( )** and **moveTo( )**, the first moves the layer
by the specified amount, while the second moves the layer to the specified
position. For instance, we took the layer from the previous example and created these buttons:

Example 14.4

```
<FORM NAME="layerForm">
<B>Movement:</B>
<INPUT TYPE="button" VALUE="offset()" onclick="layers.layer1.offset
(-100,100)">
<INPUT TYPE="button" VALUE="MoveTo()" onclick="layers.layer1.moveTo(0,300)">
</FORM>
```

The first button, the **offset( )** button, shifts the layer to the left **100** pixels and down **100** pixels. The **moveTo( )** button moves the layer to an absolute position in the window: **0** pixels from the left edge and **300** pixels down.

Visibility & Clipping

Layers have a **visibility** property, which is initially set from the **VISIBILITY** attribute of the **<LAYER>** tag. The attribute can be set to one of three values:

- **SHOW** to display the layer in the normal way.
- **HIDE** to make the layer invisible.
- **INHERIT** to make the layer's visibility follow its parent layer.

JavaScript can make a layer appear and disappear by changing the **visibility** property. The property, which is a string, may be set to **"hide"** or **"inherit"** (**"show"** is not allowed, but setting a parent layer to **"inherit"** is the equivalent of showing it, as the Web page—in effect the parent layer—is always set to show). Note that if a layer is defined in HTML with **VISIBILITY=HIDE**, it will be invisible when the page is loaded; it will not appear until some JavaScript statement makes it visible. You can see an example of all this in Example 14.5. We used the same layers, but we've added these buttons:

Example 14.5

```
<FORM NAME="layerForm">
<B>Layer 1:</B><BR>
<INPUT TYPE="button" VALUE=" Hide " onclick="layers.layer1.visibility = →
'hide'">
<INPUT TYPE="button" VALUE=" Inherit (Show)"
onclick="layers.layer1.visibility = 'inherit'"><P>
<B>Layer 1A:</B><BR>
<INPUT TYPE="button" VALUE=" Hide "
onclick="layers.layer1.layers.layer1A.visibility = 'hide'">
<INPUT TYPE="button" VALUE=" Inherit"
onclick="layers.layer1.layers.layer1A.visibility = 'inherit'">
</FORM>
```

We simply set the **visibility** property like this: **layers.layer1.visibility = 'hide'** means set the visibility of layer1 to **'hide'**, and **layers.layer1.layers.layer1A.visibility = 'inherit'** means set the **visibility** property of **layer1A** to **inherit**. (Note, by the way, that we're using single quotes around inherit and hide, because these are inside event handlers, and the event handler statement is itself enclosed in double quotes.)

Play with the example and you'll see that when the child layer inherits the parent's **visibility** property it might appear—if the parent is visible, of course. If you hide the child, then hide the parent, then click the child's Inherit button, then click the parent's Inherit button, the parent reappears, as does the child; because while they were hidden you made the child inherit the parent's **visibility** property.

If you want to hide part of a layer while leaving the rest visible, you can use clipping. Clipping allows you to set upper, lower, left, and right limits on the amount of the layer that is displayed. These limits can be set by the **CLIP** attribute of the **<LAYER>** tag, or in JavaScript via the **clip.top**, **clip.left**, **clip.bottom**, and **clip.right** properties. For example, take a look at this:

```
layers.layer1.clip.top -= 10
```

This clips the top of **layer1**. What exactly does it do? This is a negative clip (**-=**), so the top edge goes up (that is, the layer gets larger). If this were **layers.layer1.clip.bottom -= 10**, the bottom layer would go up (that is, the layer gets smaller). Think of a negative clip as always moving up or to the left, and a positive clip (**+=**) as always moving down or to the right.

Example 14.6 contains eight buttons in a table, each button moving one edge of the layer in or out:

Example 14.6

```
<FORM>
<TABLE>
 <TR>
  <TD ALIGN=center VALIGN=center> <H3> Clipping: </H3> </TD>
  <TD ALIGN=center>
        <INPUT TYPE="button" VALUE=" - top
"onclick="layers.layer1.clip.top -= 10"> <BR>
        <INPUT TYPE="button" VALUE=" + top
"onclick="layers.layer1.clip.top += 10"> </TD>
  <TD></TD>
 </TR>
  <TD ALIGN=right>
        <INPUT TYPE="button" VALUE=" - left
"onclick="layers.layer1.clip.left -= 10">
        <INPUT TYPE="button" VALUE=" + left
```

```
"onclick="layers.layer1.clip.left += 10"> </TD>
  <TD></TD>
  <TD ALIGN=left>
          <INPUT TYPE="button" VALUE=" - right
"onclick="layers.layer1.clip.right -= 10">
          <INPUT TYPE="button" VALUE=" + right
"onclick="layers.layer1.clip.right += 10"> </TD>
  </TR>
  <TR>
   <TD></TD>
   <TD ALIGN=center>
          <INPUT TYPE="button" VALUE=" - bottom
"onclick="layers.layer1.clip.bottom -= 10"> <BR>
          <INPUT TYPE="button" VALUE=" + bottom
"onclick="layers.layer1.clip.bottom += 10"> </TD>
   <TD></TD>
  </TR>
</TABLE>
</FORM>
```

If it's more convenient, you can use the **clip.width** or **clip.height** property. Setting one of these causes JavaScript to adjust the **clip.right** or **clip.bottom** value to get the specified width or height. There are also two methods, **resizeTo(*width, height*)** and **resizeBy(*horizontal, vertical*)**, that adjust both properties with one statement. These methods shift the bottom and right edges in or out to create a layer of the specified size. The first, **resizeTo( )** adjusts the size to make it the stated size; the second, **resizeBy( )**, adds the additional pixels onto the current size. You can see an example of some of these adjustments in Example 14.7.

Example 14.7

```
<form>
<INPUT TYPE="button" VALUE=" ResizeTo (narrow and deep)
"onclick="layers.layer1.resize(50,400)"><br>
<INPUT TYPE="button" VALUE=" ResizeBy (wide and shallow)
"onclick="layers.layer1.resize(400,20)"><br>
<INPUT TYPE="button" VALUE="  Width (narrow)
"onclick="layers.layer1.clip.width = '50'"><br>
<INPUT TYPE="button" VALUE=" Height (deep)
"onclick="layers.layer1.clip.height = '400'"><br>
</form>
```

The first button uses **resizeTo( )** to make the layer **50** pixels wide and **400** deep. The second uses **resizeBy( )** to *add* pixels; **400** are added to the width and **20** to the height. The final size depends on the size of the layer immediately before you click the button, of course. The fourth button uses the **clip.width** property to define the width of the layer, setting it to **50** pixels wide. And the last button uses the **clip.height** property to set the height of the layer to **400** pixels.

Example 14.8

Take a look at Example 14.8 in the Online Companion. This example shows two main layers, each with a child layer, and most of the controls that we've just looked at. You can shift these around, clip them, hide them, and so on.

Controlling Page Appearance With Style Sheets

One of the common complaints about early versions of HTML was that Web pages were boring. Everyone's documents looked the same: the authors didn't have much control over fonts and other aspects of the display. The HTML designers have worked hard to give us HTML users more creative freedom, and style sheets are one of the latest additions to the tool kit.

The term *style sheet*, like many in the electronic-publishing business, has its roots in the traditions of printing with ink and lead. Though pages created using HTML styles might never be seen on a sheet of paper, they are collections of data that control a document's appearance. There are currently two types of style sheets. First, there are *cascading style sheets*, which both Navigator and Internet Explorer can work with. You can find out about these at http://www.w3.org/pub/WWW/TR/REC-CSS1. There are also JavaScript style sheets, which are very similar to cascading style sheets but which can be directly manipulated by JavaScript, as they create JavaScript objects (they are currently only supported by Netscape Navigator 4). We're concerned here with JavaScript style sheets.

The simplest way to use style sheets is to change the properties of the HTML tags. For example, suppose you want to spice up your document a bit by having all level 1 headings be displayed in red, instead of the usual black. You could write the following:

Example 14.9

```
<STYLE TYPE="text/javascript">
  tags.H1.color = "red"
</STYLE>
```

This little style sheet starts with the **<STYLE>** tag and ends with the **</STYLE>** tag. Note the **TYPE="text/javascript"** field on the **<STYLE>** tag. HTML supports other types of style sheets, so this field is required for Java-Script styles.

TIP

> *This will work in Netscape Navigator 4, but not in Navigator 3 and Internet Explorer 3. Also note that in Navigator 3, the text between the tags will be displayed within the document, and you can't avoid this by enclosing everything in a <! > tag, as doing so stops the tags from working in a compatible browser. There's a way to avoid the problem, though, as you'll see later under "Using External Templates."*

tags is the name of a property of every **document** object. The **tags** property can hold information about the HTML tags: **<H1>** through **<H5>**, as well as **<P>**, **<B>**, **<EM>**, and many others.

In this example, we're modifying the style data for the **<H1>** tag. We have changed the **color** property to **red**. So, after this point in the document, all **<H1>** text will be red instead of the usual black.

In general, the style sheet tags can be placed anywhere, in either the HEAD or BODY of the document, but the tags will only modify items that appear after the tags. However, if you want to change a style property for your entire document, you can apply it to the BODY of the document, by placing something like this in the HEAD:

```
<STYLE TYPE="text/javascript">
  tags.BODY.color = "blue"
</STYLE>
```

This style sheet would make **blue** the default **color** for all text in the document. Note that in order for this to work, the style sheet must be placed in the header of the document (between the **<HEAD>** and **</HEAD>** tags).

When you modify the **BODY**, the other text in the document will "inherit" the **BODY**'s style. So, if you set the BODY color to red, all text in the document will be red, including Heading text. You can then modify parts of the document with style tags inserted lower down in the document.

Besides **color**, each **tags** property can contain other information that controls how tagged text is displayed, as shown in the following table:

Property	Values	Meaning
fontSize	Either a number or a keyword: **xx-small** **x-small** **small** **medium** **large** **x-large** **xx-large** **larger** **smaller**	Character size.
fontWeight	**normal** or **bold**	Character weight.
fontStyle	**normal** **italic** **oblique** **small-caps** **italic small-caps** **oblique small-caps**	Character style.
verticalAlign	**baseline** **sub** **super** **top** **text-top** **middle** **bottom** **text-bottom**	Character vertical positioning. Baseline is normal; sub is subscript; super is superscript.
textAlign	**left** **right** **center** **justify**	Text alignment on the page.
textDecoration	**none** **underline** **overline** **line-through** **blink**	Character marking or blinking.
textTransform	**none** **capitalize** **uppercase** **lowercase**	Character capitalization.
color	**number** or **keyword**	Character color.

Property	Values	Meaning
display	**inline** **block** **list-item** **none**	Controls how the text is displayed. **Inline** allows text to be on the same line as text with other tags. **Block** requires the tagged to text to occupy entire lines of text. **List-item** is like **block**, but also adds indentation like the HTML **<LI>** tag.
listType	**none** **disc** **circle** **square** **decimal** **lower-roman** **upper-roman** **lower-alpha** **upper-alpha**	If the **display** property is set to **list-item**, this property sets the type of marker or numbering placed on each paragraph.
whiteSpace	**normal** **pre**	The **pre** value makes the text appear preformatted, like the HTML **<PRE>** tag: line breaks and multiple spaces are preserved, rather than closing space and filling lines as for normal text.

The above properties can be used on any tag. There are some additional properties that can be used on any *block-level* tags: ones such as **<H1>** or **<P>** that cannot begin or end in the middle of a line of text. All block-level tags define text or images that are displayed in a rectangular region of the screen, and they have additional properties for controlling this region:

Property	Values	Meaning
marginLeft, marginRight, marginTop, marginBottom	size	Space between the text or image border (if any) and the boundaries of the enclosing window, frame, or table cell.
paddingLeft, paddingRight, paddingTop, paddingBottom	size	Space between the text or image and the border (if any).
borderLeftWidth, borderRightWidth, borderTopWidth, borderBottomWidth	size	Thickness of the border.
borderStyle	**none** **solid** **3D**	Style of the border.
width	size or **auto**	Width of the text or image.
height	size or **auto**	Height of the text or image.
lineHeight	**size**	Spacing between lines of text.
align	**left** **right** **none**	Controls how the text or image is positioned relative to other text that wraps around it.
clear	**left** **right** **both** **none**	Controls whether other text or images are allowed to appear alongside this element.
backgroundColor	**number** or **keyword** (see Appendix G)	Color of the background.
backgroundImage	**URL**	Image file for the background.

As you can see from the previous table, you can specify a size for some of these properties. The sizes can be specified in several units of measure:

Unit	Example	Meaning
pixel	**"12px"**	Size of a single dot on the computer screen, usually between 1/70 and 1/90 of an inch.
point	**"9pt"**	1/72 of an inch.
pica	**"1pi"**	1/6 of an inch (12 points).
em	**"2em"**	Width of a lower-case "m" in the current font.
ex	**"1ex"**	Height of a lower-case "x" in the current font.

Note that **em** and **ex** are relative to the current font size. This might be useful, because it means that the measurements will keep their appearance in proportion to the text.

Using External Templates

If you want to use one style sheet in many documents, you can store it in a separate file and import the styles from that "template" into other Web documents by using the **<LINK>** tag; for example:

Example 14.10

```
<LINK REL=STYLESHEET TYPE="text/javascript" HREF="myStyleSheet.htm">
```

The **REL** and **TYPE** attributes must read exactly as shown above; **myStyleSheet.htm** would of course be the URL of the file containing your style sheet statements. That file does not contain **<STYLE TYPE="text/javascript">** and **</STYLE>** tags, though. It contains only the style statements that are normally held within those tags. In Example 14.10, the document contains nothing but this statement:

```
tags.H1.color = "green"
```

You can place multiple statements in the style document; place each statement on a separate line, with a semicolon at the end of each line.

There's another way to use an external style template. You can use the **SRC=** attribute in the **<STYLE>** tag, like this:

```
<STYLE TYPE="text/javascript" SRC="myStyleSheet.htm"></STYLE>
```

You can also combine multiple template documents into a single Web page, so you can mix and match styles. Simply use a series of these **<LINK>** and **<STYLE>** tags to reference the external documents. If there are any conflicting styles, the last style takes precedence over the previous style.

Placing styles in external documents is a way to avoid problems with browsers that can't work with styles properly. As noted earlier, when Navigator 3 sees the instructions between the style tags, it displays the text in the Web page—it doesn't understand what it's supposed to do with the instructions and so regards them as normal text. If you place the style information in an external document, Navigator 3 won't see that information so it can't display it.

Creating Your Own Styles

Changing the HTML tags gives you quite a bit of control over your documents' appearance. But even more flexibility is available when you create your own styles. Each style has a name, known as its ID. Each document has an **ids** property that lets you manage your styles, just as the **tags** property lets you manage styles for HTML tags.

Here's a simple example:

Example 14.11

```
<STYLE TYPE="text/javascript">
  ids.bright.color = "orange"
  ids.bright.fontWeight = "bold"
</STYLE>
```

This creates a style called **bright**, which causes text to be displayed in orange bold characters. To apply this style to some text, use the **ID** attribute on an HTML tag, like this:

```
<P ID="bright"> Here's a brightly displayed paragraph. </P>
```

```
<H3 ID="bright"> This level 3 header can also be made bright. </H3>
```

What if you want to apply a style to text in a place, such as the middle of a paragraph, where there is no tag? In that case, you can use the **<SPAN>** tag with the **ID** attribute, like this:

```
<P> Here's a paragraph with <SPAN ID="bright"> some bright text </SPAN> in
the middle. </P>
```

Classes of Styles

So now we have created a style—named **bright**—that can make any text appear in bold orange characters. But we have already changed our **<H2>**s to red, and orange might look almost the same as red on some computers. So, it would be nice if we could define a single style that would have different properties depending on where it was used. We can, in fact, do this, using something called a *class*. A class will change characteristics depending on the type of text being modified. For example, you could create a class that changes one type of text—normal text, say—to orange, and another type of text—H2 text, for instance—to gold.

Every document has a property called **classes** to hold class information. Here's a way to create a class called **general**:

Example 14.12

```
<STYLE TYPE="text/javascript">
 classes.general.all.color = "green"
 classes.general.all.fontWeight = "bold"
 classes.general.H2.color = "gold"
 classes.general.H1.textDecoration = "blink"
 classes.general.H1.color = "blue"
</STYLE>
```

The first two lines of this style sheet define **color** and **fontWeight** properties for **general.all**, so they will apply to any tag that uses the **CLASS="general"** attribute. The third line defines a color for **general.H2**; this color, **gold**, will override the orange property when **general** is used on **<H2>** text. The last two define how to display **H1** text; it will be **blue** and will **blink** on and off.

In other words, you can use the **CLASS="general"** attribute in different places, and its effect will depend on the context. As you can see here, we can apply the same class to the different types of text and get different effects:

```
<P CLASS="general"> Here's a general class paragraph. </P>

<H2 CLASS="general"> This level 2 header can also be set to the general
class. </H2>

<H1 CLASS="general"> This level 1 header can also be set to the general
class. </H1>

<P> Here's a paragraph with <SPAN CLASS="general"> some general-class text
</SPAN> in the middle. </P>
```

As you'll see in the Online Companion example, we have three different types of text, though we've applied the same class. This allows you to create a page, then apply different styles to the page in quite a sophisticated way, quickly modifying the manner in which the document appears by changing the class or referring to a different external document containing the class information.

A tag can only have one **ID** attribute, so you can't apply two styles to one tag. But you can use both **ID** and **CLASS** on one tag; so, by using classes as well as styles, you have more flexibility in applying styles to text. For example, we can create a style that applies a black background:

```
<STYLE TYPE="text/javascript">
  ids.onBlack.backgroundColor="black"
</STYLE>
```

Then, we can apply both the **general** characters and **onBlack**'s black background to one paragraph, like this:

```
<P CLASS="general" ID="onBlack"> This paragraph has both a class and an ID.
</P>
```

You can see more style examples in Example 14.13, including the following class and ID, which place a box around text:

Example 14.13

```
<STYLE TYPE="text/javascript">
  classes.box.all.borderTopWidth = "1em"
  classes.box.all.borderRightWidth = "6pt"
  classes.box.all.borderBottomWidth = "12px"
  classes.box.all.borderLeftWidth = 24
  classes.box.all.borderStyle = "3D"

  ids.padded.paddingTop = "12pt"
  ids.padded.paddingBottom = "12pt"
  ids.padded.paddingLeft = "24pt"
  ids.padded.paddingRight = "24pt"
</STYLE>
```

The **box** class places a lined box around the text. The **padded** ID controls the distance between the text and the box. In Example 14.13, we applied just the box class, and then both the **box** class and the **padded** ID (see Figure 14-3).

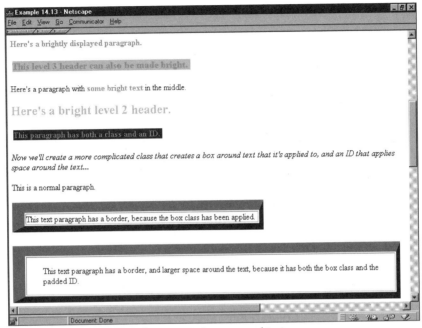

Figure 14-3: You can use styles to create boxes around text.

TIP

If you want to fool around with JavaScript styles, take a look at the Dynamic Style Sheets document at http://developer.netscape.com/library/documentation/communicator/stylesheets/jssindex.htm.

Text Manipulation Using Regular Expressions

Starting with JavaScript 1.2 (Navigator 4), JavaScript includes a feature called *regular expressions* that provides some very powerful ways to work with text. To work with regular expressions, you need to create *patterns*. These patterns can then be used to find, copy, and replace pieces of text.

A JavaScript pattern is a set of symbols enclosed by two slash (/) characters. For example:

```
txt = "This is a string."
pat = /is/

result = txt.match(pat)
```

This shows how to use the **match** method to search a string for any text that matches the pattern. We have defined a string called **txt**, and a pattern called **pat,** consisting of the letters **is**. The **match** method searches the string from left to right, trying to find a section that matches the pattern. The value returned by **match** is placed in the variable **result**. In this case, **result** will contain **is**, the text that was found and matched the pattern. If no match was found, **result** would be **null**. Try the following example to see how this works:

Example 14.14

```
function matchIt(form) {
  txt = form.data.value
  pat = /is/
  result = txt.match(pat)
  form.results.value = result
}
```

This example uses a form into which you can type some text. When you click on a button that calls this function, the text you typed (**form.data.value**) is sent to the function and loaded into **txt**. The function then creates a pattern (**pat**), and uses the **match( )** method to search the text for the characters **is**. If it finds them, it displays the number **2** in the **results** text box (**form.results.value**); if it doesn't, it displays **null**.

Besides finding text that matches a pattern, we can also replace it with a new value using the **replace** method. For example:

```
txt = "This is a string."
pat = /is/

txt2 = txt.replace(pat,"was")
```

You can see this at work in the following example:

Example 14.15

```
function matchIt(form) {
  txt = form.data.value
  pat = /is/
  txt2 = txt.replace(pat,"was")
  form.results.value = txt2
}
```

This takes the text from **txt**, modifies it, and places it into **txt2**. You might expect that this would change the text to "**This was a string**." But in fact, the result will be "**Thwas is a string**." Do you see why? A pattern will match the first occurrence in the string. The letters **is** in the word **This** come before the word **is**, so that's where the replacement occurs.

This all seems pretty basic; so far we haven't done anything that we couldn't already do with string methods. But we're just getting started. Patterns become really useful when you use their more advanced features. Suppose we want to change that last example so that it only replaces the word **is**, not an occurrence of those two letters in a longer word. We can write:

```
txt = "This is a string."
pat = / is /

txt.replace(pat," was ")
```

You can see this in the following example:

Example 14.16
```
function matchIt(form) {
  txt = form.data.value
  pat = / is /
  txt2 = txt.replace(pat," was ")
  form.results.value = txt2
}
```

Now, the pattern will only match the letters **is** if they are preceded and followed by a space. But what if **txt** contains **This is, in fact, a string.**? Now, the pattern will fail to match, because the word **is** is followed by a comma rather than a space. The solution is to change the pattern again:

```
txt = "This is, in fact, a string."
pat = /\bis\b/

txt.replace(pat,"was")
```

We have replaced the spaces in the pattern with the special symbol, **\b**, which represents a word boundary: a point where a "word" character is followed or preceded by a "nonword" character. For this purpose, a "word" character is defined as any letter or digit, or the underscore (_) character. All the others—punctuation and white space—are considered nonword characters. Note that the word boundary doesn't represent the boundary character itself; it doesn't represent the space or comma, for instance. Rather, it represents the point at which the characters meet. So, while in the previous example we had **(pat," was ")**—because we were replacing **is** and the spaces before and after—this time we have **(pat,"was")**. We're not replacing the nonword characters. The pattern has matched just the characters **is**, not the space followed by **is**.

Besides **\b**, JavaScript accepts a number of special symbols in patterns:

Symbol	Matches:
\t	Tab character.
\n	Newline character.
****	Back slash character.
\w	Any "word" character: letters, digits, or underscore (_).
\W	Any "nonword" character
\s	Any white-space character: space, tab, newline, etc.
\S	Any non-white-space character.
\d	Any digit.
\D	Any nondigit.
\b	Any word boundary: a point in the string between a word and non-word character.
\B	Any nonword boundary: a point in the string between two characters that are both word characters, or are both nonword.
.	Any character.
^	The beginning of the string.
$	The end of the string.

Note: the backslash character may be used before special pattern characters, such as **^**, **$**, and so on, in order to override their special meanings. For example, a dash (-) is a special character in patterns. To actually match a dash, use **\-**.

Here are some more types of patterns:

Pattern component	Matches:
P|Q	Either **P** or **Q**, where **P** and **Q** are patterns.
P+	One or more consecutive occurrences of pattern, **P**.
P*	Zero or more consecutive occurrences of pattern, **P**.
P?	Zero or one occurrence of pattern, **P**.
P{n}	Exactly **n** consecutive occurrences of pattern, **P**.
P{n,}	At least **n** consecutive occurrences of pattern, **P**.
P{n,m}	At least **n**, and at most **m**, consecutive occurrences of pattern, **P**.
[aeiou]	Any one of the characters, **a**, **e**, **i**, **o**, or **u** (lowercase).
[a-z]	Any lowercase letter.
[0-9]	Any digit.

Besides these symbols, there are two modifiers, **i** and **g**, that may be placed after the slash at the end of a pattern. The **i** modifier selects case-insensitive matching: it causes uppercase and lowercase letters to be considered as equivalent. So for example, the pattern **/kent/i** will match **kent**, **Kent**, **KENT**, or even **KeNt**.

The **g** modifier selects "global" operation for the **match** and **replace** methods. For **match**, this modifier means to search the entire string, rather than stopping at the first match. In this case, the result will be an array containing all the matching substrings. Similarly, the **g** modifier causes the **replace** method to replace all occurences in the string. Here's a variation on an earlier example:

```
txt = "This is a string."
pat = /\bis\b/g

txt.replace(pat,"was")
```

Because of the **g** modifier on the pattern, the call to **replace** will change both occurrences of **is**, resulting in **"Thwas was a string."**

Remembering Matches

One very useful technique to use with patterns is to have JavaScript remember parts of the matched expression. For instance, suppose you have created a form in which the user should enter a phone number. People do this in different ways: some put the area code in parentheses, some put dashes between parts of the number, and so on. You want to be able to remove any punctuation or white space, and just extract the groups of 3, 3, and 4 digits.

This is actually quite easy to do using a function like this:

Example 14.18

```
function phoneNumber(form) {
  var s = form.data.value
  var num = new Array()
  var p = /(\d{3})\D*(\d{3})\D*(\d{4})/

  num = s.match(p)
  alert("The phone number is " + num)
}
```

This function accepts a string, **s,** and returns a three-element array, **num,** containing the parts of the standard phone number. Take a look at the pattern **p.** As mentioned above, **\d** represents a digit, and **\D** represents a nondigit. So **\d{3}** matches exactly 3 digits, and **\D*** matches any group of nondigit characters, or none at all. The clever part of this pattern is the parentheses. They tell JavaScript that if a match is found for the pattern, it should remember the part of the string corresponding to the symbols in parentheses. So, this example will remember groups of 3, 3, and 4 digits, while discarding everything else.

How do we access these remembered values? Well, one way is shown above. The **match** method returns an array containing the remembered values. Note that this returned value is different from what we got in our earlier examples, where the pattern did not contain any parentheses.

Also, the remembered values are available as properties of the **RegExp** object, which we'll look at in a moment. The properties named **RegExp.$0, RegExp.$1,** and **RegExp.$2** are set to the first three remembered values whenever a pattern is matched. Additional properties **$3** through **$9** are available, so a pattern match can remember up to 10 values.

Of course, this script is limited in that it will only work properly if there are 10 digits in groups of 3, 3, and 4. Some people may not include an area code when they type a phone number; and some users who connect to your Web page from outside your home country may include a country code, or divide up the digits differently. We can give our script more flexibility by using the **split( )** method.

Example 14.19

```
function phoneNumber(form) {
  var s = form.data.value
  var num = new Array()
  var p = /\D+/
```

```
num = s.split(p)
alert("The result is " + num)
}
```

The **split** method accepts a pattern which is the separator: the separator represents the character that occurs between the parts of the string that we want to keep. In other words, it throws away the separator you specify and keeps the rest. In this case, we have used the pattern **\D+** representing one or more nondigit characters. So, **split** will remove all the nondigit characters, and return an array containing each group of digits in a separate string. This function will work with any groups of digits; it is not limited to the 3-3-and-4 format required by the previous script.

Patterns have a number of additional features which are of interest mainly to advanced programmers. Netscape's patterns are based on those in the PERL language; so, if you want more details, a PERL manual may be helpful.

The RegExp Object

We mentioned the **RegExp** object above in describing its properties $0 through $9. Another use of the **RegExp** object is as a constructor for patterns. For example, the statement:

```
pat = new RegExp("\\bis\\b", "i")
```

is equivalent to:

```
pat = /\bis\b/i
```

Either one matches the word **is**, enclosed by nonword characters, in upper-case or lowercase. Note that when using **RegExp**, there are some slight differences. There are no slashes at the beginning and end; and the back slashes are doubled, as they must be when you want to put them in a quoted string. Also, the **i** modifier is in a separate string, which is the second argument to **RegExp**.

So, why type all those extra characters if the effect is the same? The useful thing about constructing patterns with **RegExp** is that you don't have to use quoted strings. You can use variables that are passed from other parts of your script, or even typed by the user into a text field.

Example 14.20

That's how we created the demonstrator forms in Example 14.20. These forms allow you to type in a text string and a pattern, and see the results. The scripts use **RegExp** to create patterns from the characters that you type. This example allows you to play around using a variety of special-character symbols in matches, modifiers, your own strings and patterns, and so on.

Providing Security With Object Signing

Security for Web browsers is an important issue; so important that, until recently, both JavaScript and Java had a major flaw; they were intentionally limited to doing things that would not allow people to design programs that could harm the recipient's data. In other words, they couldn't change anything on the user's computer, except in the most limited way (writing cookies, for instance). There have been security bugs in the past, but these were mistakes; the intention all along was to create programming languages that could only carry out "safe" procedures.

Why is this such an important issue? It's important because the Internet became a new "input" device pouring data into our computers. In the early days of the personal computer, new programs could be introduced to our computers using floppy disks. Later, they could be introduced using networks. In both cases, there's a degree of control over these two methods. And in any case, using those methods programs were unlikely to be added to the computer very often. The Internet, and more importantly the Web, created a completely new way to bring programs into a computer. Now, programs can be downloaded to your computer frequently, very quickly, and even in such a way that you're not aware of what is going on while the transfer is taking place. And they're introduced in such a manner that they run immediately . . . unlike, for instance, a program that you get on a floppy disk, which can be virus checked, installed, and then run under controlled conditions.

Thus, the Internet provides wonderful new opportunities for our virus-writing colleagues, or at least *would* if Java and JavaScript provided unlimited access to computer resources. So, it was apparent from the beginning that these programming languages could not be allowed unrestricted access to recipient computers' hard drives, screens, e-mail systems, and so on. So, up until JavaScript 1.2, the activities of JavaScripts were limited to the browser itself, and restricted from access to the rest of the computer except where absolutely necessary.

But these restrictions introduce a real problem; in effect Java and JavaScript have been crippled. Programs *need* to be able to access the hard drive; for instance, can you imagine how useful a word processor would be if it couldn't save your work? These programs *must* have access to the computer's resources in the same way that a program you buy and install has access to computer resources. Without this access, both Java and JavaScript would eventually die out, as their utility would be severely restricted. So, what's needed is a system that can use computer resources . . . but only if you allow it access to those resources.

There is a way that this can be done, using digital signatures to identify the programs you download from the Web. Digital signatures can be used to sign any form of computer data; it can be used to sign e-mail messages, for instance, so you can receive email that is as trustworthy as a paper document with someone's signature on it. You can browse Web pages or download files with the same level of safety that you would have buying brand-name software off the shelf in a store.

Netscape has introduced the concept of *object signing* as a way to provide this security for JavaScripts and Java applets. Note that this technology is just coming out as this book goes to press. For detailed, updated information, see some of the references listed at the end of this section.

Basics of Object Signing

A digital signature may be attached to any script, Java applet, or other downloadable file. It provides the following benefits:

- Signed objects can be positively identified. Digital signatures cannot be faked; the mathematical formulas that are used to generate them ensure that even the most powerful supercomputers can't crack their codes. So, once an object's signature is verified, you know who the object came from.

- Signed objects cannot be tampered with. Users can detect any change to the data that was made after it was signed, because once the file has changed, the digital signature is no longer valid.

- Signed objects can be controlled. For instance, suppose you surf your way to a Web page with a Java applet that writes files on your hard drive. Navigator will pop up a dialog box explaining what the applet wants to do, and asking your permission. Since the applet is signed, the browser can verify where it came from. This will help you decide whether or not to let the applet access your files, and will also let you know who to contact if some problem arises.

A signature is packaged with some other data into a form called a certificate. Certificates are created by certificate authorities: public organizations that are well-known and trusted by both the authors and users. If you have the Windows version of Navigator version 4, preview release 4 or later, you already have some certificates. (At the time of publication, security was not working on the Mac browser.) Click the Security button (or select Security Info from the Communicator menu). In the dialog box that opens, select Signers under the Certificates category. You should see a menu of certificates from organizations such as telephone companies, government agencies, and some new companies that have been started specifically to act as certificate authorities. Having the authorities' certificates on your machine is the first step in verifying certificates that you receive from other sources.

If you click Yours in this dialog box, you will see a list of any certificates that you may have obtained for yourself. Initially, of course, the list will be empty. There is a Get a Certificate button (scroll to the bottom of the dialog box) that will send you to the https://certs.netscape.com/client.html Web page, where you can link to certificate authorities. There are different types of certificates, providing different levels of security; they vary from no-cost to about $400. For instance, a Class 3 Digital ID for Validating Software costs $400. The certifying authority will check that the company to which it's issuing the certificate is really who they purport to be, by checking their name and location, credit and company report, and so on, so recipients of the certificate can be sure that it comes from who it says it comes from. A $20 Class 2 Digital ID for Validating Software provides less assurance, because the certifying authority checks the company's identity in less detail.

After you obtain a certificate, you can use it to sign files and scripts that you create. To do this, you need a software tool called the JAR Packager. JAR stands for Java Archive. A JAR file can contain scripts, applets, or other files, and their signatures. The JAR packager allows you to create and work with JAR files, and to apply your signature to objects in the JAR file. You can download the JAR Packager from Netscape at http://developer.netscape.com/software/signedobj/jarpack.html.

For More Information

Object signing is both complicated and, at present at least, confusing, because it's only just been introduced and is still in development. There's a lot to read and understand, so if you'd like to find more information about object signing try this page at the Netscape developer support library: http://developer.netscape.com./library/documentation/doclist.html#security.

You will find several articles on security here, as well as what's-new documents describing the features of the latest version of Navigator. There's also an interesting plain-English article on security at http://home.netscape.com/newsref/ref/rsa.html.

Moving On

We've finished with the theory, and we're going to move on now to specific ways in which you can use all the techniques you've learned. We'll start, in the next chapter, by looking at ways to control windows and the documents within those windows. We'll learn about opening secondary windows and writing to them. Then, in subsequent chapters, we'll move on and look at how to work with frames and forms, and how to communicate with the user.

Controlling Windows & Documents With JavaScript

In this chapter you're going to learn all about working with windows—how to open them, how to write to them, how to close them, and so on. In order to work with windows, though, we need to understand the **window** and **document** objects, so we'll begin there, with a bit more theory.

The Window Object

Your JavaScripts always have a **window** object. The **window** object sits at the top of the object hierarchy and contains properties and methods designed to provide information and help you manipulate both the window itself and the document within the window. For example, there are properties that contain information about the status-bar message and the number of frames in the document.

Window Object Properties

Let's take a look at the **window** properties:

Property	Description
closed	Specifies whether a window has closed. This was added in JavaScript 1.1 (Navigator 3).
defaultStatus	The default text in the window's status bar. A read-only property.
innerHeight	The height of the window's internal document area, in pixels. Added in JavaScript 1.2 (Navigator 4).
innerWidth	The width of the window's internal document area, in pixels. Added in JavaScript 1.2 (Navigator 4).
length	The number of frames in the window.
name	The name assigned to the window when opened.
opener	Refers to the window in which a script used **window.open** to open the current window. This was introduced with JavaScript 1.1 (Navigator 3).
outerHeight	The height of the entire window, including borders, toolbar, etc. Added in JavaScript 1.2 (Navigator 4).
outerWidth	The width of the entire window, including borders, toolbar, etc. Added in JavaScript 1.2 (Navigator 4).
parent	A synonym for the parent window in a frameset. (We'll discuss this, along with **self**, **top**, and **window**, in a moment.)
self	A synonym for the current window.
status	The text currently displayed in the window's status bar. For example, you can set the following: **status="calculation complete".**
top	A synonym for the **top** window. If you have frames within a window, **top** refers to the main window—the parent of all of the windows.
window	The current window.

The **window** object also has the following properties that are objects in their own right:

Property	Description
document	The currently displayed document.
frame	A **frame** object contains information about a frame contained by the window.
frames array	This array contains a list of all the **frame** objects in the window. You can refer to a **frame** object using the **frames** array, like this: **window.frames[indexnumber]**; or by using the object's name, like this: **window.framename**.
history	An object that contains information about the history list of the current window or frame.
location	An object that contains information about the URL of the document displayed in the window.
	Don't confuse this with **document.location**, which is the URL of the currently displayed document (which is the same as **document.URL** and now undocumented, as Netscape is encouraging the use of **document.URL** rather than **document.location**). You can change **window.location** (replacing the current document with another), but you can't change the **document.location** (as that's the location of the document currently displayed).
locationbar	The window's location bar. Added in JavaScript 1.2 (Navigator 4).
menubar	The window's menu bar. Added in JavaScript 1.2 (Navigator 4).
personalbar	The window's "personal" bar (the new customizable button bar in Navigator 4). Added in JavaScript 1.2 (Navigator 4).
scrollbars	The window's scrollbars. Added in JavaScript 1.2 (Navigator 4).
statusbar	The window's statusbar. Added in JavaScript 1.2 (Navigator 4).
toolbar	The window's toolbar. Added in JavaScript 1.2 (Navigator 4).

Note also that a new object added to JavaScript 1.2 (the **screen** object) allows you to find out the screen resolution—the screen width and height in pixels—used by the display on which the browser is running.

> **TIP**
>
> *The property table—and the method table, later in this chapter—are not intended to replace the Netscape JavaScript documentation (see Appendix H, "Finding More Information," for information on where to get this). There's way too much detailed information in that documentation to be squeezed into this book. Use these tables to get an idea of what can be accomplished, then refer to the full documentation for the complete details.*

Referring to Windows

There are several properties that are used to refer to particular windows. From "inside" a window—that is, when referring to the window containing the document in which the JavaScript is placed—you can use the **window** property or you can use nothing at all. If you don't name the window, JavaScript assumes you are talking about the window holding the document in which the JavaScript is placed. If you want to refer to a secondary window, though, you will have to name it.

> **TIP**
>
> ***Important:*** *When you refer to the current window from an event handler, you* **must** *include the* **window.** *part.*

As we'll see later in this chapter, when you create a window you will name it. In fact, the window will get *two* names. One name is used by HTML tags in the **TARGET** attribute to define where a document should be placed. The other name is the one that you will use in your JavaScripts to refer to the other window.

So, here's how to refer to a window. For example, let's say you want to set a value in a text box (**text1** in the form named **form1**). If the form that contains this text box is in the current document, you can use any of these methods to refer to the text box:

```
form1.text1.value="Wednesday"
window.document.form1.text1.value="Wednesday"
self.document.form1.text1.value="Wednesday"
```

You don't have to specify which window at all (unless you are running this script from an event handler, in which case you must use one of the last two formats). But you might want to, just to make the script more readable and to keep all these window references clear in your mind. You can refer to the window as **window** or **self**—it's the same thing.

Now, how do we refer to frames within a window? Each frame in a window is considered to be a *child* of that window. And it's a **window** object in its own right, having the same properties and methods as the parent window. If the form you want to modify is in another frameset, you can refer to it by referring back to the parent window, like this:

```
parent.frame1.document.form1.text1.value="Wednesday"
```

We're going to be looking at frames in more detail in Chapter 16, "Using JavaScript With Frames."

Referring to Other Windows

You can refer to one window from another. For example, let's say you have a script in the parent window; how would you refer to a child window (a window that was created from that parent window)? You do this in the same way that you would refer to a child frame:

```
Win1.document.form1.text1.value="Wednesday"
```

This places a value into the **text1** text box in **form1** in a child window named **Win1**. What about a child of a child (a "grandchild"). That is, a child of a window created from the current window? Well, you'll have to name both windows, like this:

```
Win1.Win2.document.form1.text1.value="Wednesday"
```

Win2 (the child of the child window) is, in effect, a property of **Win1**, so you must use the complete hierarchy and name. You cannot simply name **Win2**. The parent window knows nothing about **Win2**, because it was created by a different window.

When you refer to windows from a script, think about whether the current window will know anything about the other window. If you are referring to a child, it will. If you are referring to a window created from somewhere else, though, it might not. In JavaScript 1.0 (Navigator 2) it won't know about a grandparent or a sibling—the grandparent was created by a great-grandparent, the sibling by a parent. In fact, in JavaScript 1.0 you can only refer to windows "down" the family tree, not "up" the family tree. You can refer to a child, or a grandchild, or a great-grandchild. You can't refer to a parent window (except in the case in which you are referring from a *frame* to the frame's parent; you can't refer from a window back to the window that created it). You can't refer to a grandparent. You can't even refer to a "sibling," which is another window created by the same window that created the current window. However, starting with JavaScript 1.1 (Navigator 3), there's a property that improves the way in which you refer to other windows: **opener**. This property refers to the window that opened the window the script is running in.

We have a couple of examples that show how this window-addressing system works. We created a document with a button that opens two secondary windows. One of the secondary windows has a button that opens another child window. Within the first document we have several buttons that modify the **defaultStatus** property in the three windows. (Right now don't worry about how windows are opened; we'll come back to that in a few moments.)

Example 15.1

```
<INPUT TYPE="BUTTON" VALUE="This window's status bar: self.defaultStatus"
onclick="self.defaultStatus='This is the current window\'s status bar'">
```

This button modifies the first window's status bar; notice that we've used **onclick="self.defaultStatus=**. We had to state **self.defaultStatus** because in an event handler you must state which window you are referring to, even if you are referring to the current window. (We could have used **window.defaultStatus** too, which means the same thing.)

```
<INPUT TYPE="BUTTON" VALUE="The child window's status bar:
Win1.defaultStatus" onclick="Win1.defaultStatus='The child window\'s status bar'">
```

The second button modifies the child window's status bar; we've used **Win1.defaultStatus** this time, **Win1** being the child window's name.

```
<INPUT TYPE="BUTTON" VALUE="The grandchild window's status bar:
Win1.Win2.defaultStatus" onclick="Win1.Win2.defaultStatus='The grandchild
window\'s status bar'">
```

The third button modifies the grandchild's status bar, a child window of one of the current window's child. This time we named both windows (**Win1.Win2.defaultStatus**). If you want to try an experiment you can close the child window, then try this button. It won't work (in fact you'll see an error message), because once the **Win1** window has closed there's no way to address **Win2**. The script has to address *through* **Win1**.

There are also two buttons used to close the child and grandchild:

```
<INPUT TYPE="BUTTON" VALUE="Close the grandchild window: Win1.Win2.close( )"
onclick="Win1.Win2.close( )">
<INPUT TYPE="BUTTON" VALUE="Close the child window: Win1.close( )"
onclick="Win1.close( )">
```

You'll find that if you use the second button and *then* the first button, the first button won't work. Why? Again, because once you've closed the child, there's no way to refer to the grandchild. (The current window doesn't know the grandchild's name, but has to refer to it "through" the child.)

The grandchild also has several buttons, but they won't all work correctly:

```
<FORM>
<INPUT TYPE="BUTTON" VALUE="The current window: self.defaultStatus"
onclick="self.defaultStatus='This is the current window\'s status bar'"><P>
<INPUT TYPE="BUTTON" VALUE="The parent window: Win1.defaultStatus"
onclick="Win1.defaultStatus='The previous (parent) window\'s status →
bar'"><P>
<INPUT TYPE="BUTTON" VALUE="The parent window: parent.defaultStatus"
onclick="parent.defaultStatus='The previous (parent) window\'s status →
bar'"><P>
<INPUT TYPE="BUTTON" VALUE="The top window: top.defaultStatus"
onclick="top.defaultStatus='The top (most-ancient ancestor) window\'s →
status bar'"><P>
</FORM>
```

These all try to write to various status bars. The first one works, because it's writing to **self.defaultStatus**, the status bar in the grandchild window. The second creates an error message. We've named the previous window (**Win1.defaultStatus**), but the grandchild doesn't know that name, so it won't work. The third actually works; it does set the parent window's status bar, but this window is, in effect, its own parent! In other words, the button will change the status bar in the current window, not the true parent—because when we use **parent**, we are actually talking about the parent window containing a frameset (you might think of it as the *main* window), not the window that created this window. So the current window's status bar is modified. (No, our window doesn't actually have any framesets in it; still, **parent** doesn't refer back any farther than the main window.)

And finally, we tried **top**. Again, though, when we use **top** we are referring to a situation in which a window contains nested framesets—not to a window that created another window. So again, this changes the current window's status bar.

That's JavaScript 1.0, but JavaScript 1.1 (Navigator 3) works a little differently. You can now use the **opener** property to refer back up the window hierarchy. For example:

```
window.opener.defaultStatus=
```

This means "the **defaultStatus** of the window that opened the window this script is running in." So in the next example we *can* refer to previous windows, as long as we're using a JavaScript 1.1 browser.

Example 15.2

```
<FORM>
<INPUT TYPE="BUTTON" VALUE="The parent window: window.opener.defaultStatus"
onclick="window.opener.defaultStatus='The previous (parent) window\'s →
status bar'"><P>
<INPUT TYPE="BUTTON" VALUE="The top window:
window.opener.opener.defaultStatus"
onclick="window.opener.opener.defaultStatus='The top (most-ancient →
ancestor) window\'s status bar'"><P>
<INPUT TYPE="BUTTON" VALUE="The parent's sibling window:
window.opener.opener.Win2.defaultStatus"
onclick="window.opener.opener.Win2.defaultStatus='The parent\'s sibling\'s →
window\'s status bar'"><P>
<INPUT TYPE="BUTTON" VALUE="Close this window" onclick="self.close( )">
</FORM>
```

In this example we created two child windows (**Win1** and **Win2**) and a grandchild window (**Win3**). We have referred to the parent window and the grandparent window: **window.opener.opener.defaultStatus** means "the **defaultStatus** of the window that opened the window that opened this one." Try this example and you'll see that we can, indeed, modify the status bars in the previous windows. We can even address siblings and "aunts and uncles" using this method: **window.opener.opener.Win2.defaultStatus** means "the **defaultStatus** of the child named **Win2** which is a child of the window that opened the window that opened this one." In other words, this addresses a sibling window of the parent window. We could have taken it a step further and addressed a child of that sibling, too, or another child of the parent. So as you can see, the **opener** property is very important, allowing us to pass information back up the window hierarchy, and even down other branches.

Window Object Methods

Now let's look at the **window** methods—the functions associated with the **window** object.

Method	Description
alert( )	Opens an Alert message box.
blur( )	Moves focus away from the specified window. This method was added in JavaScript 1.1 (Navigator 3).
clearTimeout( )	Cancels a delayed script that was started by **setTimeout( )**.
close( )	Closes the window. Starting with JavaScript 1.1 (Navigator 3), if you use this method to close a window other than one opened by JavaScript using the **open** method, the user sees a confirmation box, and the window is not closed unless the user confirms the close. It *will* close the window *without* confirmation if there's only one open window, though.
confirm( )	Opens a Confirm message box; the user has two choices: OK and Cancel. The method returns **true** if the user clicks on OK, **false** if the user clicks on Cancel.
focus( )	Brings the specified window to the foreground. This method was added in JavaScript 1.1 (Navigator 3).
open( )	Opens a new window.
prompt( )	Opens a Prompt message box; the user can type into this box, and the typed text is returned to the script.
scroll( )	Scrolls the document in the window to a particular position. This was added in JavaScript 1.1 (Navigator 3). It's being replaced in JavaScript 1.2 (Navigator 4) by **scrollTo( )**.
setTimeout( )	Causes a script to be executed after a specified time delay.

JavaScript 1.2 (Navigator 4) added the following methods:

Method	Description
back( )	Moves to the previous page in the history list (in effect, clicks the browser's Back button).
captureEvents( )	Captures all events of the specified type (see Chapter 12 for more information about capturing events). All objects that have event handlers have this method and the other **Event( )** methods below.
clearInterval( )	Cancels a repeating timer that was started by **setInterval( )**.
find( )	Opens the Search dialog box.
forward( )	Moves to the next page in the history list (in effect, clicks the browser's Forward button).
handleEvent( )	Invokes the event handler for the specified event. (All objects that have event handlers have this method.)

Method	Description
home( )	Displays the browser's home page (the one set in the browser's preferences).
moveBy( )	Moves the window a specified distance across the screen.
moveTo( )	Moves the window to a specific location on the screen.
print( )	Prints the contents of the window.
releaseEvents( )	Releases captured events of the specified type, sending the events further along the event hierarchy.
resizeBy( )	Changes the size of the window by a specified amount.
resizeTo( )	Changes the size of the window to a specific width and height.
routeEvent( )	Passes a captured event along the event hierarchy.
scrollBy( )	Scrolls the document being displayed in the window by specified amounts.
scrollTo( )	Scrolls the document being displayed in the window until a specific point is at the upper left corner. This is intended as a replacement for **scroll( )**, though **scroll( )** will still work and you might want to use it for a while to make sure your scripts work with older browsers.
setInterval( )	Causes a specified script to be repeatedly executed at a specified time interval.
stop( )	Stops the download (in effect clicks the browser's Stop button).

Note, by the way, that these methods were not all added at the same time. Some appeared in the second preview version of Navigator 4, while others were added in the third preview version, another reason to make sure you're always working with the latest browser software.

TIP

We've used the **prompt**, **alert**, *and* **confirm** *methods a number of times, so we won't repeat them here. Just remember that if you use one of these methods from an event handler (as opposed to putting it in a function and then calling the function from an event handler), you must write* **window.prompt**, **window.alert**, **window.confirm**.

By the way, the **location** object also has two useful methods that are related to the displaying of documents in a window and were added in JavaScript 1.1 (Navigator 3). The **location.replace( )** method is used to replace the currently displayed document with another one, while **location.reload( )** is used to reload the current document.

Now that we've got the basic information, let's take a look at what we can do with all this.

Opening Secondary Windows

We'll begin with the basics. How can you open another window using Java-Script? Simple. Let's take a look again at Example 2.4, which we saw back in Chapter 2, "A Few Quick JavaScript Tricks." First, we had this in the HEAD:

Example 2.4

```
<HEAD>
<SCRIPT LANGUAGE="JAVASCRIPT">
<!--
function WinOpen( ) {
    open("window.htm","Window1","toolbar=yes");
}
//-->
</script>
</HEAD>
```

Then we placed the following piece in the body:

```
<form>
<input type="button" name="WindowButton" value="Secondary Window--Click on
me" onclick="WinOpen( )">
</form>
```

As you can see, we began by defining a function in the HEAD; we called this function **WinOpen( )**. The function uses the **open** method to open a window (called **Window1**), to load the file **window.htm** into the window, and to add the toolbar to the window.

Why would you want to create secondary windows like this? Well, secondary windows have been used in hypertext for a long time. The earliest forms of hypertext were too simple. If you clicked on a link you saw another document. Click on another link to see yet another document, and so on. The people developing hypertext soon learned two things: that there would be many times when the reader would want to see a bit of information for a moment, then continue in the current document; and that it's very easy to get lost in hypertext! Readers reported getting totally confused about "where" they were in the network of interlinked documents.

Secondary windows were one of the things developed to make hypertext easier to use. They were intended for situations in which the developer could be fairly sure that the user would want to keep the original document open. For example, in a glossary you might have one document with a large list of entries; the user would click on an entry, and a secondary window would open that contained the definition of the entry on which you clicked. The original list would remain in view, of course, so the user could click on another one, modifying the contents of the secondary window to show the next definition.

Here's another use of secondary windows. Perhaps the developer feels that the user might want to branch off in a particular direction, but keep the original window open for some reason. In other words, the user might click on a link in the first window, opening the second. The user can then navigate through the document in the second window, going from page to page, while the original document remains open in the first window.

There are many reasons for using secondary windows and, as you've seen, secondary windows are very easy to create with JavaScript. They're also pretty easy to create in HTML, but as you'll see creating windows with JavaScript provides a lot more flexibility and options.

TIP

When you create secondary windows, make sure that you check them in a low-resolution mode, such as VGA. If you create windows in a high-resolution mode, such as 800 x 600 or 1024 x 768, they might fit nicely on your screen, but change to VGA and you might find that they are partly off screen. Also, a window that doesn't need a scroll bar in high resolution might need one in a low resolution.

Configuring the Window

JavaScript provides a number of ways for you to configure your windows. You can do so by modifying the parameters of the **open** method. So let's look at **open**. This is the basic format used by the **open** method:

```
[windowVar = ][window].open("URL", "windowName", ["windowFeatures"])
```

The various parts of the **open** method are:

- **windowVar** This is a window name. In effect, the **open** method "returns" the window to this name. We didn't use this in our earlier example, and you don't have to always do so. However, if you plan to refer to this window from another window in your scripts, then you must use this.

- **window** The **open** method is a method of the **window** object, so you can include **window.** here if you wish, but it's not necessary. (Unless, of course, this script is in an event handler, in which case you must include **window..**)

- **URL** is the URL of the document you want to place into the window. (Leave this empty—""—if you want an empty window, or if you want to write to the secondary window. We'll see how to do that later in this chapter.)

- **WindowName** is a name you give to the window. In this instance, however, this is the name used by the HTML **<FRAME>** and **<A>** tags, not by your JavaScripts.

Finally, there are the **WindowFeatures**; you can define exactly what the window should look like—whether it should have a toolbar, location bar, directories bar, and so on, and what size it should be.

The following features are set *on* using **yes**, **1**, or by simply naming the feature. They are set *off* using **no**, **0**, or by omitting the feature in its entirety:

- **alwaysLowered**—This causes the window to move to the bottom of all the other windows and not to sit above windows, even when it is active. This is a JavaScript 1.2 (Navigator 4) feature.

- **alwaysRaised**—The opposite of **alwaysLowered**, this causes the window to always appear "on top of" all other windows, even when some other window is active. (This depends on the operating system; in Windows the window is always on top; on a Macintosh it will remain above other browser windows, but not necessarily windows in other applications.) This is a JavaScript 1.2 (Navigator 4) feature.

- **dependent**—Use this to create a new window that isn't a child of the current window (by setting **dependent** to **false**). This is a JavaScript 1.2 (Navigator 4) feature.

- **directories**—Use this to include the browser's Directory Buttons bar. (The Netscape family of browsers has a Directory Button bar. Many browsers don't have such a bar, so JavaScript browsers from other companies might simply ignore this window feature.)

- **hotkeys**—This disables hotkeys if the window has no menu bar (with the exception of the Exit and Security hotkeys). This is a JavaScript 1.2 (Navigator 4) feature.

- **location**—Use this to include the browser's location or URL bar.

- **menubar**—Use this to include the browser's menu bar.

- **resizable**—Use this to allow the user to resize the window. If this is set *off*, the window size will be fixed.

- **scrollbars**—Use this to place scroll bars in the window. (The scroll bars will only appear in the window if necessary; if the contents of the window are all visible within the window, the scroll bars won't be there.)

- **status**—Use this to include the browser's status bar.

- **titlebar**—Set this to *false* to remove the title bar.

- **toolbar**—Use this to include the browser's toolbar in the window. For example, **toolbar**, **toolbar=1**, or **toolbar=yes** means "place a toolbar in the secondary window."

- **z-lock**—This creates a new window that does not rise above other windows when activated, even when it is active. This is a JavaScript 1.2 (Navigator 4) feature.

TIP

If you omit all feature names, JavaScript assumes you want them all. So if you want none of these features, simply name one like this: **toolbar=no**.

The following features control the size and position of the window and are specified in pixel values. The exact size on users' screens will depend on how their computers are set up, but as a rule of thumb you can figure about 75 to 100 pixels per inch (and, of course, you should test your scripts in different video resolutions).

- **width**—This sets the width of the viewing area of the window: the part in which documents are displayed. For example, **width=400** will give a viewing area about 4 inches wide. (This item and the following one are being replaced by the new **innerWidth** and **innerHeight** settings; see below, and the note at the bottom of this list.)

- **height**—This sets the height of the viewing area of the window, in pixels.

- **innerHeight**—Sets the height of the window's internal document area, in pixels. This and the following five items are JavaScript 1.2 features (Navigator 4); they won't work in earlier browsers.

- **innerWidth**—Sets the width of the window's internal document area, in pixels.

- **outerWidth**—This sets the width of the entire window, including borders, toolbar, and so forth. This takes precedence over innerWidth; that is, if you set both, innerWidth will be ignored.

- **outerHeight**—This sets the height of the entire window, including borders, toolbar, and so forth. This takes precedence over innerHeight; if you set both, innerHeight will be ignored.

- **screenX**—This sets the distance from the left edge of your computer screen to the left edge of the window.

- **screenY**—This sets the distance from the top of your computer screen to the top of the window.

- **type=fullWindow**—This is not in JavaScript 1.2 (Navigator 4) at the time of writing, but should be added soon. It will allow you to set *canvas mode*, which we'll talk about a little later in this chapter.

Note that the new **innerWidth** and **innerHeight** settings replace the old **width** and **height** settings. You can, if you wish, still use **width** and **height** and, in fact, should do so if you want to maintain backward compatibility—that is, to make sure your scripts work with JavaScript 1.1 and 1.0 browsers. But eventually you'll be able to give up using those settings, and they will eventually be removed from the JavaScript documentation.

You should also be aware that some of these features can only be used in *signed scripts*, as we discussed in Chapter 14: **alwaysRaised**, **alwaysLowered**, **titlebar** (if false), and **z-lock** can only be used in signed scripts. And the **outerWidth**, **outerHeight**, **innerWidth**, **innerHeight**, **screenX**, and **screenY** features must be used within a signed script if you are creating a very small window or pushing the window offscreen.

TIP

It's a good idea to put scroll bars into your window if you are unsure as to whether all the data will fit. If you don't put scroll bars in, you won't get them even if they are needed to view all the contents.

TIP

*There used to be, early in JavaScript's life, another feature, **copyhistory**, but it has been disabled for security reasons. This feature would grab the history list from the first window and give it to the new window, so the user could move back and forth through the history from that window. The Back and Forward buttons and the Go menu would then work using the original window's history list. For the present, this feature has been removed from JavaScript—though it's a handy feature to have.*

You can use all or any of these options, separating each with a comma (but *no* space between them), all enclosed within the same quotation marks. The quickest way to create a complete window is to leave all this stuff out, like this:

Example 15.3

```
<SCRIPT LANGUAGE="JAVASCRIPT">
<!--
function WinOpen( ) {
   open("window.htm","Window1");
}
//-->
</SCRIPT>
```

Try this example in the Online Companion and you'll find that you get a complete window (see Figure 15-1): all the toolbars and the status bar, it's sizeable, and it's full size. Remember, if you don't name any window features, you get them all.

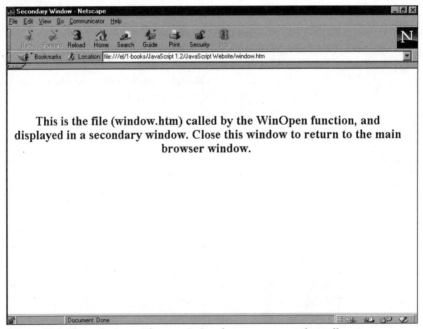

Figure 15-1: If you don't specify any window features, you get them all.

But look at the following example. In this example, we've added the **"location"** feature. Now we get a completely different window. Because we've specified one feature, JavaScript assumes all the others should be turned off; all we get this time is a window with the location bar.

Example 15.4

```
<SCRIPT LANGUAGE="JAVASCRIPT">
<!--
function WinOpen( ) {
    open("window.htm","Window1","location");
}
//-->
</SCRIPT>
```

Mix and match as you wish. What you want will depend on what you want the window to achieve. For example, you might want the location bar, so the users can see the URL or enter another one. You quite likely will want to size the window. You might want to provide a toolbar, but no other controls. Here's an example:

Example 15.5

```
<SCRIPT LANGUAGE="JAVASCRIPT">
<!--
function WinOpen( ) {
    open("window.htm","Window1","location,resize,height=250,width=450,toolbar, →
scrollbars");
}
//-->
</SCRIPT>
```

In this example you'll get a resizable window that is 250 pixels high and 450 wide, with a location bar and toolbar. Notice that all the features appear within the same quotation marks and that there are no spaces between them—features appearing after a space won't work. This is why this window *doesn't* have scroll bars, even though the word **scrollbars** appears at the end of the features.

JavaScript 1.2's Improvements

JavaScript 1.2 (Navigator 4) provides some important new features. In earlier browsers you couldn't position the window, which was a bit of a nuisance. You could size it, but not determine *where* in the screen it should appear. And in earlier versions you could determine the size of the window by stating the inner dimensions but not the outer dimensions. With JavaScript 1.2 you can tell the browser exactly where to put the window, and you can choose whether to set the outer dimensions of the window (that is, the very outside edge of the window) or the inner dimensions (the area in which the document is displayed). That's handy if you need to position a window very precisely or if you have multiple windows working together. Of course you can't use both methods at once; or rather if you do use both, the outer size (**outerHeight** and **outerWidth**) will take precedence and the inner size (**innerHeight** and **innerWidth**) will be ignored.

JavaScript 1.2 also has two more very useful features: **alwaysRaised**, which stops the secondary window from getting lost below other windows (it's "always on top"), and **alwaysLowered**, which has the opposite effect—it stops the window from ever obscuring other windows, even if it's active. (Of course you have to be careful with this feature, or windows can get completely lost.)

Example 15.6

```
function WinOpen( ) {
    open("window3.htm","Window1","location,resize,screenY=200,screenX=100, →
alwaysRaised=yes,outerHeight=450,outerWidth=450,toolbar, scrollbars");
}
```

In this example we've set the outer size of the window and also placed it where we want it on the screen using **top** and **left**. And we've used **alwaysRaised** to create an always-on-top window. You'll find, however, that **alwaysRaised** won't work. Try clicking outside the window, on a window below, and you'll find that the current window will disappear; it *doesn't* stay on top. This feature only works if it's in a signed script (which we discussed in Chapter 14).

Canvas Mode

There's a feature you can work with, known as *canvas mode,* that is similar to something you might have run across in browsers a couple of years ago: *kiosk mode* (some browsers still have this feature, though the two most popular browsers do not). Canvas mode is used to remove all the "chrome" from around the window; the toolbars, the status bar, the menu bar, and the scroll bars. You're left with a document and almost nothing around it (you'll still get the title bar and a window border). Note, however, that canvas mode will only work in signed scripts (see Chapter 14 for information about signed scripts).

For instance, you could create a canvas-mode window like this.

```
function WinOpen( ) {
    open("window4.htm","Window1","titlebar=no,left=-1,top=- →
1,width=screenWidth,height=screenHeight,alwaysRaised=yes");
}
```

At the time of writing canvas mode was created using **alwaysRaised**, by setting the **top** and **left** to **-1**, and using **width=screenWidth** and **height=screenHeight**. However, a new **type=fullWindow** feature will be added to JavaScript 1.2 soon. This will provide a simpler way to set canvas mode. You'll be able to replace everything in the example we saw with this:

```
function WinOpen( ) {
    open("window4.htm","Window1","type=fullWindow");
}
```

The Problem With Links

It would be nice to be able to open these secondary windows using links rather than buttons. Indeed, you can open secondary windows using links, but there are problems with doing so in JavaScript 1.0. In the following example we created two links that open secondary windows. The first link doesn't refer to an HTML file in the normal way, though—it uses the **onclick** instruction to do so, but there's nothing in the **HREF=** attribute. The second link uses both the **onclick** instruction and the normal URL attribute:

Example 15.7
```
<A HREF="" onclick="WinOpen( )">Open Secondary Window</A><BR>
<A HREF="window.htm" onclick="WinOpen( )">Open Secondary Window</A>
```

In both cases clicking on the link will open the secondary window. What's interesting, though, is what happens to the browser window below. If you are using Netscape Navigator, clicking on the first link displays a directory listing (as shown in Figure 15-2). In some other browsers clicking on such a link might do nothing.

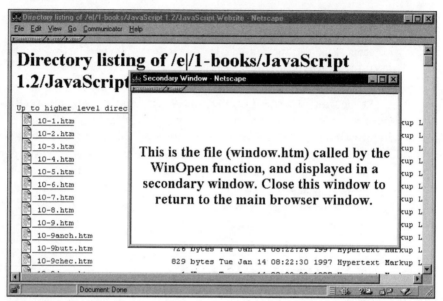

Figure 15-2: The Netscape browsers open a directory listing if you click on a link with nothing in **HREF=**.

In the second case, the one in which we have entered a filename in the **HREF=** attribute, the browser will open the same document in both windows; again, not quite what we wanted. Also, there are reports that doing this sort of thing might crash some browser versions on some operating systems (though the reports might be misidentifying the problem). Thus opening windows from links in this manner is a bit of a problem and, for the moment at least, to be avoided.

JavaScript 1.1 provides a fix for this sort of thing. As you saw in Chapter 13, you can create JavaScript tags like this:

```
<A HREF="javascript:instruction>Link text</A>
```

This creates a link that runs the JavaScript and *won't* display the directory listing we just saw. For example, you could do this:

Example 15.8

```
<A HREF="javascript:"WinOpen( )">Open Secondary Window</A><BR>
```

Closing Secondary Windows

The user can always close a window using the normal window controls—by clicking on the X button in the top right corner in Windows 95, for example. But it's a good idea to include a Close button if this is a temporary window—a window that you expect to be opened, read, and then closed. Create a button like this:

Example 15.9

```
<FORM>
<input type="button" Value="Close this Window" onclick="self.close( )">
</FORM>
```

Again, notice that we are using **self.close( )**, not **close( )**, as you must be specific in an event handler. If we had the **close( )** method in a function being called from the **onclick** event handler, though, we could use **close( )**.

Writing to the Window

We've just seen how you can open a window and place the contents of a specified Web page into that window. There's something else you can do, though—you can write from your script to the new window. Take a look at this:

Example 15.10

```
function OpenWindow( )   {
    Win1 =
open("window.htm","SecWin","scrollbars=yes,width=350,height=230");
    var sText = "<BODY>This is some text<P></BODY>"
    Win1.document.write("<H2>Secondary window</H2><HR><P>" + sText)
}
function CloseWindow( )   {
    Win1.close( )
}
```

In the HEAD we've created a function called **OpenWindow( )**. This uses the **open** method to create a new window; notice that this time we have a window name (**Win1=**) because we plan to use it later. You'll notice that we've specified **window.htm** to be placed into the window, as before. But as you'll see, this will be ignored, because we're going to write to the window using **document.write( )** instead. (You don't have to specify an .HTM document. Simply enter **open("",** etc.)

After opening the window we declare a variable (**sText**) and place a string into it. You can see that the string includes some HTML tags. Finally, we use the **document.write** method to write something to this window. We have to name the window we want to write to, so we use **Win1.document.write**. We write HTML tags, text, and the contents of the **sText** variable to the window.

The second function, **CloseWindow( )**, quite simply uses the **Win1.close( )** method to close the window we created. This example Web page has two buttons, one to call the **OpenWindow( )** function and one to call the **CloseWindow( )** function. You can see the result of clicking on the first button in Figure 15-3.

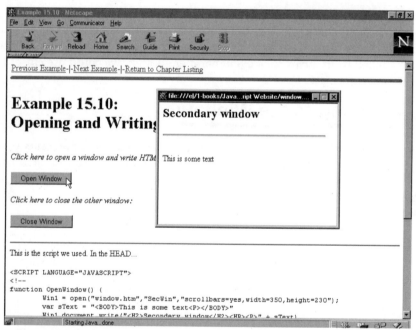

Figure 15-3: We've created a window and written text to it.

Now, try this. Click on the Open Window button in the original window. Click several times. If you have your browser window maximized, nothing appears to happen. But switch back to the window and you'll see that you've been writing to the window again . . . and again, and again; the same text is written over and over. The window was already open, so it didn't open again. Yet the text you were writing *was* sent to the window. We'll see how to deal with that little problem in a moment.

Writing to One Window From Another

Now that you have a window open, how can you write to it from the first window? Earlier we discussed how secondary windows are commonly used when you want to have two windows open at the same time, such as a glossary list in one window and a glossary definition in the other. Clicking on a button in the glossary list window could then display a related topic in the secondary window. (I say button, not link, because of the link problem we've just discussed. In most hypertext systems a glossary list would usually contain a list of links. As you've seen, you can easily do that in JavaScript 1.1, but not in JavaScript 1.0.)

Writing to the window is simple. You use the **document.write** method. In other words, rather than write directly to the **window** object, you must write to the **document** object that is a property of the **window** in which you want the text to appear. For example, we could do this:

```
function MoreText( )    {
    Win1.document.write("<P>Here's some <P>more text for you...and some →
more. Yes, and more, and yet more<BR>")
}
```

This function uses the **write** method to place text in the **Win1** window. We have to include **document**, because you can't really write to windows; you have to write to the documents inside them. Notice again that we can include HTML tags within the text we are sending.

Problems Writing to Windows

Writing to other windows in this way is a little erratic. Make sure that you place an HTML **
** tag at the end of the text you are sending or it won't be written in its entirety. (Some of it might be written some of the time—it's hard to predict what will be written.) Even if you place the text to be written in a variable, then use the variable name in the **document.write** method, you should still use a **
** at the end of the text in the variable. Also, note that there's a better way to write to a document, as we'll see under "The Document Stream" later in this chapter.

Where's That Window?

Actually the example we showed you above is not a good way to write to a window. The problem is that if the window is not visible, the user won't see anything happen and might not realize the window has been written to.

But there's a new **window** method called **focus( )**. This is not available in any of the Netscape Navigator 2.0 browsers, but was introduced in JavaScript 1.1 (Netscape Navigator 3). It's used to bring the specified window to the foreground, and we can employ this method to resolve the problem we had with the last example. In the following example, we've added a function that—when called from a button—writes more text to the window, but also brings that window to the front:

Example 15.11

```
function MoreText( )    {
    Win1.document.write("<P>Here's some <P>more text for you...and some  →
more. Yes, and more, and yet more<BR>")
    Win1.focus( )
}
```

We write to the window's document. Then, once the script's done that, it uses **Win1.focus( )** to bring the window back to the forefront. It's a good idea to use the **focus( )** method whenever you are doing something to another window to make sure that the user can see what's happening. Try it in the Online Companion and you'll see how it works. (You can also use the **alwaysRaised** window feature, as we saw before, to make the window "always on top," though this only works with JavaScript 1.2 browsers.)

By the way, in this case each time we click on the button we *add* to the document. If we'd opened a Web page in the window first, writing to it again will clear the Web page and then write the text, as you will see in the following example:

Example 15.12

```
function OpenWindow( )    {
    Win1 = open("window.htm","SecWin","scrollbars=yes,  →
width=350,height=230");
}
```

This time we've opened **window.htm** in the new window—we haven't written to it. Now, if you try this example in the Online Companion you'll see that when you click on the button that runs the **MoreText( )** function, the Web page is removed, and the new text written. Why? In effect the **document.write** command is opening a new document stream (which we'll discuss a little later in this chapter). When you open a new stream, you automatically clear the current document from the window. Each subsequent **document.write** instruction is part of the current stream, so clicking on the button several times simply adds to the document, it doesn't clear it again.

TIP

You cannot write to the end of a Web page. Once a Web page has been written it can't be modified without being rewritten. However, if you haven't finished the document "stream," the Web page has not finished, so you can continue writing to it.

The Document Object

We're not only working with the **window** object now, but with the **document** object. So before we go any further, let's take a look at the **document** object. These are the available properties:

Property	Description
alinkColor	The color of an active link (**ALINK**).
Anchor	An HTML anchor, created using the **<A NAME=>** tag. This property is also an object in its own right.
anchors array	An array listing the document anchor objects (**<A NAME=>**). This property is also an object in its own right.
Applet	An **<APPLET>** tag, used to embed a Java applet into a document. This property is an object in its own right. This property was added in JavaScript 1.1 (Navigator 3).
applets array	An array that lists the **Applet** objects. This property was added in JavaScript 1.1 (Navigator 3).
Area	An HTML tag (the **<AREA HREF=>** tag, used within the **<MAP>** tag), used to create image maps. This property is also an object in its own right and is regarded as a form of **Link** object. This property was added in JavaScript 1.1 (Navigator 3).
bgColor	The document's background color (**BGCOLOR**).
classes	A property added in JavaScript 1.2 (Navigator 4), used within the **<STYLE>** tags to set the style of multiple HTML text elements.
cookie	A piece of information stored in the cookie.txt file. (We talked about cookies in Chapter 13, "Advanced Topics.")

Property	Description
domain	The domain name of the server that sent the document. Introduced with JavaScript 1.1 (Navigator 3).
Embed	An undocumented object/property. A file type embedded into the document using the **\<EMBED\>** HTML tag. Added in JavaScript 1.1 (Navigator 3).
embeds array	A list of the **\<EMBED\>** tags in the document. Added in JavaScript 1.1 (Navigator 3).
fgColor	The document's text color (the **TEXT** attribute in the **\<BODY\>** tag).
Form	A form (**\<FORM\>**) in a document. This property is also an object in its own right.
forms array	An array listing the **Form** objects in the order in which they appear in the document. This property is also an object in its own right.
ids	A property added in JavaScript 1.2, used within the **\<STYLE\>** tags to modify the style of text that would otherwise be set using the **classes** property.
Image	An image in a document, created with an HTML **\<IMG\>** tag (used to embed an image in a document) or by using **new Image( )**. This property is an object in its own right. This property was added in JavaScript 1.1 (Navigator 3).
lastModified	The date the document was last changed.
linkColor	The color of the document's links, the **LINK** attribute in the **\<BODY\>** tag (links to documents that the user has not yet viewed).
Link	An **\<A HREF=\>** tag in the document. This property is also an object in its own right.
links array	An array of the **Link** and **Area** objects in a document, in the order in which they appear. This property is also an object in its own right.
location	The URL of the currently displayed document. You can't change the **document.location** (as that's the location of the document currently displayed). You can, however, change **window.location** (replacing the current document with another). While **window.location** *is* also an object in its own right, **document.location** is *not*. Also, note that this property will be removed in later versions of JavaScript (presumably because of this ambiguity!). Instead of **document.location** you can use **document.URL**, which will work for Navigator 2 and later, but not for Internet Explorer 3.

Property	Description
referrer	The URL of the document containing the link that the user clicked on to get to the current document.
tags	A property added in JavaScript 1.2 (Navigator 4), used within the **<STYLE>** tags to set the style of a particular HTML text element.
title	The document's title (**<TITLE>**).
URL	A string containing the complete URL of the document. This is exactly the same as **document.location**. It was in Navigator 2, but, because it wasn't documented, it's not in Internet Explorer 3, so it won't work in that browser.
vlinkColor	The text color of links pointing to documents that the user has viewed. The **VLINK** attribute of the **<BODY>** tag.

Document Methods

Now, here are the document object's methods:

Method	Property
captureEvents( )	Captures all events of the specified type. (All objects that have event handlers have this method and the other **Event( )** methods below.) Added in JavaScript 1.2 (Navigator 4).
close	Closes the document stream (we'll get to that next).
getSelection( )	Creates a string containing the currently selected text within the document. Added in JavaScript 1.2 (Navigator 4).
handleEvent( )	Invokes the event handler for the specified event.
open	Opens the document stream.
releaseEvents( )	Releases captured events of the specified type, sending the events further along the event hierarchy. Added in JavaScript 1.2 (Navigator 4).
routeEvent( )	Passes a captured event along the event hierarchy. Added in JavaScript 1.2 (Navigator 4).
write	Writes text to the document.
writeln	Writes text to the document and ends with a newline character.

The Document Stream

What's all this about the document stream? Well, using the document stream provides a better, more formal way to write to documents than the manner we've looked at so far. Previously we simply wrote straight to the document in the window. If you do that and there's no document in the window, then a document is automatically opened. In other words, you can open a blank window—simply don't specify a Web page or use **document.write** to put anything in it. Later, if you use **document.write** to send text to the document, a new document is automatically opened inside that window.

A better way to do this is to create a document "stream" using the **document.open( )** method. In the following example we've modified an earlier example to use this more formal method:

Example 15.13

```
function MoreText( )      {
    Win1.focus( )
    Win1.document.open( )
    Win1.document.write("Some guy hit my fender the other day, and I said →
unto him, \"Be fruitful, and multiply.\" But not in those words.<P>Woody →
Allen")
}
```

Here's what we've done. First, we've used **Win1.focus( )** to bring the window to the front (remember, this won't work on Netscape 2 browsers, only in JavaScript 1.1 browsers—Netscape Navigator 3 or later). Then we used **Win1.document.open( )** to open the document stream. That means "here comes a document." Unlike in the earlier examples, the original text (written with **document.write** in an earlier function) is cleared from the window, because when you open a stream, you clear the document. Next we use the **Win1.document.write** method to write the text.

Now, go to the Online Companion and try this. If you're using an early JavaScript browser you'll probably find that the end of the text is missing (Navigator 4 seems to handle this okay). Remember the problem we had earlier, with missing text? Well, here's a quick fix for that:

Example 15.14

```
function MoreText( )     {
    Win1.focus( )
    Win1.document.open( )
    Win1.document.write("Some guy hit my fender the other day, and I said →
unto him, \"Be fruitful, and multiply.\" But not in those words.<P>Woody →
Allen")
    Win1.document.close( )
}
```

Same function, except that we've added the **Win1.document.close( )** method. This closes the document stream; you'll find that all the text will appear in the document—there'll be nothing missing. In fact with the previous example you'd find that when you closed the window, the rest of the text was written to the page just before the window disappeared, because as you closed it the document stream was being closed, too.

> **TIP**
>
> *When you open a document stream, the document is automatically a text document. But the* **window.open( )** *method actually allows you to specify what type of document you want, like this:* **open("mimetype")**. *You can use* **text/html, text/plain, image/gif, image/jpeg, image/x-bitmap**, *or any plug-in that Netscape Navigator supports. Because we haven't specified anything in our examples, JavaScript assumes (rightly) that we want* **text/html**.

Here's another thing to notice, by the way. If you click on this button over and over, the text is not added to the bottom of the document. Rather, the document is cleared each time, and the text rewritten. In fact that's the case in both this and the previous example. That's because the **document.open( )** method closes the previous document stream, even if the previous stream did not use a **document.close( )** statement.

> **TIP**
>
> *Remember when, in an earlier example, we wrote to a window containing a Web page, without using* **document.open( )**? *Even so, the Web page was cleared, right? That's because once a Web page has been written, its document stream is closed.*

The clear( ) & writeln( ) Methods

Let's look at the last two methods, **clear( )** and **writeln( )**. The **clear( )** method, not surprisingly, clears the contents of a document. In our next Online Companion example we have a document that automatically opens a second window and writes to that window. Now, in theory you can use this to clear the window:

```
function ClearWindow( )    {
    Win1.focus( )
    Win1.document.clear( )
    Win1.document.close( )
}
```

Actually in some early browsers **clear( )** doesn't work well; if you created an example using this you might find that you have to call the function twice to get the window to clear. Still, there's a way around the problem. In our next example we automatically open a secondary window (using **<BODY onload="OpenWindow( )">**), then do this:

Example 15.15

```
function ClearWindow( )     {
    Win1.focus( )
    Win1.document.open( )
    Win1.document.write( )
    Win1.document.close( )
}
```

This uses the **document.write( )** method, but doesn't write anything. That's the same as clearing the document.

Finally, the **writeln** method; this is the same as the **document.write( )** method, except that a new line character is placed at the end of the text that is written. This is ignored when writing HTML, unless the text is being placed between **<PRE>** and **</PRE>** or **<XMP>** and **</XMP>** tags.

> **TIP**
>
> *As you've seen,* **window.open** *and* **window.close** *are very different from* **document.open** *and* **document.close***. Try not to confuse them!*

Pictures, Too

We can even insert pictures into a document. In fact, you can write any text or HTML tags to the document. Here's an example:

Example 15.16

```
function OpenWindow( ) {
    Win1 = open("","SecWin","scrollbars=yes,width=600,height=350");
    Win1.document.open( );
    Win1.document.write("<HEAD><TITLE>Image Document</TITLE></HEAD><IMG →
SRC='http://www.netscapepress.com/support/javascript1.2/new/bell.gif' WIDTH=144 →
HEIGHT=119 ALT='Wait a few moments and the Bell will appear...'><P>You have →
to do this just right, or the picture doesn't appear. (It may take a few →
moments for the picture to load and, of course, you have to be online to get →
it.) Make sure you use the full URL of the picture--a relative URL may not →
be good enough. You should also include the image size; although it probably →
```

```
makes no difference to Netscape 3.0, earlier browsers may choke if you don't →
include the image size.<BR><FORM><input type='button' value='Close Window' →
onclick='window.close( )'></FORM>")
    Win1.document.close( )
}
```

You can see the result of this in Figure 15-4. The image will be placed into the window at the top.

TIP

You must include the image size in your tag, or your browser might choke! (Netscape 3 and later browsers are okay, but Netscape 2 might not like it.)

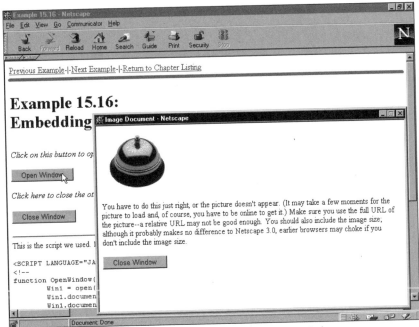

Figure 15-4: You can even write picture <IMG> tags to your windows.

To make sure this works, include an absolute URL to the image, not a relative URL; in other words, give the full URL, including the protocol (**http://**), the directory, and the filename. If you use just the filename, you might find the image is not placed into the document, even if that file is in the same directory as the original HTML document. Also, use the **document.open( )** and **document.close( )** methods to make sure everything is written correctly.

Controlling Background Colors

When JavaScript first appeared the most popular use seemed to be to provide color controls for Web pages. Why? Because they're very easy to build. You can create buttons in your documents that allow people to modify background colors. For example, if you have an unusual background color but have heard from some readers that they don't like it, you can give them the choice, like this:

Example 15.17

```
<FORM>
<INPUT TYPE="button" VALUE="Red" onclick="document.bgColor='red'">
<INPUT TYPE="button" VALUE="White" onclick="document.bgColor='white'">
<INPUT TYPE="button" VALUE="Blue" onclick="document.bgColor='blue'">
<INPUT TYPE="button" VALUE="Green" onclick="document.bgColor='green'">
<INPUT TYPE="button" VALUE="Blue (#0000FF)"
onclick="document.bgColor='#0000FF'">
</FORM>
```

TIP

Where do these colors come from? You can, if you prefer, use the color's hexadecimal values. (I'm sure you have the hexadecimal value for red, green, and blue on the tip of your tongue, don't you?) On the other hand, you can do what we did for most of these colors and use the color names built into the browser. See Appendix G, "Color Values," for a list of these names (and the corresponding hexadecimal values). Of course in most cases you won't need to refer to this list; simply type the name of the color and as long as it's nothing unusual, it's almost certainly in the list.

By the way, this:

```
<INPUT TYPE="button" VALUE="Blue" onclick="document.bgColor='blue'">
```

is just the same as this:

```
<INPUT TYPE="button" VALUE="Blue" onclick="document.bgColor='#0000FF'">
```

The hexadecimal number (**0000FF**) preceded by # is the equivalent of **blue**. Now you know that, you can forget about using hexadecimal values for colors; and if you want to see a color chart showing all the available colors, go to the Online Companion's Color Chart. (There's a link within this chapter's example links, or go directly to http://www.netscapepress.com/support/javascript1.2/colors.htm.)

Your Settings Override

The settings you make using the document object's properties: **vlink**, **bgColor**, **fgColor**, and so on, override both the document's HTML settings (the ones in the **<BODY>** tag *and* the user's own preferences). Remember, users can choose to override **<BODY>** settings in General Preferences, but if you modify the settings using JavaScript, the script wins! Also, note that it doesn't matter where in the document you make these settings, the script still takes precedence. For example, if you make the settings in a script above the **<BODY>** tag (so the **<BODY>** tag is read last), and the **<BODY>** tag has different settings, the scripts settings are still used.

Creating "Slide Shows"

There are two window methods we haven't looked at yet that can be very useful: **setTimeout** and **clearTimeout**. The first is used to add a lag to script instructions. In other words, **setTimeout** tells the browser not to run the instruction until a certain time has passed. (If the user does something to move to another page before that time has passed, the instruction will not be executed.) The other method, **clearTimeout**, is used to stop the **setTimeout** method from working.

You use **setTimeout** like this:

```
setTimeout("instruction", timedelay_in_milliseconds)
```

For example, if you want to call function **LetsMove( )** after five seconds, you would do this:

```
setTimeout("LetsMove( )", 5000)
```

Now, if you use the method in this manner, you won't be able to use **clearTimeout** to stop it. To do that, you need to provide an ID name that the **clearTimeout** method can refer to (after all, you might have several timeouts working at once, so it has to know which one you want to stop). You create this ID by preceding the statement with the ID name, like this:

```
IDname=setTimeout("instruction", timedelay_in_milliseconds)
```

So, in our example, you might do this:

```
move=setTimeout("LetsMove( )", 5000)
```

We've given the timeout the ID move, so later we can do this:

```
clearTimeout(move)
```

Here's an example that creates a little "slide show." The Web pages automatically change every five seconds:

Example 15.18

```
<HEAD>
<SCRIPT LANGUAGE="JAVASCRIPT">
<!--
function LetsMove( )    {
    location='15-18A.htm'
}
//-->
</SCRIPT>
</HEAD>
<BODY onload="setTimeout('LetsMove( )', 5000)">
</BODY>
```

The function **LetsMove( )** is very simple; it uses the **window.location** property (we've used the shorthand **location**) to load the file called **15-18A.htm**. This function is run from the **onload** event handler, which uses the **setTimeout** method. Note that we have a **5000** millisecond (5 second) delay. (See Figure 15-5.)

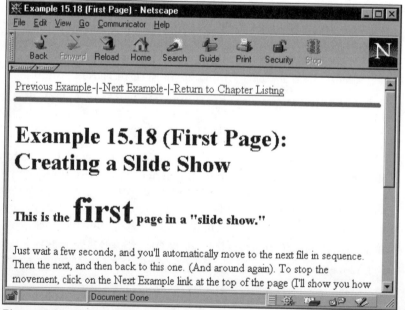

Figure 15-5: setTimeout provides a very quick and easy way to create a slide show.

TIP

Although the **setTimeout** *and* **clearTimeout** *methods are, strictly speaking, window methods, you are not restricted to using them only for window-related purposes. You can use these methods for any script you wish.*

In this case there's no way to stop the event (except by moving to another page before the delay is over). So let's see how to stop scripts run with **setTimeout( )**:

Example 15.19

```
<BODY onload="move=setTimeout('LetsMove( )', 5000)">
```

We have the same function, but we've modified the event handler. We've simply placed **move=** before **setTimeout**. Now we can create this button, to stop the motion:

```
<INPUT TYPE="BUTTON" VALUE="Stop Movement" onclick="clearTimeout(move)"><P>
```

This uses the **clearTimeout( )** method to refer to our timeout by its ID, **move**. By the way, if you create a little slide show like this, you might also want to add a button that allows the person to get started again—something like this:

```
<INPUT TYPE="BUTTON" VALUE="Next Page" onclick="window.location='15-
19A.htm'"><P>
```

This sets the **window.location** property to the name of the file you want to move to in sequence. When that file loads, a new timeout will begin, and the slide show will start up again.

JavaScript 1.2 adds two more similar methods, **clearInterval( )** and **setInterval( )**. These are used to create scripts that repeat. The script specified in **setTimeout( )** only runs once. A script run with **setInterval( )** runs over and over. It repeats after the interval specified by **setInterval( )** and continues running until the Web page closes or **clearInterval( )** is used to turn it off.

Where Do You Want to Go?

Before we move on, let's look at a couple of little systems you can use to allow the user to make choices. First, we'll look at a selection box from which the user can choose. Then we'll look at how to add a Confirmation box to a link.

There are a variety of "image previewers" that JavaScript authors have used as examples, but you don't have to use them just for images. They allow users to make choices about what to load next and where to load it—whether to load a Web page, an image, a sound, an Adobe Acrobat PDF file, a Shockwave file, or anything else. You can use a system like this to load something into the current window, or open another window and load it there. Here's what we've done:

Example 15.20

```
function Dest(form)    {
    var sGo
if (form.select1.selectedIndex == 0) sGo = "15-20a.htm";
if (form.select1.selectedIndex == 1) sGo = "15-20b.htm";
if (form.select1.selectedIndex == 2) sGo = "15-20c.htm";
if (form.select1.selectedIndex == 3) sGo = "15-20d.htm";
if (form.select1.selectedIndex == 4) sGo = "15-20e.htm";
if (form.select1.selectedIndex == 5) sGo = "15-20f.htm";
if (form.select1.selectedIndex == 6) sGo = "15-20g.htm";
if (form.select1.selectedIndex == 7) sGo = "15-20h.htm";
if (form.select1.selectedIndex == 8) sGo = "15-20i.htm";
if (form.select1.selectedIndex == 9) sGo = "15-20j.htm";
    form.select1.blur( )   ;
    Win1=open(sGo,"Window1","width=400,height=200")  ;
    Win1.focus( )
}
```

The function **Dest** takes information from the selection box (which we'll see in a moment). It declares a variable called **sGo**, and then uses a series of **if** statements to determine what to place in that variable, depending on what's been selected in the selection box. For example, if the seventh item has been clicked on, it places **15-20g.htm** into the variable.

Next, it uses the **blur( )** method to remove focus from the selection box. This is simply a little trick to avoid a problem that might occasionally occur with this selection box. You see, we've used the **onchange** event handler in the selection box, which causes a small problem. If we *don't* use the **blur( )** method, when the user reloads the page after clicking on the selection box, the **onchange** event runs again. As the page is reloading, though, the function we've created wouldn't be able to find out what's selected—because nothing has been selected. So it would open a blank window (actually your system might lock). By using the **blur( )** method we've moved focus from the selection box; if the user reloads, the **onchange** event won't run.

Next, we open a window. Note that we are placing the text from the **sGo** variable into the parameters, so whatever filename is in **sGo** is the file that will be loaded into the window.

Finally, we used **Win1.focus( )** again, to bring the window to the front. That's just in case someone clicks on several of the items in the selection box without closing the new window first.

Now, here's our selection box:

```
<form>
<select name="select1" size=4 onchange="Dest(this.form)">
<option>The White Room
<option>The Red Room
<option>The Green Room
<option>The Purple Room
<option>The Gray Room
<option>The Brown Room
<option>The Yellow Room
<option>The Blue Room
<option>The Crimson Room
<option>The Olive Room
</select>
</form>
```

When the user clicks on an item, the **onchange** event handler calls the **Dest** function, passing information from the form to the function. You can see the system in action in Figure 15-6.

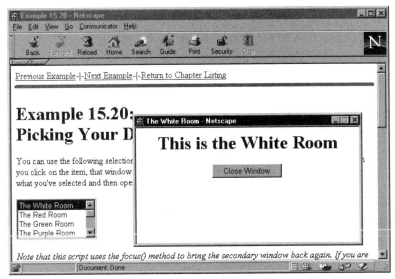

Figure 15-6: This is a very simple way to allow the user to make a choice.

This is a really simple way to let the user select what to do. Of course you can use it in many ways; you might incorporate it with a button, so the window does not open until the button's clicked. You don't have to open another window; you could use **window.location** to load another document into the current window. You could use it to run any script you want.

> **TIP**
>
> *In this script we looked at how to carry out an operation depending on the position in the selection box of the item that the user has selected. In Chapter 17 we'll look at a different way to make this decision, by actually looking at the text that has been selected in the selection list and basing the decision on that text.*

Confirmation Boxes on Links

JavaScript 1.1 (Netscape Navigator 3) has an improvement to the **onclick** event handler. You can now add a Confirmation box to the link to make the user confirm that he really wants to use the link. You can do it like this:

```
<A HREF = "URL"   onclick="return confirm('Your Text Here')">Your Text
Here</a>
```

You might try this:

Example 15.21

```
<A HREF = "adult.htm"   onclick="return confirm('Remember, this page is for →
adults only. If you are under 18 or living in an area where such images are →
illegal, please do not continue. Click on Cancel to stop the transfer, or OK →
to go to the page.')">The Naughty Bits</a>
```

When the user clicks on the link, the Confirmation box opens (see Figure 15-7). If the user clicks on Cancel, the link operation will not work. Only if the user clicks on OK will the referenced page be transferred.

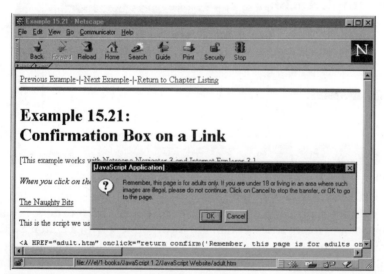

Figure 15-7: You can confirm Web page transfers.

The Image Object

An important new object was added to JavaScript 1.1 (Netscape Navigator 3): the **Image** object. This was added to JavaScript to provide some basic graphic functions. **Image** objects can be created in one of two ways. They are created automatically by Navigator when it loads an image tag in a Web page. For example:

```
<IMG name="myImage" src="http://www.mysite.com/myimage.gif">
```

This HTML tag displays the image file in the **myimage.gif** file. In effect it also creates a JavaScript **Image** named **myImage** and initializes it with the graphic data from the file specified in the **src** attribute. Once this object is created, you can change its contents by using JavaScript statements such as this:

```
document.myImage.src = "image2.gif"
```

This statement loads the new graphic file **image2.gif** into the Web page. That's right, the image that was originally in the page will now be replaced by the image stored in the **image2.gif** file.

The other way to create an image object is by declaring it with a JavaScript statement like this:

```
var image2 = new Image( )
image2.src = "portrait.jpg"
```

When you create an image object, you can specify its dimensions:

```
var image3 = new Image(150, 300)
image3.src = "portrait.jpg"
```

The above statement sets **image3** to be 150 pixels wide and 300 pixels high. When the file **portrait.jpg** is loaded, if its size is not 150 x 300, Navigator will scale it to fit the object.

Image objects created with **new**, unlike those declared in HTML text, are not a visible part of the Web page. They can be used as temporary holding areas (often called *buffers* in programming jargon), so that graphic files can be preloaded from a distant Web site and held in the browser's memory until they are needed. In other words, if you create an **Image** object like this the image in the file will be transferred to the user's computer, but the user won't see it; it will be stored in the browser's cache, ready to be called from a script.

Once transferred, images stored in the cache can be displayed much more quickly than if they had to be received across the Internet. So you can use image objects to create simple animation. For example, suppose you want to create an animated eye that blinks. You have three GIF graphics showing the eye open, half-open, and closed. You create a Web page using the **<IMG>** tag to display the open eye:

Example 15.22

```
<A HREF="javascript:void(null)" onmouseover="blink( )"><IMG name="eye"
src="eye-open.gif"></a>
```

We've actually made this image a link, so we could use the **onmouseover** event handler on the image. When the user points at the image the event handler calls the **blink( )** function, making the eye blink. We've used **javascript:void(null)** in place of the URL so that the link doesn't actually go anywhere. Note also that we've created an **Image** object named **eye**; remember, when you specify an **<IMG>** tag you're creating an image object.

Then you define image objects to hold the three graphics:

```
var eye1 = new Image( )
eye1.src = "eye-open.gif"

var eye2 = new Image( )
eye2.src = "eye-half.gif"

var eye3 = new Image( )
eye3.src = "eye-clos.gif"
```

These cause the three image files to be transferred to the user's computer, but not to be displayed. Finally, you write a function that uses **setTimeout( )** to display the images in sequence:

```
function blink( ) {
        document.eye.src = eye2.src
        setTimeout("document.eye.src = eye3.src", 100)
        setTimeout("document.eye.src = eye2.src", 200)
        setTimeout("document.eye.src = eye1.src", 300)
}
```

This function, named **blink( )**, displays the images at intervals of 100 milliseconds (1/10th of a second). It begins by assigning **eye2.src** to the image: **document.eye.src = eye2.src** means "set the **src** property of the **document.eye** object to hold **eye2.src**." Then we use **setTimeout**, which we saw earlier in this chapter; in its parentheses it provides an instruction The first one, for example, replaces the image with **eye3.src**. But it also provides a lag time, which basically means, "don't carry out this instruction yet, wait for this many milliseconds." When the instruction has been carried out, the function moves to the next one. In this way it displays each of the images, making the eye blink. The **blink( )** function is called from a button and, as just mentioned, from the link's event handler. You can see this in action in Figure 15.8.

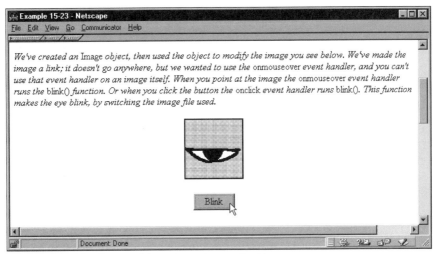

Figure 15-8: Using **Image** *objects to create an animation.*

Moving On

Manipulating windows and documents is perhaps one of the most important and useful features of JavaScript, and it's basic to virtually all JavaScript applications. These days many documents have frames, too, so you need to understand how to work with them. Each frame within a window is a property of that window. It's also an object in its own right—a window object, too! So let's move on to the next chapter and figure out how to work with frames.

16

Using JavaScript With Frames

Even if you haven't used *frames* in your own Web documents, you are
probably familiar with them by now. The frames feature is one that was introduced with the Netscape 2.0 browser family. It allows a Web author to split the
browser window into smaller parts, each part called a frame (in other
hypertext systems such frames are often known as *panes*).

We'll start by quickly reviewing how frames are created using HTML tags.
Then we'll come back to JavaScript and see how you can create scripts that
will control the frame contents.

Frame Basics

Creating frames is quite simple. First, you create the main document, one containing the HTML tags that define how the browser should create the frames.
This file will contain nothing else—it won't be displayed in the browser window, it's simply the instructions that create the frames. This file has no **<BODY>**
tag. Instead it uses a **<FRAMESET>** and **</FRAMESET>** tag pair, and nested
within that pair are **<FRAME>** tags that describe each individual frame and,
perhaps, more sets of the **<FRAMESET> </FRAMESET>** tag pairs.

A **<FRAMESET> </FRAMESET>** tag pair is used to split the browser
window into columns or rows, for example:

```
<FRAMESET COLS="50%,50%">
</FRAMESET>
```

This means "split the window into two columns, each 50 percent of the original window size." Actually this is not enough; unless we tell the browser what to put into each frame, we'll get a blank window. So we add **<FRAME>** tags:

Example 16.1

```
<FRAMESET COLS="50%,50%">
<FRAME SRC="16-1A.HTM">
<FRAME SRC="16-1B.HTM">
</FRAMESET>
```

You can see the result of this in Figure 16-1 and in the Online Companion. The first file, **16-1A.HTM,** is placed in the first column (the leftmost column), while **16-1B.HTM** is placed in the second.

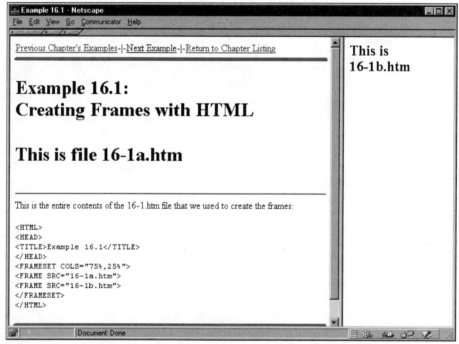

Figure 16-1: Creating frames in HTML is quick and easy. This took four lines to create.

Remember, the contents of the first file do not appear in the Web browser. In fact, here are the entire contents of that file:

```
<HTML>
<HEAD>
<TITLE>Example 16.1</TITLE>
</HEAD>
<FRAMESET COLS="75%,25%">
<FRAME SRC="16-1A.HTM">
<FRAME SRC="16-1B.HTM">
</FRAMESET>
</HTML>
```

The file does two things: it creates the frames, and it provides its **<TITLE>** to the browser. That's it. Don't bother putting any text in the document, as it won't appear in the browser (except for text between **<NOFRAMES>** **</NOFRAMES>** tags, of course, which is intended for browsers that cannot work with frames). The only visible text will be the text from the two files in the **SRC=** attributes.

Now, here's a slightly more complicated frame setup. This time we have a nested **<FRAMESET>**:

Example 16.2

```
<HTML>
<HEAD>
<TITLE>Example 16.2</TITLE>
</HEAD>
<FRAMESET COLS="75%,25%">
    <FRAME SRC="16-2A.HTM">
    <FRAMESET ROWS="50%,50%">
    <FRAME SRC="16-2B.HTM">
    <FRAME SRC="16-2C.HTM">
    </FRAMESET>
</FRAMESET>
</HTML>
```

First we split the window into two columns, as before. Then we specified the document, **16-2A.HTM**, that should go in the first frame (the leftmost). Then we nested another frameset; this time we are creating two rows. Where do these rows go? Well, we already filled the first column, so these rows go in the second column. Next we specify which documents go in those rows; **16-2B.HTM** will go in the top row (because it appears first), then **16-2C.HTM** will go in the bottom row.

Notice that you specify what goes where by its line position. You work from left to right when working with columns, and top to bottom when working with rows. Think of it like this: when you enter a **<FRAMESET>** tag you are stating how many positions there will be within the frameset (**"50%,50%"** means two positions, each taking up 50 percent of the space available; **"40%,20%,40%"** means three positions of different sizes, and so on). Immediately after the **<FRAMESET>** tag you begin filling the positions; in each position you must specify either another frameset or a frame (**<FRAME>**). The first **<FRAMESET>** or **<FRAME>** tag defines the first position (leftmost or top), the second defines the second position, and so on.

TIP

As with JavaScript, it's a good idea to indent lines when creating frames, so you can quickly see how frames and framesets are nested below other framesets.

There are a variety of things you can do with frames by entering attributes into the **<FRAME>** tag.

Frame Property	Description
NAME="window_name"	Assigns a name to the frame so it can be targeted by links in other documents (normally frames in the same document) using the **TARGET=** attribute.
MARGINWIDTH="value"	This allows you to control the size of the left and right frame margins.
MARGINHEIGHT="value"	Controls the size of the upper and lower frame margins.
SCROLLING="yes|no|auto"	Adds a scroll bar to the window (by default you get a scroll bar if it's needed).
NORESIZE	Stops the user from changing frame sizes; by default the user can change the frame sizes (by dragging the margins).

Getting Out of Frames

If you have a normal link within a frame and you click on the link, you load the referenced document into that frame. What if you want to break out of the frame system and load a document into the entire window? There are a couple of ways to do this, using the **TARGET=** attribute of the anchor tag. You can use either of these methods:

```
<A HREF="16-1.htm" TARGET="_top">Previous Example</A>
<A HREF="16-1.htm" TARGET="_parent">Previous Example</A>
```

In the first case, **TARGET="_top"**, all the frames in the window are replaced with the targeted document (in this example, with **16-1.htm**). In the second case, all the frames in the frameset holding the document that contains this link are replaced with the referenced document. If this is a nested frameset, then the parent frameset is unaffected. On the other hand, if there's only one frameset in the window, _top and _parent are, in effect, the same thing.

There's much more to learn about creating frames, but that's all we're going to cover here. If you want to learn more about frames, go to http://home.netscape.com/assist/net_sites/frames.html, or go the Netscape site at http://home.netscape.com and search for the word *frames*.

Frames Are Objects

As far as JavaScript is concerned, each frame in a frameset is an object. In addition, each frame is a property of the **window** object (or of another **Frame** object). **Frame** objects can be used in virtually the same way as **window** objects (see Chapter 15, "Controlling Windows & Documents With JavaScript"), with a few exceptions. You can think of a frame as a "subwindow," with fewer properties than a true window property (in particular, the **defaultStatus**, **history**, **opener**, and **status** properties all belong to the parent). Here, then, are the **Frame** properties:

Frame Property	Description
document	The currently displayed document. This property is also an object in its own right.
Frame	A subframe—a frame within the current frame, and an object in its own right.
frames array	An array that lists the child frames within this frame. (The **parent** window object also has a frames array.)
length	The number of frames within this frame.
name	The frame's name (the **NAME** attribute in the **<FRAME>** tag).
parent	A synonym for the **parent** window that contains this frame.
self	A synonym for the current frame.
window	A synonym for the current frame.

As for methods, **Frame** objects have some of the same methods as window objects:

Method	Description
blur()	Moves focus away from the specified frame. This method was added in JavaScript 1.1 (Navigator 3).
clearInterval()	Cancels a repeating timer that was started by **setInterval()**. This method was added in JavaScript 1.2 (Navigator 4).
clearTimeout()	Cancels a delayed script that was started by **setTimeout()**.
focus()	Moves focus onto the specified frame. This method was added in JavaScript 1.1 (Navigator 3).
print()	Prints the contents of the window. Added in JavaScript 1.2 (Navigator 4).
setInterval()	Causes a specified script to be repeatedly executed at a specified time interval. This method was added in JavaScript 1.2 (Navigator 4).
setTimeout()	Causes a script to be executed after a specified time delay.

The frames Array

The **window** object has another frame-related property, the **frames** array. Actually the array might also be a property of a **Frame** object, if that **Frame** object contains subframes. The array is a list of frames and, as with other arrays, allows you to refer to a **Frame** using an index number: **[0]** for the first frame, **[1]** for the second, and so on. The **frames** array has a single property, **length**, which is the number of frames listed within the array.

Referring to Frames

You can refer to a particular frame by name—if it has one—or by reference to the **parent** and the array index of that frame. For example, let's say you are writing a script that will appear inside the first frame (**parent.frames[0]**), and you want to refer to the third frame. You can call this **parent.frames[2]**; in other words, the third frame of the parent. (Remember, programmers count from 0! The first frame is **0**, the second is **1**, the third frame is **2**, and so on.)

Let's assume that the third frame was named **frame2** (using the tag **<FRAME NAME="frame2">**). You could then also refer to this frame as **parent.frame2**.

For example, we've created the following frames:

Example 16.3

```
<FRAMESET COLS="40%,20%,20%,20%">
<FRAME SRC=16-3a.htm NAME="frame1">
<FRAME SRC=16-3b.htm NAME="frame2">
<FRAME SRC=16-3c.htm NAME="frame3">
<FRAME SRC=16-3d.htm NAME="frame4">
</FRAMESET>
```

TIP

> *You can see in the* **<FRAME>** *tags that we've counted from 1 up. These are the frame names—you can call them whatever you want. The* **frames** *array, though, will count from 0 up, without asking what you prefer!*

As you can see, we have four frames within the frameset, each holding a different document. Notice that each **<FRAME>** tag has a **NAME=** attribute; we've given each of the frames a name. You can see what this looks like in Figure 16-2.

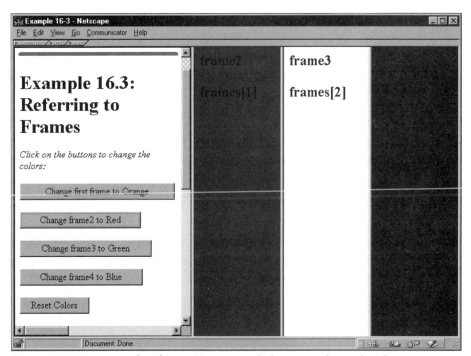

Figure 16-2: Here are our four frames. You can use the buttons to change the colors.

The first document, in the first frame, contains a number of buttons. (We won't bother looking at the other three documents, as they contain no Java-Script. They are little more than placeholders.) Here are the buttons we used:

```
<FORM>
<INPUT TYPE="button" VALUE="Change first frame to Orange"
onclick="parent.frames[0].document.bgColor='orange'"><P>
<INPUT TYPE="button" VALUE="Change frame2 to Red"
onclick="parent.frames[1].document.bgColor='red'"><P>
<INPUT TYPE="button" VALUE="Change frame3 to Green"
onclick="parent.frame3.document.bgColor='green'"><P>
<INPUT TYPE="button" VALUE="Change frame4 to Blue"
onclick="top.frames[3].document.bgColor='blue'"><P>
<INPUT TYPE="button" VALUE="Reset Colors" onclick="resetColors()">
</FORM>
```

The first three buttons change the background colors of the documents in the frames. We have referred to the frames in two different ways, however:

```
onClick="top.frames[3].document.bgColor='blue'"
```

This means, "when the user clicks on the button, change the background color (**bgColor**) in the document in the fourth frame in the **frames** array held by the **top** window to **blue**." Remember, we're using the **frames** array and counting from **0**, so **3** is actually the fourth frame. Here's another way you can refer to a frame:

```
onClick="parent.frame3.document.bgColor='green'"
```

This time we are modifying **frame3**. This is the name we gave to the third frame in the third **<FRAME>** tag. The last button calls the **resetColors()** function:

```
function resetColors()    {
    self.document.bgColor="white"
    top.frames[1].document.bgColor="white"
    top.frames[2].document.bgColor="white"
    top.frames[3].document.bgColor="white"
}
```

This function changes all the colors back to **white** again. Notice that this time we used **self.document.bgColor** to change the color in the first frame. As the button is in the first frame, it's quicker to refer to the frame as **self**. We could also have used **window.document.bgColor** or **current.document.bgColor**. In fact, we could have just used **document.bgColor**, as we're referring here to the current window. Although they are optional, you might want to use **self** or **current** to make your scripts a little easier to read.

TIP

Don't use the word **reset** *for a function name. This is an undocumented reserved word.*

What About top?

But how about **top.document.bgColor**? Couldn't we use that to set the background color of the first document? Well, no, because **top** refers to the window containing the frameset. There is no document in **top**; **top** contains frames which contain documents, but **top** itself cannot hold a document.

To demonstrate this, try the following example, in which we have three buttons that address **top**:

Example 16.4

```
<FORM>
<INPUT TYPE="button" VALUE="Change top frame to Orange"
onclick="top.document.bgColor='orange'"><P>
<INPUT TYPE="button" VALUE="Change Status Bar" onclick="top.status='Ah ha, →
you've just changed the status bar.'"><P>
 <INPUT TYPE="button" VALUE="Change Status Bar: top.frames[2].status="
onclick="top.frames[2].status='And again.'">
</FORM>
```

The first button can't do anything. The **top** window has no viewable document, so it can't change the color; **top** is not the same as **self** or **window**. The second button *will* work, however. The **top** window has a status bar, so **top.status=** will work. However, so would **top.frames[2].status=** (see the last button); changing the status property of any frame changes the status bar message. (We're using **status**, which is a temporary status-bar message; it will disappear when you move the mouse pointer away from the button, except in Internet Explorer 3.)

Changing a Frame's Contents

We can modify the contents of one frame from another, by specifying into which frame a particular document should be loaded. The easiest way to do this is actually with HTML, like this:

```
<A HREF="16-5b.htm" TARGET="frame2">Change Frame2</A>
```

You simply name the frame using the **TARGET=** attribute. When the user clicks on this link, the document named **16-5b.htm** is loaded into **frame2**. For instance, here's an example in the Online Companion:

Example 16.5

```
<A HREF="16-5b.htm" TARGET="frame2">Change frame2</A><BR>
<A HREF="16-5b.htm" TARGET="frame3">Change frame3</A><BR>
<A HREF="16-5b.htm" TARGET="frame4">Change frame4</A><BR>
```

Click on each link, and you'll see the text in the appropriate frame change (see Figure 16-3).

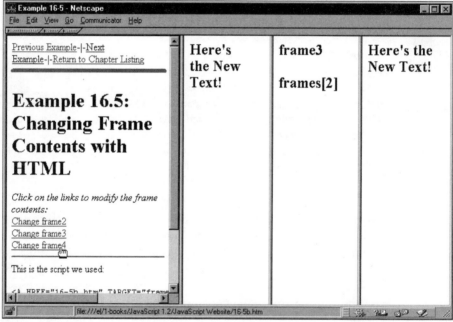

Figure 16-3: The easiest way to change contents is by using HTML.

But we can also write to a frame using JavaScript in much the same way that you can write to windows (see Chapter 15, "Controlling Windows & Documents With JavaScript"). For example, take a look at this script:

Example 16.6

```
<SCRIPT LANGUAGE="JAVASCRIPT">
<!--
function new1()    {
```

```
    parent.frame2.document.write("<P>Here's some more text for you...and  →
some more. Yes, and more, and yet more<BR>")
}
function new2()    {
    parent.frame3.document.write("Making predictions is very difficult,  →
especially about the future.<BR>")
}
function new3()    {
    parent.frame4.document.write("Um...what else can I say? Oh, I know,  →
I'll omit the line break and see what happens.")
}
//--->
</SCRIPT>
```

The Online Companion example has three buttons to run these three functions. You can see in Figure 16-4 what happens when you use them.

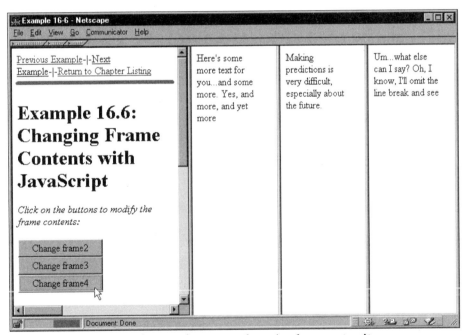

Figure 16-4: You can write from one frame to another using **document.write**.

Notice that there's part of the last document missing. Remember the problem with writing documents that we looked at in Chapter 15? In the last function we forgot the **
** tag, so some of the text was not written.

Of course we should really be using the more formal method for writing these things, like this:

Example 16.7

```
function new1()    {
    parent.frame2.document.open()
    parent.frame2.document.write("<P>Here's some more text for you...and  →
some more. Yes, and more, and yet more<BR>") parent.frame2.document.close()
}
function new2()    {
    parent.frame3.document.open()
    parent.frame3.document.write("Making predictions is very difficult,  →
especially about the future.<BR>") parent.frame3.document.close()
}
function new3()    {
    parent.frame4.document.open()
    parent.frame4.document.write("Um...what else can I say? Oh, I know,  →
I'll omit the line break and see what happens.") parent.frame4.document.close()
}
```

This time we used **document.open()** and **document.close()**, and the text was written to the frames correctly.

Calling Functions in Other Frames

You can also call functions that are inside documents in other frames. For instance, in our next example we have placed the same functions in the first frame. But we now have a document in the fourth frame with buttons to call those functions:

Example 16.8

```
<FORM>
<INPUT TYPE="BUTTON" VALUE="Change frame2"
onclick="parent.frame1.new1()"><BR>
<INPUT TYPE="BUTTON" VALUE="Change frame3"
onclick="parent.frame1.new2()"><BR>
<INPUT TYPE="BUTTON" VALUE="Change frame4"
onclick="parent.frame1.new3()"><BR>
</FORM>
```

You can see this in action in Figure 16-5. As you can see, we are calling the same functions, but we have to tell the **onclick** event handler *where* the functions are: **parent.frame1**.

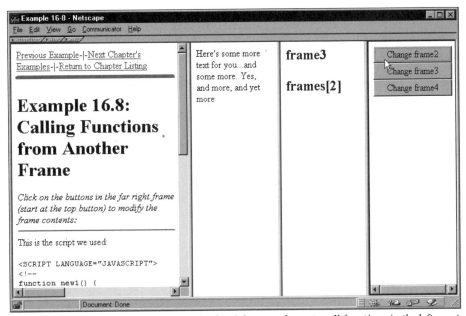

Figure 16-5: This example uses buttons in the right-most frame to call functions in the left-most frame's document.

Moving On

Working with frames is really quite straightforward; it's just like working with other windows, except that those "windows" are all together within the same "body." In fact, as we mentioned before, **Frame** objects are really almost the same as **window** objects.

The next thing we're going to look at is working with forms. This is one of the most important uses for JavaScript. You can get JavaScript to do things for you on the user's computer that before would have required the use of a CGI script on the server. For example, you can use JavaScript to search for information held in arrays within your document. You can also use it to verify that the user is entering the correct information into the form's text elements.

17

Forms & JavaScript

We've already worked with forms quite a bit throughout this book. What we haven't done, however, is look closely at how we are passing information from a form to a script. In order to do that we need to understand the way that forms fit into the object hierarchy, so we'll begin by going over that quickly.

Form Objects

A **Form** object is a property of the **document** object. There's also a **forms** array—another property of the **document** object. As you already know, the **forms** array is essentially a list of forms within the document that allows you to refer to a form by index number; **forms[0]** is the first form in the document, **forms[1]** is the second, and so on. (By first we mean closest to the top, of course. We count from the top down.)

Form objects have their own properties, of course:

Object	Property
action	A string that contains the destination URL for a form submission.
Button	A button in a form, created using the **\<INPUT TYPE="BUTTON"\>** tag. This property is also an object in its own right.
Checkbox	A checkbox, created using the **\<INPUT TYPE="CHECKBOX"\>** tag. This property is also an object in its own right.
elements array	An array that lists form elements in the order in which they appear in the form.
encoding	The MIME encoding of the form.
FileUpload	A file upload element (**\<INPUT TYPE="FILE"\>**) in a form. This property is also an object in its own right. This property was added in JavaScript 1.1 (Navigator 3).
Hidden	A hidden (**\<INPUT TYPE="HIDDEN"\>**) element in a form. This property is also an object in its own right.
length	The number of elements in the form.
name	Starting with JavaScript 1.1 (Navigator 3) there's a **name** property; the **NAME=** attribute.
method	How data inputted in a form is sent to the server; the **METHOD=** attribute in a **\<FORM\>** tag.
Password	A password field (**\<INPUT TYPE="PASSWORD"\>**) in a form. This property is also an object in its own right.
Radio	A radio (option) button set (**\<INPUT TYPE="RADIO"\>**) in a form. This property is also an object in its own right.
reset	A reset button (**\<INPUT TYPE="RESET"\>**) in a form. This property is also an object in its own right.
select	A selection box (**\<SELECT\>**) in a form. This property is also an object in its own right.
submit	A submit button (**\<INPUT TYPE="SUBMIT"\>**) in a form. This property is also an object in its own right.
target	The name of the window that displays responses after a form has been submitted.
text	A text element in a form (**\<INPUT TYPE="TEXT"\>**). This property is also an object in its own right.
textarea	A textarea element (**\<TEXTAREA\>**) in a form. This property is also an object in its own right.

As you can see, a number of these properties are objects themselves; each element within a form is an object, for example.

Forms have several methods. They have the **eval()**, **toString()**, and **valueOf()** methods, of course, as all objects have these methods. But they have two of their own, the **submit()** and **reset()** methods.

The **submit()** method, available in all versions of JavaScript, submits the form. It's the equivalent of clicking on the Submit button. In effect, it provides a way for your scripts to "click" the Submit button. The **reset()** handler was added to JavaScript 1.1 (Navigator 3) and is the equivalent of clicking the Reset button.

Forms also have two event handlers. All versions of JavaScript have **onsubmit**. This event handler runs when the script is submitted (either because the user clicks Submit or because a script uses the **submit()** method). Although this event handler operates when the user clicks on the submit button, the event handler is actually placed within the **<FORM>** tag (not within the **<INPUT TYPE="SUBMIT">** tag). We saw an example of this event handler in use in Chapter 12, "JavaScript Events—When Are Actions Carried Out?" The **onreset** event handler was added in JavaScript 1.1 (Navigator 3); it runs when the user clicks on a Reset button or a script uses the **reset()** method.

Note, however, that the elements within the form have event handlers, too:

Element	Handler
button (**<INPUT TYPE="BUTTON">**)	onclick
checkbox (**<INPUT TYPE="CHECKBOX">**)	onclick
hidden element (**<INPUT TYPE="HIDDEN">**)	none
radio (**<INPUT TYPE="RADIO">**)	onclick
reset button (**<INPUT TYPE="RESET">**)	onclick
selection list (**<SELECT>**)	onblur, onchange, onfocus
submit button (**<INPUT TYPE="SUBMIT">**)	onclick
text box (**<INPUT TYPE="TEXT">**)	onblur, onchange, onfocus, onselect
textarea (**<TEXTAREA>**)	onblur, onchange, onfocus, onselect

Passing Information From Forms

By now you've probably got the idea of how to address something using the object hierarchy, and working with forms is no different. If you want to refer to an element in the form, you can use the element name or you can use the

elements array. To refer to a form, you can use the **Form** name or the **forms** array. For example, you might refer to a form element like this:

```
document.form1.radio1
```

or like this:

```
document.forms[0].radio1
```

or like this:

```
document.forms[0].elements[0]
```

One thing we haven't really discussed yet is how information is passed from a form to a function. Actually we've done this a lot throughout the book's examples, but we need to come back and explain exactly how that information is passed from forms.

For example, take a look at this form:

Example 17.1

```
<FORM>
<input type="text" size="30"><P>
<input type="button" value="What Did You Type" onclick="What(this.form)">
</FORM>
```

This is a simple form with a text box and a button. Note that we haven't named either element—we'll use the element's array to refer to them. When the user clicks on the button, the **onclick** event handler calls the **What()** function. Notice that in the parentheses we typed **this.form**, which means "pass a reference concerning this form to the function named **What()**." The function can then use the reference to retrieve the information it needs from the form. You can see it in action in Figure 17-1.

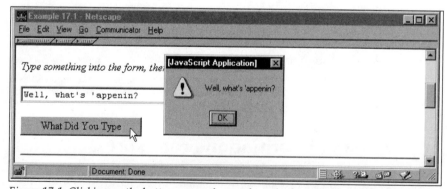

Figure 17-1: Clicking on the button passes the text from the form to a function, which is then displayed in an Alert box.

Now, as in most of the examples in this book, we've created functions something like this:

```
function functionname(form)
```

What does **form** mean? Does it mean "this information is coming from a form?"; "treat this information in a special manner reserved for forms?"; "warning, this stuff comes from a **form** object?" Actually, it means nothing so complicated. It's simply a name. In fact, here's the function we used in the Online Companion example:

```
function What(gertrude)    {
    alert(gertrude.elements[0].value)
}
```

What's **gertrude**? Just a name like any other—such as **form**. The text within the parentheses is simply a name. It means, in this case, this function is being passed some information, and we're going to refer to that information as **gertrude**. In most of our scripts we use the word **form** because it's simple and descriptive, but we want you to understand that there's nothing magic about **form**.

So what does this function do? It opens an Alert box and displays the value held by the **elements[0]** object—the first element in the form. That element is a text box, so the **value** is whatever you've typed into the box. Remember, **gertrude** is just a name; so **gertrude.elements[0].value** means "look at the information that was passed to this function—information that we are going to refer to as **gertrude**—look for information about the first element, and grab the **value**."

Incidentally, although we haven't given the form a name, we could have. We could call it **fred**, for example (**<FORM NAME="fred">**). Still, that doesn't necessarily mean we could use **fred.elements[0].value**. Nor could we have used **forms[0].elements[0].value**, as you can see in this example:

Example 17.2

```
function What1(gertrude)    {
    alert(fred.elements[0].value)
}
function What2(gertrude)    {
    alert(forms[0].elements[0].value)
}
function What3(gertrude)    {
    alert(gertrude.elements[0].value)
}
```

We put three buttons in our Online Companion example to call these three functions. They do not refer to the objects quite correctly because we are not using **gertrude**, nor do they use the full object hierarchy—**document.** is missing (we'll look at this next). If you are using an early JavaScript browser (Navigator 2 or an early Navigator 3 beta) you will get an error. If you click on the first button to call **What1()**, you might get an error message saying *fred is not defined*. Click on the second button to call **What2()**, and you might see *forms is not defined*. On later browsers (starting with Netscape Navigator 3 and Internet Explorer 3) you won't see the error messages. Only the third button works consistently, because we are referring to the form using the correct name—the one we put in parentheses, **gertrude**. So although all these methods of referring to the form might work on your browser, the first two are not, strictly speaking, correct, and should be avoided.

You Don't Need to Pass a Reference

But you don't need to pass a reference at all. You can simply refer to the form and its elements by the full name, adding the **document.** part. For example:

Example 17.3

```
function What1()    {
    alert(document.fred.elements[0].value)
}
function What2()    {
    alert(document.forms[0].elements[0].value)
}
```

As you can see, this time we are not passing information—there's nothing in the parentheses. In fact, take a look at these buttons:

```
<FORM NAME="fred">
<input type="text" size="30"><P>
<input type="button" value="document.fred.elements[0].value" →
onclick="What1()"><P>
<input type="button" value="document.forms[0].elements[0].value" →
onclick="What2()"><P>
</FORM>
```

Notice that we called the function, but haven't placed anything in parentheses. So why do we bother passing **this.form** sometimes, if we really don't need to pass the reference? Well, it can make it easier by allowing us to type less. We can write a single function that is called from more than one form, each form passing the relevant information—using **this.form**—to the function.

In some cases this isn't appropriate, though; for example, if the function is operating on several forms at once or operating on a different form from the one it's called from, you might want to use the full element names.

Passing Information Between Forms

Let's see an example of how we might pass information from one form to another:

Example 17.4

```
function Pass()    {
    document.joe.elements[0].value = document.fred.elements[0].value
}
```

Then we have these buttons:

```
<FORM NAME="fred">
<input type="text" size="30"><P>
</FORM>
<I>Now click on this button in the second form:</I>
<FORM>
<input type="button" value="Pass the Text" onclick="Pass()">
</FORM>
<I>You'll see the text in the third form:</I>
<FORM NAME="joe">
<input type="text" size="30"><P>
</FORM>
```

We've actually got three separate forms here. Type something into the first form, **fred**; click on the button, and the text is passed to **joe**, as you can see in Figure 17-2. Really very simple.

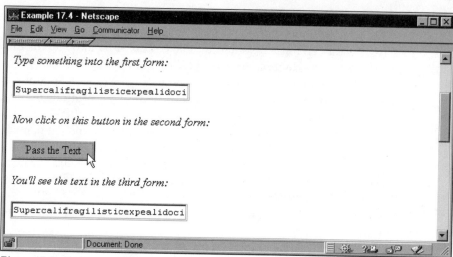

Figure 17-2: Clicking on the button passes the text from the first text box to the second.

Using simple scripts such as this, plus all the various techniques we've seen earlier in this book, you can see how to manipulate the data in forms. You can take data from one form, carry out calculations, pass it back to the same form or another form, and so on.

Form Validation

One big issue when working with forms is form validation. How can you be sure that what the user typed in makes sense? Until JavaScript, there was only one way to know—the user would submit the data, then a script at the server would check it to see if it was okay. If it wasn't, a document would be sent back to the user's browser saying that the form is incorrectly filled out.

That system is a nuisance, for a few reasons. First, it takes up server re-sources—wouldn't it be better to make sure that the form was okay *before* the server dealt with it? Also, it's irritating to the user. He fills out the form, clicks on Submit, and then waits, and waits, and waits only to be told that the he has messed up and has to do it over again.

With JavaScript you can create simple validation scripts for each field, then run the scripts before the data from the form is submitted. You could validate the form when the user moves from one element to another (using **onblur**) or when the user clicks on the Submit button (by using **onsubmit** in the <FORM> tag). If the form validation fails—and returns **false** to **onsubmit**— then the data is not sent back to the server.

Also, you can use form validation to check data that will be used by the scripts themselves. As we'll see in Chapter 19, "The Area Code & Telephone Directory Applications," our programs do everything internally—there's no communication with the server. However, we use validation to make sure that the user is entering information that is valid.

How do we validate data, then? Well, you've already seen the basic components. We take data from a form element—usually a text box—and pass it to a function. The function then checks that the data is valid (that it is within a range of valid ranges) and, based on what it finds, performs an action. For example, you might wish to check that a user types a number and not letters, which would be meaningless in a calculation and could cause an error. The function could then display an Alert, warning the user that the data is incorrect.

Checking a Number

We're going to look at the input in a text box, check that the number is within a certain range (100 to 200 inclusive), and then decide what to do: either display an Alert box telling the user that the input is a wrong number, or pass the number to another form. We've used the same **Pass()** function—well, with a few additions.

Example 17.5

```
function Pass()   {
var nCheck = document.fred.elements[0].value
        if (nCheck >= 100)           {
                if (nCheck >=201) {
                        alert("You entered a number that's too high. You must →
enter a number within the range of 100 to 200 inclusive.")
                }
                else {
                  document.joe.elements[0].value = document.fred.→
elements[0].value
                }
        }
        else {
            alert("You entered a number that's too low. You must enter a →
number within the range of 100 to 200 inclusive.")
        }
}
```

We used the same buttons in our Online Companion for this example as in the previous example: the button called **Pass()**. So what does **Pass()** do? Well, we started by taking the value typed into the text box and placing it in a variable called **nCheck**. Next we started an **if** statement. The first line looks at the value in **nCheck**. It checks to see if the value is greater than or equal to **100**. If it is, the number might be okay—it's above the lower limit, after all. So if the number is **100** or more, we move to the next line, which checks to see if it's **201** or more. If it is, then it's out of bounds—it's supposed to be 100, 200, or anything in-between. So if this line evaluates to **true**, we carry out the next instruction, which is to display an Alert box (see Figure 17-3).

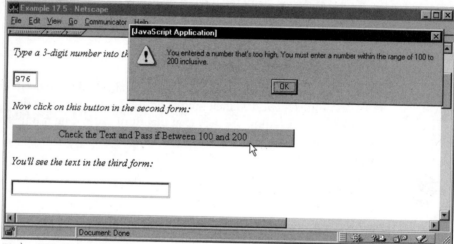

Figure 17-3: We've called a function that checked to see if the number was okay—but it was too high.

If the line evaluates to **false**, though, it means the number is okay, so we carry out the **else** clause: **document.joe.elements[0].value = document.fred.elements[0].value**.

This, of course, takes the value and passes it to the other text box, as we saw earlier.

And the final **else** clause? That's related to the first **if** statement, of course, and is used if the number is less than **100**. It displays an Alert box with a different message.

All quite simple—except there's a problem. Try typing non-numeric characters into that text box, and then click on the button. You'll get an error message.

Is It a Number?

Well, we'd better check to see if the text is numeric. If it's not, this script crashes. So here's a new version:

Example 17.6

```
function Pass()   {
    var sCheck = document.fred.elements[0].value
    nCheck = parseInt(sCheck, 10)
    if (nCheck <=99 || nCheck == 0 )   {
       alert("This is not a 3-digit number.")
    }
    else {
          if (nCheck >= 100)    {
             if (nCheck >=201)   {
                 alert("You entered a number that's too high. You must →
enter a number within the range of 100 to 200 inclusive.")
             }
             else {
                 document.joe.elements[0].value = nCheck
             }
          }
    }
}
```

We started this script a little differently. This time we placed the text into **sCheck** (rather than **nCheck**). Strictly speaking, the stuff coming from the text box is text, not a number (text boxes contain text strings, remember). Then we added **nCheck = parseInt(sCheck)**. Now, you'll remember **parseInt()** from Chapter 7, "More on Functions." This function looks at the value in the parentheses and tries to extract a number from it. In our example, **parseInt** is evaluating **sCheck,** which is whatever the user typed into the text box (the **10** simply means "try to extract a number in base **10** from the string"). And we're passing the value to another variable, **nCheck**. Now, if it can't extract a number, it passes 0. If the user types a few numbers followed by non-numeric characters, it throws those characters away and keeps the numbers; and if the user types non-numeric characters followed by numbers, it throws it all away. For example:

12egty = 12

12 = 12

agj12 = 0 (JavaScript 1.0) or **NaN** (JavaScript 1.1)

So we end up with a number, or, if the text isn't a number we'll get **0** (in JavaScript 1.0) or **NaN** (in JavaScript 1.1). Then we check the result. The **if** statement looks at the number to see if it's less than or equal to **99**—as it will be if the user has not typed three digits. It also checks to see if the number is equal to **0**. If **parseInt** is unable to extract a number from **sCheck,** it will set **nCheck** to **0** in JavaScript 1.0 browsers. In most JavaScript 1.1 browsers it sets it to **NaN**, which must be evaluated using the **isNaN** function. We'll come back to that in a moment.

If **nCheck** holds **99** or less, or if it holds **0**, we see the Alert box. Otherwise (if it's **100** or more), we move on to the **else** statement. Why are we checking to see if it's less than **99** *and* if it holds **0**? Isn't **0** less than **99**? Well, yes it is, but unless we did it this way the script simply wouldn't work correctly. If the user types letters instead of a number into a JavaScript 1.0 browser on Windows or the Macintosh, **parseInt** appears to pass **0** (if you added **alert(nCheck)** at this point in the script the Alert box would display **0**), but it's not a true **0**. The script apparently won't recognize the contents of **nCheck** as being less than **99**. It will, however, recognize that **nCheck** contains **0**. Weird, but true.

Now, the else clause holds the rest of the function that we've already seen, with one exception. We changed this:

```
document.joe.elements[0].value = document.fred.elements[0].value
```

to this:

```
document.joe.elements[0].value = nCheck
```

Why did we make this change? Well, assume, for example, that the user typed in **213khk;jh**. The **parseInt()** function would evaluate this to **213**, which is a valid number within our range. Then, using the old script, we would copy the text from the first text box (**213khk;jh**) into the second text box. Instead, we've copied the text from **nCheck**, the evaluated number, into the checkbox. So we decided that if the user typed three numbers followed by garbage, we would accept the numbers.

Now, back to **NaN**. The **parseInt()** function has changed between JavaScript versions. The **parseInt()** function running on most Netscape Navigator 2 browsers returns **0** if it evaluates a non-numeric value. On Solaris and Irix Navigator 2 browsers it would return **NaN**. All Navigator 3 and 4 browsers return **NaN** for non-numeric values. Internet Explorer 3, however, returns **0**. So we could check to see if **NaN** is returned rather than **0**, like this:

```
function Pass()   {
   var sCheck = document.fred.elements[0].value
   nCheck = parseInt(sCheck, 10)
   if (isNaN(nCheck)) {
     alert("You did not type a number")
   }
```

```
else {
    if (nCheck <=99 || nCheck == 0 )   {
        alert("This is not a 3-digit number.")
    }
```

We can use **isNaN**, as you saw in Chapter 7. If **nCheck** contains **NaN**, **isNaN** returns true, so the alert box is displayed. If **nCheck** doesn't contain **NaN**, the **else** clause runs, carrying out the script that we've already seen. The problem with doing this is that browsers using the old-style **parseInt**, the **parseInt** that returns **0** rather than **NaN**, will not understand **isNaN** and choke on it. You could, of course, check the **navigator.AppVersion** property to find out which sort of browser the person is using and run a script accordingly, but that's probably overkill. In the original script if the browser returns **NaN** the user won't see an alert box, nor will the text he or she types be transferred to the second text box.

How Long Is It?

Another condition you might want to check is length: how long is the text that the user has typed? In fact it might be a good idea to check the number of characters typed in the example we've just seen. Here's how you could do that:

Example 17.7
```
function Length()   {
var sCheck = document.fred.elements[0].value
    if (sCheck.length > 3)   {
    alert("You have typed too many characters")
    }
     else {
         Pass()
     }
}
```

We've added a new function (the other one was getting a bit long and complicated), and we changed the button to call this function instead of **Pass( )**.

We declared a variable called **sCheck** again and gave it the contents of the text box. Then we have a simple **if** statement to check the number of characters in **sCheck**; **sCheck.length > 3** is checking the **length** property of the **sCheck** object (remember, a string variable is a string object). If it's greater than 3 characters, an Alert box is opened. If it's not, the **else( )** clause calls **Pass( )** and we continue checking the number.

Of course with a very slight modification, we can check to make sure that the number's neither too long nor too short.

Example 17.8

```
function Length()    {
var sCheck = document.fred.elements[0].value
   if (sCheck.length > 3 || sCheck.length < 3)    {
     alert("You must type 3 characters: no more, no less")
   }
   else {
   Pass()
   }
}
```

The **if (sCheck.length > 3 | | sCheck.length < 3)** bit checks to see if the string is greater than three characters or less than three characters.

Finding Selection Box Text

In Chapter 15, Example 15.17, you saw a way that you could base decisions on the selection made in a selection box. In that example we based the decision on the position of the item that the user selected in a selection box. Let's quickly see another method. In this example we're going to actually look at the selected text in the box and use that text in a script.

Example 17.9

```
<SCRIPT LANGUAGE="JAVASCRIPT">
<!--
function DisplayItem(Myform) {
  var i = Myform.lstOption.selectedIndex
  var sText = Myform.lstOption.options[i].text
  alert(sText)
}
//-->
</SCRIPT>
```

We've begun by creating a function called **DisplayItem**, which we'll be calling from the form. Then we create a variable called **i**, which we fill with the index position of the **selectedIndex**, the property that shows us which option the user has selected in the select box. (**Myform.lstOption.selectedIndex** means "get the **selectedIndex** number from the component called **1stOption** in **Myform**, which is the form passed to the function.") We then use that variable to fill the **sText** variable with the text held at that index position.

Finally, we display the contents of the variable **sText** using **alert**. Here's the form we're using:

```
<FORM>
Pick an option from the Select box:
<BR>
<SELECT name="1stOption">
    <OPTION>Text at Index=0
    <OPTION>Text at Index=1
    <OPTION>Text at Index=2
    <OPTION>Text at Index=3
    <OPTION>Text at Index=4
    <OPTION>And here's more...
</SELECT>
<BR>
<INPUT TYPE="button" VALUE="Click to display the text from the selected
option" onclick="DisplayItem(this.form)">
</FORM>
```

As you can see, the Select box is called **1stOption**. And the button uses **onclick** to call **DisplayItem(this.form)**, passing information from the form to the function.

We used this system in a little JavaScript applet we call The Color Chart, which you can see in Example 17.10. We began with this function in the HEAD:

Example 17.10

```
function PickColor(form)    {
        var sWhichSelect = form.select1.selectedIndex
        var sThisColor = form.select1.options[sWhichSelect].text
        form.select1.blur()
        document.bgColor = sThisColor
}
```

As you can see, we've declared a function called **PickColor**. We began by creating a variable named **sWhichSelect**, which holds the **selectedIndex** value from the component named **select1**. We then grab the text from that index position and place it in a variable named **sThisColor**. Next, we've used the **blur()** method, a method of the **select** object, to remove focus from the Select box named **select1**. (We did this because some earlier versions of Navigator did strange things if we didn't move focus away from the box.) Finally, we set the **bgColor** property of the **document** object (the background color) to the value set in **sThisColor**.

Here's the form we used:

```
<form>
<select name="select1" size="15" onchange="PickColor(this.form)">
        <option>aliceblue
        <option>antiquewhite
        <option>aqua
        <option>aquamarine
        <option>azure
        <option>beige
        <option>bisque
        <option>black
[many more color options go here]
        <option>whitesmoke
        <option>yellow
        <option>yellowgreen
</select>
</form>
```

As you can see, we used the **onchange** event handler. When the user clicks on something in this list, the **onchange** event handler calls the **PickColor** function, sending information from the form to that function. The function figures out what is selected, then grabs the text from that position. It then changes the background color, using that text (the color name).

Changing the Option Text

If you are writing scripts for use in Netscape Navigator 3, there's a fancy new trick you can try. You can actually change the text in the Select box, replacing it with text that you want to appear in the box (depending on some user action, for example).

In Example 17.11 we've shown you how this works. We've started with this function in the HEAD:

Example 17.11

```
function ChangeItem(Myform) {
  var i = Myform.txtIndex.value
  Myform.1stOption.options[i].text = Myform.txtNewText.value
}
```

The form we'll see in a moment passes information to the function named **ChangeItem**. We're taking the information in the **txtIndex** component (which, as you'll see, is a text box) and placing it in the variable named **i**, then using variable **i** with the **options** array to refer to an option in the Select box named **1stOption**. We're placing the text from the text box named **txtNewText** into that array position. Now here's the form we've got:

```
<FORM>
<SELECT name="1stOption" SIZE=5>
    <OPTION>Text at Index=0
    <OPTION>Text at Index=1
    <OPTION>Text at Index=2
    <OPTION>Whatever text you want
</SELECT>
<BR>
Change this index position: <INPUT TYPE="text" NAME="txtIndex" VALUE="0"
SIZE=2> to the following text: <INPUT TYPE="text" NAME="txtNewText"
VALUE="Type your text here"SIZE=20>
<BR>
<INPUT TYPE="button" VALUE="Change text" onclick="ChangeItem(this.form)">
</FORM>
```

Type a number into the **txtIndex** box, type some text into the **txtNewText** box, click the button, and **ChangeItem** will replace the old text with the new.

There's a problem with this script, though. If you enter an index number that doesn't actually exist in the **options** array, you'll get an error message. There's another way to modify text in a Select box, though, using JavaScript 1.1's (Navigator 3) new **Option** object. Take a look at Example 17.12:

Example 17.12

```
function AddItem(Myform) {
 var sText = Myform.txtItem.value;
 var iIndex = Myform.txtIndex.value;
 NewItem = new Option(sText, iIndex, false, true);
 Myform.1stOption.options[iIndex]=NewItem;
 history.go(0);
}
```

The **AddItem** function begins by creating the **sText** and **sIndex** variables, which hold the values from the **txtItem** and **txtIndex** text boxes. Then it creates a new object instance called **NewItem**. You can see that we've created this instance using the **new** keyword (see Chapter 11): **NewItem = new Option(sText, iIndex, false, true)** means "create a new instance of the **Option** object class called **NewItem** and create four properties: **sText** and **iIndex** (taken from the variables we've just created) and **false** and **true**." Finally the function places the new object, **NewItem**, into the Select box, the object called **1stOption**, using the **options** array.

We've ended with **history.go(0)**; this refreshes the page. If you don't do this, you might find that the Select box is not set to the correct size.

Note that these are the four properties that you must specify when creating an **Option** instance.

Property Position	Purpose
1st	The text that will appear in the Select box (in this case the text held by **sText**).
2nd	The information that will be submitted back to the server if this option is selected by the user before clicking on the Submit button. In our example we've used the index position held in the **iIndex** variable.
3rd	A value, **true** or **false**, indicating whether this new option will be the **defaultSelected** option in the Select box.
4th	A value, **true** or **false**, indicating whether this new option is selected or not.

Moving On

We'll come back to form validation later, in Chapter 19, "The Area Code & Telephone Directory Applications." In that chapter you'll see an example of validation integrated into an actual application.

For now, though, we're going to move on to the next chapter, "Communicating With the User," where you can learn more about how to send messages to the user.

Communicating With the User

JavaScript allows you to create interactive Web pages—rather than simply providing static information that the user reads or views. Your pages can ask the user to take an active role, to "make things happen" in direct response to user actions. So communicating with the user is an important part of working with JavaScript. We've already seen many examples of how you can communicate with the user, from using the Alert box to putting messages into the status bar. In this chapter we want to put it all together and see how these different methods can be employed.

First, here are a number of different ways that you can communicate with the user:

■ The Alert box—shows the user a message.

■ The Confirm dialog box—shows a message and asks the user to make a two-option choice.

■ The Prompt dialog box—shows a message, asks the user to make a two-option choice and, if choosing the OK option, asks the user to type information.

■ Mix and match—by using a mix of different boxes, you can make more complicated decision "trees."

■ Default status-bar messages—display a message in the status bar.

■ Status-bar messages—display a message in the status bar that only appears under specific circumstances (when the user points at a link or makes a choice in a Prompt or Confirm box, for example).

- Write information to text boxes and textareas.
- Open secondary windows and display messages.

We've already seen many of these individual components in action (we've used the Alert box dozens of times, for example), but let's take a look at a few ways that you might communicate with your readers.

Incorporating User Information

You can collect information from users in a couple of ways: they can type the information into forms or into a Prompt dialog box. Once you have the information stored in variables or simply held in the form itself, you can use it any way you want. For example, you might have a user fill information into a form, then click on a button at the bottom of the page to open a new document and incorporate the information that was typed into the form in a new document. In fact, let's see how that might be done. We created this form in which the user types information:

Example 18.1

```
<FORM>
First Name: <input type="text" size="30"><BR>
Last Name: <input type="text" size="30"><BR>
Address: <input type="text" size="30"><BR>
City: <input type="text" size="30"><BR>
State/Province/Region: <input type="text" size="30"><BR>
Zip/Postal Code: <input type="text" size="30"><BR>
Country: <input type="text" size="30"><BR>
<input type="button" value="Next Page" onclick="Use(this.form)">
</FORM>
```

As you can see, there are a number of text boxes, plus a button. The button uses an **onclick** event handler to call the **Use()** function. Here is that function:

```
function Use(form)    {
    var sFname = form.elements[0].value
    var sLname = form.elements[1].value
    var sAddr = form.elements[2].value
    var sCity = form.elements[3].value
    var sState = form.elements[4].value
    var sZip = form.elements[5].value
    var sCou= form.elements[6].value
    if (confirm("Let's just check that we got the right information, shall →
we? Your name is " + sFname + " " + sLname + ". Your address is " + sAddr + →
```

in blue ⟩

```
", " + sCity + ", " + sState + ", " + sZip + ", " + sCou + ". Is that all →
correct?"))  {
        alert("We've open an alert box if you click on OK, but you could →
do anything you want, such as move to another page using location='url'.")
    }
}
```

This is really quite simple. We've taken the information typed by the user and placed that information into variables. Then we've displayed a Confirm dialog box that shows the user what he typed and asks for confirmation, as you can see in Figure 18-1. If the user clicks on OK, the Alert box opens. We could do anything at this point, though, such as move to another page or call another function that uses the data.

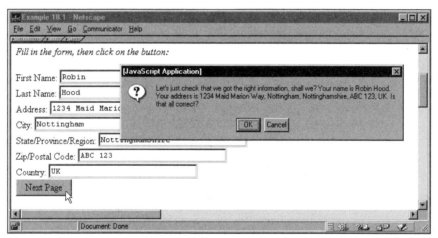

Figure 18-1: We are communicating with the user; we've taken the user's words and asked the user to confirm that they are correct.

Using the Prompt Box

Another way to collect information is with the Prompt dialog box. Rather than giving the user a form to fill in, you can ask the user a series of questions, one by one, as in the following example:

Example 18.2
```
<SCRIPT LANGUAGE="JAVASCRIPT">
<!--
```

```
var sFname = prompt("What is your first name?","")
var sLname = prompt("What is your last name?","")
var sAddr = prompt("What is your street address?","")
var sCity = prompt("What is your city?","")
var sState = prompt("What is your state, province, or region?","")
var sZip = prompt("What is your zip or postal code?","")
var sCou= prompt("What is your country?","")
//-->
</SCRIPT>
```

We put this script in the HEAD of the document, so it runs before the document is loaded. We're going to write this information to the document itself. So we couldn't put this script in a function and call it with the **onload** event handler, as that would run the script after the document has loaded. Notice the **prompt()** method. We are taking the value from the Prompt dialog box and placing it in a variable. We now have two things in parentheses: the text that will appear in the Prompt dialog box as a question, followed by "" (which means "don't use a default value in the text box"; take out the quotation marks and you'll see **undefined** in the text box).

Next we have this in the BODY of the document:

```
Now we've collected all that information, we can write it to the document if
we wish:
```

```
<P>
<SCRIPT LANGUAGE="JAVASCRIPT">
<!--
document.write("Let's just check that we got the right information, shall  →
we? Your name is " + sFname + " " + sLname + ". Your address is " + sAddr + →
", " + sCity + ", " + sState + ", " + sZip + ", " + sCou + ". Is that all  →
correct?")
//-->
</SCRIPT>
```

We're simply writing all variable contents to the document using **document.write**; you can see the result in Figure 18-2.

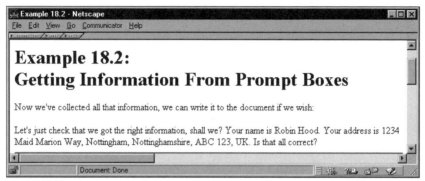

Figure 18-2: This time we collected information from the user via Prompt dialog boxes, then used the information in the document.

Status Bar Messages

There are three forms of status bar messages. First, there's the type that we are all used to and which we have no control over: those inserted by the browser. When you point at a link or load a Web page, the browser displays information in the status bar. It can be the URL of the link you are pointing at or information about the progress of the document transfer.

Then there's something called the *default* status-bar message. This is a JavaScript feature that lets you set a message that will be displayed at any time that something else is not being displayed there. It's set using the **windows.defaultStatus** property.

Finally, there's a *temporary* status-bar message (also known as a *transient* or *priority* status-bar message). This is set using the **windows.status** property, and is a message that will appear for a short time—while the user points at a link, for example.

defaultStatus

We'll begin by setting the **defaultStatus** property. You can set this at any time: when the user loads the page, when the user clicks on a button to carry out some JavaScript operation, and so on. For example, try something like this in a script:

Example 18.3

```
defaultStatus = "Hello, how y'all doing?"
```

In our Online Companion example we put this script in the HEAD. This message will appear as soon as the browser reads the HEAD—before it's even had a chance to load the remainder of the document. Of course you could also put this into the **onload** event handler, but then the message won't appear until after the document has loaded; or you can combine both, like this:

Example 18.4

```
<HEAD>
<SCRIPT LANGUAGE="JAVASCRIPT">
<!--
defaultStatus = "Hold on, we're loading..."
//-->
</SCRIPT>
</HEAD>
<BODY onload="defaultStatus = 'Hello, how y\'all doing?'">
```

This displays *Hold on, we're loading…* when the document begins loading, then the *Hello, how y'all doing?* message after it's finished. Of course if the page loads very quickly, you might never see the first message.

You can change the **defaultStatus** message at any time, in different ways. You could, for example, change it when the user enters information into a form element, like this:

Example 18.5

```
<FORM>
Type something, then press Tab: <INPUT TYPE="TEXT" SIZE="30"
onblur="self.defaultStatus='Here\'s what you typed: ' + →
document.forms[0].elements[0].value"><P>
<INPUT TYPE="TEXT" SIZE="30">
</FORM>
```

We are using an **onblur** event handler here to set the **defaultStatus** value. Notice a couple of things. First, we haven't used **defaultStatus**, but **self.defaultStatus**. You may remember that when you refer to something in the object hierarchy from an event handler, you must include the **window** part (actually in this case we used **self**, which is a synonym for "current window").

We've also taken the information typed into the text box, along with some extra text (*Here\'s what you typed:*), and passed that to the status bar.

You can change the **defaultStatus** any way you want. Here are a couple more ways you can change it:

Example 18.6

```
<FORM>
<INPUT TYPE="BUTTON" VALUE="Change" onclick="self.defaultStatus='Let\'s →
change the status message from this button!'">
</FORM>
<A HREF="nowhere" onmouseover="self.defaultStatus='Now from this link!'; →
return true">Or just point at this link (which doesn't go anywhere) to →
change the status message.</A>
```

This time we used an **onclick** event handler on a button to change the **defaultStatus** and an **onmouseover** on the link. Notice anything strange about the link? First, we included **; return true** at the end of the message that we want to display. In theory you need this bit to make the **onmouseover** event handler work with **defaultStatus**. It works *without* this bit on some browsers, but leave it in to make sure it works in all JavaScript browsers.

TIP

How do you "cancel" a **defaultStatus** *message? Simply write a blank* **defaultStatus** *message.*

Working With Status

The status message overrides other messages, but it is only temporary. It's commonly used to display a message when the user points at a link, like this:

Example 18.7

```
<A HREF="nowhere" onmouseover="self.status='This link takes you to ... ';
return true">Point at the link to see another message.</A>
```

This is easy to do; simply use **onmouseover**, remembering to include **; return true** at the end (you definitely must include this in the case of the **status** property).

As we've discussed earlier, these status messages set on links can be a bit of a nuisance. For a while after the introduction of JavaScript we saw a lot of these messages, because many people operate under the theory that "if you can, you should, and it's fun doing new stuff anyway." Since then I think people have realized how irritating they can be, and we haven't noticed quite so many. Think carefully before you use these messages, and consider whether the benefits outweigh the possible irritation. And take a look at Chapter 12, "JavaScript Events—When Are Actions Carried Out?" for an example of when it really does make sense to put a message over the link, that is, to mask the link (see "onmouseover" in that chapter).

Can we change **status** from elsewhere? Well, yes, but it rarely makes sense, because the message is temporary. For example, you could put it on a button, like this:

Example 18.8

```
<FORM>
<INPUT TYPE="BUTTON" VALUE="Try to Change Status Bar"
onclick="self.status='You\'ll see this message until you move the mouse →
from the button.'">
</FORM>
```

You'll find when you click on the button, the new message appears and then, when you move the mouse, it disappears. Remember, it's only temporary.

> **TIP**
>
> *You can see an example of a more advanced status bar message—one that moves along the status bar—in Chapter 20, "Ready-to-Use Scripts."*

Writing to the Current Page

You'll remember that you can't write to the current page. Once the source HTML document has been loaded, trying to write to it won't add text to the display; instead the document will be cleared and a *new* document written. (In some old browsers a bug might stop the new text from being written, but the old text will be cleared.) For example, we can try this:

Example 18.9

```
function Rewrite()    {
    document.open()
    document.write("Write this to the document<BR>")
    document.close()
}
```

What happens if we call this from within the document? The document is cleared, and the new text written to the document (click on Reload to come back).

There is a simple way around this problem, though—a way to write to a document without losing it. Write to a textarea. Try this example:

Example 18.10

```
<FORM>
First Name: <input type="text" size="30"><BR>
Last Name: <input type="text" size="30" onfocus="elements[7].value = s1 →
"><BR>
Address: <input type="text" size="30" onfocus="elements[7].value = s2 "><BR>
City: <input type="text" size="30" onfocus="elements[7].value = s3 "><BR>
State/Province/Region: <input type="text" size="30"
onfocus="elements[7].value = s4 "><BR>
Zip/Postal Code: <input type="text" size="30" onfocus="elements[7].value →
= s5 "><BR>
Country: <input type="text" size="30" onfocus="elements[7].value = s6 "><P>
<B>See the instructions here:</B><BR>
<TEXTAREA COLS="40" ROWS="2" WRAP="virtual">Type your first name in the text
box.</TEXTAREA>
</FORM>
```

We created a form similar to one we saw earlier in this chapter. This time, though, we have a textarea at the bottom; we'll use this to display information about each field. Notice that we have the text *Type your first name in the text box* in the textarea to begin—we're using this script to move focus to the first text box when we load the file:

```
document.forms[0].elements[0].focus()
```

So the text in the textarea refers to the first text box. Then, we have a series of **onfocus** event handlers, such as this:

```
onFocus="elements[7].value = s4 "
```

In this case we are placing the contents of variable **s4** into the 8th element within the current form, when the user moves focus to this text box. Here are the variables we are using (we defined them in the HEAD):

```
var s1 = "Type your last name here."
var s2 = "Type your street address."
var s3 = "Your city name, please."
var s4 = "Yes, yes, you know--state, province, etc."
var s5 = "Okay, zip or postal code."
var s6 = "Yep, now your country."
```

So each **onfocus** displays a different message within the textarea—each message related to the text box that focus is moving to—as you can see in Figure 18-3.

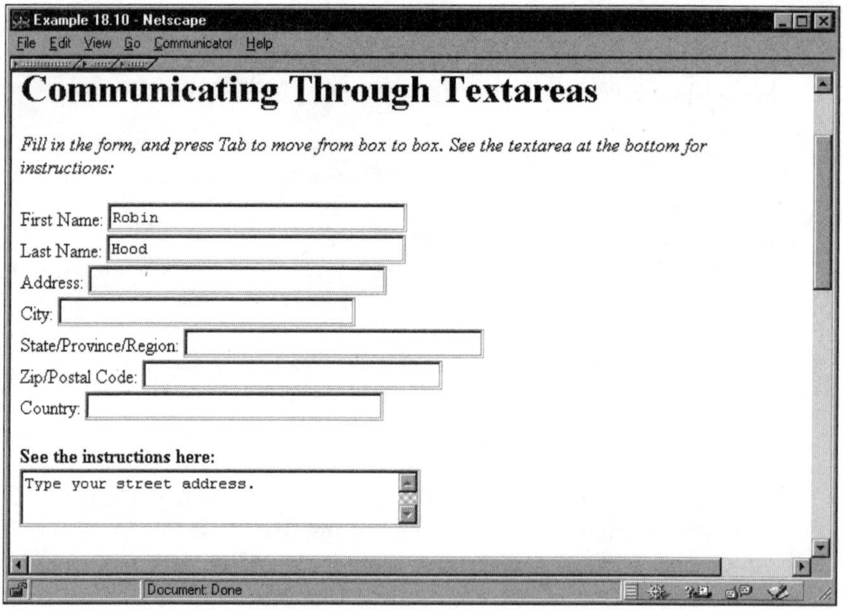

Figure 18-3: Writing to the textarea provides a very simple way to communicate with a user.

Writing to the textarea provides a very simple way to communicate with the user. This is a simple example, but you can get fancy and send messages to the user related to operations carried out by the JavaScript. You can use this system to carry out calculations and display the result, for example.

TIP

*We used a textarea in this example, but we could just as easily have used a text box, instead. The textarea has the advantage of providing more space. However, remember that there's a problem with the line breaks that must be placed in long messages. You can see Chapter 11, "More About Built-in Objects," to find out how to set the line breaks so that the correct break is used regardless of the browser being used to view the document. We'll be looking at this again in the following chapter, too. Or there's an easier method you can use to solve the problem. Simply set the textarea to word wrap using the **WRAP=** attribute. In our example we used **WRAP="virtual"**, which wraps the text onto the next line.*

Moving On

Tired of theory yet? Want to put it all into action? That's what we will be doing in the next couple of chapters.

In the next chapter, we'll examine two programs we've created, the area-code program and the telephone directory. The first lets you search for information about a particular area code in the North American Dialing Plan. You can search by area code, city, or region (state, province, or island nation in the Caribbean). The second lets you create a little telephone directory—an office directory, for example—and search on multiple keywords for the person you want. These two programs will show you how the skills you've learned so far can create actual JavaScript applications.

The Area Code & Telephone Directory Applications

We're now going to see several examples of how you can put together everything you've learned and actually create a JavaScript that does something! The first example we're going to use is our little area-code program. This is an application that allows you to search for an area code within the North American Numbering Plan (NANP) and find out where that code is. You can also search for a state (in the U.S.A), a province (in Canada), an island nation (in the Caribbean), or a city and find the corresponding area codes. Or you can see the entire NANP list of area codes.

Example 19.1

In Figure 19-1 you can see what this looks like. Why not go to the Online Companion and try it out? It's very simple. Type an area code into the Search Text box and click on Search. Or click on an option button, then type the appropriate text into the Search Text box and click on Search. The result of the search will be seen in the text area at the bottom of the page. You can also click on the Display ALL Area Codes option button to display the entire list in the text area.

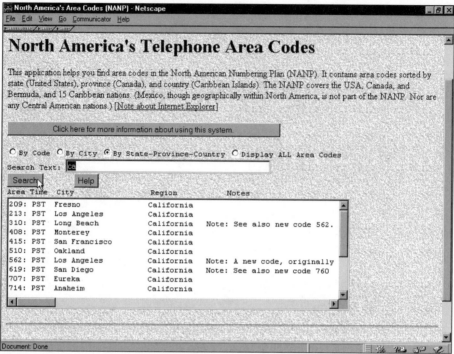

Figure 19-1: The Area Code program in action.

The other program is similar to the Area Code program. It's a Telephone Directory, containing fake information—a sample employee database. There are several important differences between this and the Area Code program. First, the Telephone Directory allows you to enter multiple search criteria; you can search for all the people whose first names begin with **b** in the **Admin** department, for example. And it also shows how you can use drop-down list boxes to allow the user to select from a group of options. Finally, we've handled a blank search differently, as we'll explain later.

Both these programs will work in Netscape Navigator 2 and 3, and in Internet Explorer 3. However, Netscape Navigator uses a nonproportional font in textareas, so the information that is found by the search lines up correctly in the textarea box. Internet Explorer, on the other hand, uses a proportional font, so the text does not line up in columns correctly. Also, the textarea will be much wider in Netscape Navigator, so the headings above the textareas will not line up properly.

Finally, we'll show you a JavaScript 1.1 version of the Telephone Directory. This will work in Netscape Navigator 3 or 4 (not in Internet Explorer). It uses the true **Array** object to create the array of telephone-directory entries.

Why These Applications?

JavaScript gives you a way to make your Web pages interactive. Computer systems consist of code that provides functional behavior, but by itself this is not enough to be of any real use. The bit that you also need in order to have a program that actually *does* something is *data*.

There are many JavaScript examples on the Web that demonstrate function, but where you have to provide the data. For example, there are calculators created using JavaScript. You provide the data by typing it in. Examples that require you to key in all of the data each time tend to be just that, examples, and not of any real use. We wanted to give you a *real world* example of a JavaScript application that someone might actually want to *use* for a reason other than to find out how JavaScript works. So we needed data.

Our example applications have all the data they need stored in arrays within the code. This might not be the most elegant way to input data into a program, but it suits our purposes because it is simple. And it's a real-world application. Right now we're talking with a record company about putting a simple JavaScript "database" on the Web, one that would allow users to search for a band's concert dates and locations. An application based on the concepts shown in these two sample applications is ideally suited to that kind of purpose.

TIP

We've used a lot of comment lines within the script to make the script easier to read. You can see the script in its entirety by opening the Area Code application and viewing the source. You can find this application in the Online Companion (http://www.netscapepress.com/support/javascript1.2/, or go directly to http://www.netscapepress.com/support/javascript1.2/areacode.htm).

We're going to begin by looking at the Area Code application in some detail. Then we'll look at the Telephone Directory application. Both programs share many features, so you need to read about the Area Code application first; we won't be covering the same ground when we get to the Telephone Directory.

Where's the Data?

Where is the Area Code application's information stored? Well, you'll remember from Chapter 9, "Building Arrays," that we can store information such as this area-code stuff in an array, and that's just what we did. In fact, we began by creating an **array** object like this:

Example 19.1

```
function makeArray(n) {
    this.length = n
    return this
}
```

You'll remember that this is how you start creating an array. (Yes, there's now a built-in **Array** object, but this object only works in Navigator 3.0 or later—so we are using the earlier method for creating arrays so that the script will work in all JavaScript browsers.) Once we've created the **makeArray** object class, we can create the actual arrays—the instances—themselves, like this:

```
var cde = new makeArray(187)
var area = new makeArray(187)
var cit = new makeArray(187)
var tz = new makeArray(187)
var no = new makeArray(187)
```

TIP

As mentioned in Chapter 9, we've broken one of our rules: we haven't placed a letter before a variable name to indicate the variable type (sArea, for example, instead of area). We wanted to use a small name, because we're going to be using it many times. And because we're using it so often in the script, we're not likely to forget what type of data it holds.

We now have five arrays:

- **cde**   The area codes.
- **area**   The area each code represents (state, province, island, and so on).
- **cit**   The city names.
- **tz**   The time zone.
- **no**   The notes related to that area code.

Then we had to place the information into the arrays, like this:

```
area[1]="Alabama";cde[1]=205;tz[1]="CST ";cit[1]="Birmingham →
";no[1]="See also the new code 334."
area[2]="Alabama";cde[2]=334;tz[2]="CST ";cit[2]="Montgomery →
";no[2]="A new code; originally within the 205 area."
area[3]="Alaska";cde[3]=907;tz[3]="-09 ";cit[3]="Anchorage";no[3]=""
area[4]="Alberta";cde[4]=403;tz[4]="MST ";cit[4]="Edmonton";no[4]=""
area[5]="Antigua";cde[5]=268;tz[5]="-04 ";cit[5]="St. Johns →
";no[5]="A new  code, originally within the 809 area. The old code may be →
used until March 31 1997."
```

TIP

It's very important to make sure that you get the array numbers correct, or you will mess up the program. For example, if you mistype a number—for example, 19 instead of 119—you will place the information into the wrong array position, perhaps writing over something else.

As we showed you in Chapter 9, "Building Arrays," we placed each array one after another on the same line for each index number (187 index positions). For example, take a look at this:

```
area[5]="Antigua";cde[5]=268;tz[5]="-04 ";cit[5]="St. Johns →
";no[5]="A new code, originally within the 809 area. The old code may be →
used until March 31 1997."
```

We start by placing the word **Antigua** into position **5** in the **area** array. The number **268** goes into position **5** in the **cde** array; **-04** goes into position **5** in the **tz** array; **St. Johns** goes into position **5** in the **cit** array; and the note at the end goes into position **5** in the **no** array. Notice that we separated each of these with a *;*.

Now, you don't have to place all of these on the same line. You could do all of the **area** array, then do all of the **cde** array, and so on with each array in a separate block. We like to have all the arrays together, so we can quickly enter information for each area code at one time and can quickly see all the information in one place. However, in some cases we weren't able to use this method, so we had to move some of the array assignments down.

You see, we ran into a size limitation. When we first wrote this program, using a beta of Navigator 3.0, JavaScript had, under some circumstances, a 255-character limitation on a line, and a number of our lines exceeded this limit. Look at this line:

```
area[6]="Arizona";cde[6]=520;tz[6]="MST";cit[6]="Tucson →
";no[6]="A new code, originally within the 602 area. The old code has →
expired for much of Arizona. In Tucson it expires on Dec 31 1996, in →
Flagstaff, Prescott, Yuma it expires on June 30 1996."
```

JavaScript just didn't like this. The entire line was too long. Luckily there's a quick fix. We simply removed the **;** before the **no[6]** and moved the **no[6]** assignment down onto another line, like this:

```
area[6]="Arizona";cde[6]=520;tz[6]="MST";cit[6]="Tucson";
no[6]="A new code, originally within the 602 area. The old code has →
expired for much of Arizona. In Tucson it expires on Dec 31 1996, in →
Flagstaff, Prescott, Yuma it expires on June 30 1996."
```

Now it works fine. We had a slightly more complicated problem with this entry:

```
area[30]="Caribbean";cde[30]=809 ;tz[30]="CCT";cit[30]=" ";no[30]="These →
are the countries currently covered by this code (with their new codes if →
changing soon): Anguilla, Bahamas (242), Barbados (246), Bequla, British →
Virgin Islands, Cayman Islands, Dominica, Dominican Republic, Jamaica, →
Montserrat (664), Mustique, Nevis, Palm Island, St. Kitts, St. Lucia (758), →
St. Vincent, Trinidad and Tobago, Union Island, US Virgin Islands"
```

Not only is the entire line too long, but the note itself is too long to be assigned to a variable in one block. So we simply did this:

```
var ex1="A code covering a number of Caribbean nations. This is gradually →
being split into smaller areas. See also new codes 242, 246, 268, 284, →
441, 473, 664, 787, 869, 758, 868."

var ex2="These are the countries currently covered by this code (with →
their new codes if changing soon): Anguilla, Bahamas (242), Barbados →
(246), Bequla, British Virgin Islands, Cayman Islands, Dominica, Dominican →
Republic, Jamaica, Montserrat (664), Mustique, Nevis, Palm Island"

var ex3=", St. Kitts, St. Lucia (758), St. Vincent, Trinidad and Tobago, →
Union Island, US Virgin Islands"

area[30]="Caribbean";cde[30]=809 ;tz[30]="CCT";cit[30]=" ";no[30]=ex1 + ex2 + ex3
```

First we declared three variables, **ex1**, **ex2**, and **ex3**, and split the note into those variables. Then we concatenated these on the last line when we assigned them to **no[30]**.

That's how we put the data into the script, and there's quite a bit of it—almost 190 entries, with 5 arrays, so it's almost 950 array assignments. It's often easier to work with this sort of data in a good word processor and then copy it to your HTML editor later. A good word processor will have the sort of text-management tools that can really speed things up with lists like this: really good search and replace tools, the ability to copy and paste columns, and so on.

The Form

Now let's see the form we created:

```
<FORM NAME="form1">
<INPUT TYPE="BUTTON" VALUE="Click here for more information about using this
system." onclick="Info( )"><P>
<INPUT TYPE="radio" NAME="radSearchType"CHECKED VALUE =
"CODE"onclick="ClearAll(this.form);">By Code
<INPUT TYPE="radio" NAME="radSearchType"  VALUE = "CITY"
onclick="ClearAll(this.form);">By City
<INPUT TYPE="radio" NAME="radSearchType"  VALUE = "STATE"
onclick="ClearAll(this.form);">By State-Province-Country
<INPUT TYPE="radio" NAME="radSearchType"  VALUE = "ALL"
onclick="ShowAll(form)">Display ALL Area Codes
<BR> Search Text:
<INPUT TYPE="text" NAME="txtSearch" SIZE=50>
<INPUT TYPE="button" VALUE="Search"
onclick="SearchType(this.form)">
<BR>
Area / Time / City / State-Province-Country / Notes <INPUT TYPE="button"
VALUE="Help" onclick="Help( )">
<BR>
<TEXTAREA NAME="txtResults" ROWS=10 COLS=73></TEXTAREA>
</FORM>
```

You can see the form created by this in Figure 19-2. We start with a large button that calls the **Info( )** function. This function opens a new window and displays information about using the system. (We'll show you this and the other functions as we go through the script.)

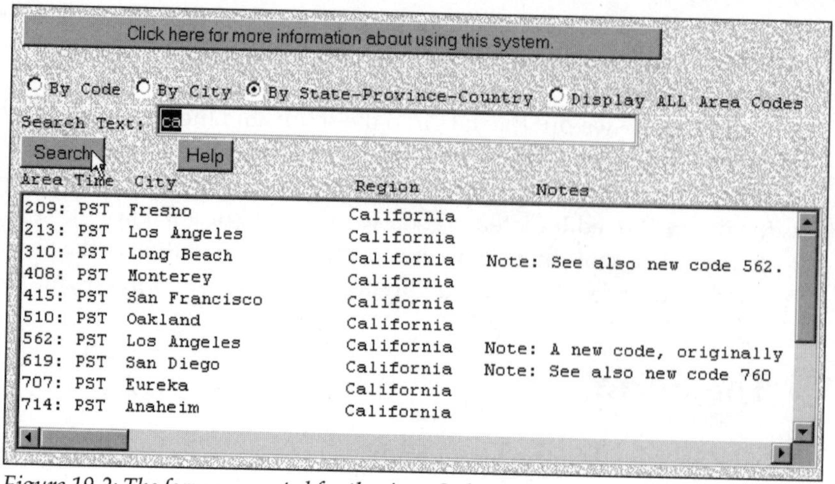

Figure 19-2: The form we created for the Area Code application.

Next we have several option buttons. These are used to determine how the data is searched: by code, city, or state-province-country. There's also a button that displays the entire list of entries. Now, the first three of these buttons call the **ClearAll( )** function; this function is used to clear the contents of the textarea at the bottom of the page, to move focus to the Search Text box, and to select the contents of that box.

The last option button is a little different. It calls the **ShowAll( )** function, which clears the contents of the textarea, displays a Confirm box that asks if you want to continue, and writes all the information from the arrays into the textarea.

Then we have the **txtSearch** text box—this is where the user types the text to be searched for—and a button that the user clicks on to call the **SearchType( )** function. This function determines which type of search should be carried out and calls the appropriate function to do so.

Next we have the **Help** button. This calls the **Help( )** function, another one used to open an information window. Finally, we have a large textarea at the bottom of the form, the **txtResults** element. This is where the results of the search are placed.

Setting Focus on the Form

After the form, we have this script:

```
<SCRIPT LANGUAGE="JavaScript">
<!--
    //set the focus to the txtSearch box:
    document.form2.txtSearch.focus( )
    document.form2.txtSearch.select( )
//-->
</SCRIPT>
```

This simply sets the focus on the **txtSearch** box once the form has been loaded. In other words, the cursor is placed in the **txtSearch** box. The expression **document.form2.txtSearch.focus( )** indicates that we wish to use the **focus( )** method on the **txtSearch** element of the form named **form2.txt** in the **document**. You'll also notice that we used the **select( )** method in addition to **focus( )**. That's so if there's any text in the text box when the document is loaded (for example, if the user does a search, then comes back later to do another), then that text will be highlighted. All the user has to do is type, and the existing text is replaced.

> **TIP**
>
> *If you create a "database" program like this, be careful not to run into an inherent size limitation. While JavaScript itself doesn't have a built-in script-size limitation, Windows 3.1 does. You should avoid producing a Web page anywhere near 64K because, thanks to the way that Windows handles memory, Windows 3.1 browsers can have problems with the JavaScript.*

The Functions

Now let's take a look at the functions that actually make this application work. (We've already seen the **makeArray( )** function, so we won't revisit that one.) We placed all the functions in the HEAD of the document—not necessarily in the order that they are run, since the order of their definitions doesn't matter. We have these functions:

Function	Definition
info( )	Opens a window that contains information about the program. Called from the large button at the top of the form.
Help( )	Opens a window that explains the information returned. Called from the Help button.
ClearAll( )	Clears the contents of the textarea, moves focus back to the text box, and highlights the text in the text box.
ShowAll( )	Writes all the area code information to the textarea. Called when the user clicks on the Show ALL Area Codes option button.
AddText( )	Grabs information from the arrays and passes it back to the calling function. Called by the **ShowAll( )**, **CodeSearch( )**, **CitySearch( )**, and **StateSearch( )** functions.
SearchType( )	Checks to see which option button the user clicked on and then calls the appropriate function (**CodeSearch( )**, **CitySearch( )**, or **StateSearch( )**). Called when the user clicks on the Search button.
CodeSearch( )	Searches for a particular area code. Called by the **SearchType( )** function, if the By Code option button is selected.
ValidateAreaCode( )	Called by the **CodeSearch( )** function to determine whether the user typed a three-digit number.
CitySearch( )	Searches for a particular city. Called by the **SearchType( )** function, if the By City option button is selected.
StateSearch( )	Searches for a particular state, province, or island nation. Called by the **SearchType( )** function, if the By State-Province-Country option button is selected.

You can see how these functions are linked together. For example, clicking on the Search button calls **SearchType( )**, which might call **CodeSearch( )**, which calls both **AddText( )** and **ValidateAreaCode( )**. Let's see how each of these functions works.

info( ) & Help( )—Viewing Information Windows

When you click on the large button labeled **Click Here for More Information About Using This System**, the **info( )** function is called. Here's the **info( )** function:

```
function Info( ) {
        WinInfo = open("area1.htm","Info","menubar,scrollbars, →
toolbar,height=350,width=600")
}
```

This is a simple little function. It opens a window and loads the **area1.htm** file into that window. The window has a menubar, scroll bars, and toolbar.

The **Help** button is similar; it calls the **Help( )** function:

```
function Help( ) {
        WinInfo2 = open("area2.htm","Info2","height=400,→
width=600,scrollbars")
}
```

This time we loaded **area2.htm**. This window has only scroll bars. We added a menubar and toolbar to the first window (**WinInfo**) because we have a link in **area1.htm** that takes people to the Bellcore Web site, to find more information about the North American Numbering Plan. The second window (**WinInfo2**) is intended to be opened, read, and closed, so we have fewer components.

By the way, we checked both windows in VGA mode, to make sure that the windows wouldn't be too large in a low resolution video mode. Unfortunately that makes them smaller than they could be in a higher resolution—but that's just one of the tradeoffs you have to make now and then. (We could have chosen to have the windows maximized, full size. But you risk confusing users when you do that, as they might not realize that a new window has opened and the old one is below the current one. We wanted the user to be able to see the old window below.)

ClearAll( )—Clear the Textarea

When you click on one of the first three option buttons, the textarea is cleared and the text in the Search Text box is highlighted. This is done by calling the **ClearAll( )** function:

```
function ClearAll(form) {
    form.txtResults.value = ""
    form.txtSearch.focus( )
    form.txtSearch.select( )
}
```

First we set the value held in **form.txtResults**—in other words, "the value in the **txtResults** element in the **form**." Which form? Notice that the word **form** appears in parentheses after **ClearAll**. If you look at the option buttons in the form, you'll see that **this.form** is being passed to the function. The form is identifying itself, so the function knows which form to work with. We're setting the value in the textarea to ""; in other words, we're putting an empty string into the textarea, so it's cleared.

Next we use the **focus( )** and **select( )** methods, as we saw a moment ago, to place the cursor inside the text box and highlight any text that might be left over from an earlier search.

ShowAll( )—Display All the Entries

The **ShowAll( )** function is called from the last option button:

```
<INPUT TYPE="radio" NAME="radSearchType"    VALUE = "ALL"
        onclick="ShowAll(form)">Display ALL Area Codes
```

This function gets the entire area code list and places it into the textarea. Here's how:

```
function ShowAll(form)    {
  var sText = ""
  form.txtResults.value = ""
  if (!confirm("Displaying all of the area codes may take twenty seconds →
or more (and you won't see any \"busy\" indicator while retrieving the →
information). Do you wish to continue?"))    {
            //if user clicks on cancel we do this:
            form.radSearchType[0].checked = true
            form.txtSearch.focus( )
            form.txtSearch.select( )
            return
      }
      //if user clicks on OK we do this:
      for (var i = 1; i <= area.length; i++) {
          sText = AddText(sText, i)
  }
  form.txtResults.value = sText
  form.txtSearch.focus( )
  form.txtSearch.select( )
}
```

We begin by declaring a variable, **sText**. Then we use the same **form.txtResults.value = ""** instruction (that we've just seen in **ClearAll( )**), to clear the contents of the textarea.

Next we have an **if** statement. We begin the statement by displaying a Confirm box with a message that warns the user that it will take a while to display all the information. Currently JavaScript has no way to display a "busy" or "at work" indicator. Displaying all the area codes can take 20 seconds or more; therefore, we thought we should warn people what was happening. Without the Confirm box, it appears as if nothing is happening after the textarea has been cleared. (Unfortunately there are some browser bugs at work here; with some browsers, on some systems, it can take a *very* long time.)

What happens if the user clicks on the Cancel button? Well, notice that we have **!confirm**; this means if **confirm** is not true, carry out the following instructions (the instructions in the { }). You'll remember that if the user clicks on OK, **confirm** returns true. So if the user clicks on Cancel (if **confirm** is not true), then we run the instructions in the { }:

```
form.radSearchType[0].checked = true
form.txtSearch.focus( )
form.txtSearch.select( )
return
```

The first line uses the **checked** property, which is a property of a **form** element. The **radSearchType** element is the set of radio buttons in our form. We've used the **radio** object; **radSearchType** is the name of our **radio** object, and **radSearchType[0]** means "the first radio button in the set." And as we are setting the property to **true**, it means that we are selecting the first radio button. In other words, if the user decides not to go ahead and display the entire list of area codes, we reset the form, selecting the By Code radio button again. Then we use the **focus( )** and **select( )** methods, which we've seen before, to move focus to the Search Text box and highlight any text that's there. Then the **return** statement exits this function.

What happens if the user clicks on OK? We do this:

```
        //if user clicks on OK we do this:
        for (var i = 1; i <= area.length; i++) {
            sText = AddText(sText, i)
    }
    form.txtResults.value = sText
    form.txtSearch.focus( )
    form.txtSearch.select( )
}
```

We have a **for** loop here. We declare a variable named **i** and initialize it with the value **1**. That represents the first value ([1]) in our arrays. (Remember from Chapter 6, "Conditionals & Loops—Making Decisions & Controlling Scripts," this is the *initial expression*, and we are initializing counter **i**.) Next the *conditional expression* is evaluated: **i<=area.length**. This means, "as long as the value held by variable **i** is the same or less than the **length** property of the area array is **1** or greater." The **length** property of the array object is the number of index positions in the array. Remember when we created the **array** object? We did this:

```
function makeArray(n) {
    this.length = n
}
```

That means "the **length** property of **this** object is equal to **n**." Where does **n** come from? It's passed to the **makeArray** object in parentheses. Then, when we created the instance of the **area** array object, we did this:

```
var area = new makeArray(187)
```

We are passing the number **187** to the **makeArray** object, so the **length** of the **area** array is **187**. Now, back to the **ShowAll( )** function. You can now see that **i <= area.length** means, "if the counter **i** contains the number **187** or less, continue. If it contains **188**, stop."

We are beginning with the value **1**, of course, so the **for** loop now continues and runs the code between the { } brackets, as shown in this piece:

```
sText = AddText(sText, i)
```

We are taking the value returned by the **AddText( )** function to the **sText** variable. We'll look at **AddText( )** in a moment; this function is used to grab the information from the arrays. In parentheses, we pass this function the current value held by **sText**, along with the value in the counter **i**. **AddText( )** then grabs the information from that array position (if the counter **i** holds **15**, for example, it grabs the information from position **15**), adds that information to the information it was given by **sText**, then returns the information back to the **sText** variable. So **sText** is collecting each array entry, one by one. When this part of the code has run, the **for** loop then runs the *update expression:*

```
i++
```

This increments the value in **i**. So we begin with **1**, then after the first loop we go to **2**, then after the second loop we go to **3**, and so on, all the way to **188** when the loop stops running because **i** will no longer be less than or equal to **area.length**. At that point we run the rest of the instructions:

```
form.txtResults.value = sText
form.txtSearch.focus( )
form.txtSearch.select( )
```

First we set the value property of **txtResults** (the textarea); we place the contents of **sText** into the box. Then we use the **focus( )** and **select( )** methods to move focus to the Search Text box and highlight the text in the box.

That's it. Let's take a look at **AddText( )** to see how it managed to grab the information for us.

AddText( )—Grabbing Information From the Arrays

This function is called by the **ShowAll( )**, **CodeSearch( )**, **CitySearch( )**, and **StateSearch( )** functions. It's the heart of the application—the function that actually grabs the information from the arrays and hands it back to the functions so they can display it in the textarea.

```
function AddText(sText, i) {
   sText = sText + cde[i] + ": " + tz[i] + " " + cit[i] + " " + area[i]
   if ( no[i] != "" )    {
      sText = sText + "   Note: " + no[i] + nl
   }
   else  {
      sText = sText + nl
   }
   return sText
}
```

When a function calls **AddText( )**, it passes two items: the contents of the **sText** and **i** variables. As we just saw, **sText** is the variable containing the information that will be placed in the textarea, while **i** is a counter. (The other functions that call **AddText( )** work in a similar way to the **ShowAll( )** function we've just seen.)

AddText( ) begins by assigning several things to the **sText** variable. First, it assigns **sText**—that's right, it assigns itself. We want to keep the information that's already in **sText**, and in the same position, so **sText = sText** is the same as saying "keep the current contents." Then we add the value held by **cde[i]**; this is the **cde** array (the array holding the area codes). We are looking in array position **i**; remember, **i** is being passed to **AddText( )**, so the other function is telling **AddText( )** which array position to look in.

Then we add a colon and a space (**:**), followed by the data in the same position from the **tz** array (time zone). Then we add a space, followed by the information from the **cit** array (city), then a space followed by the information from the same position in the **area** array (the state, province, or island nation).

Next we have an **if** statement. We want to know if there's something in the **no** array, the notes. So we do this:

```
if ( no[i] != "" )    {
```

This means, "if the item in the **no** array at position **i** is not equal to '''', run the instructions after the **{** bracket." If it's not equal to '''', that means there *is* something in the **no** array at that position. So what do we do if there is something there? This:

```
sText = sText + "   Note: " + no[i] + nl
```

We assign **sText** to itself again, then add several spaces and **Note:**, followed by another space and the value from the **no** array. Finally we add **nl**. This is a variable that contains the characters required to create a line break at the end of all this information, so when we write to the textarea all the information is not written to one long line. (Instead, each area code's information appears on its own line.) So where does the value in **nl** come from? Well, the value required depends on the browser you are using, so we set the value in **nl** when the browser first opens the document. We'll look at that later in this chapter, in "The Line Break Problem."

What do we do if there *isn't* anything in the **no** array at that position? We have this instruction:

```
sText = sText + nl
```

Again, we assign **sText** to **sText**, then add the **nl** variable's value.

Finally, when the **if** statement has finished, what happens? We have this line:

```
return sText
```

We return the value held by **sText** to the function that called **AddText( )**. Remember the following from the **ShowAll( )** function:

```
sText = AddText(sText, i)
```

The value returned by **AddText( )**—the **sText** variable with the additional information—is returned to **ShowAll( )** and placed back into the **sText** variable.

So you can see that in this way a function can request information from particular array positions (or, in the case of **ShowAll( )**, all the array positions), and **AddText( )** will add the information one position at a time.

Searching the Arrays

We've now seen how the Display ALL Area Codes option button works. Now let's see how we can search for specific entries. We can search for a particular area code, city, or region (state, province, country). We do this by clicking on the appropriate option button and then clicking on the Search button. So let's see what the Search button does:

```
<INPUT TYPE="button" VALUE="Search" onclick="SearchType (this.form)">
```

As you can see, when you click on the Search button, the **onclick** event handler calls the **SearchType( )** function and passes the information from **this.form** to that function. So we'll begin there, by seeing what **SearchType( )** does.

SearchType( )—Which Search Do You Want?

We used the **SearchType( )** function to look at the option buttons and figure out what type of search the user wants and then call that search. This function is called when the user clicks on the Search button. Here's how we did it:

```
function SearchType(form) {
    //Clear the textarea box:
    form.txtResults.value = ""

    if (form.radSearchType[0].checked) {
        CodeSearch(form)
            return
    }
    if (form.radSearchType[1].checked) {
        CitySearch(form)
            return
    }
    if (form.radSearchType[2].checked) {
        StateSearch(form)
            return
    }
}
```

We've actually begun by clearing the contents of the textarea; you've seen **form.txtResults.value = ""** a number of times already. Then we use a series of nested **if** statements to decide which type of search to carry out: **if (form.radSearchType[0].checked){** means "look at the **checked** property for the **radSearchType** radio button in position **0**—the first button." If the radio button is selected, then the value held by **checked** is **true**, so the **if** statement continues and runs the instructions after the { brace. The first instruction is **CodeSearch(form)**, which means "call the **CodeSearch( )** function and pass the contents of the **form** to that function." The next instruction, **return**, exits the function.

If the radio button is not selected, **checked** contains **false**—so the **if** statement moves on and runs the next **if** statement. We have two more **if** statements: the first looking at radio button **[1]** (the second one), and the other looking at button **[2]** (the third one). If button **[1]** is selected (so **checked** is **true**), then the script calls the **CitySearch( )** function. If button **[2]** is selected, it calls **StateSearch( )**.

And that's all there is to **SearchType( )**. Once it's made its decision, we move to the selected function and carry out the search.

CodeSearch( )—Searching for an Area Code

The **CodeSearch( )** function is called by the **SearchType( )** function, if the By Code radio (option) button is selected. Here's the function:

```
function CodeSearch(form) {
  var bFound = false
  var nCode = 0
  var sText = ""
  var sSearch = form.txtSearch.value

    if (ValidateAreaCode(sSearch)) {
        nCode = sSearch
        for (var i = 1; i <= cde.length; i++) {
            if (nCode == cde[i]) {
                bFound = true
                break
            }
        }
        if (bFound) {
            sText = AddText(sText, i)
                    form.txtResults.value = sText
        }
        else {
          alert("Area code not found");
        }
    }
    form.txtSearch.focus( )
    form.txtSearch.select( )
}
```

We begin by declaring several variables: **bFound**, **nCode**, **sText**, and **sSearch**. We've assigned various values to these variables: **bFound** is set to **false**, **nCode** is **0**, **sText** is an empty string, and **sSearch** takes the value from **form.txtSearch.value**—the information that the user typed into the Search Text box.

Next we have an **if** statement. This begins by using the **ValidateAreaCode( )** function, which looks at the area code that the user typed and checks it to make sure that it's okay. (Notice that we pass the value from **sSearch** to the function.) We'll look at this function in a moment, but for now all you need to know is that it returns **true** if the area code is okay and **false** if it is not.

If the area code is valid, the next statement takes the value in **sSearch** (the area code the user typed) and places it into **nCode**. Then we have a **for** loop that will run its instructions if the value in **cde.length** (the number of items in the **cde** array) is less than or equal to the value in counter **i**; as before, we're going to go through each array position, starting at **1**. If **i** *is* less than or equal to **cde.length**, the **if** statement runs. This compares the value in **nCode** (the value the user typed) with the value in the **cde** array at position **i** (position **1**, then **2**, and so on). When the two values match—that is, when we've found the area code that the user typed in—**true** is assigned to the **bFound** variable; then use the **break** keyword, which stops the loop from continuing. Otherwise, as long as **nCode** does not equal the value in **cde** at that position, the **i++** incremental expression runs, increasing the value in **i** and trying again. So in this way the function examines the **cde** array entries, stopping when it finds the area code that the user typed.

When the **for** loop ends—when **break** runs, or when we get all the way to the end of the array and **i** exceeds the **cde.length** value—we move to the next **if** statement. This examines **bFound**. Remember, if we found a matching area code, **bFound** contains **true**, in which case we do this:

```
sText = AddText(sText, i)
form.txtResults.value = sText
```

We call the **AddText( )** function in the same way that we called the **ShowAll( )** function. **AddText( )** grabs the information from the arrays in position **i** and returns them to the **sText** variable. Then we write the contents of **sText** to the **txtResults** textarea.

What happens if **bFound** is **false**? We set **bFound** to **false** when we initialized it, and if we didn't find a match then it's still **false**. Well, we use this **else** statement:

```
else {
  alert("Area code not found");
}
```

This opens an Alert box and tells the user that the area code was not found. Finally, whatever the outcome of the search, we end the **CodeSearch( )** function with the usual:

```
form.txtSearch.focus( )
form.txtSearch.select( )
```

We move focus to the Search Text box and highlight the text.

ValidateAreaCode( )—Is the Area Code Okay?

The **ValidateAreaCode( )** function is called by the **CodeSearch( )** function. It's used to examine the information typed into the Search Text box and to make sure that it is valid—that is, that it's a three-digit number. Here's the script:

```
function ValidateAreaCode(sText) {
    //Make sure it is a number:
    for (var i = 0; i < sText.length; i++) {
        var sChar = sText.substring(i, i + 1)
        if (sChar < "0" || sChar > "9") {
            alert("Not a valid number. Enter an area code")
            return false
        }
    }
//Check to see if the number is less than 100 or more than 999
i = parseInt(sText, 10)
    if (i < 100 || i > 999) {
        alert("Area code should be a 3-digit number")
        return false
    }
    //Validation passed:
    return true
}
```

First, notice that **CodeSearch( )** passed **sText** to this function. The **sText** variable contains the text that the user typed into the Search Text box (the text that we want to look at). We begin with a **for** loop. We set the counter **i** to 0. Then we use the conditional expression **i < sText.length**. This means continue if the value held by **i** is less than the length of the **sText** variable. If the user types a 3-digit number, as he should, then when **i** increments to 3 (from 0 to 1, 2, 3—0 represents the first digit, 1 the second, 2 the third, so 3 would be the fourth, which we don't want), the loop stops. Next we declare a variable called **sChar** and use the **substring( )** method on the **sText** variable. The **substring( )** method is a string-object method that is used to grab a character (or several characters) from a string. The statement **substring(i, i + 1)** means grab the text starting at position **i** in the string, and finishing at position **i + 1**. In other words, "grab one character, the character at position **i**." (You have to give **substring( )** an ending position, which is actually the position immediately after the last character you want to grab, thus **i + 1**.) This character is then placed into the **sChar** variable.

Next we have an **if** statement nested within the **for** loop. This takes the value in **sChar** and examines it. The statement **sChar < "0" || sChar > "9"** means that if the value held by **sChar** is less than **0** or greater than **9**, continue. In other words, if the character contains anything but a digit from **0** to **9** (for example, if the user typed a letter or some other character), the **if** statement displays the Alert box; then, when the user clicks on OK, it returns **false** to the **CodeSearch( )** function, telling that function that the text the user typed is invalid.

If the character is not less than **0** or more than **9**, then it must be valid, so the loop goes around again and checks the next character. When it has checked all the characters (when **i** has incremented above the **sText.length** value), the script moves on to the next part:

```
//Check to see if the number is less than 100 or more than 999
i = parseInt(sText, 10)
    if (i < 100 || i > 999) {
        alert("Area code should be a 3-digit number")
        return false
    }
    //Validation passed:
    return true
}
```

This takes the value from **sText** and uses **parseInt** to extract a number from it, placing that number into the variable **i**. (We use **parseInt** to make sure we've got a number; if the user typed text instead of a number, **parseInt** will return 0.) Then we use an **if** statement to check to see if the value held by **i** is less than **100** (**99** or less, in which case it's a two-digit number or less), or greater than **999** (**1000** or more, in which case it's a four-digit number or more). If it is, then the Alert box is displayed informing the user, and the function returns **false** to the **CodeSearch( )** function, telling that function that the text the user typed is invalid. If it's not, then we continue to the end of the script and return **true** to the **CodeSearch( )** function, telling that function that the text the user typed is valid.

CitySearch( )—Searching for a City

The **CitySearch( )** function is called by the **SearchType( )** function, if the By City radio (option) button is selected. Here's the function:

```
function CitySearch(form) {
  var bFound = false
  var sSearch = form.txtSearch.value
  var sCity
  var sText = ""
  var nStringLength = sSearch.length

  if (nStringLength == 0){
        form.txtSearch.focus( )
        return
  }
  sSearch = sSearch.toLowerCase( )
```

```
for (var i = 1; i <= cit.length; i++) {
        sCity = cit[i]
    //get the city name to the same length of string
        sCity = sCity.substring(0,nStringLength);
        sCity = sCity.toLowerCase( )
        if (sSearch == sCity) {
            bFound = true;
            sText = AddText(sText, i)
        }
    }
}
if (bFound) {
        form.txtResults.value = sText
}
else {
    alert("No Cities exist which match your search text")
}
form.txtSearch.focus( )
form.txtSearch.select( )
}
```

We start by declaring five variables: **bFound** (**false**); **sSearch** (containing the value from the **txtSearch** text box—that is, the value typed by the user); **sCity** (we placed nothing in here); **sText** (an empty string); and **nStringLength** (the value from the **length** property of the **sSearch** string object—that is, the number of characters that the user typed).

Next we use a quick **if** statement to see if we should bother to continue. If **nStringLength** is equal to **0**—that is, if the user didn't type anything into the Search Text box—all we do is move the focus back to the Search Text box and stop. Next, **return** means "exit out of the function and go back to where the function was called." In other words, don't go any further in this function.

However, if the user did type something into the text box, we continue to the next part of the script. First we change the text that the user typed to lower-case, using the **toLowerCase( )** method. **sSearch = sSearch.toLowerCase( )** means "convert the text in **sSearch** to lowercase, then put it back into the **sSearch** variable."

Then we use a **for** loop; as long as the value in counter **i** is less than or equal to the **cit.length** value (the number of items in the **cit** array), the loop continues. What does the loop do? Well, it starts by copying the contents of the **cit** array, at position **i**, into variable **sCity**. Then it cuts this value down to size, using the **substring( )** method (which we just looked at, in the **ValidateAreaCode( )** function). **sCity = sCity.substring(0,nStringLength)** means "grab all the text starting at the first position in the **sCity** variable and ending at the **nStringLength** position, and copy it into the **sCity** variable." Remember, **nStringLength** is the length of the text that the user typed into the Search text box.

Next we take that text and convert it to lowercase using the **toLowerCase( )** method. Now both strings—the text we've found in the array and the text that the user typed into the text box—are the same size and both lowercase. So it's an easy matter to compare the two:

```
if (sSearch == sCity) {
    bFound = true;
    sText = AddText(sText, i)
}
```

The **if** statement looks at the two strings, **sSearch** and **sCity**. If they are exactly the same, it sets **bFound** to equal **true** and then uses the **AddText( )** function that we reviewed earlier to add the text for that city into the **sText** variable. If the two don't match, nothing happens; **bFound** is not set to **true** (so it remains unchanged—remember, we initialized **bFound** as **false**), and we don't use the **AddText( )** function. Either way the code is now at the end of the loop and it returns to the top (it increments the counter **i** in the **for** line). The script loops around adding cities to the **sText** variable.

Once the loop has finished going around (when **i** = **cit.length**), we move on to the next part of the script:

```
if (bFound) {
        form.txtResults.value = sText
}
```

Here we look at **bFound** and decide what to do. If **bFound** contains **true**, then that means at least one match was found and we copy the contents of **sText** to the **txtResults** textarea. If it contains **false**, we use the **else** clause:

```
        else {
        alert("No Cities exist which match your search text")
    }
```

This displays an Alert box which tells the user that there's no match. Finally, whatever the result of the search, we do the usual thing:

```
form.txtSearch.focus( )
form.txtSearch.select( )
```

We move **focus** to **txtSearch** and highlight the text.

StateSearch( )—Searching for a Region

The **StateSearch( )** function is called by the **SearchType( )** function, if the By State-Province-Country radio (option) button is selected. Here's the function:

```
function StateSearch(form) {
  var bFound = false
  var sSearch = form.txtSearch.value
  var sState
  var sText = ""
  var nStringLength = sSearch.length

    if (nStringLength == 0){
        form.txtSearch.focus( )
        return
    }
    sSearch = sSearch.toLowerCase( )
    for (var i = 1; i <= area.length; i++) {
                sState = area[i]
            //get the state name to the same length of string
                sState = sState.substring(0,nStringLength);
                sState = sState.toLowerCase( )
                if (sSearch == sState) {
            bFound = true;
                    sText = AddText(sText, i)
// only use the following if the State data is entered into the arrays in →
alphabetical order
        }
        else {
            if (sSearch < sState) {
            //State is in alphabetical order so if we are here,
            //we have gone past where the search string would
            //have been in the list. No need to look further.
            break;
                }
            }
        }
    if (bFound) {
            form.txtResults.value = sText
    }
    else {
        alert("No states, provinces, or island nations exist which match →
your search text");
    }
    form.txtSearch.focus( )
    form.txtSearch.select( )
}
```

This is very similar to the **CitySearch( )** function that we just looked at, with a few differences, starting here:

```
else {
        if (sSearch < sState)
        //State is in alphabetical order so if we are here
            //we have gone past where the search string would
            //have been in the list. No need to look further.
            break;
}
```

As you see, we entered the information into our arrays in alphabetical order by state/province/island-nation order. So we can add a little bit of code that speeds up a search slightly. This code stops the search as soon as it has passed the point at which it makes sense to search. For example, if you are searching for Utah, once the script gets to Vermont it stops, because V comes after U. Of course this is only good if you have everything in alphabetical order—which is why we didn't do this for the **CitySearch( )** function.

This extra bit of code simply adds an **else** clause. If **sSearch** does not equal **sState**, the **else** clause looks at it and uses the following **if** statement (we've removed the comment lines):

```
if (sSearch < sState) {
        break;
        }
```

This means "if **sSearch** is less than **sState**, then use the **break** command." The **sSearch** variable contains the text the user typed, and **sState** contains the contents of the **area** array at the current position. So if **sSearch** is (alphabetically speaking) less than **sState**, we've gone past the position at which the text we are looking for could be. The **break** command will break out of the **for** loop.

The Line Break Problem

There's a small problem with line breaks in JavaScript. The way you create a line break varies, depending on which browser has loaded the document containing your JavaScript. Windows browsers use one method, UNIX and Macintosh browsers use another method. In our example we wanted to put a line break at the end of each line of data written to the textarea. In a Windows browser, we must use **\r\n** at the end of a line to push the next line down. In Macintosh browsers we have to use **\r**, and with UNIX browsers we have to use **\n**. That's tricky. How can we write two scripts and get the browser to pick one? Well, we saw how to do this in Chapter 11, "More About Objects," and we've used the same method we saw there. Right at the top of the HTML document we used this script:

```
//Set up the newline characters to be used in the textarea box –

//this depends on which platform
//the browser is running on
var nl=null
        if (navigator.appVersion.lastIndexOf('Win') != –1) {
            nl = "\r\n"
        }
        else    {
            if (navigator.appVersion.lastIndexOf('Mac') != – 1)    {
                nl = "\r"
            }
            else {
                nl = "\n"
            }
        }
```

We declared a variable called **nl**. Now we have an **if** statement. The statement uses the **lastIndexOf** method to see if **Win** is in the string. If it is, the method returns some number, indicating where in the string **Win** is found. If it isn't in the string, it returns **-1**. Then we compare this result to **-1**. The **!= -1** piece means, "not equal to **-1**." So if it's not equal (if **Win** *is* in the string), the next line is executed—and we place \r\n into the **nl** variable. If the letters **Win** don't appear in the string, though, we get **-1**, so the **else** line is executed and we use a nested **if** statement to see if the letters **Mac** are in the string. If they are we place \r into **nl**. If they aren't, we move on and place \n into the variable (if it's not a Windows or Macintosh computer, it must be UNIX). As we saw earlier in this chapter, later in our script we use **nl** to place the correct characters into the strings when we write to the textarea (using the text from the **AddText( )** function).

The Telephone Directory Application

Now let's look at another example of a JavaScript application, this time a Telephone Directory. You can take this one and modify it to suit your own needs, creating any kind of directory you wish. It allows you to store several pieces of information about each item, then search for entries by entering search criteria or selecting search criteria from a drop-down list box. It also uses selection boxes, so the user can select from a group of possible search criteria.

Example 19.2

You can see this program in action in Figure 19-3 and view it in the Online Companion. You can use multiple search criteria with this program. For example, you might select a department from the first drop-down list box, a country from the second, then click Search to see the names of all the people in the specified department and country.

Customize this program for whatever you want. It could be a directory of a publisher's author events, for instance: select an author name to see where that author will be and when, select a region to see which authors will be in your area, and so on. You could use this program as a product database, with each entry a particular characteristic of your products; the users can then search for just what they are looking for. It could be a skills database, providing information about the skills of your company's employees, consultants, contractors, and so on, so you can search for the people who are right for a particular job. Or you can use it the way we've designed it, as a directory of employees.

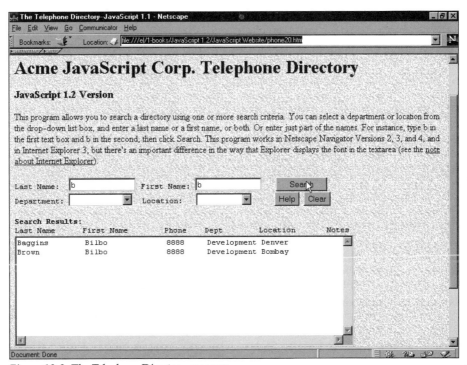

Figure 19-3: The Telephone Directory program.

There's another important difference, the way that we handle a blank search. In the Area Code application we allowed the user to display the entire database. All the user has to do is click the Display ALL Area Codes option button and the program will, after displaying a warning message, place all entries into the text area. Unfortunately that causes problems on some computers. If a user's computer is slow or has too little RAM, the program might never finish its work; it might simply churn away without achieving anything. So we've set up the Telephone Directory so that users can only search for particular people; they can't display *everyone* in the database.

Much of this program is the same as the Area Code program, so we won't go through this one in as much detail—we'll just look at a few important differences.

Creating the Arrays

We began by creating our arrays:

```
function makeArray(n) {
    this.length = n
    return this
}
```

```
//Create the array instances:
var N = new makeArray(139)     //N is Last name
var N1 = new makeArray(139)    //N1 is  First name
var X = new makeArray(139)     //X is Phone Number
var D = new makeArray(139)     //D is Department
var L = new makeArray(139)     //L is Location
var no = new makeArray(139)    //no is Notes
```

```
//Assign the data to the arrays:
N[1]="Abbot";N1[1]="John";X[1]="3456";L[1]="Hong →
Kong";D[1]="Support";no[1]="Big nose, red hair."
N[2]="Acbar";N1[2]="Rodney";X[2]="2345";L[2]="Hong Kong";D[2]="Help →
Desk";no[2]="A real idiot."
N[3]="Adder";N1[3]="Heinrich";X[3]="4566";L[3]="Hong →
Kong";D[3]="Development";
N[4]="Agar";N1[4]="Agar";X[4]="5676";L[4]="London";D[4]="Development";
N[5]="Agoth";N1[5]="Umbridge";X[5]="4567";L[5]="New York";D[5]="Help Desk";
N[6]="Albert";N1[6]="Peter";X[6]="3254";L[6]="Denver";D[6]="Development";
```

Our variable names are not terribly distinctive, but we're trying to keep them short so that we can save space. Large scripts like this one can upset some JavaScript browsers. Notice also that when we assigned the data to the array elements we left out the space. We'll show you how we have adjusted the spacing of the search result in the textarea in a few moments.

Using gsFoundText

We've used a new method for storing the information that the search function found. We created a global variable called **gsFoundText**. We discovered that the method we've shown in the Area Code application can cause problems with some browsers on some computers—if the browser is running on a slow computer with little RAM, doing several large searches can slow the script down dramatically. Through experimentation we discovered that if we used a global variable to store the data this didn't happen. So we modified the **AddText( )** function that we showed you in the Area Code application. We now have this:

```
//Add in the text for this index:
function AddText(i) {
gsFoundText = gsFoundText + SpaceCat(N[i],13)+ "  " + SpaceCat(N1[i],17)+ " →
" + SpaceCat(X[i],8) + " " + SpaceCat(D[i],11)+ " " + SpaceCat(L[i],15)

    if (( no[i] != "" ) && ( no[i] != null ))   {
        gsFoundText = gsFoundText + "*  " + no[i] + nl
    }
    else {
        gsFoundText = gsFoundText + nl
    }
}
```

Now, when we call **AddText( )**, something quite different happens. First we take the text that's stored in **gsFoundText** and add to it the result of using another new function, the **SpaceCat( )** function (which we'll look at in a moment). **SpaceCat( )** is the function we're using for adding the correct number of spaces to the results text so it lines up in the textarea. **SpaceCat( )** takes the text that the search has found, adds any necessary blank spaces, and passes them back to the **AddText( )** function, which places them into **gsFoundText** global string variable. What values are we passing to **SpaceCat( )**? The value from the different array elements, plus the total number of characters that the text should fill—each **N** element (last name) should be **13** characters long, each **N1** element (first name) should be **17** characters, and so on. We use **SpaceCat( )** to provide the text for all of the elements with the exception of the **no** field (notes).

Adding Spaces With SpaceCat( )

Let's see how **SpaceCat( )** (that's short for "space concatenation," if you're wondering) works:

```
//Concatenate spaces to the end of a string up to the correct length:
function SpaceCat(sText, iLen) {
var sSpaces = "";
    if ( sText.length < iLen ) {
        iLen = iLen - sText.length
        for (var i = 1; i <= iLen; i++) {
            sSpaces = sSpaces + " "
        }
    sText = sText + sSpaces
    }
    return sText
}
```

As you just saw, **AddText( )** passes two values to **SpaceCat( )** (for example: **SpaceCat(N[i],13)**). The first value, which **SpaceCat( )** is calling **sText**, is the text taken from the array element; in this case the text taken from the **N** element, the last name. The second value, which **SpaceCat( )** calls **iLen**, is the total length of the field: the total number of characters we want to use in the textarea for that column of data. **SpaceCat( )** creates a variable called **sSpaces** and begins by clearing it. Next it uses an **if** statement that is carried out if the length of the text placed in **sText** is less than the total number of characters for that field. (If the length is the same we don't want to add any more spaces, of course.) We then change the value held by **iLen** to the difference between **iLen** and **sText**; this is the total number of spaces we need to add to the text to bring it to the correct length. Then we use a **for** loop to add the spaces; as long as the value held by **i** is less than or equal to **iLen**, we add a space to the **sSpaces** text. As soon as we reach a value that is greater than **iLen**—in other words, as soon as we've added all the spaces we need, we end the loop. So, for example, if **iLen** equals five, this loops around five times and adds five spaces.

Finally, we use **sText = sText + sSpaces** to add the spaces to the text already held in **sText**, and we return **sText** back to the **AddText( )** function.

Searching

There's nothing terribly complicated in this form. We've created two text boxes and two selection lists; we've used the **size="1"** attribute, so these are created as drop-down list boxes. Each has a blank space at the top, then several options below. There's also a textarea that, as in the Area Code application, we use to display the results of the search.

The heart of this form is the **Search( )** function, which runs when you click the Search button. Here's that function:

```
//Search
function Search(form) {
    var bSurNameFlg = true;
    var blstNameFlg = true;
    var bDFlg = true;
    var bLocnFlg = true;
    var sSurNameDB;
    var slstNameDB;
    var sDeptDB;
    var sLocnDB;
    var sSurName = form.txtSurName.value;
    var slstName = form.txtlstName.value;
    var sDept = GetItem(form.cmbDept);
    var sLocn = GetItem(form.cmbLocn);
    var sText = ""
    sSurName = sSurName.toLowerCase( )
    slstName = slstName.toLowerCase( )
    sDept    = sDept.toLowerCase( )
    sLocn    = sLocn.toLowerCase( )
    var nLenSurName = sSurName.length
    var nLenlstName = slstName.length
    var nLenD = sDept.length
    var nLenLocn = sLocn.length

    gsFoundText = ""
    form.txtResults.value = ""

 // need to check that we are checking for something.

    if ((nLenSurName == 0) && (nLenlstName == 0) && (nLenD == 0) && →
(nLenLocn == 0))    {
        alert("You have not input any search criteria.")
        return
    }
    //Loop around data arrays doing search:
    //-----------------------------------
    for (var i = 1; i <= N.length; i++) {
        if (nLenSurName > 0)    {
            bSurNameFlg = false;        //search is on
            sSurNameDB = N[i]
            //get the Surname name to the same length of string
```

```
        sSurNameDB = sSurNameDB.substring(0,nLenSurName);
        sSurNameDB = sSurNameDB.toLowerCase( )
        if (sSurNameDB == sSurName) {
            bSurNameFlg = true;
        }
        else {
            if (sSurNameDB > sSurName) {
                //Surname is in alphabetical order so if we are here,
                //we have gone past where the search string would
                //have been in the list. No need to look further.
                break;
            }
        }
    }
    if (nLen1stName > 0)    {
        b1stNameFlg = false;
        s1stNameDB = N1[i]
        s1stNameDB = s1stNameDB.substring(0,nLen1stName);
        s1stNameDB = s1stNameDB.toLowerCase( )
        if (s1stNameDB == s1stName) {
            b1stNameFlg = true;
        }
    }
    if (nLenD > 0)    {
        bDFlg = false;
        sDeptDB = D[i]
        sDeptDB = sDeptDB.substring(0,nLenD);
        sDeptDB = sDeptDB.toLowerCase( )
        //Do not need to shorten department as search on full text
        if (sDept == sDeptDB) {
            bDFlg = true;
        }
    }
    if (nLenLocn > 0)    {
        bLocnFlg = false;
        sLocnDB = L[i]
        sLocnDB = sLocnDB.substring(0,nLenLocn);
        sLocnDB = sLocnDB.toLowerCase( )
        //Do not need to shorten location as search on full text
        if (sLocn == sLocnDB) {
            bLocnFlg = true;
        }
    }
    if ((bSurNameFlg == true) && (b1stNameFlg == true) && (bLocnFlg == →
true) && (bDFlg == true))    {
```

```
            AddText(i);
        }
        else    {
            bSurNameFlg = true;
            blstNameFlg = true;
            bDFlg = true;
            bLocnFlg = true;
        }
    }
    //End of search loop

    if (gsFoundText.length > 0) {
        form.txtResults.value = gsFoundText
    }
    else {
        form.txtResults.value = ""
        alert("No entries exist which match your search criteria");
    }
    form.txtSurName.focus( )
    form.txtSurName.select( )
}
```

This function is more complicated than anything we saw in the Area Code program, because we're trying to do something that's more complicated: we're searching for several things at once, so if the user enters multiple search criteria, we have to make sure that they all match. Let's see what's going on in this script.

```
//Search
function Search(form) {
    var bSurNameFlg = true;
    var blstNameFlg = true;
    var bDFlg = true;
    var bLocnFlg = true;
```

We've begun by creating four Boolean variables, one for each of the items for which the user can search (Last Name, First Name, Department, Location), and we've set each to true.

```
    var sSurNameDB;
    var slstNameDB;
    var sDeptDB;
    var sLocnDB;
```

We've created four more variables, which we're going to use to store the data we are examining from each element in the array.

```
var sSurName = form.txtSurName.value;
var s1stName = form.txt1stName.value;
var sDept = GetItem(form.cmbDept);
var sLocn = GetItem(form.cmbLocn);
var sText = ""
```

Then we created four more that hold the data from the form: the information typed into the form or selected from the two drop-down list boxes. And we created **sText**, which we saw earlier.

```
sSurName = sSurName.toLowerCase( )
s1stName = s1stName.toLowerCase( )
sDept    = sDept.toLowerCase( )
sLocn    = sLocn.toLowerCase( )
```

Then we set all the information taken from the form to lowercase; we're going to do the same to the information from the array in a few moments, too, so we can compare the two sets of information.

```
var nLenSurName = sSurName.length
var nLen1stName = s1stName.length
var nLenD = sDept.length
var nLenLocn = sLocn.length

gsFoundText = ""
form.txtResults.value = ""
```

Finally, four more variables, to hold the length of the data taken from the form. And we cleared the **gsFoundText** variable, to clear out the results of any earlier searches (remember, **gsFoundText** is a global variable, which is not always a good way to do things, but as we mentioned earlier, using a global variable seemed to help when doing large searches on slow machines). And we cleared the contents of the textarea.

Then we check to see that we are actually searching for something (that is, that the user hasn't clicked the Search button without entering any search criteria), as you can see here:

```
// need to check that we are checking for something.
    if ((nLenSurName == 0) && (nLen1stName == 0) && (nLenD == 0) && →
(nLenLocn == 0))    {
        alert("You have not input any search criteria.")
        return
    }
```

We've used an **if** statement to see if anything has been entered or selected. We've looked at each of the variables containing the values taken from the text boxes and drop-down list boxes and used the == operator (equal to) to see if the variables contain **0**. We've tied them all together with **&&**, a Boolean AND. So if both text boxes are empty and nothing's selected in either drop-down list box, the **if** condition has been met and the **alert** statement runs. If the condition has not been met—if the user typed something into a box or selected something from a drop-down list box—we move on to the next part of the script. We've used a **for** statement, with a series of nested **if** statements:

```
//Loop around data arrays doing search:
    //-------------------------------------
    for (var i = 1; i <= N.length; i++) {
```

The for statement simply tells the script to look at each entry in the array one at a time and run the **if** statements on each entry. Let's look at just the first **if** (they're all similar):

```
if (nLenSurName > 0)    {
            bSurNameFlg = false;      //search is on
            sSurNameDB = N[i]
```

If the user typed something into the **nLenSurName** text box, then the length of the variable is greater than **0**, so the if statement sets the **bSurNameFlg** variable to **false** and begins the process of comparing what the user typed into the text box and the values held in the array, by placing the data from the first element in the N array into **sSurNameDB**.

```
            //get the Surname name to the same length of string
            sSurNameDB = sSurNameDB.substring(0,nLenSurName);
            sSurNameDB = sSurNameDB.toLowerCase( )
```

The user might have typed just a few characters of a name: sm instead of smith, for example. So we use the substring method to remove all the text in **sSurNameDB** that is longer than the amount of text stored in **nLenSurName**. And we've also changed the text to lowercase (remember, we changed the text from the form's text box to lowercase earlier. Then we carry out the comparison:

```
            if (sSurNameDB == sSurName) {
                bSurNameFlg = true;
            }
```

If the text in **sSurNameDB** and **sSurName** matches, we've found what we're looking for, so we set the **bSurNameFlg** to true again. Finally, the corresponding **else**:

```
<Computer Code>             else {
                if (sSurNameDB > sSurName) {
                    //Surname is in alphabetical order so if we are here,
                    //we have gone past where the search string would
                    //have been in the list. No need to look further.
```

```
            break;
        }
    }
}
```

If the last name text does *not* match, we check to see if we should continue by comparing **sSurNameDB** with **sSurName**; if **sSurNameDB** (the text in the array) is greater than **sSurName** (the text typed into the text box) it means that we've now passed the point at which there can possibly be any more matches (this assumes that the entries are stored alphabetically). If **sSurNameDB** *is* greater, alphabetically speaking, we **break**, so the script won't continue with the other if statements (which check the other three search criteria).

By the way, if you look back at the Area Code application you might notice that we did the same thing, comparing **sSearch** and **sState** like this: **(sSearch < sState)**. Just now we compared **sSurNameDB** with **sSurName** like this: **(sSurNameDB > sSurName)**. Why use < in one case and > in the other? Well, you can do it any way you want, really, but in some cases it just sounds right the other way around, and when you are reading scripts trying to debug them or remember how you wrote them, that helps. Saying **(sSurNameDB > sSurName)** ("if the value in the array element is greater than the value typed into the text box") might, to some ears, sound better than **(sSurName > sSurNameDB)** ("if the value in the text box is less than the value in the array element"), especially if we are trying to figure out if we've gone too far along the list, as we are in this example.

If we haven't gone too far, the script then runs the other **if** statements to see if there's a match on the other three search criteria. Then it does this:

```
if ((bSurNameFlg == true) && (blstNameFlg == true) && (bLocnFlg == true) && →
(bDFlg == true))    {
```

For each of the four search criteria it checks to see if the Boolean variable has been set to **true**. It's set to **true** if something's been found, remember. And as all search criteria must match—the user is looking for entries that match all the information he's entered, not just some of them—we check here to make sure that all the variables are set to **true**. If so we run **AddText( )**, which we saw earlier.

```
            AddText(i);
        }
        else    {
            bSurNameFlg = true;
            blstNameFlg = true;
            bDFlg = true;
            bLocnFlg = true;

        }
    }
```

If a single variable is set to **false**, that's the end of it—the data is not a true match, so we run the above **else** statement, which sets the Boolean variables back to **true** so they're ready to check the next array element.

Finally, we finish up the **Search( )** function with this:

```
if (gsFoundText.length > 0) {
form.txtResults.value = gsFoundText
}
else {
form.txtResults.value = ""
alert("No entries exist which match your search criteria");
}
form.txtSurName.focus( )
form.txtSurName.select( )
}
```

This checks to see if **gsFoundText** has anything stored in it; if it has, we place the text from **gsFoundText** into the form's textarea. If it hasn't, we clear the textarea and display an **alert** box explaining that nothing was found. Then we finish up by moving focus to the **txtSurName** element, the Last Name text box, and select the contents of that box.

The JavaScript 1.1 Version

We've also provided a version of the Telephone Directory that works with a couple of JavaScript 1.1 features. Of course this means it won't work in many JavaScript browsers—it won't work in Netscape Navigator 2 and Internet Explorer 3.

In this example we've started by using a source file. Take a look at the source code and you'll see this:

```
<SCRIPT language="JavaScript" src="phonelst.js"></SCRIPT>
```

This simply tells the browser to go to the **phonelst.js** file and insert the script from that file. What's in that file? Well, we have this:

```
//Create the array instances:
var N  = new Array( )    //N is Last name
var N1 = new Array( )    //N1 is  First name
var X  = new Array( )    //X is Phone Number
var D  = new Array( )    //D is Department
var L  = new Array( )    //L is Location
var no = new Array( )    //no is Notes
```

```
//Assign the data to the arrays:
N[1]="Abbot";N1[1]="John";X[1]="3456";L[1]="Hong
Kong";D[1]="Support";no[1]="Big nose, red hair."
N[2]="Acbar";N1[2]="Rodney";X[2]="2345";L[2]="Hong Kong";D[2]="Help →
Desk";no[2]="A real idiot."
N[3]="Adder";N1[3]="Heinrich";X[3]="4566";L[3]="Hong →
Kong";D[3]="Development";
N[4]="Agar";N1[4]="Agar";X[4]="5676";L[4]="London";D[4]="Development"; →
N[5]="Agoth";N1[5]="Umbridge";X[5]="4567";L[5]="New York";D[5]="Help Desk";
```

We used the new Array object to create array object instances, as explained in Chapter 9. The **var N = new Array( )** means "create a new array named **N**." As you can see from the comment, **N** is the Last Name field.

So the **phonelst.js** file contains all the data; the Web page itself contains the code. This is a great way to use one Web page in different situations. You might have different directories for different corporate departments, for example. Place each in a separate directory with a different phonelst.js file (or if you want all the pages in the same directory, have several different **.js** files and rename the **src="phonelst.js"** attribute in each Web page). (By the way, if you want to see the **phonelst.js** script in the Online Companion, click the link at the bottom of the Telephone Directory page; this links to **phonelst.js.txt**, a copy of the phonelst.js file.)

There's another change, too. In the **Search( )** function we used this:

```
for (var i = 1; i <= N.length - 1; i++) {
```

You'll remember from Chapter 9 that the new **Array** object counts array elements starting at **0**. But we've been creating our arrays starting at **1**; that way we can use the same set of data with the new **Array** object *and* with the old form of array that will work in the early JavaScript browsers. So we've taken **N.length** and removed **1** from it to get the number we really need.

JavaScript Generators

A program such as the one we've just looked at in this chapter would work well in conjunction with a JavaScript generator, a little program that could generate JavaScript from a database. For example, anyone who is familiar with programming a database such as Access or FoxPro could write a little script that would take information out of the database and put it into a text file, with all the JavaScript coding already in place (for information about just such a generator, see John's Web page at **http://www.arundel.com/ciss/gen.htm**).

The problem with JavaScript, as we've seen, is that on its own it's a one-way street. You can send data to the browser, but you can't easily get information back from the browser, without reverting to CGIs for example. So in our examples, users can easily get the information *from* the databases, but it's harder to get new information *into* the database. To add information to a script you have to modify the script, inserting the data in the right place and hoping that you don't make any mistakes.

There's an old programming rule that says you should avoid embedding data into programs. Doing so often results in errors being made when the data is updated, and in fact makes it much harder to update the information. It's better to keep the program and data separate. One way to do that is to keep the information in a true database program and use a JavaScript generator to periodically rewrite the script with the new data.

To simplify the process of generating a JavaScript you could even write the generator to create a **.js** file, a script file that can hold the array and be inserted into your JavaScript at the correct point using the **SRC=** attribute in the **<SCRIPT>** tag (see Chapter 3). Remember, though, that attribute only works in Netscape Navigator 3 and 4, not in Internet Explorer 3 or Netscape Navigator 2.

Using an automatic generator is much safer than making modifications by hand. Once the generator has been written and debugged, it will always work correctly. The human hand, however, is a capricious and faulty tool that seems to love creating typos and other errors. An automatic generator makes updating your scripts with data much quicker, easier, and less likely to introduce errors.

Moving On

Was that a lot of work? You've learned everything you need to know to create a script like the one we've just looked at—but something might have occurred to you: creating big JavaScripts can take a lot of time. Still, there are other ways to go about creating JavaScripts. You can borrow bits of code from real JavaScript programmers, people who've probably been programming for years and have the experience and skills that help them throw together scripts in half the time it would take a new programmer.

In the next chapter we're going to look at where you can find JavaScript code "libraries" from which you can borrow. In many cases you can quickly copy a script, drop it into your Web page, and customize just one or two things to get it to work for you.

Ready-to-Use Scripts

If you've never programmed anything before JavaScript, you've learned something by now. Programming JavaScript is no simple task. (That's why programmers get paid so much. Programming is a skill that takes a lot of learning and just the right type of person!) You might have decided that you'll never build anything large or complicated in JavaScript, although you've also learned how to do lots of little things to spruce up your pages.

If building large or complicated scripts is not your thing, there's something else you can do: you can take other people's JavaScripts, modify them, and drop them into your pages. Now, I'm not suggesting that you steal anyone's work—you don't have to. There are plenty of JavaScript programmers quite willing to provide JavaScripts to the public. And that's the subject of this chapter, how you can find the JavaScripts you need and import them into your own pages.

Of course you've got to know *what* to modify in a script. Often the authors will include comments pointing out the bits you must change. But even if they don't, if you've read the rest of the book you should be able to identify the different parts of a JavaScript, figure out how it works, and modify just the bits that need to change.

Finding JavaScripts

In Appendix H, "Finding More Information," we've listed all sorts of Java-Script resources. (You can also find this appendix in the Online Companion, so you don't need to type all those URLs.) Spend a little time moving around these sites and you'll run into lots of useful samples. You'll notice that many authors have given permission to the public to use these scripts. Read the permission statements, however, as there might be some restrictions. (For example you can use some for personal pages, but not for commercial sites. Others have been placed into the public domain, which means that you can do anything with them that you like.)

There are also sites that have actual libraries of JavaScripts from which you can grab pieces. Try these sites:

JavaScript 411
http://www.freqgrafx.com/411/
Among other things, this site has a Snippet Library.

The JavaScript Library at the JavaScript Index
http://www.sapphire.co.uk/javascript/lib/
The JavaScript Index maintains a library of JavaScript source code.

JavaScript: Simple Little Things to Add to Your Pages
http://tanega.com/java/java.html
A lot of simple things that you can add to your pages. (We've looked at most of the things the author of this page has described, but check to see if he's added more.)

The JavaScript Archive
http://planetx.bloomu.edu/~mpscho/jsarchive/
A couple of calculators, a script used to test browsers to see if they work with JavaScript, and much more.

JavaScript Applets
http://www.oz.net/~alden/javascript/jsintro.html
Currently a small collection, though unusual stuff; a Blackjack game, for example, and a compound-interest calculator.

Timothy's JavaScript Page
http://www.essex1.com/people/timothy/index.html
A small collection of interesting scripts.

You might find more libraries listed at the JavaScript Index (at http://www.sapphire.co.uk/javascript/lib/). You'll find lots of scripts in these libraries and many more at individual programmer's sites. You'll find different types of banners, games, calculators, color-changing utilities, clocks and timers, and more. Before you take a script, however, check to see if you can use it. If the site gives explicit permission, then fine, use it. If not, you'd better contact the author first.

Adding a Clock

Want to add a clock to your Web page? Here's how. Go to the Snippet Library at JavaScript 411 (http://www.freqgrafx.com/411/library.html) and find the link to the Clock page (or go directly to http://www.freqgrafx.com/411/clock.html). You'll find the page shown in Figure 20-1. You can see the digital clock in the text box near the bottom of the page. This clock is actually taken from the Netscape Communications documentation.

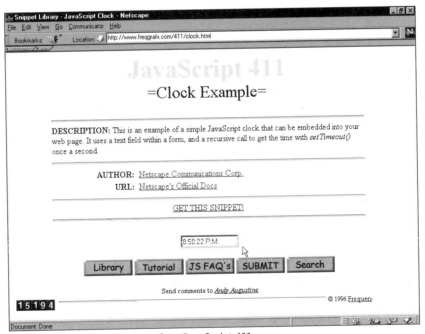

Figure 20-1: The Clock snippet from JavaScript 411.

Notice the *GET THIS SNIPPET!* link above this clock. Click on the link and Netscape loads the CLOCK.JS file. When it opens, you'll notice that the very first tag in the page is **<XMP>**; the **<XMP> </XMP>** tag pair tells the browser to display everything between the tags—without interpreting the HTML tags—so you can see the entire script (see Figure 20-2). We used the **<XMP>** tags in the Online Companion to display the scripts used in our pages.

```
http://www.freqgrafx.com/411/library/clock.js - Netscape
File  Edit  View  Go  Communicator  Help
Bookmarks:      Location:  http://www.freqgrafx.com/411/library/clock.js

<XMP>
<HTML>
<HEAD>
<TITLE>Clock Snippet</TITLE>

<SCRIPT LANGUAGE="JavaScript">
<!-- HIDE ME FROM THAT BROWSER
var timerID = null
var timerRunning = false

function stopclock(){
    // cannot directly test timerID on DEC OSF/1 in beta 4.
    if(timerRunning)
        clearTimeout(timerID)
    timerRunning = false
}

function startclock(){
    // Make sure the clock is stopped
    stopclock()
    showtime()
}

function showtime(){
    var now = new Date()
    var hours = now.getHours()
    var minutes = now.getMinutes()
    var seconds = now.getSeconds()
    var timeValue = "" + ((hours > 12) ? hours - 12 : hours)
    timeValue  += ((minutes < 10) ? ":0" : ":") + minutes
    timeValue  += ((seconds < 10) ? ":0" : ":") + seconds

Document: Done
```

Figure 20-2: Highlight the script and copy it.

Now highlight the script; you'll have to take the script from the top—the code that does the actual work—plus the form in the BODY of the document that is used to create the text box that holds the clock. You'll also notice that there's an onload instruction in the **<BODY>** tag; you'll need that too, of course.

Example 20.1

Now simply paste all this into your Web document. This is a very simple example, because there's really nothing to change. Drop the entire first script into the HEAD of your document, modify the **<BODY>** tag (to show **<BODY onload="startclock( )">**, with the current script), and then drop the **<FORM>** into the body of your page just where you want it. Open the document in your browser and you've got a clock!

Scrolling Status-Bar Messages

The last example was very simple, because there was nothing to change. You don't even have to look closely at the script, you simply drop it into the right place. Let's look at another example, though, one that takes a little more thought.

Take a look at the scrolling status-bar message in the same library at http://www.freqgrafx.com/411/scroller.html. (While it might be confusing, these messages have become known to many as *scrollbars* or *scrollers*, so if you see these terms used in JavaScript sites they are often referring to status-bar messages—not window scroll bars.) You can see this page in Figure 20-3.

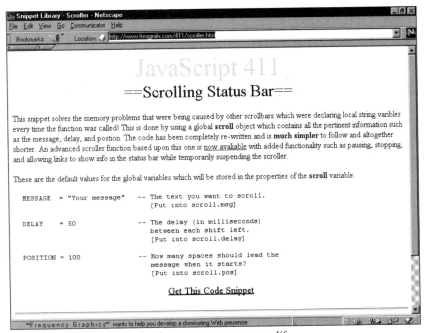

Figure 20-3: A scrolling status-bar message you can modify.

In this case you can see that the author has actually provided instructions telling you what you'll need to change. There's the **MESSAGE**, the **DELAY**, and the **POSITION**. Click on the *Get This Code Snippet* link to open the code. This time you'll have to be a bit more selective about what you take. First, you'll see that the author has included the following comment at the top:

```
/*
 Copyright (C) 1996 Frequency Graphics All Rights Reserved.
  Feel free to reuse this code snippet
```

```
    provided this header remains intact
*/
```

In other words, this code snippet is not in the public domain. It doesn't belong to you, although the author is giving you permission to use it as long as the copyright header remains with the code. So make sure that you include this header with the script you copy.

You'll also notice that there's nothing in the BODY of the document that you need. Everything is in the script in the HEAD and in the **<BODY>** tag, which looks like this:

```
<body onload="scroller( )">
```

So the script in the HEAD creates a **scroller( )** function, which is called by the **onload** instruction in the <BODY> tag. In other words, as soon as the browser has finished loading the document, it starts the status-bar message.

So, modify the **<BODY>** tag in your Web document and copy the entire script from the snippet's HEAD into the HEAD of your Web document. Then save the document and take a look in your browser. There it is, your Web page with the ***Frequency Graphics** wants to help you create a dominating Web presence* scrolling message. Now you know it's working, and all you need to do is make it display your message at the rate you want it displayed.

The first step, then, is to substitute your message. That's easy enough; just search for ****** or for ****F r e q u** (you'll notice that the scrolling message has spaces between each letter in **F r e q u e n c y G r a p h i c s**). You'll find several lines like this:

```
var MESSAGE = "**F r e q u e n c y  G r a p h i c s**"
        + " wants to help you develop"
        + " a dominating Web presence"
```

Replace this with your own text. You can do one long line if you wish, like this:

```
var MESSAGE = "*^*^*SLUG FEST*^*^* You want slugs, we got 'em. The best →
slug site in Cyberspace!"
```

However, there's a bug in early versions of Netscape Navigator (some of the beta versions of 3.0 and earlier) in which very long lines of text—255 characters or more—can cause errors. So you can break it up, like the original script:

Example 20.2

```
var MESSAGE = "*^*^*SLUG FEST*^*^*"
        + " You want slugs, we got 'em."
        + " The best slug site in Cyberspace!!!"
```

Make sure that your text has quotation marks around it, of course.

Now save your file, reload it into the browser, and see what it looks like. Your message will scroll along the bottom in place of Frequency Graphics' message.

Next, let's change the delay. This controls how quickly the message moves across the status bar. The instructions in the Snippet Library said that you need to change the **DELAY** = setting, so search for the word **DELAY**. You'll find it in a couple of places, but you need to find where the **DELAY** variable is declared:

```
var DELAY  = 50
```

Change this value. For example, replace **50** with **200**. Save the file, reload in the browser, and see what happens. It's now much slower. Experiment with different values until you have the one you think works best.

Finally, we can change the starting position—the point at which the message first appears on the status bar. The instructions said that this is controlled through the **POSITION** = setting, so look around for **POSITION**. Again, you'll find the word **POSITION** several places in this script, but you are looking for where the variable is declared (close to where the **DELAY** variable is declared, actually):

```
var POSITION = 100
```

Substitute some other value for **100**; try **50**, for example. Save and reload, and see what it does. If the value's too small, the message scrolls too quickly to be read, because it will start all the way over at the left side of the scroll bar. The larger the value, the more to the right the message begins. If it's too large, though, the message won't appear for a few seconds, as it's starting "off" the status bar. In fact this is a good way to make the message appear a few moments after the page has loaded, rather than right away.

TIP

The JavaScript 411 Snippet Library contains other more advanced scrolling status-bar message examples, which give you more control over the messages.

Don't Steal, Borrow

Although you can't simply take someone's script without permission and drop it straight into your pages, there's nothing to stop you from "borrowing" a script and seeing how it works. In the same way that a writer might read notable authors and poets to learn how they produced their great works, you should examine the JavaScripts you like. Copy a script from the source document to your hard disk, then play with it to see how it functions. You'll then see how you can do similar things in your own scripts.

To do this, of course, you'll need to understand JavaScript, even if you are no master of the art. You'll need to understand what we've studied in the first part of this book; all about functions, variables, objects, and so on. Once you know that stuff, though, you'll be able to read scripts and understand them and learn.

Conclusion

Well, that's it. If you've made it this far you've got a good grounding in Java-Script. You won't be a JavaScript guru, but you will understand the basics: enough to add many types of scripts to your Web pages, to read and understand other people's scripts, and to continue with your JavaScript education.

The rest of this book contains a variety of reference materials. You'll find summaries of JavaScript's objects, properties, and event handlers, a list of reserved words, and the colors you can use. You'll also find a reference table showing the different symbols used by JavaScript, to help you understand the scripts you find on the Web.

Most important, there's an appendix providing information about finding more information. Your education is not over, after all. There's plenty more to learn! You can also find this appendix in our Online Companion at http://www.netscapepress.com/support/javascript1.2/

Finally, we've included a script index. This is a list of scripts, sorted by purpose. Look in this list for the kinds of things that we've covered in this book, and for each one you'll find the page containing the script and the Online Companion example script number.

About the Online Companion

Included on the Online Companion for the *Official Netscape JavaScript 1.2 Book* are all the scripts in this book, in the order in which they appear in the book. Please go to the http://www.netscapepress.com/support/javascript1.2/ Web page to access these examples. Don't waste time typing in the scripts; copy them directly from the Online Companion.

The Online Companion also includes all the links found in this book, sorted by chapter and appendix so you can find them easily. There's no need to type those, either, just click on the links at the Online Companion. Or download a Bookmarks or Favorites file, and load them into your browser.

The Online Companion also includes the Color Chart, and our Area Code and Telephone Directory programs.

Netscapepress.com (http://www.netscapepress.com/) features a catalog of other Netscape Press titles, technical support information, and news about the Internet.

Also found at http://www.netscapepress.com/ is *Navigate!*, the official electronic publication of Netscape Press. Netscape Press is a joint effort between Ventana and Netscape Communications Corp., and serves as the publishing arm of Netscape. *Navigate!* is a monthly online publication that offers a wide range of articles and reviews aimed at Netscape users. *Navigate!* features interviews with industry icons and experts, as well as articles excerpted from upcoming Netscape Press titles.

The JavaScript Objects & Arrays

This appendix lists the various JavaScript objects and arrays. For each one you will find associated properties, methods, and event handlers with a short description of what each one does. We've also noted the parent object of each.

The following **methods** are methods of all objects, so we haven't mentioned them each time:

eval( )	Starting with JavaScript 1.1 (Navigator 3) all objects have this method. Used to evaluate a string of JavaScript code and evaluate any statements it finds in relation to the object.
handleEvent( )	This invokes the event handler that has been specified for the object. (A method of all objects that use event handlers.)
toString( )	Used to convert an object to a string.
valueOf( )	Starting with JavaScript 1.1 (Navigator 3) all objects have this method. Used to convert an object to a primitive value.

Anchor

An HTML anchor, created using the **<A NAME=>** tag. It can be targeted by a link. If the anchor includes the **HREF=** attribute, it is also a **Link** object. The **Anchor** object is a property of the **document** object. It has no properties or event handlers.

anchors array

The **anchors** array is a property of the **document** object and is a list of all the **Anchor** objects in a document. If an **Anchor** is also a **link**, then it appears in *both* the **anchors** and the **links** arrays.

Properties

length	The number of anchors in the document.

Applet

A property of the **document** object. An HTML tag (**<APPLET>**) used to embed a Java applet into a Web page. The **MAYSCRIPT** attribute is used to allow a Java applet access to a JavaScript script. This object was added in JavaScript 1.1 (Navigator 3).

Properties

name	The **NAME=** attribute in the **<APPLET>** tag.

Methods

The **Applet** object has all the public methods of the applet referenced by the **<APPLET>** tag.

applets array

A property of the **document** object. An array listing the **Applet** objects (the **<APPLET>** tags) in a document. This array was added in JavaScript 1.1 (Navigator 3).

Properties

length	The number of **<APPLET>** tags in the document.

Area

A property of the **document** object. An HTML tag (**<AREA HREF=>**), within the **<MAP>** tag, used to create an image map from an image, so that when the user clicks on the defined part of the image the specified HTML document is loaded. Each **<AREA HREF=>** tag specifies one "hot spot" in the image map, so the **Area** object refers to a single hot spot.

Area objects' behavior in JavaScript is equivalent to **Link** objects (they're regarded as a form of **Link** object). There's no **area** array; rather, the **<AREA HREF=>** tags are included along with the **<A HREF=>** link tags in the **links** array. You can only reference an **Area** object using the **links** array; you can't refer to it by name. This object was added in JavaScript 1.1 (Navigator 3).

Properties
The **Area** objects have the same properties as the **Link** objects.

Event Handlers
The **Area** objects have the same event handlers as the **Link** objects.

arguments array

A list of the arguments in a function. This is a property of any **Function** object or user-created function.

Properties

length	The number of arguments in the function.

Array

This is a built-in object, not a property of another object. It's used to define arrays of data, two or more values in an ordered list. This object was added in JavaScript 1.1 (Navigator 3).

Properties

length	The number of values held in the array.
prototype	Used to add properties to an **Array** object.

Methods

join(sep)	Used to join the elements of an array together, creating a single string. The value of **sep** is used as a separator between elements.
reverse( )	Switches the elements in an array; the first becomes the last, and the last becomes the first.
sort( )	Sorts the elements held by the array, using the system specified by a function.

Boolean

An object used for working with Boolean values; can be used to convert non-Boolean values to Boolean. This is a built-in object, so it is not a property of another object. This object was added in JavaScript 1.1 (Navigator 3).

Properties

prototype	Used to add properties to the **Boolean** object.

Button

This is a property of a **Form** object. It's created using the **<INPUT TYPE="BUTTON">** tag.

Properties

form	Specifies the form holding the button.
name	The **NAME=** attribute in the HTML tag.
value	The **VALUE=** attribute in the HTML tag.
type	The **TYPE=** attribute in the HTML tag. This property was added in JavaScript 1.1 (Navigator 3).

Methods

click( )	Simulates a mouse click on a button.
blur( )	Removes focus from the button. Added in JavaScript 1.1 (Navigator 3).
focus( )	Moves focus to the button. Added in JavaScript 1.1 (Navigator 3).

Event Handlers

onblur	Added in JavaScript 1.1 (Navigator 3).
onclick	
onfocus	Added in JavaScript 1.1 (Navigator 3).
onmousedown	Added in JavaScript 1.2.
onmouseup	Added in JavaScript 1.2.

Checkbox

This is a property of a **Form** object. It is created using the **<INPUT TYPE="CHECKBOX">** tag.

Properties

checked	The selection state of the check box.
defaultChecked	The tag's **CHECKED=** attribute.
form	Specifies the form holding the check box.
name	The tag's **NAME=** attribute.
type	The **TYPE=** attribute in the HTML tag. This property was added in JavaScript 1.1 (Navigator 3).
value	The tag's **VALUE=** attribute.

Methods

click( )	Simulates a mouse click on a button.
blur( )	Removes focus from the check box. Added in JavaScript 1.1 (Navigator 3).
focus( )	Moves focus to the check box. Added in JavaScript 1.1 (Navigator 3).

Event Handlers

onblur	Added in JavaScript 1.1 (Navigator 3).
onclick	
onfocus	Added in JavaScript 1.1 (Navigator 3).

Date

A built-in object—not a property of another object. Allows you to carry out a variety of procedures using dates and times. An instance of a **Date** object is created using the **new** keyword.

Properties

prototype	Used to add properties to a **Date** object. This property was added in JavaScript 1.1 (Navigator 3).

Methods

getDate( )	Looks in the **Date** object and returns the day of the month.
getDay( )	Returns the day of the week.

getHours( )	Returns the hours.
getMinutes( )	Returns the minutes.
getMonth( )	Returns the month.
getSeconds( )	Returns the seconds.
getTime( )	Returns the complete time.
getTimeZone Offset( )	Returns the time-zone offset (the number of hours' difference between Greenwich Mean Time and the time zone set in the computer running the script).
getYear( )	Returns the year.
parse( )	Returns the number of milliseconds in the **Date** string since January 1, 1970 00:00:00. (The **Date** object stores times and dates in the form of milliseconds since this date.)
setDate( )	Changes the **Date** object's day of month.
setHours( )	Changes the hours.
setMinutes( )	Changes the minutes.
setMonth( )	Changes the month.
setSeconds( )	Changes the seconds.
setTime( )	Changes the complete time.
setYear( )	Changes the year.
toGMTString( )	Converts the **Date** object's date (a numeric value) to a string in GMT time, returning, for example, Weds, 15 June 1997 14:02:02 GMT (the exact format varies depending on the operating system that the computer is running).
toLocaleString( )	Converts the **Date** object's date (a numeric value) to a string, using the particular date format the computer is configured to use.
UTC( )	Use **Date UTC(year, month, day, hrs, min, sec)** to return that date in the form of the number of milliseconds since January 1, 1970 00:00:00. (The hrs, min, and sec are optional.)

document

A property of the **window** and **Frame** objects; the document displayed in the window or in the frame.

Properties

alinkColor	The color of an active link (**ALINK**).
Anchor	An HTML anchor, created using the **<A NAME=>** tag. This property is also an object in its own right.

anchors array	An array listing the document anchor objects (**<A NAME=>**). This property is also an object in its own right.
Applet	An **<APPLET>** tag, used to embed a Java applet into a document. This property is an object in its own right. This property was added in JavaScript 1.1 (Navigator 3).
applets array	An array that lists the **Applet** objects. This property was added in JavaScript 1.1 (Navigator 3).
Area	An HTML tag (the **<AREA HREF=>** tag, used within the **<MAP>** tag) used to create image maps. This property is also an object in its own right and is regarded as a form of **Link** object. This property was added in JavaScript 1.1 (Navigator 3).
bgColor	The document's background color (**BGCOLOR**).
classes	A property added in JavaScript 1.2 (Navigator 4), used within the **<STYLE>** tags to set the style of multiple HTML text elements.
cookie	A piece of information stored in the cookie.txt file. A property of the **document** object.
domain	The domain name of the server that sent the document. Introduced with JavaScript 1.1 (Navigator 3).
Embed	An undocumented object/property. A file type embedded into the document using the **<EMBED>** HTML tag. Added in JavaScript 1.1 (Navigator 3).
embeds array	A list of the **<EMBED>** tags in the document. Added in JavaScript 1.1 (Navigator 3).
fgColor	The document's text color (the **TEXT** attribute in the **<BODY>** tag).
Form	A form (**<FORM>**) in a document. This property is also an object in its own right.
forms array	An array listing the **Form** objects in the order in which they appear in the document. This property is also an object in its own right.
ids	A property added in JavaScript 1.2 (Navigator 4), used within the **<STYLE>** tags to modify the style of text that would otherwise be set using the **classes** property.
Image	An image in a document, created with an HTML **<IMG>** tag (used to embed an image in a document) or by using **new Image( )**. This property is an object in its own right. This property was added in JavaScript 1.1 (Navigator 3).
lastModified	The date the document was last changed.
linkColor	The color of the document's links, the **LINK** attribute in the **<BODY>** tag (links to documents that the user has not yet viewed).
Link	An **<A HREF=>** tag in the document. This property is also an object in its own right.
links array	An array of the **Link** and **Area** objects in a document, in the order in which they appear. This property is also an object in its own right.

location	The URL of the currently displayed document. You can't change the **document.location** (as that's the location of the document currently displayed). You can, however, change **window.location** (replacing the current document with another). While **window.location** *is* also an object in its own right, **document.location** is *not*. Also, note that this property will be removed in later versions of JavaScript (presumably because of this ambiguity!); instead of **document.location** you can use **document.URL**, which will work for Navigator 2 and later, but not for Internet Explorer 3.
referrer	The URL of the document containing the link that the user clicked on to get to the current document.
tags	A property added in JavaScript 1.2, used within the **<STYLE>** tags to set the style of a particular HTML text element.
title	The document's title (**<TITLE>**).
URL	A string containing the complete URL of the document. This is exactly the same as **document.location**. It was in Navigator 2, but because it wasn't documented it's not in Internet Explorer 3, so it won't work in that browser.
vlinkColor	The text color of links pointing to documents that the user has viewed. The **VLINK** attribute of the **<BODY>** tag.

Methods

captureEvents( )	Captures all events of the specified type. Added in JavaScript 1.2 (Navigator 4).
close( )	Closes the document stream.
getSelection( )	Creates a string containing the currently selected text within the document. Added in JavaScript 1.2 (Navigator 4).
handleEvent( )	This invokes the event handler that has been specified for the object. Added in JavaScript 1.2 (Navigator 4).
open( )	Opens the document stream.
releaseEvents( )	Releases captured events of the specified type, sending the events further along the event hierarchy. Added in JavaScript 1.2 (Navigator 4).
routeEvent( )	Passes a captured event along the event hierarchy. Added in JavaScript 1.2 (Navigator 4).
write( )	Writes text to the document.
writeln( )	Writes text to the document and ends with a newline character.

Event Handlers

Beginning with JavaScript 1.2 (Navigator 4), the document object has event handlers:

onkeydown

onkeypress

onkeyup

onmousedown

onmouseup

elements array

A property of the **Form** object. An array listing the elements in a form.

Properties

length   The number of elements in the form.

Embed

An undocumented object. A file type embedded into the document using the **<EMBED>** HTML tag. A property of the **document** object, listed in the **embeds** array. Added in JavaScript 1.1 (Navigator 3).

embeds array

A property of the **document** object. A listing of the **<EMBED>** tags. This array was added in JavaScript 1.1 (Navigator 3).

Properties

length   The number of **<EMBED>** tags in the HTML document.

event

An object created whenever an event occurs, which is passed to JavaScript event handlers. The object can then be queried to determine information about the event. Added in JavaScript 1.2 (Navigator 4).

Properties

data	An array of strings representing URLs passed by the **ondragdrop** event handler.
height	The height of a window or frame.
layerX	A number that usually specifies the cursor's horizontal position in pixels, relative to the document layer in which the event occurred. For a resize event, this number specifies the width of the resized object.
layerY	A number that usually specifies the cursor's vertical position in pixels, relative to the document layer in which the event occured. For a resize event, this number specifies the height of the resized object.
modifiers	A number containing bit values that indicate whether keys such as Alt or Shift were pressed (see "Mask Values," below).
pageX	A number that specifies the cursor's horizontal position in pixels, relative to the Web page in which the event occurred.
pageY	A number that specifies the cursor's vertical position in pixels, relative to the Web page in which the event occurred.
screenX	A number that specifies the cursor's horizontal position in pixels, relative to the top left corner of the computer screen.
screenY	A number that specifies the cursor's vertical position in pixels, relative to the top left corner of the computer screen.
target	A link's target if the event is run from a hypertext link.
type	A string that identifies the type of event.
which	For keyboard events, a number giving the ASCII code for the pressed key. For mouse events, this property is **1** for the left button, or **3** for the right button.
width	The width of a window or frame.
x	Provided for compatibility with earlier versions; use **screenX** (**onmove**) or **width** (**onresize**) instead.
y	Provided for compatibility with earlier versions; use **screenY** (**onmove**) or **height** (**onresize**) instead.

Event object

A built-in object that serves as a holder for mask values used by event handlers and the **captureEvent** method; not to be confused with the **event** object (see above). This object was added in JavaScript 1.2 (Navigator 4).

Properties

ALT_MASK	For keyboard events, this indicates that the Alt key was held by the user.
CONTROL_MASK	For keyboard events, this indicates that the Ctrl key was held by the user.
SHIFT_MASK	For keyboard events, this indicates that the Shift key was held by the user.
META_MASK	For keyboard events, this indicates that the Meta key was held by the user.
MOUSEDOWN	Used by event capturing (the **captureEvents( )** method of the **window** and **document** objects), to capture all **onmousedown** events.
MOUSEUP	Used by event capturing to capture all **onmouseup** events.
MOUSEOVER	Used by event capturing to capture all **onmouseover** events.
MOUSEOUT	Used by event capturing to capture all **onmouseout** events.
MOUSEMOVE	Used by event capturing to capture all **onmousemove** events.
CLICK	Used by event capturing to capture all **onclick** events.
KEYDOWN	Used by event capturing to capture all **onkeydown** events.
KEYUP	Used by event capturing to capture all **onkeyup** events.
KEYPRESS	Used by event capturing to capture all **onkeypress** events.
DRAGDROP	Used by event capturing to capture all **ondrapdrop** events.
MOVE	Used by event capturing to capture all **onmove** events.
RESIZE	Used by event capturing to capture all **onresize** events.

FileUpload

A property of a **Form** object. An HTML tag (**<INPUT TYPE="FILE">**) used to create a file-upload element in a form. This object was added in JavaScript 1.1 (Navigator 3).

Properties

form	Specifies the form holding the form element.
name	The **NAME=** attribute in the HTML tag.
type	The **TYPE=** attribute in the HTML tag.
value	The **VALUE=** attribute in the tag, or the text typed into the field by the user.

Methods

blur( )	Removes focus from the file-upload element.
focus( )	Moves focus to the file-upload element.

Event Handlers

onblur

onchange

onfocus

Form

A property of the **document** object. A form within the document.

Properties

action	A string containing the destination URL for a form submission.
Button	A button in a form, created using the **<INPUT TYPE="BUTTON">** tag. This property is also an object in its own right.
Checkbox	A check box, created using the **<INPUT TYPE="CHECKBOX">** tag. This property is also an object in its own right.
elements array	An array listing form elements in the order in which they appear in the form. This property is also an object in its own right.
encoding	The MIME encoding of the form.
FileUpload	A file upload element (**<INPUT TYPE="FILE">**) in a form. This property is also an object in its own right. This property was added in JavaScript 1.1 (Navigator 3).

Hidden	A hidden (**<INPUT TYPE="HIDDEN">**) element in a form. This property is also an object in its own right.
length	The number of elements in the form.
method	How data input into a form is sent to the server; the **METHOD=** attribute in a **<FORM>** tag.
name	The **NAME=** attribute. Added in JavaScript 1.1 (Navigator 3).
Password	A password field (**<INPUT TYPE="PASSWORD">**) in a form. This property is also an object in its own right.
Radio	A radio button (**<INPUT TYPE="RADIO">**) set in a form. This property is also an object in its own right.
Reset	A Reset button (**<INPUT TYPE="RESET">**) in a form. This property is also an object in its own right.
Select	A selection box (**<SELECT>**) in a form. This property is also an object in its own right.
Submit	A Submit button (**<INPUT TYPE="SUBMIT">**) in a form. This property is also an object in its own right.
target	The name of the window that displays responses after a form has been submitted.
Text	A text element in a form (**<INPUT TYPE="TEXT">**). This property is also an object in its own right.
Textarea	A textarea element (**<TEXTAREA>**) in a form. This property is also an object in its own right.

Methods

submit( )	Submits a form (the same as using the Submit button).
reset( )	Resets the form to its default value, in effect simulating a mouse click on the form's Reset button (though it still works even if no Reset button has been defined). This method was added in JavaScript 1.1 (Navigator 3).

Event Handlers

onreset	Added in JavaScript 1.1 (Navigator 3).
onsubmit	

forms array

A property of the **document** object. An array that lists the forms in the document.

Properties

length	The number of forms in the document.

Frame

A property of the **window** object. A frame within the window. A **Frame** object functions in the same way as a window object, with a few exceptions.

Properties

document	The document within the frame. This property is also an object in its own right.
Frame	A frame (**<FRAME>**) within the frame. This property is also an object in its own right.
frames array	An array listing the child frames within this frame. This property is also an object in its own right.
length	The number of frames within this frame.
name	The frame's name (the **NAME** attribute in the **<FRAME>** tag).
parent	A synonym for the parent window containing this frame.
self	A synonym for the current frame.
window	A synonym for the current frame.

Methods

blur( )	Moves focus away from the specified frame. This method was added in JavaScript 1.1 (Navigator 3).
clearInterval( )	Cancels a repeating timer that was started by **setInterval( )**. This method was added in JavaScript 1.2 (Navigator 4).
clearTimeout( )	Cancels a delayed script that was started by **setTimeout( )**.
focus( )	Moves focus to the specified frame. This method was added in JavaScript 1.1 (Navigator 3).
print( )	Prints the contents of the frame. Added in JavaScript 1.2 (Navigator 4).
setInterval( )	Causes a specified script to be repeatedly executed at a specified time interval. This method was added in JavaScript 1.2 (Navigator 4).
setTimeout( )	Causes a script to be executed after a specified time delay.

Event Handlers

The **Frame** event handlers can only be used in **<FRAMESET>** tags, not **<FRAME>** tags. (However, note that they have no effect in MS Windows browsers. You can use them as **window** event handlers, though, in the **<BODY>** tag.) To create **onblur** and **onfocus** events for frames rather than framesets, use the **blur( )** and **focus( )** methods.

onblur	Added in JavaScript 1.1 (Navigator 3).
onfocus	Added in JavaScript 1.1 (Navigator 3).
onmove	Added in JavaScript 1.2 (Navigator 4).
onresize	Added in JavaScript 1.2 (Navigator 4).

frames array

A property of both the **window** and **Frame** objects. Lists the frames within the **window** or within the **Frame**.

Properties

length	The number of frames within the **window** or **Frame** object.

Function

The **Function** object is a function that has been created by compiling a string of JavaScript into the object using the **new Function( )** *statement*. This is a built-in function and is not a property of any other object. This object was added in JavaScript 1.1 (Navigator 3).

Properties

arguments array	The elements of the function, compiled into the new function using the **Function** object.
caller	Specifies the function calling the **Function** object.
prototype	Used to add properties to a **Function** object. This property was added in JavaScript 1.1 (Navigator 3).

Hidden

A property of a **Form** object. A hidden (**<INPUT TYPE="HIDDEN">**) element in a form.

Properties

name	The name (the **NAME=** attribute) in the tag.
form	Specifies the form holding the form element.
type	The **TYPE=** attribute in the HTML tag. This property was added in JavaScript 1.1 (Navigator 3).
value	The **VALUE=** attribute in the tag.

history

A property of the **window** object. The window's history list.

Properties

current	The complete URL of the history object. This was added in JavaScript 1.1 (Navigator 3).
length	The number of items in the history list.
next	The complete URL of the next history entry. Added in JavaScript 1.1 (Navigator 3).
previous	The complete URL of the previous history entry. Added in JavaScript 1.1 (Navigator 3).

Methods

back( )	Loads the previous document in the history list.
forward( )	Loads the next document in the history list.
go( )	Loads a document in the history list, specified by its position in the list.

history array

A list of the entries in the history entries stored by the browser window (that is, in the **history** object). A property of the **window** object.

Properties

length	The number of entries in the window's history list.

Image

An image embedded into a document with the **<IMG>** tag. or an image created using the **new** keyword (**imagename = new Image( )**). A property of the **document** object. Introduced with JavaScript 1.1 (Navigator 3).

Properties

border	The **<IMG>** tag's **BORDER=** attribute.
complete	A Boolean value indicating whether the browser has completely loaded the image.
height	The **HEIGHT=** attribute.
hspace	The **HSPACE=** attribute.
lowsrc	The **LOWSRC=** attribute.
name	The **NAME=** attribute.
prototype	Enables you to add properties to image objects created using **Images( )**.
src	The **SRC=** attribute.
vspace	The **VSPACE=** attribute.
width	The **WIDTH=** attribute.

Event Handlers

onabort	
onerror	
onkeydown	Added in JavaScript 1.2 (Navigator 4).
onkeypress	Added in JavaScript 1.2 (Navigator 4).
onkeyup	Added in JavaScript 1.2 (Navigator 4).
onload	

images array

A property of the **document** object. A list of all the images in the document.

Properties

length	The number of images in the document, created with the **<IMG>** tag or using the **Images( )** object.

Layer

A property of the **document** object. A movable segment of a document that sits above the main Web page but can sit above or below other layers or be hidden. Created using the **<LAYER>** and **<ILAYER>** tags. Added to JavaScript 1.2 (Navigator 4).

Properties

above	The layer above the current layer in the z-order among all layers in the document.
background	The image used as the layer's background image.
below	The layer below the current layer in the z-order among all layers in the document.
bgColor	The layer's background color.
clip.bottom	Used to move the bottom edge of the layer in or out.
clip.height	Used to modify the height of the layer to a specific size, by moving the bottom edge.
clip.left	Used to move the left edge of the layer in or out.
clip.right	Used to move the right edge of the layer in or out.
clip.top	Used to move the top edge of the layer in or out.
clip.width	Used to modify the width of the layer to a specific size, by moving the right edge.
document	The layer's equivalent of the window's **document** object.
left	The distance, in pixels, from the left edge of the parent layer to the left edge of the layer.
name	The layer name (the **NAME=** attribute in the **<LAYER>** tag).
pageX	The distance, in pixels, from the left edge of the page to the left edge of the layer.
pageY	The distance, in pixels, from the top edge of the page to the top edge of the layer.
parentLayer	The layer of which this layer is a child.
siblingAbove	The layer above the current layer in the z-order among layers sharing the same parent.
siblingBelow	The layer below the current layer in the z-order among layers sharing the same parent.
src	The content of the layer; the layer's content can come from an external file.
top	The distance, in pixels, from the top edge of the parent layer to the top edge of the layer.

visibility	Determines layer visibility; **show** means display the layer; **hide** means hide the layer; **inherit** means use the same visibility status as the parent.
zIndex	The position of the layer in relation to its parent and siblings. The lower the **zindex** number, the lower the position in the stack.

Methods

load(*url, width*)	Loads the specified file into the layer and modifies the width of the layer at the same time.
moveAbove (*layer*)	Changes Z indexes so that this layer is immediately above the specified one.
moveBelow (*layer*)	Changes Z indexes so that this layer is immediately below the specified one.
moveBy(*x, y*)	Moves the layer by the specified distances (in pixels) horizontally and vertically.
moveTo(*x, y*)	Changes a layer's horizontal and vertical positions to the specified values within the parent layer.
moveToAbsolute (*x, y*)	Changes a layer's horizontal and vertical positions to the specified values within the Web page.
ResizeBy (*width, height*)	Adjusts the clipping boundaries, adding the specified width and height to the existing width and height.
ResizeTo (*width, height*)	Adjusts the clipping boundaries to make the displayed portion have the specified size.

Event Handlers

onmouseout

onmouseover

layers array

A property of the **document** object. An array listing all the layers in a document.

Properties

length	The number of layers in the document.

Link

An <A HREF=> (hypertext link) tag in the document. A property of the **document** object.

Properties

hash	A string beginning with a hash mark (**#**) that specifies an anchor within the URL.
host	The host name part of the URL which includes a colon and the port number.
hostname	The same as the host property, except that the colon and port number are not included.
href	The entire URL.
pathname	The directory path portion of a URL.
port	The **:port** portion of a URL.
protocol	The URL type (**http:**, **ftp:**, **gopher:**, and so on).
search	Part of the URL beginning with a **?** that specifies search information.
target	The window that displays the content of the referenced document when the user clicks on a link (the **TARGET** attribute).

Event Handlers

onclick	Link objects only.
onkeydown	Added in JavaScript 1.2 (Navigator 4).
onkeypress	Added in JavaScript 1.2 (Navigator 4).
onkeyup	Added in JavaScript 1.2 (Navigator 4).
onmousedown	Added in JavaScript 1.2 (Navigator 4).
onmouseout	Added in JavaScript 1.1 (Navigator 3).
onmouseover	Link and Area objects.

links array

A property of the **document** object. A list of all the links (<A HREF=>) and image map hot spots (<AREA HREF=>) in the document (the **Link** and **Area** objects).

Properties

length	The number of links in the document.

location

A property of the **window** object. Information about the URL of the document currently displayed in the window. Do not confuse this with the **document.location** property, which can be used to load a new document. The **document.location** property is *not* an object in its own right. Also, while **window.location** can be modified by a script, **document.location** cannot.

Properties

hash	A string beginning with a hash mark (**#**) that specifies an anchor within the URL.
host	The host name part of the URL which includes a colon and the port number.
hostname	The same as the host property, except that the colon and port number are not included.
href	The entire URL.
pathname	The directory path portion of a URL.
port	The :port portion of a URL.
protocol	The URL type (**http:**, **ftp:**, **gopher:**, and so on).
search	Part of the URL beginning with a **?** that specifies search information.

Methods

reload( )	Forces the document specified by **location.href** to reload. This was added in JavaScript 1.1 (Navigator 3).
replace( )	Similar to **reload**, except that after the document has reloaded the user cannot use Back to return to the previous document. This was added in JavaScript 1.1 (Navigator 3).

locationbar

The window's location bar. This is a property of the **window** object, added in JavaScript 1.2 (Navigator 4). This can only be used in a signed script.

Properties

visible	A Boolean value showing whether the bar is visible.

Math

This is not a property of another object; it's a built-in object. The **Math** object contains mathematical constants and functions.

Properties

E	Euler's constant and the base of natural logarithms (approximately 2.718).
LN2	The natural logarithm of 2 (approximately 0.693).
LN10	The natural logarithm of 10 (approximately 2.302).
LOG2E	The base 2 logarithm of e (approximately 1.442).
LOG10E	The base 10 logarithm of e (approximately 0.434).
PI	The value of pi (approximately 3.14159).
SQRT1_2	The square root of one-half, or 1 over the square root of 2 (approximately 0.707).
SQRT2	The square root of 2 (approximately 1.414).

Methods

abs( )	Returns a number's absolute value (its "distance from zero"; for example, both 2 and -2 have absolute values of 2).
acos( )	Returns the arc cosine of a number (in radians).
asin( )	Returns the arc sine of a number (in radians).
atan( )	Returns the arc tangent of a number (in radians).
atan2( )	The angle (the theta component) of the polar coordinate (r,theta) corresponding to the specified cartesian coordinate (x,y).
ceil( )	Returns the integer equal to or immediately above a number (**ceil(-22.22)** would return **-22**; **ceil(22.22)** would return **23**; **ceil(22)** would return **22**).
cos( )	Returns the cosine of a number (in radians).
exp( )	Returns e^{number}.
floor( )	The opposite of ceil. (**floor(-22.22)** would return **-23**; **floor(22.22)** would return **22**; **floor(22)** would return **22**).
log( )	Returns the natural logarithm (base e) of a number.
max( )	Returns the greater of two numbers.
min( )	Returns the lesser of two numbers.
pow( )	Returns $base^{exponent}$.
random( )	Returns a pseudo-random number between zero and one. (This method only worked on UNIX versions of Netscape Navigator in the early JavaScript releases; it works on all platforms in Navigator 3.)

round( )	Returns a number that is rounded to the nearest integer.
sin( )	Returns the sine of a number (in radians).
sqrt( )	Returns the square root of a number.
tan( )	Returns the tangent of a number.

menubar

The window's menu bar. This is a property of the **window** object, added in JavaScript 1.2 (Navigator 4). This can only be used in a signed script.

Properties

| visible | A Boolean value showing whether the bar is visible. |

MimeType

A MIME file type that the browser can work with. This is a property of the **navigator** object and was added in JavaScript 1.1 (Navigator 3).

Properties

description	A description of the specified MIME type (**MPEG Audio**, **GIF Image**, and **TIFF Image**, for example).
enabledPlugin	Indicates whether a plug-in has been installed to handle the specified MIME type.
suffixes	A list of all the file suffixes (file extensions) for a MIME type.
type	Indicates the name of the specified MIME type.

mimeTypes array

A list of all the MIME types that the browser can handle (the **MimeType** objects). A property of the **navigator** object. This object was added in Java-Script 1.1 (Navigator 3).

Properties

| length | The number of MIME types (**MimeType** objects) recognized by the browser. |

navigator

This is not a property of another object; it is a built-in object containing information about the browser that has loaded the document.

Properties

appCodeName	The browser's code name (*Mozilla*, for example).
appName	The browser's name.
appVersion	The browser's version number.
language	The language version of the browser. This property was added in JavaScript 1.2 (Navigator 4).
MimeType	A MIME type that can be handled by the browser. This property is an object in its own right and was added in JavaScript 1.1 (Navigator 3).
mimeTypes	An array of the **MimeType** objects. This property was added in JavaScript 1.1 (Navigator 3).
platform	The operating system for which the Navigator was compiled. This property was added in JavaScript 1.2.
Plugin	A plug-in "viewer" installed in the browser. This property is an object in its own right and was added in JavaScript 1.1 (Navigator 3).
plugins	An array of the plug-ins installed in the browser (the **Plugin** objects). This property was added in JavaScript 1.1 (Navigator 3).
userAgent	The user-agent header text sent from the client to the server. A property of the **navigator** object.

Methods

javaEnabled( )	A Boolean value indicating whether Java has been enabled in the browser. (Note that it does not indicate the status of JavaScript, only Java.) This property was added in JavaScript 1.1 (Navigator 3).
taintEnabled( )	Specifies whether data tainting is enabled for the browser. This property was added in JavaScript 1.1 (Navigator 3).

Number( )

An object designed to help you work with numbers. This is a built-in object, so it is not a property of another object. It was introduced with JavaScript 1.1 (Navigator 3).

Properties

MAX_VALUE The maximum numeric value that can be represented in JavaScript (approximately 1.79E+308).

MIN_VALUE The minimum numeric value that can be represented in JavaScript (approximately 2.22E-308).

NaN A value meaning Not a Number.

NEGATIVE_INFINITY
A special value (**"-Infinity"**) representing negative infinity.

POSITIVE_INFINITY
A special value (**"Infinity"**) representing infinity.

prototype Used to add properties and methods to the **Number** object.

Option

An option (**<OPTION>**) within a selection box (**<SELECT>**). The option might be created automatically, when the page is read and the selection box is built according to the HTML tags. Or it might be created using the **new Option( )** constructor. The option can then be placed into the selection box by assigning it to an index position in the **options** array. This is a property of the **Select** object. The new **Option( )** constructor was added in JavaScript 1.1 (Navigator 3).

Properties

defaultSelected A Boolean value indicating whether the **Option** object has been selected.

index The index position of the option in the selection list.

prototype Used to add properties to an **Option** object created using **new Option( )**.

selected The current selection state.

text The text held by this option.

value The value associated with this option, that is, the one returned to the server when the user submits the form (**VALUE=**).

options array

A property of a **Select** object. A list of all the options (**<OPTION>**) within the selection box.

Properties

length The number of options in a **Select** object.

selectedIndex The position of the selected option.

Password

A property of a **Form** object. An **<INPUT TYPE="PASSWORD">** tag.

Properties

defaultValue	The default value of the **password** object (the **VALUE=** attribute).
form	Specifies the form holding the form element.
name	The name (the **NAME=** attribute) of the object.
type	The **TYPE=** attribute in the HTML tag. This property was added in JavaScript 1.1 (Navigator 3).
value	The current value held by the field. Initially it's the same as the **VALUE=** attribute (**defaultValue**); but if a script modifies the value held by the field, **value** will change.

Methods

blur( )	Removes focus from the field.
focus	Moves focus to the field.
select( )	Selects the input area.

Event Handlers

onblur	Added in JavaScript 1.1 (Navigator 3).
onfocus	Added in JavaScript 1.1 (Navigator 3).

personalbar

The window's personal bar (the new customizable button bar in Navigator 4). This is a property of the **window** object, added in JavaScript 1.2. This can only be used in a signed script.

Properties

visible	A Boolean value showing whether the bar is visible.

Plugin

A plug-in "viewer" installed in the browser. A property of the **navigator** object. This object was added in JavaScript 1.1 (Navigator 3).

Properties

name	The plug-in name.
description	A description of the plug-in.
filename	The path and filename of the file that runs the plug-in.
length	The number of MIME file types that the plug-in can handle.

plugins array

A list of the plug-in "viewers" installed in the browser (the **Plugin** objects). A property of the **navigator** object. This object was added in JavaScript 1.1 (Navigator 3).

Properties

length	The number of plug-ins installed.

Methods

refresh	Makes newly installed plug-ins available to the browser, updates the **plugins** array, and (optionally) reloads the document.

Radio

A property of a **Form** object. A set of radio buttons (option buttons) in the form (**<INPUT TYPE="RADIO">**).

Properties

checked	The state of a check box or option button (radio button).
defaultChecked	The default state of a check box or option button (radio button).
form	Specifies the form holding the form element.
length	The number of buttons in the set.
name	The name (the **NAME=** attribute) of the object.
type	The **TYPE=** attribute in the HTML tag. This property was added in JavaScript 1.1 (Navigator 3.)
value	The **VALUE=** attribute.

Methods

blur( )	Removes focus from the radio buttons. Added in JavaScript 1.1 (Navigator 3).
click( )	Simulates a mouse click on a radio button.
focus( )	Moves focus to the radio buttons. Added in JavaScript 1.1 (Navigator 3).

Event Handlers

onblur	Added in JavaScript 1.1 (Navigator 3).
onclick	
onfocus	Added in JavaScript 1.1 (Navigator 3).

RegExp

A built-in object used for creating patterns and working with regular expressions. The expression **new RegExp(s, m)** creates a pattern based on the pattern string **s** and modifier string **m**. (Regular expressions are patterns that are used to match combinations of characters in strings.) This object was added in JavaScript 1.2 (Navigator 4).

Property

$0, $1, $2, ... $9

These properties are set to any values remembered by JavaScript while matching a pattern that contains parentheses.

Method

compile(s, m) Set the variable to the pattern defined by the pattern string **s** and the modifier string **m**. Note that this is equivalent to **new RegExp(s, m)**, except that it uses an existing object instead of creating a new one.

exec(s) Attempts to match the pattern in the string **s**. Note that **p.exec(s)** is equivalent to **s.match(p)**, where **p** is a pattern and **s** is a string.

Reset

A property of a **Form** object. A reset button (**<INPUT TYPE="RESET">**)

Properties

form	Specifies the form holding the form element.
name	The name (the **NAME=** attribute) of the object.
type	The **TYPE=** attribute in the HTML tag. This property was added in JavaScript 1.1 (Navigator 3).
value	The **VALUE=** attribute.

Methods

blur( )	Removes focus from the button. Added in JavaScript 1.1 (Navigator 3).
click( )	Simulates a mouse click on the button.
focus( )	Moves focus to the button. Added in JavaScript 1.1 (Navigator 3).

Event Handlers

onblur	Added in JavaScript 1.1 (Navigator 3).
onclick	
onfocus	Added in JavaScript 1.1 (Navigator 3).

Note also that there's an **onreset** event handler, but it belongs to the **Form** object, not the **reset** object, and is placed in the **<FORM>** tag.

screen

An object containing information about the screen in which the browser is running. This is a built-in object, and was added in JavaScript 1.2 (Navigator 4).

Properties

colorDepth	The number of colors that can be displayed.
height	The height of the screen in pixels.
pixelDepth	The number of bits per pixel in the display.
width	The width of the screen in pixels.

scrollbars

The window's scroll bars. This is a property of the **window** object, added in JavaScript 1.2 (Navigator 4). This can only be used in a signed script.

Properties

visible	A Boolean value showing whether the bar is visible.

Select

A property of a **Form** object. A selection box (**<SELECT>**). See also the **Option** object.

Properties

form	Specifies the form holding the form element.
length	The number of options (**<OPTIONS>**) in the selection list.
name	The name (the **NAME** attribute) of the selection list.
Option	An **<OPTION>** tag, or an option created using the **new Option( )** constructor. An object in its own right.
options	The number of options in the list.
selectedIndex	The index (position) of the selected **<OPTION>** in the selection list.
text	The text after an **<OPTION>** tag in the selection list. Added in JavaScript 1.1 (Navigator 3).
value	The **VALUE=** attribute of the selection list.

Methods

blur( )	Removes focus from the selection list.
focus( )	Moves focus to the selection list.

Event Handlers

onblur

onchange

onfocus

statusbar

The window's status bar. This is a property of the **window** object, added in JavaScript 1.2 (Navigator 4). This can only be used in a signed script.

Properties

visible   A Boolean value showing whether the bar is visible.

String

This is not a property of another object; it is a built-in object. Each string is a **String** object; String objects might be created automatically when you create a string or, starting with JavaScript 1.1 (Navigator 3), using the **new String( )** constructor.

Properties

length   The number of characters in the string.

prototype   Used to add properties to a **string** object, if created using **new String( )**. This property was added in JavaScript 1.1 (Navigator 3).

Methods

anchor(*name*)   Used to turn the string into an HTML anchor tag (**<A NAME=**).

big( )   Changes the text in the string to a big font (**<BIG>**).

blink( )   Changes the text in the string to a blinking font (**<BLINK>**).

bold( )   Changes the text in the string to a bold font (**<B>**).

charAt(*index*)   Finds the character in the string at a specified position.

fixed( )   Changes the text in the string to a fixed-pitch font (**<TT>**).

fontcolor(*color*)   Changes the text in the string to a color (**<FONT COLOR=>**).

fontsize(*size*)   Changes the text in the string to a specified size (**<FONTSIZE=>**).

indexOf( )   Used to search the string for a particular character and returns the index position of that character.

italics( )   Changes the text in the string to italics (**<I>**).

lastIndexOf( )   Like **indexOf**, but searches backward to find the last occurrence of the character.

link( )   Used to turn the string into an HTML link tag (**<A HREF=>**).

match(*p*)   Returns a value indicating whether a regular expression matching the pattern **p** occurs in the string. Added in JavaScript 1.2 (Navigator 4).

replace(p, s)	Searches the string for a regular expression matching the pattern **p**; if found, replaces it with the string **s**. Added in JavaScript 1.2 (Navigator 4).
small( )	Changes the text in the string to a small font (**<SMALL>**).
split(*sep*)	Returns an array created by splitting the string into separate sections at each occurrence of the separator string **sep**. Added in JavaScript 1.1 (Navigator 3).
strike( )	Changes the text in the string to a strikethrough font (**<STRIKE>**).
sub( )	Changes the text in the string to a subscript font (**<SUB>**).
substring(*indexA,indexB*)	
	Returns a portion of the string between specified positions within the string.
sup( )	Changes the text in the string to a superscript font (**<SUP>**).
toLowerCase( )	
	Changes the text in the string to lowercase.
toUpperCase( )	
	Changes the text in the string to uppercase.

Submit

A property of a **Form** object. A submit button in the form (**<INPUT TYPE="SUBMIT">**).

Properties

form	Specifies the form holding the button.
name	The name (the **NAME=** attribute) of the object.
type	The **TYPE=** attribute in the HTML tag. This property was added in JavaScript 1.1 (Navigator 3).
value	The **VALUE=** attribute.

Methods

blur( )	Removes focus from the button. Added in JavaScript 1.1 (Navigator 3).
click( )	Simulates a mouse click on a button.
focus( )	Moves focus to the button. Added in JavaScript 1.1 (Navigator 3).

Event Handlers

onblur	Added in JavaScript 1.1 (Navigator 3).
onclick	
onfocus	Added in JavaScript 1.1 (Navigator 3).

Text

A property of a **Form** object. A text field in the form (**<INPUT TYPE="TEXT">**).

Properties

defaultValue	The default value of the text object (the **VALUE=** attribute).
form	Specifies the form holding the form element.
name	The name (the **NAME=** attribute) of the object.
type	The **TYPE=** attribute in the HTML tag. This property was added in JavaScript 1.1 (Navigator 3).
value	The current value held by the field. Initially it's the same as the **VALUE=** attribute (**defaultValue**); but if a script modifies the value held by the field, **value** will change.

Methods

blur( )	Removes focus from the text box.
focus( )	Moves focus to the text box.
select( )	Selects the input area.

Event Handlers

onblur

onchange

onfocus

onselect

Textarea

A property of a **Form** object. A textarea field in the form (**<TEXTAREA>**).

Properties

defaultValue	The default value of the **textarea** object (the **VALUE=** attribute).
form	Specifies the form holding the form element.
name	The name (the **NAME=** attribute) of the object.
type	The **TYPE=** attribute in the HTML tag. This property was added in JavaScript 1.1 (Navigator 3).
value	The current value held by the field. Initially it's the same as the **VALUE=** attribute (**defaultValue**); but if a script modifies the value held by the field, **value** will change.

Methods

blur( )	Removes focus from the textarea.
focus( )	Moves focus to the textarea.
select( )	Selects the input area.

Event Handlers

onblur	
onchange	
onfocus	
onkeydown	Added in JavaScript 1.2 (Navigator 4).
onkeypress	Added in JavaScript 1.2 (Navigator 4).
onkeyup	Added in JavaScript 1.2 (Navigator 4).
onselect	

toolbar

The window's toolbar. This is a property of the **window** object, added in JavaScript 1.2 (Navigator 4). This can only be used in a signed script.

Properties

visible	A Boolean value showing whether the bar is visible.

window

The browser window. This is not a property of another object; it is the top-level object.

Properties

closed	Specifies whether a window has closed. This was added in JavaScript 1.1 (Navigator 3).
defaultStatus	The default status-bar message.
document	The currently displayed document. This property is also an object in its own right.
Frame	A frame (**<FRAME>**) within a window. This property is also an object in its own right.
frames array	An array listing the window's **Frame** objects in the order in which they appear in the document. This property is also an object in its own right.

history	The window's history list. This property is also an object in its own right.
innerHeight	The height of the window's internal document area, in pixels. Added in JavaScript 1.2 (Navigator 4).
innerWidth	The width of the window's internal document area, in pixels. Added in JavaScript 1.2 (Navigator 4).
length	The number of frames in the window.
location	The full (absolute) URL of the document displayed by the window. This property is also an object in its own right.
	Don't confuse this with **document.location**, which is the URL of the currently displayed document (the same as **document.URL**). You can change **window.location** (replacing the current document with another), but you can't change the **document.location** (as that's the location of the document currently displayed).
locationbar	The window's location bar. This is an object in its own right. Added in JavaScript 1.2 (Navigator 4).
menubar	The window's menu bar. This is an object in its own right. Added in JavaScript 1.2 (Navigator 4).
name	The name assigned to the window when opened.
opener	Refers to the window in which a script used **window.open** to open the current window. Evaluating a window's **window.opener** property will tell you which window opened it. This property was added in JavaScript 1.1 (Navigator 3).
outerHeight	The height of the entire window, including borders, toolbar, etc. Added in JavaScript 1.2 (Navigator 4).
outerWidth	The width of the entire window, including borders, toolbar, etc. Added in JavaScript 1.2 (Navigator 4).
parent	A synonym for the window containing the current frame. A property of the frame and window objects.
personalbar	The window's "personal" bar (the new customizable button bar in Navigator 4). This is an object in its own right. Added in JavaScript 1.2 (Navigator 4).
self	A synonym for the current window or frame.
scrollbars	The window's scrollbars. This is an object in its own right. Added in JavaScript 1.2 (Navigator 4).
status	A message in the status bar.
statusbar	The window's status bar. This is an object in its own right. Added in JavaScript 1.2 (Navigator 4).
toolbar	The window's toolbar. This is an object in its own right. Added in JavaScript 1.2 (Navigator 4).

top	A synonym for the topmost browser window containing the current frame.
window	A synonym for the current window or frame. The same as **self**.

Methods

alert( )	Opens an Alert message box.
back( )	Moves to the previous page in the history list (in effect, clicks the browser's Back button). Added in JavaScript 1.2 (Navigator 4).
blur( )	Moves focus away from the specified window. This method was added in JavaScript 1.1 (Navigator 3).
captureEvents( )	Captures all events of the specified type. Added in JavaScript 1.2 (Navigator 4).
clearInterval( )	Cancels a repeating timeout set with **setInterval( )**. Added to JavaScript 1.2 (Navigator 4).
clearTimeout( )	Cancels a delayed script that was started by **setTimeout( )**.
close( )	Closes the window. Starting with JavaScript 1.1 (Navigator 3), if you use this method to close a window other than one opened by JavaScript using the **open** method, the user sees a confirmation box, and the window is not closed unless the user confirms the close. It *will* close the window *without* confirmation if there's only one open window, though.
confirm( )	Opens a Confirm message box; the user has two choices, OK and Cancel—the method returns **true** if the user clicks on OK, **false** if on Cancel.
find( )	Opens the Search dialog box. Added in JavaScript 1.2 (Navigator 4).
focus( )	Brings the specified window to the foreground. This method was added in JavaScript 1.1 (Navigator 3).
forward( )	Moves to the next page in the history list (in effect, clicks the browser's Forward button). Added in JavaScript 1.2 (Navigator 4).
home( )	Displays the browser's home page (the one set in the browser's preferences. Added in JavaScript 1.2 (Navigator 4).
moveBy( )	Moves the window by the specified number of pixels horizontally and vertically. Added to JavaScript 1.2 (Navigator 4).
moveTo( )	Moves the top left corner of the window to the specified position. Added to JavaScript 1.2 (Navigator 4).
open( )	Opens a new window.
print( )	Prints the contents of the window. Added in JavaScript 1.2 (Navigator 4).

prompt( )	Opens a Prompt dialog box; the user can type into this box, and the typed text is returned to the script.
releaseEvents( )	Releases captured events of the specified type, sending the events further along the event hierarchy. Added in JavaScript 1.2 (Navigator 4).
resizeBy( )	Resizes the window by moving the bottom right corner the specified amount. Added to JavaScript 1.2 (Navigator 4).
resizeTo( )	Resizes the window to the specified height and width. Added to JavaScript 1.2 (Navigator 4).
routeEvent( )	Passes a captured event along the event hierarchy. Added in JavaScript 1.2 (Navigator 4).
scroll( )	Scrolls the document in the window to a particular position. This was added in JavaScript 1.1 (Navigator 3).
scrollBy( )	Scrolls the document in the window by the specified number of pixels. Added to JavaScript 1.2 (Navigator 4).
scrollTo( )	Scrolls the document in the window to the specified position. Added to JavaScript 1.2 (Navigator 4); this method replaces **scroll( )**.
setInterval( )	Causes a specified script to be repeatedly executed at a specified time interval. The interval is specified in milliseconds. Added to JavaScript 1.2 (Navigator 4).
setTimeout( )	Causes a script to be executed after a specified time delay.
stop( )	Stops the download (in effect clicks the browser's Stop button). Added in JavaScript 1.2 (Navigator 4).

Event Handlers

onblur	Added in JavaScript 1.1 (Navigator 3).
ondragdrop	Added in JavaScript 1.2.
onerror	Added in JavaScript 1.1 (Navigator 3).
onfocus	Added in JavaScript 1.1 (Navigator 3).
onload	
onmove	Added in JavaScript 1.2 (Navigator 4).
onresize	Added in JavaScript 1.2 (Navigator 4).
onunload	

JavaScript Properties

Properties are related to objects, and many properties work with multiple objects. This Appendix is a quick summary of the different properties available. It's a good idea to read through this list simply to get an idea of what's available to you.

The list tells you which object or objects may use each property. (See Appendix B, "The JavaScript Objects & Arrays," for more information about each object and its related properties, methods, and event handlers.) Remember, many properties are objects in their own right; they have their own properties. We've indicated which properties are also objects.

Of course a number of objects are not properties; the **Array**, **Boolean**, **Date**, **event**, **Function**, **Math**, **navigator**, **Number**, **RegExp**, **screen**, and **String** objects are "built-in" objects—objects that are available from anywhere because they are not related to other objects.

Property	Description
$0, $1, $2, … $9	These properties are set to any values remembered by Javascript while matching a pattern that contains parentheses. Properties of the **RegExp** object.
action	A string that contains the destination URL for a form submission. A property of the **Form** object.
alinkColor	The color of an active link (**ALINK**). A property of the **document** object.

➡

Property	Description
ALT_MASK	For keyboard events, this indicates that the Alt key was held by the user. A property of the **Event** object.
Anchor	An HTML anchor, created using the **<A NAME=>** tag. A property of the **document** object. This property is also an object in its own right.
anchors array	An array which lists the document **anchor** objects (**<A NAME=>**). A property of the **document** object.
appCodeName	The browser's code name (*Mozilla*, for example). A property of the **navigator** object.
Applet	An **<APPLET>** tag, used to embed a Java applet into a document. A property of the **document** object. This property is an object in its own right. This property was added in JavaScript 1.1 (Navigator 3).
applets array	An array that lists the **Applet** objects. This property was added in JavaScript 1.1 (Navigator 3).
appName	The browser's name. A property of the **navigator** object.
appVersion	The browser's version number. A property of the **navigator** object.
Area	An HTML tag (the **<AREA>** tag, used within the **<MAP>** tag), used to create image maps. A property of the **document** object. This property is also an object in its own right. This property was added in JavaScript 1.1 (Navigator 3).
arguments array	An array used to list specific arguments within the **Function** object. A property of the **Function** object.
bgColor	The document's background color (**BGCOLOR**). A property of the **document** object. Also the background color of a layer (a property of the **Layer** object).
border	The **<IMG>** tag's **BORDER** attribute. A property of the **Image** object.
Button	A button in a form, created using the **<INPUT TYPE="BUTTON">** tag. A property of the **Form** object. This property is also an object in its own right.
caller	This property returns the name of the function invoking the current function. This is a property of the **Function** object.
Checkbox	A checkbox, created using the **<INPUT TYPE="CHECKBOX">** tag. A property of the **Form** object. This property is also an object in its own right.
checked	The state of a checkbox or option button (radio button). A property of the **Checkbox** object and the **Radio** object.

Property	Description
classes	A property of the **document** object, used within the **<STYLE>** tags to set the style of multiple HTML text elements. Added to JavaScript 1.2 (Navigator 4).
CLICK	Used by event capturing to capture all **onclick** events. A property of the **Event** object.
closed	Specifies whether the window is closed. A property of the **window** object, added to JavaScript 1.1 (Navigator 3).
colorDepth	The number of colors that can be displayed. A property of the **screen** object.
complete	A Boolean value indicating whether the browser has completely loaded an image. A property of the **Image** object.
constructor	This specifies the function that creates an object prototype. A property of any prototype object, added to JavaScript 1.1 (Navigator 3).
CONTROL_MASK	For keyboard events, this indicates that the Ctrl key was held by the user. A property of the **Event** object.
cookie	A piece of information stored in the cookie.txt file. A property of the **document** object.
current	The complete URL of the history object. This is a property of the **history** object and was added in JavaScript 1.1 (Navigator 3).
data	An array of strings representing URLs passed by the **ondragdrop** event handler. A property of the **event** object.
defaultChecked	The default state of a checkbox or option button (radio button). A property of the **Checkbox** object and the **Radio** object.
defaultSelected	The default selection in a selection list (**<SELECT>**) and, starting with JavaScript 1.1 (Navigator 3), a Boolean value indicating whether an **Option** object (which is a property of the **Select** object) has been selected A property of the **Select** and **Option** objects.
defaultStatus	The default status-bar message. A property of the **window** object.
defaultValue	The default value of a **Password**, **Text**, or **Textarea** object (the **VALUE=** attribute). A property of the **Password**, **Text**, and **Textarea** objects.
description	A description of the specified MIME type (**MPEG Audio**, **GIF Image**, and **TIFF Image**, for example). A property of the **mimeType** and **Plugin** objects.

➡

Property	Description
document	The currently displayed document. A property of the **window** and **Frame** objects. Also the document displayed with a layer (a property of the **Layer** object). This property is also an object in its own right.
domain	The domain name of the server that sent the document. A property of the **document** object, introduced with JavaScript 1.1 (Navigator 3).
DRAGDROP	Used by event capturing to capture all **ondrapdrop** events. A property of the **Event** object.
E	Euler's constant and the base of natural logarithms (approximately 2.718). A property of the **Math** object.
elements array	An array that lists form elements in the order in which they appear in the form. A property of the **Form** object.
Embed	An undocumented object/property. A file type embedded into the document using the **<EMBED>** HTML tag. A property of the **document** object and an object in its own right. Added in JavaScript 1.1 (Navigator 3).
embeds array	A list of all the **<EMBED>** tags in the document. This was added in JavaScript 1.1 (Navigator 3).
enabledPlugin	Indicates whether a plug-in has been installed to handle the specified MIME type. A property of the **mimeTypes** object.
encoding	The MIME encoding of the form. A property of the **Form** object.
fgColor	The document's text color (the **TEXT** attribute in the **<BODY>** tag). A property of the **document** object.
filename	The name of a plug-in file. A property of the **Plugin** object, added in JavaScript 1.1 (Navigator 3).
FileUpload	A fileupload element (**<INPUT TYPE="FILE">**) in a form. A property of the **Form** object. This property is also an object in its own right. This property was added in JavaScript 1.1 (Navigator 3).
form	A property of the **Button**, **Checkbox**, **FileUpload**, **Hidden**, **Password**, **Radio**, **Reset**, **Select**, **Submit**, **Text**, and **Textarea** objects, this property (not to be confused with the Form property, which is an object in its own right) refers to the form holding the object, as in **this.form** or **document. Form1.TextObject1.form**.
Form	A form (**<FORM>**) in a document. A property of the **document** object. This property is also an object in its own right.
forms array	An array that lists the **Form** objects in the order in which they appear in the document. A property of the **document** object.

Property	Description
Form	A form (**<FORM>**) in a document. A property of the **document** object. This property is also an object in its own right.
forms array	An array that lists the **Form** objects in the order in which they appear in the document. A property of the **document** object.
Frame	A frame (**<FRAME>**) within a window. A property of the **window** and **Frame** objects. This property is also an object in its own right.
frames array	An array that lists the window's **Frame** objects in the order in which they appear in the document. A property of the **window** object.
hash	A string beginning with a hash mark (**#**) that specifies an anchor within the URL. A property of the **Area, location,** and **Link** objects.
height	The **HEIGHT** attribute of an **<IMG>** tag. A property of the **Image** object.
	The height of a window or frame. A property of the **event** object.
	Also a property of the **screen** object: the height of the screen in pixels.
Hidden	A hidden (**<INPUT TYPE="HIDDEN">**) element in a form. A property of the **Form** object. This property is also an object in its own right.
history	The window's history list. A property of the **window** object. This property is also an object in its own right.
history array	All the history entries stored by the browser window. A property of the **window** object.
host	The hostname part of the URL that includes a colon and the port number. A property of the **Area, location,** and **Link** objects.
hostname	The same as the **host** property, except that the colon and port number are not included. A property of the **Area, location,** and **Link** objects.
href	The entire URL. A property of the **Area, location,** and **Link** objects.
hspace	The **HSPACE** attribute of the **<IMG>** tag. A property of the **Image** object.
ids	A property of the **document** object, used within the **<STYLE>** tags to modify the style of text that would otherwise be set using the **classes property**. Added to JavaScript 1.2 (Navigator 4).

Property	Description
Image	An image embedded with the **<IMG>** tag. A property of the **document** object. This property is also an object in its own right. This property was added in JavaScript 1.1 (Navigator 3).
images array	An array that lists the embedded **Image** objects. A property of the **document** object.
index	The index position of an option in a selection list (the **<SELECT>** tag). A property of the **options** array and, starting with JavaScript 1.1 (Navigator 3), of the **Option()** object.
innerHeight	The height of the window's internal document area, in pixels. A property of the **window** object, added in JavaScript 1.2 (Navigator 4).
innerWidth	The width of the window's internal document area, in pixels. A property of the **window** object, added in JavaScript 1.2 (Navigator 4).
KEYDOWN	Used by event capturing to capture all **onkeydown** events. A property of the **Event** object.
KEYPRESS	Used by event capturing to capture all **onkeypress** events. A property of the **Event** object.
KEYUP	Used by event capturing to capture all **onkeyup** events. A property of the **Event** object.
lastModified	The date the document was last changed. A property of the **document** object.
language	The language version of the browser. This is a property of the **navigator** object and was added in JavaScript 1.2 (Navigator 4). See "JavaScript Layers Properties" at the end of this appendix for descriptions of this object's properties.
Layer	A movable segment of a document that sits above the main Web page but can sit above or below other layers or be hidden. Created using the **<LAYER>** and **<ILAYER>** tags. A property of the **document** object. This property is an object in its own right and was introduced with JavaScript 1.2 (Navigator 4).
layers array	An array listing all the layers in a document. A property of the **document** object.
layerX	A number that usually specifies the cursor's horizontal position in pixels, relative to the document layer in which the event occured. For a resize event, this number specifies the width of the resized object. A property of the **event** object.
layerY	A number that usually specifies the cursor's vertical position in pixels, relative to the document layer in which the event occured. For a resize event, this number specifies the height of the resized object. A property of the **event** object.

Property	Description
length	A number that is related to the object or array using the property, such as the number of elements in a form or the number of frames in a window. A property of the **Array**, **Frame**, **history**, **Plugin**, **Radio**, **Select**, **String**, and **window** objects; and a property of the **anchors**, **applets**, **arguments**, **elements**, **embeds**, **forms**, **frames**, **images**, **layers**, **links**, **mimeTypes**, **options**, and **plugins** arrays.
Link	An **<A HREF=>** tag in the document. A property of the **document** object. This property is also an object in its own right.
linkColor	The color of the document's links. The **LINK** attribute in the **<BODY>** tag (links to documents that the user has not yet viewed). A property of the **document** object.
links array	An array of the **Link** objects in a document, in the order in which they appear. A property of the **document** object.
LN2	The natural logarithm of 2 (approximately 0.693). A property of the **Math** object.
LN10	The natural logarithm of 10 (approximately 2.302). A property of the **Math** object.
location	The full (absolute) URL of the document displayed by the window. A property of the **window** object. This property is also an object in its own right.
	Also, a property of the **document** object. The URL of the currently displayed document. Thus you can change **window.location** (replacing the current document with another), but you can't change the **document.location** (as that's the location of the document currently displayed). While **window.location** *is* also an object in its own right— **document.location** is *not*. The **document.location** property is no longer documented in the JavaScript Guide, as Netscape Communications is encouraging the use of **document.URL** instead. However, **document.location** still works, and you might want to use it for compatibility with Internet Explorer 3.
locationbar	The window's location bar. This is an object in its own right. A property of the **window** object, added in JavaScript 1.2 (Navigator 4).
menubar	The window's menu bar. This is an object in its own right. A property of the **window** object, added in JavaScript 1.2 (Navigator 4).
LOG2E	The base 2 logarithm of e (approximately 1.442). A property of the **Math** object.

Property	Description
LOG10E	The base 10 logarithm of e (approximately 0.434). A property of the **Math** object.
lowsrc	The **LOWSRC=** attribute of an **<IMG>** tag. A property of the **Image** object.
MAX_VALUE	The maximum numeric value that can be represented in JavaScript (approximately 1.79E+308). This is a property of the **Number** object.
META_MASK	For keyboard events, this indicates that the Meta key was held by the user. A property of the **Event** object.
method	How data input in a form is sent to the server; the **METHOD=** attribute in a **<FORM>** tag. A property of the **Form** object.
MimeType	A MIME type that can be handled by the browser. A property of the **navigator** object. This property is an object in its own right and was added in JavaScript 1.1 (Navigator 3).
mimeTypes array	An array of the **MimeType** objects. A property of the **navigator** object. This property was added in JavaScript 1.1 (Navigator 3).
MIN_VALUE	The minimum numeric value that can be represented in JavaScript (approximately 2.22E-308). This is a property of the **Number** object.
modifiers	A number containing bit values that indicate whether keys such as Alt- or Shift- were pressed. A property of the **event** object.
MOUSEDOWN	Used by event capturing (the **captureEvents()** method of the **window** and **document** objects), to capture all **onmousedown** events. A property of the **Event** object.
MOUSEMOVE	Used by event capturing to capture all **onmousemove** events. A property of the **Event** object.
MOUSEOUT	Used by event capturing to capture all **onmouseout** events. A property of the **Event** object.
MOUSEOVER	Used by event capturing to capture all **onmouseover** events. A property of the **Event** object.
MOUSEUP	Used by event capturing to capture all **onmouseup** events. A property of the **Event** object.
MOVE	Used by event capturing to capture all **onmove** events. A property of the **Event** object.

Property	Description
name	The name (the **NAME=** attribute) of an object. A property of the **Applet**, **Button**, **Checkbox**, **FileUpload**, **Frame**, **Hidden**, **Image**, **Password**, **Plugin**, **Radio**, **Reset**, **Select**, **Submit**, **Text**, and **Textarea** objects, and of the **images** and **options** array. Also of the **Form** object in JavaScript 1.1 (Navigator 3). For the **window** object, name is the name assigned to the **window** when opened.
	Also a layer name (the **NAME=** attribute in the **<LAYER>** tag). A property of the **Layer** object.
NaN	A value meaning Not a Number. A property of the **Number** object.
NEGATIVE_INFINITY	A special value (**"-Infinity"**) representing negative infinity. A property of the **Number** object.
next	The complete URL of the next history entry. A property of the **history** object, added in JavaScript 1.1 (Navigator 3).
opener	Refers to the **window** in which a script used **window.open** to open the current window. A property of the **window** object. This property was added in JavaScript 1.1 (Navigator 3).
Option	A **Select** object option created by the HTML **<OPTION>** tag or by using the **new Option()** constructor. This property is a property of the **Select** object in its own right, and the **new Option()** constructor was added in JavaScript 1.1 (Navigator 3).
options array	An array of the options (**<OPTION>**) in a selection list (**<SELECT>**), in the order in which they appear. A property of the **Select** object.
outerHeight	The height of the entire window, including borders, toolbar, and so on. A property of the **window** object, added in JavaScript 1.2 (Navigator 4).
outerWidth	The width of the entire window, including borders, toolbar, and so on. A property of the **window** object, added in JavaScript 1.2 (Navigator 4).
pageX	A number that specifies the cursor's horizontal position in pixels, relative to the Web page in which the event occured. A property of the **event** object.
pageY	A number that specifies the cursor's vertical position in pixels, relative to the Web page in which the event occured. A property of the **event** object.
parent	A synonym for the window that contains the current frame. A property of the **Frame** and **window** objects.
parentLayer	The layer of which this layer is a child. A property of the **Layer** object.

Property	Description
Password	A password (**<INPUT TYPE="PASSWORD">**) object in a form. A property of the **Form** object. This property is also an object in its own right.
pathname	The directory path portion of a URL. A property of the **Link**, **location**, and **Area** objects.
personalbar	The window's "personal" bar (the new customizable button bar in Navigator 4). This is an object in its own right. A property of the **window** object, added in JavaScript 1.2 (Navigator 4).
PI	The value of pi (approximately 3.14159). A property of the **Math** object.
pixelDepth	The number of bits per pixel in the display. A property of the **screen** object.
platform	The operating system for which the Navigator was compiled. This is a property of the **navigator** object and was added in JavaScript 1.2 (Navigator 4).
Plugin	A plug-in "viewer" installed in the browser. A property of the **navigator** object. This property is an object in its own right and was added in JavaScript 1.1 (Navigator 3).
plugins array	An array of the plug-ins installed in the browser (the **Plugin** objects). A property of the **navigator** object. This property was added in JavaScript 1.1 (Navigator 3).
port	The :port portion of a URL. A property of the **Link, location**, and **Area** objects.
POSITIVE_INFINITY	A special value (**"Infinity"**) representing infinity. A property of the **Number** object.
previous	The complete URL of the previous history entry. A property of the **history** object, added in JavaScript 1.1 (Navigator 3).
protocol	The URL type (**http:, ftp:, gopher:**, and so on). A property of the **Link, location**, and **Area** objects.
prototype	Used to add properties and methods to objects. A statement of the form **ObClass.prototype.NewPropName = value** creates a new property or method for the specified object class. A property of any object defined using the **new** keyword, including the **Array, Boolean, Date, Function, Image, Number, Option**, and **String objects**. This property was added in JavaScript 1.1 (Navigator 3).
Radio	A radio button set (**<INPUT TYPE="RADIO">**) in a form. A property of the **Form** object. This property is also an object in its own right.
referrer	The URL of the document that contains the link that the user clicked on to get to the current document. A property of the **document** object.

Property	Description
Reset	A reset button (**<INPUT TYPE="RESET">**) in a form. A property of the **Form** object. (This property is also an object in its own right.)
RESIZE	Used by event capturing to capture all **onresize** events. A property of the **Event** object.
screenX	A number that specifies the cursor's horizontal position in pixels, relative to the top left corner of the computer screen. A property of the **event** object.
screenY	A number that specifies the cursor's vertical position in pixels, relative to the top left corner of the computer screen. A property of the **event** object.
scrollbars	The window's scrollbars. This is an object in its own right. A property of the **window** object, added in JavaScript 1.2 (Navigator 4).
search	Part of the URL beginning with a **?** that specifies search information. A property of the **Link**, **location**, and (in JavaScript 1.1—Navigator 3) **Area** objects.
Select	A selection box (**<SELECT>**) in a form. A property of the **Form** object. This property is also an object in its own right.
selected	A Boolean value that indicates the selection state of an option **<OPTION>** in a selection list (**<SELECT>**). A property of the **options** array. In JavaScript 1.1 (Navigator 3) it's also a property of the **Option** object.
selectedIndex	The index (position) of the selected **<OPTION>** in a selection list (**<SELECT>**). A property of the **Select** object and **options** array.
self	A synonym for the current window or frame. A property of the **Frame** and **window** objects.
SHIFT-MASK	For keyboard events, this indicates that the Shift key was held by the user. A property of the **Event** object.
SQRT1_2	The square root of one-half, or 1 over the square root of 2 (approximately 0.707). A property of the **Math** object.
SQRT2	The square root of two (approximately 1.414). A property of the **Math** object.
src	The **SRC** attribute of an **<IMG>** tag. A property of the **Image** object.
	Also, the content of a layer; the layer's content can come from an external file. A property of the **Layer** object.
status	A message in the status bar. A property of the **window** object.
statusbar	The window's statusbar. This is an object in its own right. A property of the **window** object, added in JavaScript 1.2 (Navigator 4).

Property	Description
Submit	A submit button (**<INPUT TYPE="SUBMIT">**) in a form. A property of the **Form** object. This property is also an object in its own right.
suffixes	A list of all the file suffixes (file extensions) for a MIME type. A property of the **MimeType** object. This property was added in JavaScript 1.1 (Navigator 3).
tags	A property of the **document** object, used within the **<STYLE>** tags to set the style of a particular HTML text element. Introduced with JavaScript 1.2 (Navigator 4).
target	The name of the window that displays responses after a form has been submitted; or, the window that displays the content of the referenced document when the user clicks on a link (the **TARGET** attribute). A property of the **Form**, **Link**, and **location** objects. In JavaScript 1.1 (Navigator 3) it's also a property of the **Area** object. A link's target if the event is run from a hypertext link. A property of the **event** object.
text	The text after an **<OPTION>** tag in a selection list (**<SELECT>**). A property of the **options** array. In JavaScript 1.1 (Navigator 3) it's also a property of the **Option** object. Also, a text element in a form (**<INPUT TYPE="TEXT">**). A property of the **Form** object. This property is an object in its own right.
Textarea	A textarea element (**<TEXTAREA>**) in a form. A property of the **Form** object. This property is also an object in its own right.
title	The document's title (**<TITLE>**). A property of the **document** object.
toolbar	The window's toolbar. This is an object in its own right. A property of the **window** object, added in JavaScript 1.2 (Navigator 4).
top	A synonym for the top-most browser window that contains the current frame. A property of the **window** object. Also, the distance in pixels from the top edge of the parent layer to the top edge of the current layer. A property of the **Layer** object.

type	A form element's **TYPE=** attribute or tag name. A property of the **Text**, **Radio**, **Checkbox**, **FileUpload**, **Hidden**, **Submit**, **Reset**, **Password**, **Button**, **Select**, and **Textarea** objects.
	    Also, in JavaScript 1.1 (Navigator 3), a property of the **MimeType** object, indicating the name of the specified MIME type.
	    Also a property of the **event** object that identifies the event type.

Property	Description
URL	A string containing the complete URL of the document. This is a property of the **document** object and is exactly the same as **document.location**. However, although **document.URL** was present in Navigator 2.0 it was not documented, so Microsoft missed it. That means it will work in Navigator 2.0 and later, but not in Internet Explorer 3.0.
userAgent	The user-agent header text sent from the client to the server. A property of the **navigator** object.
value	The current value held by the related object. Initially it's the same as the **VALUE=** attribute (**defaultValue**), but if the user or a script modifies the value held by the object then the value will change. A property of the **Button, Checkbox, FileUpload, Hidden, Password, Radio, Reset, Submit, Text,** and **Textarea** objects and the **options** array. Starting with JavaScript 1.1 (Navigator 3) it's also a property of the **FileUpload** and **Option** objects.
visible	Indicates whether a particular screen component is visible; a property of the **locationbar, menbuar, personalbar, scrollbars, statusbar,** and **toolbar** objects.
vlinkColor	The text color of links pointing to documents that the user has viewed. The **VLINK** attribute of the **<BODY>** tag. A property of the **document** object.
vspace	The **VSPACE** attribute of an **<IMG>** tag. A property of the **Image** object.
which	For keyboard events, a number giving the ASCII code for the pressed key. For mouse events, this property is **1** for the left button, or **3** for the right button. A property of the **event** object.
width	The **WIDTH** attribute of an **<IMG>** tag. A property of the **Image** object. The width of a window or frame. A property of the **event** object. Also, the width of the screen in pixels: a property of the **screen** object.
window	A synonym for the current window or frame. The same as **self**. Not to be confused with the **window** object, which is not a property of anything.
x	Provided for compatibility with earlier versions; use **screenX** (**onmove**) or **width** (**onresize**) instead. A property of the **event** object.
y	Provided for compatibility with earlier versions; use **screenY** (**onmove**) or **height** (**onresize**) instead. A property of the **event** object.

JavaScript Layers Properties

Property	Description
above	The layer above the current layer in the z-order among all layers in the document.
background	The image used as the layer's background image.
below	The layer below the current layer in the z-order among all layers in the document.
bgColor	The layer's background color.
clip.bottom	Used to move the bottom edge of the layer in or out.
clip.height	Used to modify the height of the layer to a specific size, by moving the bottom edge.
clip.left	Used to move the left edge of the layer in or out.
clip.right	Used to move the right edge of the layer in or out.
clip.top	Used to move the top edge of the layer in or out.
clip.width	Used to modify the width of the layer to a specific size, by moving the right edge.
document	The layer's equivalent of the window's **document** object.
left	The distance, in pixels, from the left edge of the parent layer to the left edge of the layer.
name	The layer name (the **NAME=** attribute in the **<LAYER>** tag).
pageX	The distance, in pixels, from the left edge of the page to the left edge of the layer.
pageY	The distance, in pixels, from the top edge of the page to the top edge of the layer.
parentLayer	The layer of which this layer is a child.
siblingAbove	The layer above the current layer in the z-order among layers sharing the same parent.
siblingBelow	The layer below the current layer in the z-order among layers sharing the same parent.
src	The content of the layer; the layer's content can come from an external file.
top	The distance, in pixels, from the top edge of the parent layer to the top edge of the layer.
visibility	Determines layer visibility; **show** means display the layer; **hide** means hide the layer; **inherit** means use the same visibility status as the parent.
zIndex	The position of the layer in relation to its parent and siblings. The lower the **zIndex** number, the lower the position in the stack.

The JavaScript Event Handlers

This appendix provides a summary of the event handlers that are available for use in JavaScript. Examples are given in Chapter 12. Events are actions a user can take, such as clicking on a button or link, opening or closing a document, and moving focus to and from form elements. The event handlers are placed within HTML tags.

Note that while the Netscape documentation uses mixed case for event-handler names, this is a little ambiguous, and we've used all lowercase event-handler names. When you place an event handler into an HTML tag it can be uppercase, lowercase, or mixed case—it really doesn't matter. However, starting with JavaScript 1.1 (Navigator 3) you can also use event-handler names within JavaScripts themselves to assign a particular script to an event handler. When you use event handlers within JavaScripts, they *must* be lowercase—at least for scripts that will run in Navigator 3. This changed again with Java-Script 1.2, though; now you can use mixed case. By mixed case we mean you could write, for example, **onclick** or **onClick**. You could not, however, use something like **OnClick** or **Onclick** or **OnCliCK**.

Should you use mixed case, though? Probably not. If you use mixed case the handlers will work fine in Navigator 4, but won't work in Navigator 3, so it's a good idea to stick with lowercase event handlers.

The event handlers are:

■ **onabort**—The JavaScript is executed if the user stops an image from loading (by clicking on the Stop button or a link, for instance). This works with the **<IMG>** tag, but it's a new event handler, introduced with JavaScript 1.1 (Navigator 3).

- **onblur**—The JavaScript is executed when a particular form component loses focus, that is, when the component is selected (the cursor inside it, for instance) and the user moves focus to another component by clicking elsewhere or pressing Tab. The **onblur** event handler works with the selection list (**<SELECT>**), multi-line text input (**<TEXTAREA>**), and text input (**<INPUT TYPE="TEXT">**) components. Starting with JavaScript 1.1 (Navigator 3) it also works with the **window** object (placed in the **<BODY>** tag) and the **frame** object (**<FRAMESET>**), carrying out a function when the focus changes from a particular window or frame. (However, it has no effect on MS Windows browsers when placed in a **<FRAMESET>** tag.) You can also create an **onblur** event handler for frames (**<FRAME>**) using the **onblur** property of the **frame** object; you can't use the **onblur** event handler within the **<FRAME>** tag. It also now works with **button**, **checkbox**, **fileupload**, **radio**, **reset**, and **submit** objects.

- **onchange**—The same as the **onblur**, with the exception that something must have been changed in the form components for the JavaScript to run.

- **onclick**—The JavaScript is executed when the user clicks on a button (**<INPUT TYPE="BUTTON">**), a check box (**<INPUT TYPE="CHECKBOX">**), an option (radio) button (**<INPUT TYPE="RADIO">**), a link (**<A HREF=>**), or a Reset (**<INPUT TYPE="RESET">**) or Submit (**<INPUT TYPE="SUBMIT">**) button. Starting with JavaScript 1.1 (Navigator 3) you can associate confirmation boxes with the **onclick** event handler to allow the user to confirm whether the click action should be carried out (to confirm whether the link should be followed, for instance). Use this syntax: **onclick="return confirm('*message*')"**. The confirmation box returns **true** or **false**. (This currently does not work for buttons.)

- **ondragdrop**—The JavaScript is executed when the user drops something (a file, for instance), onto the Navigator window. This is an event of the **window** object, and was added to JavaScript 1.2 (Navigator 4).

- **onerror**—The JavaScript is executed if a JavaScript or image error occurs while loading a document or an image (this event handler has no effect on other browser errors, just JavaScript and image errors). This event handler works with the **<IMG>** tag or, to use it as a **window** event handler, in a script. This event handler was introduced with JavaScript 1.1 (Navigator 3). You can use **null** to turn off the reporting of all JavaScript error messages (**onerror="null"** in an **<IMG>** tag or **window.onerror=null** in a script—notice that when used in a script there are no " " around **null**, and remember that you *must* use lowercase). You can also name a function that handles errors, **window.onerror=funerror,** for example.

■ **onfocus**—The same as **onblur**, except that the focus is moving *to* the component, not away from it.

■ **onkeydown**—The JavaScript is executed when the user presses a key. This is an event of the **document**, **Image**, **Link**, and **Textarea** objects, and was added to JavaScript 1.2 (Navigator 4).

■ **onkeypress**—The JavaScript is executed when the user holds down a key (this event is always preceded by an **onkeydown** event). This is an event of the **document**, **Image**, **Link**, and **Textarea** objects, and was added to JavaScript 1.2 (Navigator 4).

■ **onkeyup**—The JavaScript is executed when the user releases a key. This is an event of the **document**, **Image**, **Link**, and **Textarea** objects, and was added to JavaScript 1.2 (Navigator 4).

■ **onload**—The JavaScript is run when the page is loaded into the browser (specifically, once the browser has finished loading the page and any frames) or when an image is displayed. (Not when it's loaded into memory, but when it's actually displayed— which, if you're using an image created with the **Image( )** object, is not the same.) Used within the **<BODY>**, **<FRAMESET>**, and **<IMG>** HTML tags. This event handler was added to the **<IMG>** tag with JavaScript 1.1 (Navigator 3).

■ **onmousedown**—The JavaScript is executed when the user presses a mouse button. This is an event of the **Button**, **document**, and **Link** objects, and was added to JavaScript 1.2 (Navigator 4).

■ **onmousemove**—The JavaScript is executed when the user moves the mouse cursor. This is not associated with a particular object, but occurs when a capture of events is requested using the event capturing methods. This event was added to JavaScript 1.2 (Navigator 4).

■ **onmouseout**—The JavaScript is run when the mouse pointer moves away from an area of an imagemap (**<AREA>**) or from a link (**<A HREF=>**). You'll get an **onmouseout** event each time the pointer moves away from the hotspot on the image map. This event handler was added in JavaScript 1.1 (Navigator 3). Starting with JavaScript 1.2 (Navigator 4) it's also an event of the **Layer** object.

■ **onmouseover**—The JavaScript executes when the user simply points at a link (**<A HREF=>**) with the mouse pointer. Starting with JavaScript 1.1 (Navigator 3) it also works with image maps (**<AREA>**). You'll get an **onmouseover** event each time the pointer moves over the hotspot on the image map.

■ **onmouseup**—The JavaScript is executed when the user releases a mouse button. This is an event of the **Button**, **document**, and **Link** objects, and was added to JavaScript 1.2 (Navigator 4).

■ **onmove**—The JavaScript is executed when the user or a JavaScript moves a window or frame. This is an event of the **window** and **Frame** objects, and was added to JavaScript 1.2 (Navigator 4).

■ **onreset**—The JavaScript is executed when the user clicks on a Reset button in a form (it's placed in the **<FORM>** tag) or if you use the form's **reset( )** method. This event handler was added in JavaScript 1.1 (Navigator 3).

■ **onresize**—The JavaScript is executed when the user or a JavaScript resizes a window or frame. This is an event of the **window** and **Frame** objects, and was added to JavaScript 1.2 (Navigator 4).

■ **onselect**—The JavaScript is executed when the user selects text in a text (**<INPUT TYPE="TEXT">**) or textarea (**<TEXTAREA>**) form component.

■ **onsubmit**—The JavaScript is executed when the user submits a form. It's placed in the **<FORM>** tag, but runs when the user clicks on a Submit button (the **<INPUT TYPE="SUBMIT">** tag).

■ **onunload**—The JavaScript is run when the user does something to load another page into the browser—forcing unload of the current page. Used within the **<BODY>** and **<FRAMESET>** HTML tags.

Reserved Words

The words listed below cannot be used when you are naming variables, functions, methods, or objects. Also avoid the names of built-in objects, functions, and methods, such as, **Date**, **getDate**, **math**, and **sqrt**. See Appendices B and C for a more exhaustive list. While you can sometimes use such names, you might run into a conflict.

abstract	do	if	package	this
boolean	double	implements	private	throw
break	else	import	protected	throws
byte	extends	in	public	transient
case	false	instanceof	reset	true
catch	final	int	return	try
char	finally	interface	short	typeof
class	float	long	static	var
const	for	native	super	void
continue	function	new	switch	while
default	goto	null	synchronized	with
delete				

Symbol Reference

I t can be tricky for a newcomer to programming to keep all those little symbols straight. So here's a quick-reference table that will help you quickly identify the different symbols you'll run across while viewing JavaScripts. *Note:* bitwise operations listed below are not described in this book.

Symbol	Definition
+	Addition/concatenation operator; adds two numerical values together, joins two strings together.
*	Multiplication operator; multiplies two values together.
/	Division operator; divides one value by another.
%	Modulus operator; shows the remainder after dividing one number into another equally.
–	Subtraction operator; subtracts one value from another or changes a value to a negative value (unary negation).
++	Increment operator; increments a value (adds one to it).
--	Decrement operator; decrements a value (subtracts one from it).
!	Boolean NOT; tells you what value the variable *doesn't* contain. **X = !Y** would mean that if **Y** is **true**, **X** is set to **false**; and if **Y** is **false**, **X** is set to **true**.

Symbol	Definition
&&	Boolean AND; "ands" two variables together. **X**=**Y** && **Z**, means that **X** is only **true** if **Y** *and* **Z** are both **true**.
||	Boolean OR. **X**=**Y** || **Z**, means that **X** is **true** if **Y** *or* **Z** (or both of them) are **true**.
^	Boolean Exclusive OR. **X** = **Y** ^ **Z**, means that **X** is set to **true** if **Y** *or* **Z** is **true**—but not if both **Y** *and* **Z** are **true**.
&=	Boolean AND assignment. **X** &= **Y** means that **X** is set to **true** only if **X** *and* **Y** are both **true** before the expression is evaluated.
^=	Boolean Exclusive OR assignment. **X** ^= **Y** means that **X** is set to **true** if **X** *or* **Y** is **true**—but not both **true**—before the expression has been evaluated.
|=	Boolean OR assignment. **X** |= **Y**, means that **X** is set to **true** if either **X** *or* **Y** is **true** before the expression has been evaluated.
=	Assignment operator; assigns values to variables.
+=	Addition assignment; adds the variables together and modifies the variable on the left side.
-=	Subtraction assignment; subtracts the variable on the right from the one on the left and modifies the variable on the left.
*=	Multiplication assignment; multiplies the variables together, then modifies the variable on the left.
/=	Division assignment; divides the variable on the left by the one on the right, then modifies the one on the left.
%=	Modulus assignment; divides the variable on the left by the one on the right, then assigns the remainder to the variable on the left.
<	Conditional operator. Less than.
<=	Conditional operator. Less than or equal to.
>	Conditional operator. Greater than.
>=	Conditional operator. Greater than or equal to.
==	Conditional operator. Equal to. Works slightly differently in JavaScript 1.2 from the way it worked in JavaScript 1 and 1.1.
!=	Conditional operator. Not equal to. Works slightly differently in JavaScript 1.2 from the way it worked in JavaScript 1 and 1.1.
?:	Shorthand **if** statement operator, or ternary operator (**?** is used in combination with :, as in **variable** = (**condition**) **?** **value1** : **value2**).
" "	Double-quotation marks—enclose string literals and instructions in event handlers.

Symbol	Definition
' '	Single-quotation marks—enclose string literals when the statement is already enclosed in double-quotation marks.
;	Separates individual statements within a function.
.	Divides up parts of object property or method name, e.g., **document.write**
,	Separates parameters and features within feature list.
( )	Enclose parameters (arguments) after function name and set operator precedence.
[ ]	Enclose item position number in array.
{ }	Enclose blocks of script within statements, functions, and loops.
~	Bitwise complement.
<<=	Bitwise left shift assignment.
&	Bitwise operator, And.
<<	Bitwise operator, left shift.
|	Bitwise operator, Or.
>>	Bitwise operator, right shift.
^	Bitwise operator, Xor.
>>>	Bitwise operator, zero-fill right shift.
>>=	Bitwise right shift assignment.
>>>=	Bitwise zero-fill right shift assignment.
<!- -	HTML comment tags, used in JavaScripts to hide
//- ->	scripts from non-JavaScript browsers; everything between the symbols is ignored by non-JavaScript browsers.
//	JavaScript comment line; everything to the right of the symbol is assumed to be a comment and ignored.
/*	JavaScript comment block; everything between the
*/	asterisks is assumed to be a comment and ignored.

JavaScript Colors

Several properties and methods require that you specify a color. You can do this either by entering the hexadecimal representation of the color or by entering the color names.

Colors are used by these properties: **alinkColor**, **bgColor**, **fgColor**, **linkColor**, and **vlinkColor**.

Colors are used by the **fontcolor** method, a method of the **String** object.

In Netscape Navigator, Internet Explorer, and some other browsers, you can also use these color names in the HTML tags, such as **<BODY BGCOLOR="bisque">**, and **<FONT COLOR="*colorname*">*Text*</font>**. The actual color displayed varies between browsers and, of course, also depends on the video mode, video card, and video monitor.

Listed below are the colors you can use. We've also shown each color's red, green, and blue hexadecimal values. To see what these colors actually look like, see our Color Chart page in the Online Companion at http://www.netscapepress.com/support/javascript1.2/colors.htm/.

Color	Red	Green	Blue
aliceblue	F0	F8	FF
antiquewhite	FA	EB	D7
aqua	00	FF	FF
aquamarine	7F	FF	D4
azure	F0	FF	FF
beige	F5	F5	DC
bisque	FF	E4	C4
black	00	00	00
blanchedalmond	FF	EB	CD
blue	00	00	FF
blueviolet	8A	2B	E2
brown	A5	2A	2A
burlywood	DE	B8	87
cadetblue	5F	9E	A0
chartreuse	7F	FF	00
chocolate	D2	69	1E
coral	FF	7F	50
cornflowerblue	64	95	ED
cornsilk	FF	F8	DC
crimson	DC	14	3C
cyan	00	FF	FF
darkblue	00	00	8B
darkcyan	00	8B	8B
darkgoldenrod	B8	86	0B
darkgray	A9	A9	A9
darkgreen	00	64	00
darkkhaki	BD	B7	6B
darkmagenta	8B	00	8B
darkolivegreen	55	6B	2F
darkorange	FF	8C	00
darkorchid	99	32	CC
darkred	8B	00	00
darksalmon	E9	96	7A
darkseagreen	8F	BC	8F
darkslateblue	48	3D	8B

Color	Red	Green	Blue
darkslategray	2F	4F	4F
darkturquoise	00	CE	D1
darkviolet	94	00	D3
deeppink	FF	14	93
deepskyblue	00	BF	FF
dimgray	69	69	69
dodgerblue	1E	90	FF
firebrick	B2	22	22
floralwhite	FF	FA	F0
forestgreen	22	8B	22
fuchsia	FF	00	FF
gainsboro	DC	DC	DC
ghostwhite	F8	F8	FF
gold	FF	D7	00
goldenrod	DA	A5	20
gray	80	80	80
green	00	80	00
greenyellow	AD	FF	2F
honeydew	F0	FF	F0
hotpink	FF	69	B4
indianred	CD	5C	5C
indigo	4B	00	82
ivory	FF	FF	F0
khaki	F0	E6	8C
lavender	E6	E6	FA
lavenderblush	FF	F0	F5
lawngreen	7C	FC	00
lemonchiffon	FF	FA	CD
lightblue	AD	D8	E6
lightcoral	F0	80	80
lightcyan	E0	FF	FF
lightgoldenrodyellow	FA	FA	D2
lightgreen	90	EE	90
lightgrey	D3	D3	D3
lightpink	FF	B6	C1

Color	Red	Green	Blue
lightsalmon	FF	A0	7A
lightseagreen	20	B2	AA
lightskyblue	87	CE	FA
lightslategray	77	88	99
lightsteelblue	B0	C4	DE
lightyellow	FF	FF	E0
lime	00	FF	00
limegreen	32	CD	32
linen	FA	F0	E6
magenta	FF	00	FF
maroon	80	00	00
mediumaquamarine	66	CD	AA
mediumblue	00	00	CD
mediumorchid	BA	55	D3
mediumpurple	93	70	DB
mediumseagreen	3C	B3	71
mediumslateblue	7B	68	EE
mediumspringgreen	00	FA	9A
mediumturquoise	48	D1	CC
mediumvioletred	C7	15	85
midnightblue	19	19	70
mintcream	F5	FF	FA
mistyrose	FF	E4	E1
moccasin	FF	E4	B5
navajowhite	FF	DE	AD
navy	00	00	80
oldlace	FD	F5	E6
olive	80	80	00
olivedrab	6B	8E	23
orange	FF	A5	00
orangered	FF	45	00
orchid	DA	70	D6
palegoldenrod	EE	E8	AA
palegreen	98	FB	98
paleturquoise	AF	EE	EE

Color	Red	Green	Blue
palevioletred	DB	70	93
papayawhip	FF	EF	D5
peachpuff	FF	DA	B9
peru	CD	85	3F
pink	FF	C0	CB
plum	DD	A0	DD
powderblue	B0	E0	E6
purple	80	00	80
red	FF	00	00
rosybrown	BC	8F	8F
royalblue	41	69	E1
saddlebrown	8B	45	13
salmon	FA	80	72
sandybrown	F4	A4	60
seagreen	2E	8B	57
seashell	FF	F5	EE
sienna	A0	52	2D
silver	C0	C0	C0
skyblue	87	CE	EB
slateblue	6A	5A	CD
slategray	70	80	90
snow	FF	FA	FA
springgreen	00	FF	7F
steelblue	46	82	B4
tan	D2	B4	8C
teal	00	80	80
thistle	D8	BF	D8
tomato	FF	63	47
turquoise	40	E0	D0
violet	EE	82	EE
wheat	F5	DE	B3
white	FF	FF	FF
whitesmoke	F5	F5	F5
yellow	FF	FF	00
yellowgreen	9A	CD	32

Finding More Information

This appendix lists a variety of sources of JavaScript information. Note that this information is also available in the Online Companion, which you can reach at http://www.netscapepress.com/support/javascript1.2/. That site has a Web page containing this information, as well as Bookmark and Favorites files that you can download and import into your own browser system.

Netscape's JavaScript Authoring Guide

You will want to get a copy of Netscape's JavaScript Authoring Guide. It contains a wealth of information—all the funky little details you really need to work with the various objects, properties, methods, and so on. There are various versions available:

Netscape 2 Version
http://www.netscape.com/eng/mozilla/2.0/handbook/javascript/ or
http://home.netscape.com/eng/mozilla/Gold/handbook/javascript/

Netscape 3 Version
http://home.netscape.com/eng/mozilla/3.0/handbook/javascript/

Netscape 4 Version
http://home.netscape.com/eng/mozilla/4.0/handbook/javascript/
(This link currently doesn't work, but may eventually.)

What's New in Javascript 1.2 for Navigator 4.0

http://developer.netscape.com/library/documentation/communicator/js1_2.htm
You can also download the documentation from Netscape to your hard disk, though it's not always up to date. Try http://developer.netscape.com/library/documentation/ or directly at http://developer.netscape.com/library/documentation/jshtm.zip.

You can also find the Netscape documentation in a variety of other formats, though again, not always completely up to date:

JavaScript Authoring Guide in WinHelp Format

http://www.jchelp.com/javahelp/javahelp.htm
This site has the Netscape documents placed into a Windows Help file.

JavaScript Authoring Guide in Adobe Acrobat (PDF)

http://www.ipst.com/docs.htm
This site has the authoring guide in Adobe Acrobat (PDF) format.

Other Documentation

Here are some other documents that may be useful:

DevEdge Online

http://developer.netscape.com/
Netscape's developer's support site has links to lots of useful information, directly and indirectly related to JavaScript. Some areas of this site are free, some are open only to registered DevEdge members.

DevEdge Documentation Library

http://developer.netscape.com/library/documentation/
Links to lots of useful documentation.

Netscape DevEdge ONE News Subscription

http://developer.netscape.com/subscription_reg.html
Subscribe to a free newsletter related to Netscape development topics.

JavaScript 1.1 Specification in a PostScript File

http://home.netscape.com/eng/javascript/

JavaScript-Based Style Sheets

http://developer.netscape.com/library/documentation/ or
http://developer.netscape.com/library/documentation/communicator/stylesheets/jssindex.htm

Creating Multiple Layers of Content
http://developer.netscape.com/library/documentation/communicator/
layers/index.htm

Codestock on JavaScript 1.2 Enhancements
http:// developer.netscape.com/library/documentation/communicator/
codestock.html
Information about the new JavaScript 1.2 features, from a developer's conference.

Netscape Object Signing
http://developer.netscape.com./library/documentation/signedobj/
overview.html
http://home.netscape.com/assist/security/objectsign/datasheet.html
Documents about the new object-signing technology being introduced
to JavaScript 1.2.

Netscape Security Solutions
http://home.netscape.com/assist/security/
More leads to information about Netscape security, including object signing
and related subjects.

JavaScript Syntax
http://home.netscape.com/comprod/products/navigator/version_3.0/
building_blocks/jscript/how.html

Other JavaScript Resources
http://home.netscape.com/comprod/products/navigator/version_2.0/
script/script_info/

Introduction to JavaScript by Stefan Koch (was known as "Voodoo")
http://rummelplatz.uni-mannheim.de/~skoch/js/script.htm
This site contains good tutorials, plus background information and useful
links. It's also mirrored at the US and New Zealand sites listed below as well
as at various other sites in other languages.
http://www.webconn.com/java/javascript/intro/
http://www.cit.ac.nz/smac/ma200/cgi/javascr/script.htm

Persistent Client State HTTP Cookies Preliminary Specifications
http://www.netscape.com/newsref/std/cookie_spec.html
Background information about working with cookies.

The JavaScript FAQ
http://www.freqgrafx.com/411/jsfaq.html
Frequently asked questions about JavaScript. Useful information on JavaScript
bugs, too.

JavaScript Libraries

Here are a few JavaScript libraries from which you can borrow scripts (see Chapter 20, "Ready-to-Use Scripts"):

JavaScript 411
http://www.freqgrafx.com/411/

The JavaScript Library at the JavaScript Index
http://www.sapphire.co.uk/javascript/lib/

JavaScript: Simple Little Things to Add to Your Pages
http://tanega.com/java/java.html

The JavaScript Archive
http://planetx.bloomu.edu/~mpscho/jsarchive/

JavaScript Applets
http://www.oz.net/~alden/javascript/jsintro.html

Timothy's JavaScript Page
http://www.essex1.com/people/timothy/

JavaScript Index
http://www.sapphire.co.uk/javascript/collections.html
A list of more libraries.

Resource Sites

These are currently the best JavaScript link sites:

Gamelan JavaScript List
http://www.gamelan.com/pages/Gamelan.related.javascript.html
Lots of JavaScript stuff. Gamelan has a Java list, too.

The JavaScript Index
http://www.sapphire.co.uk/javascript/
Links to many JavaScript samples and resources.

Yahoo's JavaScript Category
http://www.yahoo.com/Computers_and_Internet/
Programming_Languages/JavaScript/
Not as much stuff as the first two sites listed, but pretty good nonetheless.
    Here are other JavaScript sites worth checking, not so many links, but often good examples, tutorials, and so on:

Netscape's JavaScript Introduction page
http://www.netscape.com/comprod/products/navigator/version_2.0/script/
An introductory promotional page for JavaScript, with links to the authoring guide and resources page.

Netscape's JavaScript Resources page
http://www.netscape.com/comprod/products/navigator/version_2.0/script/script_info/
A small list of links to example JavaScripts and JavaScript resources.

Unofficial JavaScript Resource Center
http://www.ce.net/users/ryan/java/
Useful samples, loads of links.

LiveSoftware's JavaScript Resource Center
http://jrc.livesoftware.com/
JavaScript examples, two newsgroups, and a chat room.

JavaScript 411
http://www.freqgrafx.com/411/
Very useful site. It has a snippets library (take bits of JavaScript code for your Web pages), the JavaScript FAQ, and tutorials.

TeamJava's Home Page
http://www.teamjava.com/
Java and JavaScript consultants, plus lots of links to JavaScript stuff.

Eric's JavaScript Page
http://www.pass.wayne.edu/~eric/javascript/
A small JavaScript links page.

Discussion Groups

The JavaScript Mailing List
There is an unofficial repository of information in the form of a mailing list for people interested in JavaScript. For more information about the list or to view old messages, point your Web browser to http://www.obscure.org/javascript/. To join, send e-mail to **majordomo@obscure.org** with this in the body of the message: **subscribe javascript**.

To get a digest—a single message each day containing all the list's messages pasted together—send e-mail to **majordomo@obscure.org** with the following in the body of the message: **subscribe javascript-digest**.

Java Message Exchange

http://porthos.phoenixat.com/~warreng/WWWBoard/wwwboard.html
A Web-based discussion group.

Internet Relay Chat

The #javascript channel on Internet Relay Chat is used for JavaScript discussions.

Netscape's JavaScript Newsgroup

This newsgroup is on the secnews.netscape.com secure news server. You can enter the following URL into Netscape Navigator's Location bar and press Enter to access this newsgroup.
snews://secnews.netscape.com/netscape.devs-javascript

Netscape's LiveWire Newsgroup

Netscape also has a LiveWire newsgroup; again, only for the developers.
snews://secnews.netscape.com/netscape.devs-livewire

Java Message Exchange

A Web-based discussion group: http://porthos.phoenixat.com/~warreng/
WWWBoard/wwwboard.html

comp.lang.javascript Newsgroup

This newsgroup is available at many local news servers.

LiveSoftware's JavaScript Newsgroups

JavaScript Development Group: news://news.livesoftware.com/
livesoftware.javascript.developer
JavaScript Examples Group: news://news.livesoftware.com/
livesoftware.javascript.examples
Go to the LiveSoftware news server (news.livesoftware.com) to participate in these newsgroups. In Netscape, for instance, just type the full URL—news://
news.livesoftware.com/livesoftware.javascript.examples, for instance—into the Location box and press Enter to open the Newsgroup window, connect to the server, and open the newsgroup. For more information, go to the LiveSoftware site: http://jrc.livesoftware.com/

Internet Relay Chat

You may find a #javascript channel on Internet Relay Chat.

For more information about JavaScript chat groups, newsgroups, and mailing lists, see the JavaScript Index: http://www.sapphire.co.uk/javascript/.

And you can also search for the word **javascript** at the major search engines to find yet more sources of information.

The Scripts We Used

You'll find loads of sample scripts scattered through this book. Many of them can be taken and pasted into your HTML pages (some might require modifications to make them work with your data).

This appendix contains a list of the scripts we've used. Go to the chapter and find the script, read the text, and if it's what you want you can either quickly type it into your HTML document or go to the Online Companion (http://www.netscapepress.com/support/javascript1.2/) and copy the text from our documents. There's no need to copy the whole source document (though you can do that if you wish)—all you need to do is copy the script from the "face" of the document itself. (Go take a look, you'll see what we mean.)

Script Purpose	Example
<NOSCRIPT>	3.5
Aborted image loading—onabort	12.10
Adding numbers	5.1
Adding numbers	5.8
Alert box, opens when user clicks on Submit button, onsubmit	12.9
Alert box, opens when user points at link, onmouseover	12.5

Script Purpose	Example	
Communicating with the user; setting status from a button	18.8	
Communicating with the user; status	18.7	
Communicating with the user; using forms	18.1	
Communicating with the user; using prompt boxes	18.2	
Communicating with the user; writing to a textarea	18.10	
Communicating with the user; writing to the current document	18.9	
Concatenation	5.8	
Conditionals, = instead of ==	6.2	
Conditionals, else clause	6.4	
Conditionals, Greater Than (>)	6.7	
Conditionals, Greater Than or Equal To (>=)	6.8	
Conditionals, if statements without brackets	6.5	
Conditionals, nesting if statements	6.9	
Conditionals, Not Equal To (!=)	6.6	
Conditionals, the ? operator	6.12	
Conditionals, the if statement	6.1	
Confirmation box, adding to link	15.21	12.17
continue—returning to the top of a loop	6.20	
Cropping (clipping) layers	14.6	
Date object methods	11.2	
Date object, creating instances	11.1	
Date; document-modified, inserted into page	2.1	3.1
Dividing numbers	5.4	
Document stream, closing	15.14	
Document stream, opening	15.13	
do while loop, JavaScript 1.0 & 1.1	6.17	
do while loop, JavaScript 1.2	6.18	
else clause	6.4	
enabledPlugin	13.10	
errors, JavaScript, suppressing	12.12	
errors run the script—onerror	12.11–12.13	
escape	7.14	

Script Purpose	Example	
eval	7.11	
event handlers, various	Chapter 12	
event handlers, adding functions to	7.18	
event handlers, resetting	12.18	
event object properties	12.19	
event object, passing properties to a function	12.20	
File support in browser	13.10	13.11
focus( )	15.11	
Focus, changing to a window	15.11	
for loops	6.13	
for loops, mimicking with nested ifs	6.14	
Form validation, onsubmit	12.8	
Form validation, using onblur	12.1	
Form validation, using onchange	12.2	
Form validation, using onfocus	12.3	
Form validation: see also the Area Code Application	Chapter 18	
Form validation; making sure it's not too long	17.7	
Form validation; checking that it's a number	17.6	
Form validation; making sure it's not too long nor too short	17.8	
Form validation; verifying a number within range	17.5	
Forms, passing data from one to another	17.4	
Forms, passing data to functions	17.1	
Forms, using information from a form in documents	18.1	
Forms; no need to pass information	17.3	
Forms; you can't simply name the form within the function	17.2	
Forwarding users to another page, with a Confirm dialog box	2.12	
Forwarding users to another page	2.11	
Frames, calling functions from another frame	16.8	
Frames, changing contents with HTML	16.5	
Frames, changing contents with JavaScript	16.6	
Frames, creating with HTML	16.1	16.2

Script Purpose	Example	
Frames, referring to	16.3	
Frames, using _top	16.4	
Frames, using document.close	16.7	
Function object()	7.17–7.19	
functions, build your own with Function	7.17–7.19	
Functions, "call by value"	7.9	
Functions, defining	3.2	7.1
Functions, defining and calling	3.3	
Functions, defining in the wrong place	7.2	7.3
Functions, escape	7.14	
Functions, eval	7.11	
Functions, multiple returns	7.6	
Functions, parseFloat	7.13	
Functions, parseInt	7.12	
Functions, passing multiple values to	7.8	
Functions, passing values to	7.7–7.9	
Functions, returning values	7.4	7.5
Functions, unescape	7.15	
Functions, working with multiple	7.10	
Grabbing text from a selection box	17.9	17.10
grandparent windows, referring to	15.2	
Greater Than (>)	6.7	
Greater Than or Equal To (>=)	6.8	
Hiding and showing layers	14.5	
Hiding scripts from non-JavaScript browsers	2.2	
HTML tags and JavaScript entities	13.12	
if statement	6.1	
if statements with boolean variables	6.3	
if statements, nesting	6.9	
if statements, the ? shorthand	6.12	
if statements, without brackets	6.5	
Image object	15.22	
Images, writing to a document	15.16	15.22
isNaN—using to evaluate the result of parseInt	7.16	
Java Console	13.8	

Script Purpose	Example	
Methods	10.3	
Methods, creating	13.3	
MIME types	13.10	
mimeTypes array	13.10	
Modulus	5.5	
Moving from page to page automatically—starting	15.18	
Moving from page to page automatically—stopping	15.19	
Moving layers	14.3	14.4
Moving mouse away runs script—onmouseout	12.14	
multidimensional, arrays	9.10	
Multiplying numbers	5.3	
NaN, isNan, and parseInt	7.16	
Navigation buttons	2.5	
navigator.javaEnabled	13.9	
navigator object and properties	10.1	
Not Equal To (!=)	6.6	
Object arrays, using to refer to things	10.5	10.6
Object array, viewing properties with	13.6	
Object hierarchy	10.8	
Object methods, using	11.2	
Object properties are sometimes strings	11.7	
Objects, creating your own	13.1	
Objects, creating methods for your	13.3	
Objects, creating properties for your	13.2	
Objects, creating instances	11.1	
Object prototypes, creating	13.4	
Objects, referring to	10.4	
Objects, string	11.5–11.7	
onabort	12.10	
onblur	12.1	
onchange	12.2	
onclick confirmation box	12.17	
onerror	12.11–12.13	

Script Purpose	Example	
Windows, controlling background colors	15.17	
Windows, opening a complete window	15.3	
Windows, opening a window with just the location bar	15.4	
Windows, opening a window with various components	15.5	15.6
Windows, opening from a link—the problems	15.7	15.8
Windows, referring to	15.1	
Windows, writing to	15.10	15.11
Windows, writing images to a document	15.16	
Windows, writing to—the document stream	15.13	15.14
word boundaries in regular expressions	14.17	
Z-INDEX and layers	14.2	

Index

Official Netscape Communicator Book

$39.99, 800 pages
Beginning to Intermediate
Windows Edition: part #: 1-56604-617-3
Macintosh Edition: part #:1-56604-620-3

The sequel to Ventana's blockbuster international bestseller
Official Netscape Navigator Book! Discover the first suite to integrate
key intranet and Internet communications services into a single,
smart interface. From simple e-mail to workgroup collaboration, from
casual browsing to Web publishing, from reading text to receiving
multimedia Netcaster channels—learn to do it all without leaving
Communicator! Covers:

• All Communicator components: Navigator, Netcaster, Messenger,
  Collabra, Composer and Conference.
• Complete, step-by-step instructions for both intranet and Internet
  task.
• Tips on using plug-ins, JavaScript and Java applets.

The CD-ROM includes a fully-supported version of Netscape
Communicator plus hyperlinked listings.

Official Netscape Communicator Professional Edition Book

$39.99, 608 pages, part #:1-56604-739-0

Windows Edition • Intermediate

**Your Guide to Business Communications Over the
Intranet & the Web!** Unlock the immeasurable potential of
Web technologies for improving and enhancing day-to-day
business tasks. Netscape Communicator and your office
intranet provide the tools and the environment. This easy-to-
use, step-by-step guide opens the door to each key module—and its most effective use. Covers:

• Navigator 4, Messenger, Collabra, Conference, Composer,
  Calendar, Netcaster and AutoAdmin.
• Key business tasks: e-mail, workgroups, conferencing and
  Web publishing.
• Step-by-step instructions, tips and guidelines for working
  effectively.

VENTANA

Official Online Marketing With Netscape Book

$34.99, 544 pages, illustrated, part #: 1-56604-453-7

The perfect marketing tool for the Internet! Learn how innovative marketers create powerful, effectove electronic newsletters and promotional materials. Step-by-step instructions show you how to plan, deisgn and distribute professional-quality pieces. With this easy-to-follow guide, you'll soon be flexing Netscape Navigator's marketing muscle to eliminate paper and printing costs, automate market research and customer service, and much more.

Official Netscape Guide to Online Investments

$24.99, 528 pages, illustrated, part #: 1-56604-452-9

Gain the Internet investment edge! Here's everything you need to make the Internet a full financial partner. Features an overview of the Net and Navigator; in-depth reviews of stock and bond quote services, analysts, brokerage houses, and mutual fund reports. Plus a full listing of related financial services such as loans, appraisals, low-interest credit cards, venture capital, entrepreneurship, insurance, tax counseling, and more.

Official Netscape Guide to Internet Research

$29.99, 480 pages, illustrated, part #: 1-56604-604-1

Turn the Internet into your primary research tool. More than just a listing of resources, this official guide provides everything you need to know to access, organize, cite and post information on the Net. Includes research strategies, search engines and information management. Plus timesaving techniques for finding the best, most up-to-date data.

VENTANA

Official Netscape Messenger & Collabra Book

$39.99, 408 pages, part #: 1-56604-685-8

Windows, Macintosh • Intermediate to Advanced

The Power of Web-based Communications—Without a Web Site!
Stay in touch with customers; promote products and services visually; share the latest market trends—with simple Internet dial-up access! This step-by-step guide helps you harness Netscape Communicator's e-mail, newsreader, HTML authoring and real-time conference tools to achieve faster, more powerful business communications—without the effort or expense of a Web site. Learn how to:
• Integrate Messenger, Collabra, Conference and Composer for efficient business communications.
• Distribute eye-catching, HTML-based marketing materials without a Web site.
• Use the Net to gather, organize and share information efficiently.

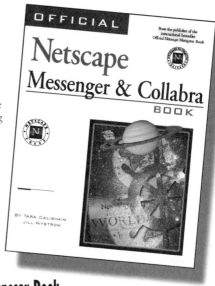

Official Netscape Composer Book

$39.99, 600 pages, part #: 1-56604-674-2

Windows • Beginning to Intermediate

Forget about tedious tags and cumbersome code! Now you can create sophisticated, interactive Web pages using simple, drag-and-drop techniques. Whether you want to create your personal home page, promote your hobby, or launch your business on the Web, here's everything you need to know to get started:
• Step-by-step instructions for designing sophisticated Web sites with no previous experience.
• JavaScript basics and techniques for adding multimedia, including animation and interactivity.
• Tips for businesses on the Web, including creating forms, ensuring security and promoting a Web site.
The CD-ROM features a wide selection of Web tools for designing Web pages, adding multimedia, creating forms and building image maps.

Official Netscape Plug-in Book, Second Edition

$39.99, 700 pages, part #: 1-56604-612-2

Windows, Macintosh • All Users

Your One-Stop Plug-in Resource & Desktop Reference!
Why waste expensive online time searching the Net for the plug-ins you want? This handy one-stop reference includes in-depth reviews, easy-to-understand instructions and step-by-step tutorials. And you avoid costly download time—the hottest plug-ins are included! Includes:
• In-depth reviews & tutorials for most Netscape plug-ins.
• Professional tips on designing pages with plug-ins.
• Fundamentals of developing your own plug-ins.

The CD-ROM includes all the featured plug-ins available at press time.

Microsoft Windows NT 4 Workstation Desktop Companion

$39.99, 1016 pages, illustrated, part #: 1-56604-472-3

Workstation users become masters of their own universe with this step-by-step guide. Covers file management, customizing and optimizing basic multimedia, OLE, printing and networking. Packed with shortcuts, secrets, productivity tips and hands-on tutorials. The CD-ROM features dozens of valuable utilities and demos for Windows NT. Innovative web-site designs, reference information, wallpaper textures, animated cursors, custom utilities and more.

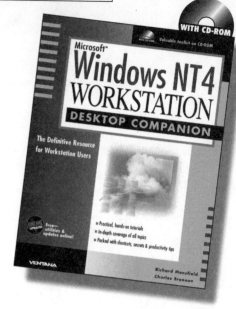

Microsoft Office 95 Companion

$34.95, 1136 pages, illustrated, part #: 1-56604-188-0

The all-in-one reference to Microsoft's red-hot suite is a worthy sequel to Ventana's bestselling *Windows, Word & Excel Office Companion*. Covers basic commands and features, and includes a section on using Windows 95. The companion disk features examples, exercises, software and sample files from the book.

SmartSuite Desktop Companion

$24.95, 784 pages, illustrated, part #: 1-56604-184-8

Here's "Suite success" for newcomers to the critics' choice of business packages. This introduction to the individual tools and features of Lotus' star software packages—1-2-3, Ami Pro, Approach, Freelance Graphics and Organizer—has been updated for the latest versions. Features new enhancements for Windows 95. The companion disk features sample exercises and files that follow the lessons in the book.

VENTANA

The Comprehensive Guide to SmartSuite 97

James Meade
$34.99, 528 pages, illustrated, part #: 1-56604-651-3

Here's Suite relief for business users at all levels. Step by step, learn to use applications together, work collaboratively, and maximize Internet and intranet connectivity. Packed with tips and shortcuts.

For Windows 95/NT • Beginning to Intermediate

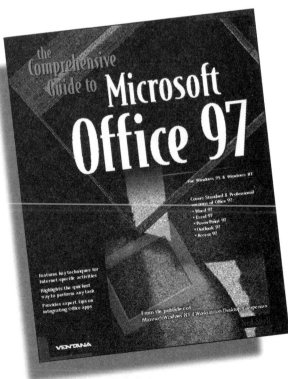

The Comprehensive Guide to Microsoft Office 97

Ned Snell
$39.99, 848 pages, illustrated, part #: 1-56604-646-7

The "right-size" guide to the world's hottest suite! Easy enough for beginners, yet in-depth enough for power users. Covers all five applications, plus tips, shortcuts, Internet techniques and more.

For Windows 95/NT • Beginning to Intermediate

VENTANA

HTML Publishing on the Internet, Second Edition

$39.99, 700 pages, illustrated, part #: 1-56604-625-4

Take advantage of critical updates and technologies that have emerged since this book's bestselling predecessor was published. Learn to create a home page and hyperlinks, and to build graphics, video and sound into documents. Highlighted throughout with examples and templates, and tips on layout and nonlinear organization. Plus, save time and money by downloading components of the new technologies from the Web or from the companion CD-ROM. The CD-ROM also features HTML authoring tools, graphics and multimedia utilities, textures, templates and demos.

The HTML Programmer's Reference

$39.99, 376 pages, illustrated, part #: 1-56604-597-5

The ultimate professional companion! All HTML categories, tags and attributes are listed in one easy-reference sourcebook, complete with code examples. Saves time and money testing—all examples comply with the top browsers! Provides real-world JavaScript and HTML examples. The CD-ROM features a complete hyperlinked HTML version of the book, viewable with most popular browsers.

VENTANA

Web Publishing With Adobe PageMill 2

$34.99, 480 pages, illustrated, part #: 1-56604-458-8

Now, creating and designing professional pages on the Web is a simple, drag-and-drop function. Learn to pump up PageMill with tips, tricks and troubleshooting strategies in this step-by-step tutorial for designing professional pages. The CD-ROM features Netscape plug-ins, original textures, graphical and text-editing tools, sample backgrounds, icons, buttons, bars, GIF and JPEG images, Shockwave animations.

Web Publishing With QuarkImmedia

$39.99, 552 pages, illustrated, part #: 1-56604-525-8

Use multimedia to learn multimedia, building on the power of QuarkXPress. Step-by-step instructions introduce basic features and techniques, moving quickly to delivering dynamic documents for the Web and other electronic media. The CD-ROM features an interactive manual and sample movie gallery with displays showing settings and steps. Both are written in QuarkImmedia.

VENTANA

The Mac OS 8 Book

Maximize your Mac with this worthy successor to Ventana's bestselling *The System 7.5 Book*! Comprehensive chapters cover installing, updating, third-party add-ons and troubleshooting tips for Mac OS 8, along with full instructions on how to connect to the Net and publish on the Web with Mac OS 8.

This thorough look at what's new also provides a complete overview of all commands and features, including

- High level of backward compatibility.
- Increased performance, stability and ease of use.
- Streamlined and enhanced programming model to simplify the job of writing software for the Mac OS 8 platform.
- Technologies that enable users to add new features to their software that were impossible or inconvenient to add with earlier System 7 generations.
- User interface themes.
- V-Twin searching and indexing technology.

The Mac OS 8 Book

Getting the most from your Macintosh operating system

Mark R. Bell   VENTANA

Plus—online updates for up-to-the-minute patches and fixes for Mac OS 8, as well as updates to the book.

part #: 56604-490-1

658 pages $29.99

Looking Good in Print, Deluxe CD-ROM Edition

$34.99, 416 pages, illustrated, part #: 1-56604-471-5

This completely updated version of the most widely used design companion for desktop publishers features all-new sections on color and printing. Packed with professional tips for creating powerful reports, newsletters, ads, brochures and more. The companion CD-ROM featues Adobe® Acrobat® Reader, author examples, fonts, templates, graphics and more.

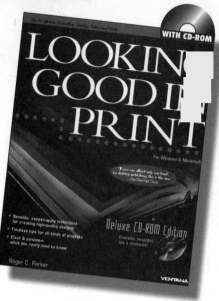

Looking Good Online

$39.99, 384 pages, illustrated, part #: 1-56604-469-3

Create well-designed, organized web sites—incorporating text, graphics, digital photos, backgrounds and forms. Features studies of successful sites and design tips from pros. The companion CD-ROM includes samples from online professionals; buttons, backgrounds, templates and graphics.

Looking Good in 3D

$39.99, 384 pages, illustrated, part #: 1-56604-494-4

Become the da Vinci of the 3D world! Learn the artistic elements involved in 3D design—light, motion, perspective, animation and more—to create effective interactive projects. The CD-ROM includes samples from the book, templates, fonts and graphics.

TO ORDER ANY VENTANA TITLE, COMPLETE THIS ORDER FORM AND MAIL OR FAX IT TO US, WITH PAYMENT, FOR QUICK SHIPMENT.

TITLE	PART #	QTY	PRICE	TOTAL

SHIPPING

For orders shipping within the United States, please add $4.95 for the first book, $1.50 for each additional book.
For "two-day air," add $7.95 for the first book, $3.00 for each additional book.
Email: vorders@kdc.com for exact shipping charges.
Note: Please include your local sales tax.

SUBTOTAL = $ _____

SHIPPING = $ _____

TAX = $ _____

TOTAL = $ _____

Mail to: International Thomson Publishing • 7625 Empire Drive • Florence, KY 41042
☎ **US orders 800/332-7450 • fax 606/283-0718**
☎ **International orders 606/282-5786 • Canadian orders 800/268-2222**

Name _____

E-mail _____ Daytime phone _____

Company _____

Address (No PO Box) _____

City_____ State_____ Zip_____

Payment enclosed ____VISA ____MC ____ Acc't # _____ Exp. date_____

Signature _____ Exact name on card _____

Check your local bookstore or software retailer for these and other bestselling titles, or call toll free:

800/332-7450
8:00 am - 6:00 pm EST

Technical support for installation related issues only provided by Ventana. The Ventana technical support office is open from 8:00 A.M. to 6:00 P.M. (EST) Monday through Friday and can be reached via the following methods:

World Wide Web: http://www.netscapepress.com/support

E–mail: help@vmedia.com

Phone: (919) 544-9404 extension 81

FAX: (919) 544-9472

America Online: keyword **Ventana**